REFUGEE LAW

Colin Yeo

First published in Great Britain in 2022 by

Bristol University Press
University of Bristol
1-9 Old Park Hill
Bristol
BS2 8BB
UK
t: +44 (0)117 954 5940
e: bup-info@bristol.ac.uk

Details of international sales and distribution partners are available at bristoluniversitypress.co.uk

© Bristol University Press 2022

British Library Cataloguing in Publication Data
A catalogue record for this book is available from the British Library

ISBN 978-1-5292-1996-8 hardcover
ISBN 978-1-5292-1997-5 paperback
ISBN 978-1-5292-1998-2 ePub
ISBN 978-1-5292-1999-9 ePdf

The right of Colin Yeo to be identified as author of this work has been asserted by him in accordance with the Copyright, Designs and Patents Act 1988.

All rights reserved: no part of this publication may be reproduced, stored in a retrieval system, or transmitted in any form or by any means, electronic, mechanical, photocopying, recording, or otherwise without the prior permission of Bristol University Press.

Every reasonable effort has been made to obtain permission to reproduce copyrighted material. If, however, anyone knows of an oversight, please contact the publisher.

The statements and opinions contained within this publication are solely those of the author and not of the University of Bristol or Bristol University Press. The University of Bristol and Bristol University Press disclaim responsibility for any injury to persons or property resulting from any material published in this publication.

Bristol University Press works to counter discrimination on grounds of gender, race, disability, age and sexuality.

Cover design: Qube Design
Front cover image: Russell Burden

Contents

Preface	vii
Introduction	**1**
Evolution of the refugee definition	4
United Nations High Commissioner for Refugees	8
The Refugee Convention	11
Entitlement to refugee status	11
Rights of refugees	13
Nature of refugeehood	14
Purpose of the Refugee Convention	16
Criticisms of the Refugee Convention	20
Global Compact on Refugees	24
Structure of the book	26
1 Legal Framework	**31**
International community of refugee law and practice	32
Role of UNHCR	35
Academic works	37
Judicial dialogue	38
Regional and domestic refugee definitions	39
Africa	40
Latin America	46
European Union	53
Domestic definitions	59
International human rights law	61
Interpretation and interplay	63
Non-refoulement in human rights cases	66
Jurisdiction and international human rights law	72
Rights and status under international human rights law	73
Trafficking victims	75
Statelessness	78

2	**Well-founded Fear**	**82**
	Burden of proof	83
	Standard of proof	84
	Meaning of 'fear'	86
	Credibility and truthfulness	88
	Plausibility	91
	Corroboration	93
	Quality of narrative	95
	Future risk	98
	Relevance of past events	99
	Identifying risk	100
	Future activities	102
	Refugees *sur place*	105
	Bad faith claims	106
3	**Being Persecuted**	**108**
	Individual impact	109
	The bifurcated approach	111
	Actors of persecution	114
	Concept of serious harm	115
	Role of human rights standards	116
	Nature or repetition	121
	Discrimination	122
	European Union Qualification Directive definition	124
	Examples of persecution	125
	Physical harm	127
	Liberty and freedom	131
	Dignity and autonomy	134
4	**Protection and Relocation**	**140**
	Dual and multiple nationality	141
	Internal or external protection	143
	Unwilling or unable	146
	Agents of the state	147
	Source of protection	149
	Degree of protection	150
	Internal flight, relocation or protection	155
	Internal flight or relocation	156
	Internal protection	159

5	**Reasons for Persecution**	**162**
	Causation	162
	Intention of persecutor	163
	Predicament of persecuted person	164
	Multiple grounds	165
	Imputed or attributed convention grounds	165
	Concealment of convention grounds	166
	Role of the convention grounds	167
	Transformative effect	168
	Prosecution and persecution	169
	Military service cases	170
	The convention grounds	173
	Race	174
	Religion	174
	Nationality	176
	Membership of a particular social group	178
	Political opinion	183
6	**Cessation and Exclusion**	**186**
	Cessation clauses	187
	Voluntary acquisition of protection	188
	Change of circumstances	191
	Exclusion clauses	193
	Article 1D: Palestinian refugees	194
	Article 1E: Equivalent protection	201
	Article 1F: Exclusion on moral grounds	202
7	**Rights of Refugees**	**214**
	Scheme of refugee rights	215
	Reservations	215
	Degree of attachment	216
	Standards of equivalence	220
	Substance of rights	221
	Right to asylum	222
	Entry without penalization	223
	Non-refoulement	225
	Non-expulsion	228
	Rights to integration	230
	Family unity	230
	Rescue at sea	233

8	**Refugee Status Determination**	**238**
	Entry and off-shoring	240
	Asylum claim and support	243
	Claim for asylum	244
	Streaming	244
	Detention	246
	Support and accommodation	247
	Refugee status determination process	248
	Administrative stage	249
	Appeal stage	250
	Refusal	252
	Unauthorized residence	253
	Removal or return	253
	Fresh asylum claims	255
	Integration	255
	Residence status	256
	Return reviews	256
	Settlement	257

Conclusion		**258**
	Attempts to reform: the Global Compacts	259
	Climate displacement	261
	Last words	265

Index		267

Preface

The job of an asylum lawyer can be by turns highly fulfilling and deeply distressing. As a barrister in the United Kingdom representing refugees in tribunals and courts for over 20 years, I have certainly experienced both extremes of emotion. It is wonderful to share the moment when a judge tells a nervous refugee they have won their battle for recognition. It is frustrating and sometimes infuriating to sit alongside refugees as they are exposed to the ritualized performances of the court system. It is beyond awful when an asylum seeker receives their final refusal but you feel they could and should have succeeded. But this is nothing as to what it must be like to experience these highs and lows yourself as a refugee in a strange land. While I sit alongside refugees, as a barrister I often only meet them at their hearing. I can only imagine what they go through.

This book is a product of my experiences as an asylum lawyer in the United Kingdom, first working for a charity as an on-site adviser at a detention centre for refugees, then for another charity preparing and presenting cases at appeals, then as a self-employed barrister. I set out to write an accessible textbook that would have helped me earlier in my own career and would assist students and early stage lawyers today. The main focus of the book is on refugee law, in the sense of the interpretation and application of the 1951 Refugee Convention. I have also touched on human rights law, complementary protection and protection for victims of trafficking. Criticism has justifiably been levelled at writing on refugee law which centres excessively on the experiences of the Global North. This book is aimed primarily at law students and lawyers in the United Kingdom and therefore focuses primarily on the law governing asylum in the United Kingdom. The highlighted key cases are nearly all United Kingdom cases, for example. I have nevertheless endeavoured to widen out my references to other common law jurisdictions and, where possible, beyond. Refugee law is by its nature international, after all. I have also consciously restricted my references mainly to judgments of supreme courts. Material is drawn from a number of journal articles, reports and websites, and, reflecting my own interests, I have occasionally strayed into territory that is strictly speaking not refugee law, as such, so much as history, policy or practice. I have included an entire chapter on the refugee status determination process in the United Kingdom in order not just to explain and describe that process but also to illustrate some themes of state response to refugee claims in the Global North. Implicitly, that chapter points to the important reality that the precise terms of the Refugee Convention may mean little to a refugee who is experiencing the refugee status determination process.

I am heavily indebted to excellent and comprehensive prior texts including the first edition of James Hathaway's *The Law of Refugee Status* (1991) and his second edition of 2014 co-written with Michelle Foster, the second edition of James Hathaway's *The Rights of Refugees under International Law* (2021), the first edition of Guy Goodwin-Gill's *The Refugee in International Law* (1983), his fourth edition of 2021 co-written with Jane McAdam, and the second edition of Mark Symes and Peter Jorro's *Asylum Law and Practice* (2011). These are far from the only texts to which I have referred during my research and writing, but I owe these a special debt. Refugee law is more stable now that the great Cambrian Explosion of exciting and exploratory case law in the 1990s and 2000s has exhausted itself. The job of bringing the law up to date from those seminal texts is a far more straightforward one than researching and writing the original ground-breaking material. The existence of the various Legal Information Institute case law databases has been invaluable and it is hard to imagine now how case law research was conducted before they sprang into being.

Very quickly on language, I have referred here to the Global North and Global South. Some readers may not be familiar with this terminology. A reference to the Global North is to the industrialized and wealthy countries generally (but not exclusively: see Australia, for example) situated in the northern hemisphere. A reference to the Global South is to the developing and poorer countries generally (but not exclusively) in the southern hemisphere. It is a useful shorthand, but the dichotomy inevitably breaks down under closer consideration of where the border between the two extremes may lie. When I refer to refugee law or otherwise refer to refugees I am usually referring to the Refugee Convention and those who meet the definition at Article 1A(2) of the convention. When I refer to asylum I am often referring to refugee protection and other forms of international protection as well: asylum is generally understood as a broader concept than refugee status. When I refer to an asylum assessor, this may be read as a reference to a government official tasked with assessing an asylum claim, a judge deciding an asylum claim in a tribunal or court or even a lawyer or UNHCR (United Nations High Commissioner for Refugees) employee, depending on context. I have generally referred to refugees rather than asylum seekers or asylum applicants but have used the latter terms where it seemed appropriate. As discussed in Chapter 1, whether a person is a refugee flows from meeting the legal definition, not from formal assessment and declaration of status. In the context of Chapter 8, I have broken this rule and decided to use the label 'asylum applicant' for a person who has applied for recognition as a refugee but has not yet received a positive decision on their application.

I owe a big thank you to Helen Davis, who very patiently helped guide me through the publishing process, and to the rest of the team at Bristol University Press. A more existential thanks goes to my wife Clare Mercer for taking on so much more work at home while I was focusing on this project and to my colleague CJ McKinney for keeping the show on the road at my Free Movement website (freemovement.org.uk). I am hugely grateful to James Hathaway for his comments on an earlier draft, David Cantor for his very helpful comments and suggested further reading, Alexandra Defresne for her help with aspects of United States asylum law, Phil Cole for helping me get started on the issue of 'climate refugees', Bridget Anderson for very kindly and generously inviting me to observe the Migration Mobilities Bristol short course, Tim Jebb for very politely reminding me that the system in England and Wales is not that of Northern Ireland or Scotland, Jack Sommers for his plain-reading points, Sophie Capicchiano Young and Chris Bertram for their incredibly helpful suggestions, and to Natasha Carver, Rebecca Chapman, Jeff Crisp, Chris Cole, Helena Wray, Shoaib M. Khan and Adam Tear for their feedback. The anonymous review of my first and second drafts commissioned by Bristol University Press was enormously useful and I am hugely indebted, whoever you are.

Introduction

The word 'refugee' is both evocative and contested; it means different things to different people. To some, a refugee is a vulnerable person who needs help. To others, a refugee is a threatening figure who belongs in a faraway land. In a newspaper column or news report, a refugee may be a person fleeing from a natural disaster or a repressive regime. Images of refugees can be visceral and are regularly used to evoke sympathy or provoke unease, to raise funds or to secure political advantage. These images often tell us more about the opinion or purpose of the person using them and the society and social order in which they are deployed than the nature, condition or legal status of the majority of the world's refugees. The publicity materials of international agencies seeking to promote their work or raise funds are a case in point. They depict small groups of women and children from the Global South physically situated in the Global South, often accompanied by a logo-emblazoned aid worker from the Global North. Newspaper articles and political parties in advanced economies routinely choose to represent stories about refugees with images of groups of men travelling or somehow seeking entry to a wealthy country. Neither is representative, given that women are estimated to constitute just under half and children four out of ten of the refugee population. The vast majority of the world's refugees remain close to their country of origin in designated or informal refugee camps.[1]

For lawyers, asylum assessors and judges, the meaning of the word 'refugee' at first appears straightforward. The main legal reference point is the UN Convention relating to the Status of Refugees of 1951; Article 1A of that convention defines the meaning of the word 'refugee' and its second paragraph (referred to as 'Article 1A(2)') states that the term refugee shall apply to any person who:

> … owing to well-founded fear of being persecuted for reasons of race, religion, nationality, membership of a particular social group or

---

[1] UNHCR (2021) *Global Trends in Forced Displacement in 2020*, Brussels, UNHCR.

political opinion is outside the country of his nationality and is unable or owing to such fear, is unwilling to avail himself of the protection of that country; or who, not having a nationality and being outside the country of his former habitual residence is unable or, owing to such fear, unwilling to return to it.[2]

This definition has itself changed over time. Originally, Article 1A(2) began with the words 'As a result of events occurring before 1 January 1951 and …'. Article 1B included an option for a state party to amend that wording to 'As a result of events occurring in Europe before 1 January 1951 and …'. Most state parties to the 1951 Refugee Convention have, by ratifying the Protocol Relating to the Status of Refugees of 1967 without reservation, agreed to remove the temporal and geographical limitations to the refugee definition.[3] The protocol requires state parties 'to apply articles 2 to 34 inclusive of the [Refugee] Convention to refugees as hereinafter defined'.[4] These two international legal instruments read together are referred to throughout this book as 'the Refugee Convention'. Today there are a handful of states which have ratified the 1951 convention but not the 1967 protocol and some – including the United States – which have ratified the protocol but not the convention. Meanwhile, Turkey, which in 2021 hosted some four million refugees, has ratified both the convention and protocol but maintains the original geographical limitation to 'events in Europe'. The effect is that Turkey does not consider refugees from outside Europe as refugees as defined in the Refugee Convention. Turkey is therefore not obliged by the refugee law treaties to offer non-European refugees the rights discussed in Chapter 7 of this book.

While the definition at Article 1A(2) of the Refugee Convention, as amended by the 1967 protocol, can and should be considered the principal definition of a refugee for the purposes of international law, it is not the only available definition in public discourse, scholarship or even in law.

As hundreds of thousands of Syrians fled civil war in their country and travelled to Europe in 2015, a war of words broke out over whether they should be labelled 'refugees' or 'migrants'. Those in favour of offering them sanctuary argued they should be called refugees. Those advocating for their exclusion preferred to call them migrants. The sharp distinction both supporters and opponents of refugee rights often draw between these two words is referred to as the refugee/migrant binary. Whether or not a person formally satisfies

---

[2] UN General Assembly, *Convention Relating to the Status of Refugees* (28 July 1951), United Nations, Treaty Series, Vol. 189, p 137.

[3] UN General Assembly, *Protocol Relating to the Status of Refugees* (31 January 1967), United Nations, Treaty Series, Vol. 606, p 267.

[4] UN General Assembly, *Protocol Relating to the Status of Refugees* (31 January 1967), United Nations, Treaty Series, Vol. 606, p 267, Article 1.

the definition of a refugee in the Refugee Convention may well be arbitrary, though. In international law, a refugee must be outside their country of origin. A person whose home is destroyed and moves within the same country is labelled an 'internally displaced person' or 'IDP'. A person fleeing the same disaster and crossing an international border may be a refugee. A person may not fear 'being persecuted' as such and therefore may not be a refugee but may well still fear for their life for other reasons. The International Organization for Migration (IOM), noting that there is no universally agreed or international law definition of 'migrant', suggests a broad definition: 'a person who moves away from his or her place of usual residence, whether within a country or across an international border, temporarily or permanently, and for a variety of reasons'. Refugees can therefore be considered a subset of the wider class of international migrants. They are sometimes grouped together with others as 'forced migrants', people who in the short term at least would have remained in their country of origin but for some external cause, be it persecution, war, famine, natural disaster or something else. The term 'survival migration' has also been coined to offer a more inclusive conception of those forced to leave their country because of 'an existential threat for which they have no access to a domestic remedy or resolution'.[5] Ultimately, these are modified versions of the refugee/migrant binary and all have been dismissed as 'categorical fetishism'.[6] Any attempt to draw sharp distinctions between individuals based on their motivation ultimately founders on the complexities of mixed motives and marginal cases.

Nevertheless, a great deal rests on how the word 'refugee' is understood and defined. A 'refugee' is widely considered deserving of admission to another country but it is almost universally considered legitimate to exclude a 'migrant'. Advocates on behalf of refugees worry that confusing refugees with migrants undermines the already precarious rights of refugees.[7] As Hamlin writes, the binary distinction is considered by many to reassure the public in the Global North that they can support admitting and protecting refugees without having to support open borders or massively increased immigration.[8] Hamlin and others are critical of this position, though. It can be argued that the distinction between refugees and migrants is an expedient but false legal fiction; it excludes

---

[5] Betts, A. (2013) *Survival Migration: Failed Governance and the Crisis of Displacement*, New York: Cornell University Press, p 23.

[6] Crawley, H. and Skleparis, D. (2018) 'Refugees, Migrants, Neither, Both: Categorical Fetishism and the Politics of Bounding in Europe's "Migration Crisis"', *Journal of Ethnic and Migration Studies*, 44(1): 48–64.

[7] See for example Hathaway, J. (2007) 'Forced Migration Studies: Could We Agree Just to "Date"?', *Journal of Refugee Studies*, 20(3): 349–369.

[8] Hamlin, R. (2021) *Crossing: How We Label and React to People on the Move*, Stanford: Stanford University Press, p 74.

from protection highly vulnerable migrants who do not satisfy the strictures of refugee status and it serves to reinforce harsh border control measures which harm all border crossers, including those defined as refugees.

Ultimately, this book addresses refugee law and with some wider laws of international asylum for those who do cross international borders. The main focus here is therefore on the existing refugee definition and the rights of refugees, not on whether that definition could or should be modified or even abandoned. We will, though, return to the issue of reform in the Conclusion.

Evolution of the refugee definition

The idea of international asylum has long legal precedents. The first known international treaty, the Kadesh Treaty, concluded between Ramses II and Hatusil III, King of the Hittites in the 13th century BC, included protection clauses.[9] Greek and Roman law and custom recognized the right of asylum as a form of sanctuary from unjust persecution and protection against extradition.[10] The theoretical founders of modern international law, figures such as Francisco de Vitoria (1480–1546), Francisco Suárez (1548–1617), Hugo Grotius (1583–1645), Samuel Pufendorf (1632–94), Christian Wolff (1679–1754) and Emerich de Vattel (1717–17), discuss the concept of asylum. The word 'refugee' first came into usage in Europe in the 17th century to describe the Huguenot Protestants who fled religious persecution in France and settled in England. Being a refugee was not a formal status; it did not need to be. In the United Kingdom, the power of the Crown to expel a person was ancient, but it was seldom used: prior to the Aliens Act 1905, there were virtually no laws governing admission to or residence in England or elsewhere at that time, so there were no legal barriers to people coming and going as they pleased.[11] When that legislation was adopted, it allowed for a right of admission for a migrant fleeing 'prosecution or punishment on religious or political grounds or for an offence of a political character, or persecution, involving danger of imprisonment or danger to life or limb, on account of religions belief'.[12] The word 'refugee' had by then become part of common usage, denoting a person who had fled religious or political persecution in their own country and who it was accepted should not be

---

[9] Gil-Bazo, M.-T. and Guild, E. (2021) 'The Right to Asylum', in Costello, C., Foster, M. and McAdam, J. (eds) *The Oxford Handbook of International Refugee Law*, Oxford: Oxford University Press, pp 868–869.

[10] Price, M. (2009) *Rethinking Asylum: History, Purpose, and Limits*, Cambridge: Cambridge University Press, Chapter 1.

[11] See discussion in *R v Immigration Officer at Prague Airport, ex p European Roma Rights Centre* [2004] UKHL 55, [2005] 2 AC 1 [11]-[12] (Lord Bingham).

[12] Aliens Act 1905, s 1(3).

sent back to that country. Formal borders, admission laws and eventually passports became more entrenched in the 19th and early 20th centuries, a trend accelerated by the First World War. At the same time, persecution and targeting of minorities and political opponents in Russia and eastern Europe led to increasing movement of people across those borders. As Hannah Arendt observed, forced migrations of people were hardly a new phenomenon in human history, but the impossibility of finding a new home was unprecedented: 'Suddenly, there was no place on earth where migrants could go without the severest restrictions, no country where they would be assimilated, no territory where they could found a new community of their own.'[13]

The sometimes desperate plight of considerable numbers of Russians who had fled their country in the years following the revolution of 1917 attracted international attention. A more formal footing for the assistance of refugees was required and, in 1921, a League of Nations High Commissioner for Refugees was appointed. This was the Norwegian Fridtjof Nansen, who by lending his name to the 'Nansen passport' was to become eponymous with refugee protection in the interwar years. The term 'refugee' emerged to describe a special category of migrant in Europe. At this stage, remedies for the situation experienced by refugees focused on filling the vacuum left by effective loss of diplomatic protection to a person outside their own country and repairing lost personal legal rights by providing identity and travel documents, and personal status for the purposes of marriage, divorce and taxation.[14] That said, the principle of no involuntary return to their country of origin, now referred to as *non-refoulement*, was from the outset considered an essential protection.[15]

The first formal international definition of a refugee was adopted by the Council of the League of Nations in 1926. This adopted what might be described as a group-status approach, applying specifically and exclusively to those of Russian or Armenian national or ethnic origin who were outside their country of nationality, did not 'enjoy the protection' of their own government and who had not acquired any other nationality. Some had fled their countries for political reasons, some had been driven from

---

[13] Arendt, H. (2017) *The Origins of Totalitarianism*, London: Penguin, p 384.
[14] Hathaway, J. (1984) 'The Evolution of Refugee Status in International Law: 1920–1950', *International and Comparative Law Quarterly*, 33(2): 348–380; Skran, C. (2011) 'The Historical Development of International Refugee Law', in Zimmermann, A. (ed.) *The 1951 Convention Relating to the Status of Refugees and Its 1967 Protocol: A Commentary*, Oxford: Oxford University Press.
[15] Goodwin-Gill, G. (2021) 'International Refugee Law in the Early Years', in Costello, C., Foster, M. and McAdam, J. (eds) *The Oxford Handbook of International Refugee Law*, Oxford: Oxford University Press, p 41.

their homes, many of the Russians had been stripped of their citizenship and all were unable to approach their own governments for assistance while abroad. The main purpose of the agreement, which was voluntary and initially signed by only 22 states, was to provide those affected with an identity certificate in lieu of a passport to enable their onward travel. The identity certificate scheme was extended in 1928 to other, smaller groups of exiles, again explicitly identified by reference to their national origins. These arrangements were then formalized in the Convention Relating to the International Status of Refugees in 1933, described by Professor Guy Goodwin-Gill, one of the leading scholars of refugee law, as 'an important marker on the road to a rights-based system of protection'.[16] In practice, the success of the new regime was limited. Only eight states ratified the treaty, several with major reservations, and by the time it came into force in 1936, it had already been overtaken by events: the rise of Nazism and election of Adolf Hitler in Germany. Nonetheless, the 1933 convention was to form the model for the post-war framework of refugee rights.[17]

The group-status approach was extended specifically to German refugees by an intergovernmental conference in 1936. When this arrangement was formalized in the Convention Concerning the Status of Refugees Coming from Germany of 1938, the definition was modified to require a more careful individual examination of personal circumstances.[18] To qualify for a certificate of identity a person would have to prove that 'in law or in fact, they do not enjoy the protection of the Government of the Reich' and that they had not left Germany 'for reasons purely of purely personal convenience'. A proposal to restrict status only to those who had fled on political, religious or racial grounds, which would have required much closer individual consideration of a person's situation, was rejected. The group-status approach was then applied also to Czechs and Slovaks and Austrians fleeing German incorporation in 1938. The Intergovernmental Committee on Refugees, formed at the Evian Conference of 1938, initially continued to focus on national groups but dispensed with the language of national protection, adopting instead a definition requiring that a refugee had emigrated 'on account of their political opinions, religious beliefs and racial origin'. This definition was in 1943 amended to abandon references to particular national groups and instead refer to any person who had been

---

[16] Goodwin-Gill, G. (2021) 'International Refugee Law in the Early Years', in Costello, C., Foster, M. and McAdam, J. (eds) *The Oxford Handbook of International Refugee Law*, Oxford: Oxford University Press, p 37.

[17] Hathaway, J. (2021) *The Rights of Refugees under International Law* (2nd edn), Cambridge: Cambridge University Press, pp 26, 29.

[18] League of Nations Treaty Series, Vol. CXCII, No. 4461, p 59.

forced to leave their country of residence 'because of the danger to their lives or liberties on account of their race, religion or political beliefs'.

Tens of millions of people were displaced within Europe during the Second World War.[19] The initial response was led by the United Nations Relief and Rehabilitation Agency (UNRRA), created in 1943 to provide immediate humanitarian relief to civilian populations once the anti-Axis counteroffensive began. Three-quarters of all displaced people in Europe were rapidly repatriated, irrespective of their individual wishes. No specific provision was made for refugees and some of those who returned to Soviet countries found themselves interned in Stalin's labour camps.[20] Increasing awareness among Western powers of the reluctance of some to return and the fate of those who did slowed the pace of transfer after 1945. Funding for UNRRA was eventually terminated by the main donor, the United States. Early in 1946, the United Nations General Assembly passed a resolution recognizing that some displaced persons were refugees who should not be forced to return to their country of origin.[21] A new body which focused on resettlement rather than repatriation was created in late 1946, the International Refugee Organization (IRO).[22] This was another powerful and well-funded institution. During the four years of its existence, the IRO assisted more than 1.6 million people, mainly by resettling them to the United States, Australia, Israel, Canada, the United Kingdom, third countries in Europe and South America.[23] Its constitution offered assistance to six protected groups, including those who had 'valid objections' to repatriation based on 'persecution, or fear, based on reasonable grounds, of persecution because of race, religion, nationality or political opinions' or objections 'of a political nature, judged by the organization to be valid'.[24] There had been no cessation or exclusion clauses included in earlier refugee conventions addressed to national groups of refugees, but the statute of the IRO explicitly excluded 'war criminals, quislings and traitors'. These exclusions reflected the more individual approach to

---

[19] Marrus, M. (1985) *The Unwanted: European Refugees from the First World War through the Cold War*, Oxford: Oxford University Press.

[20] Loescher, G. (2001) *The UNHCR and World Politics: A Perilous Path*, Oxford: Oxford University Press, p 36.

[21] UN General Assembly Resolution 8(1) on the question of refugees (UN Doc A/RES/8(I)).

[22] UN Economic and Social Council resolution 18 (III) of 3 October 1946.

[23] Einarsen, T. (2011) 'Drafting History of the 1951 Convention and the 1967 Protocol', in Zimmermann, A. (ed.) *The 1951 Convention Relating to the Status of Refugees and Its 1967 Protocol: A Commentary*, Oxford: Oxford University Press, p 46.

[24] Constitution of the International Refugee Organization, approved by the General Assembly of the United Nations in resolution 62 (I) of 15 December 1946 (United Nations, Treaty Series, Vol. 18, p 3), Annex I, Part I, Section A(1).

refugee status, moral anxiety that those responsible for perpetrating the horrors committed by Nazi and Axis regimes be held to proper account, and the increased politicization of refugees, repatriation and resettlement between Western and Soviet governments.

Despite the massive scale of the repatriation and then resettlement programmes, by the time the IRO ceased operating in 1952, there were still some 400,000 refugees remaining in camps in Europe, mainly sick, elderly and disabled people and others unable to undertake physical labour. In turn, the IRO was replaced by a much smaller organization with a tiny budget: the UNHCR.

United Nations High Commissioner for Refugees

Two mechanisms were envisaged to protect refugees: an internationally agreed legal framework in the form of a convention and an agency of the United Nations. The negotiations and drafting for the creation of both initially proceeded in parallel but the work on the agency was completed first. A resolution passed by the General Assembly of the United Nations in 1950 gave birth to the UNHCR, with effect from 1 January 1951.[25] UNHCR is both an individual, in that there is a single High Commissioner, and an office or organization. Taking over from the IRO, the new High Commissioner was charged with promoting the protection, voluntary repatriation or assimilation of remaining post-war refugees and 'such additional activities, including repatriation and resettlement, as the General Assembly may determine'.[26] The founding statute adopted the various refugee definitions of the interwar years and added a new definition which was similar but not identical to that later used in the Refugee Convention.[27] The UNHCR definition did not include an option to restrict recognition to European refugees only, did not include membership of a particular social group as a ground for refugee status, excluded those who refused to return for reasons of personal convenience or economic reasons and included past as well as present fear of persecution. The UNHCR definition was though, like the Refugee Convention, essentially backwards-looking, applying to existing refugees only or those who became refugees 'as a result of events occurring before 1 January 1951'. Despite its initially limited remit and funding and the requirement that its work 'shall

---

[25] Resolution 319 (IV) of 3 December 1949 of the United Nations General Assembly; Statute of the Office of the United Nations High Commissioner for Refugees, adopted by the General Assembly on 14 December 1950 as Annex to Resolution 428 (V).

[26] Statute of the Office of the United Nations High Commissioner for Refugees, UNGA Res 428(V), 14 December 1950, Articles 8 and 9.

[27] Statute of the Office of the United Nations High Commissioner for Refugees, UNGA Res 428(V), 14 December 1950, Article 6.

be of an entirely non-political character', UNHCR established a leading role in responding to post-war refugee crises.[28] From the start, the UNHCR statute made clear that the organization could 'engage in such additional activities, including repatriation and resettlement, as the General Assembly may determine, within the limits of the resources placed at his disposal'.[29] Appointed lead agency by the United Nations for responding to the Hungarian refugee crisis of 1956, UNHCR displayed 'considerable innovation' in maintaining that the crisis arose from events occurring before 1951.[30] A United Nations General Assembly resolution in 1959 authorized the High Commissioner to use his 'good offices' to provide future assistance to refugees who fell outside the formal definition.[31] Responding increasingly to events outside Europe, UNHCR's activities, staff and budget expanded exponentially during the 1970s under the leadership of High Commissioner Sadruddin Aga Khan.

Today, UNHCR performs multiple functions, from direct provision of aid to millions of refugees in camps around the world to carrying out refugee status determination in many countries, running refugee resettlement schemes, publishing legal guidance and intervening in court proceedings. As Gil Loescher wrote in 2001 in his landmark study of UNHCR, 'committed staff members are willing to place their lives in danger to defend the proposition that persecuted individuals need protection'.[32] UNHCR's mandate has been extended by the United Nations General Assembly beyond refugees to asylum seekers, stateless persons and returnees. In other situations, UNHCR relies on its 'good offices' function to render assistance to those forced from their homes but remaining within their country of origin or where forced from their homes by natural disaster. Neither of these groups would meet the criteria defining a refugee at Article 1A(2) of the Refugee Convention. Where UNHCR offers protection to an individual, state parties to the Refugee Convention are therefore not obliged to do likewise.[33]

UNHCR is no longer alone on the international stage. Alexander Betts argues that a 'refugee regime complex' has emerged in recent years, consisting

---

[28] See Loescher, G. (2001) *The UNHCR and World Politics: A Perilous Path*, Oxford: Oxford University Press.

[29] Statute of the Office of the United Nations High Commissioner for Refugees, UNGA Res 428(V), 14 December 1950, Article 9.

[30] Loescher, G. (2017) 'UNHCR's Origins and Early History: Agency, Influence, and Power in Global Refugee Policy', *Refuge*, 33(1): 77–86, 79.

[31] UNGA Res 1388 (XIV), 20 November 1959.

[32] Loescher, G. (2001) *The UNHCR and World Politics: A Perilous Path*, Oxford: Oxford University Press, p 1. Just two years after publication, Loescher himself suffered life-changing injuries in a suicide bombing in Baghdad while undertaking humanitarian work.

[33] *IA v The Secretary of State for the Home Department* [2014] UKSC 6 [28]–[29].

of overlapping and nested legal frameworks and organizations.[34] UNHCR competes for both function and funding, for example with the IOM, a body originally created and operating outside the UN system but later absorbed by the UN in 2018. This institutional proliferation has enabled some states, particularly in the Global North, to bypass the Refugee Convention and UNHCR without necessarily violating their legal obligations. Having led the development of the UN Global Compact on Refugees between 2016 and 2018, UNHCR appeared at the time of writing to have consolidated its position at the forefront of international refugee protection and policy.[35] Given the investment of credibility in the project discussed in more detail later, this position may prove to be vulnerable should the Compact prove ineffective. UNHCR has also been subject to criticism by refugee rights advocates and civil society. Management and oversight of the organization is unwieldy because of the growth in membership of its Executive Committee ('ExCom').[36] UNHCR has been slow to censure states in the Global North for shortcomings in their protection of refugee rights because of its institutional dependence, written into its founding statute, on voluntary contributions from wealthy countries.[37] Freedom to allocate resources is constrained by the practice of these donor states to 'earmark' funds for specific purposes. Similarly, UNHCR's dependence on the voluntary cooperation of states in the Global South in whose territories the organization must operate has led to criticism for complicity with breaches of refugee rights, for example, by encampment of refugees.[38] Finally, it has been observed that UNHCR's supervisory role is called into question when it assumes responsibilities that are properly those of states and therefore require supervision themselves.[39]

---

[34] Betts, A. (2010) 'The Refugee Regime Complex', *Refugee Survey Quarterly*, 29(1): 12–37.
[35] Global Compact on Refugees (UN Doc A/73/12) (2 August 2018).
[36] Loescher, G. (2021) *Refugees: A Very Short Introduction*, Oxford: Oxford University Press, pp 62–63.
[37] Milner, J. and Ramasubramanyam, J., 'The Office of the United Nations High Commissioner for Refugees', in Costello, C., Foster, M. and McAdam, J. (eds) *The Oxford Handbook of International Refugee Law*, Oxford: Oxford University Press, pp 189–192.
[38] Milner, J. and Ramasubramanyam, J., 'The Office of the United Nations High Commissioner for Refugees', in Costello, C., Foster, M. and McAdam, J. (eds) *The Oxford Handbook of International Refugee Law*, Oxford: Oxford University Press, p 190. Slaughter, A. and Crisp, J. (2008) 'A Surrogate State? The Role of UNHCR in Protracted Refugee Situations', in Loescher, G., Milner, J., Newman, E. and Troeller, G. (eds) *Protracted Refugee Situations: Political, Human Rights and Security Implications*, Tokyo: United Nations University Press, pp 123–140.
[39] Zieck, M. (2011) 'Executory and Transitory Provisions, Article 35 of the 1951 Convention/Article II of the 1967 Protocol', in Zimmermann, A. (ed.) *The 1951 Convention Relating to the Status of Refugees and Its 1967 Protocol: A Commentary*, Oxford: Oxford University Press, pp 1507–1508.

The Refugee Convention

The drafting process for a new convention on refugees to replace those of the interwar years was prolonged. It began in earnest with the creation at the UN of the Ad Hoc Committee on Statelessness and Related Problems in 1949. This body was tasked with considering 'the desirability of preparing a revised and consolidated convention relating to the international status of refugees and stateless persons' and, if considered desirable, drafting a text.[40] The UN Secretary-General prepared a memorandum prior to the first meeting of the committee urging that a universal refugee definition be adopted rather than one applicable only to defined national groups.[41] This proved to be a matter of considerable controversy, with the United States, in particular, opposing a universal definition but Belgium, Canada, Egypt, Lebanon, Pakistan, Turkey, the United Kingdom and others advocating in favour.[42] Most of the drafting work took place in 1950 and 1951 in the renamed Ad Hoc Committee on Refugees and Stateless Persons, including the drafting of the core of the definition later to be enshrined in the new convention. Adjustments to the text were made by the later Conference of Plenipotentiaries, including the addition of the 'membership of a particular social group' ground for being persecuted. As a compromise between the defined group and universalist positions, the final text included a temporal restriction to events occurring before 1 January 1951 and an optional geographical restriction to events in Europe. The conference formally adopted the new Convention Relating to the Status of Refugees on 28 July 1951 and it came into force on 1 January 1954. As discussed earlier, the temporal and geographical restrictions were removed by a protocol in 1967. At the time of writing, there were 149 countries around the world which were state signatories to one or both these legal instruments.

Entitlement to refugee status

The words used to define the meaning of the word 'refugee' at Article 1A(2) of the 1951 UN Convention Relating to the Status of Refugees (and set out earlier in this text) can for pedagogical purposes be broken down and arranged into its constituent parts. As we will see though, some of these elements of the definition overlap and interact with one another:

---

[40] UN Economic and Social Council Resolution 248 (IX) B of 8 August 1949.
[41] Memorandum by the Secretary-General, 3 January 1950 (UN Doc E/AC.32/2).
[42] Oberoi, P. (2001) 'South Asia and the Creation of the International Refugee Regime', *Refuge*, 19(5): 36–45.

(i) well-founded fear;
(ii) of treatment which amounts to being persecuted;
(iii) for one of five reasons, often referred to collectively as the convention grounds or reasons: race, religion, nationality, membership of a particular social group or political opinion;
(iv) where the person cannot be protected in their own country;
(v) and the person is outside their country of origin.

These elements have been described as posing a 'single composite question' with it being said to be 'a mistake to isolate the elements of the definition, interpret them, and then ask whether the facts of the instant case are covered by the sum of those individual interpretations'.[43] For example, as discussed in Chapter 5, whether or not some forms of harm amount to being persecuted may depend on the reason the harm is inflicted. This creates a problem for the author (and reader) of a book on refugee law, given that some sequencing is necessary for narrative exposition. Bundling together of issues also risks analytically defective decision-making. As Lord Justice Sedley has said, 'experience shows that adjudicators and tribunals give better reasoned and more lucid decisions if they go step by step rather than follow a recital of the facts and arguments with a single laconic assessment which others then have to unpick, deducing or guessing at its elements rather than reading them off the page'.[44] The different elements of the definition are therefore addressed in different chapters in this book but with cross-referencing between them.

The words of the refugee definition create several layers of limitation to entitlement to protection: it is not easy to qualify as a refugee and many people around the world in the direst humanitarian need are ineligible for refugee status. In the landmark Australian case of *Applicant A*, Dawson J emphasized the exclusionary nature of the refugee definition:

> No matter how devastating may be the epidemic, natural disaster or famine, a person fleeing them is not a refugee within the terms of the Convention. And by incorporating the five Convention reasons the Convention plainly contemplates that there will even be persons fearing persecution who will not be able to gain asylum as refugees.[45]

---

[43] *Ravichandran and Sandralingham v Secretary of State for the Home Department* [1996] Imm AR 97 (UK CA) (Simon Brown LJ); *Applicant A v Minister for Immigration and Ethnic Affairs* [1997] HCA 4 (Aus HC) (McHugh J).

[44] *Svazas v Secretary of State for the Home Department* [2002] EWCA Civ 74, [2002] WLR 1891 [30].

[45] *Applicant A v Minister for Immigration & Ethnic Affairs* [1997] HCA 4 (Aus HC) (Dawson J).

That said, the causes of flight are seldom straightforward and may well overlap, and there may be elements of discrimination or persecution in the way in which a state responds to a disaster. The most obvious and absolute limitation to refugee status is that a person can only become a refugee if outside their country of origin in a state of what is sometimes called 'alienage'. At a stroke, this excludes the millions of internally displaced people who remain within their own country, no matter how perilous or parlous their situation and no matter how badly their own country has failed them. Even for those who have managed to flee abroad, protection only becomes available if the person has a 'well-founded fear', which imposes the probability or risk threshold discussed in Chapter 2. Essentially, a person who flees their country must show there was a good reason for doing so, or at least that there is a good reason for not now returning. The words 'being persecuted' are interpreted as requiring a high level of ill-treatment or harm, as discussed in Chapter 3. The threshold has been expressed as 'serious harm' and 'a sustained and systemic denial of human rights'.[46] Coupled with that, as discussed in Chapter 4, many jurisdictions require that a person demonstrate failure of state protection as an added component of 'being persecuted'. Even if a person can show sufficient risk of sufficiently serious harm and insufficient state protection at home, the convention grounds discussed in detail in Chapter 5 restrict protection to those who can show their predicament is a consequence of certain protected characteristics. Not only does the definition limit the range of people entitled to protection, but the cessation clauses of the Refugee Convention state when a person ceases to be a refugee and the exclusion clauses prevent some individuals from claiming protection based on their conduct either in their own country or elsewhere; both are discussed in Chapter 6.

Rights of refugees

After defining who is and is not a refugee, the Refugee Convention goes on to require state parties to provide refugees with various rights. Addressed in Chapter 7, these include the most important right of all, the right of *non-refoulement*: the right not to be returned either directly or indirectly to a country in which the refugee might face persecution.[47] The rights afforded by the Refugee Convention are intended to protect refugees from the physical harm from which they fled, at least until their claim to be a

---

[46] Respectively Lord Hoffman in *R v Immigration Appeal Tribunal, ex p Shah* [1999] 2 AC 629 (UK HL) and Hathaway, J. (1991) *The Law of Refugee Status*, Toronto: Butterworths Canada, pp 104–105.
[47] Refugee Convention, Article 31.

refugee has been determined, to ensure that they have a personal legal status in the absence of diplomatic or consular recognition by their home country, to ensure humane treatment of refugees in the country of refuge and, in the long term, to promote the integration and assimilation of the refugee into that country.

The rights of refugees are engaged at different stages of the refugee's journey. Some, like the rights of *non-refoulement* and the right of non-discrimination, are relevant at all times that the refugee is within the jurisdiction of a state party. Other rights only become relevant at different stages of 'attachment' of the refugee to the country of refuge: physically within the territory whether lawfully or otherwise, lawfully present, lawfully staying, habitually resident or settled. The right to freedom of religion applies to refugees within the territory of a country, for example, but the right to wage-earning employment on the same terms as other foreign nationals is only engaged when a refugee is lawfully staying in the country concerned.

Nature of refugeehood

The Refugee Convention is notably silent as regards a procedure for recognition of refugees. This omission is simultaneously both a strength and a weakness for the regime of refugee protection. It is a strength because it follows that the definition of a refugee has an immediate and automatic effect. To put it another way, a grant or declaration of 'refugee status' is declaratory of a status that was in truth already held:

> A person is a refugee within the meaning of the 1951 Convention as soon as he fulfils the criteria contained in the definition. This would necessarily occur prior to the time at which his refugee status is formally determined. Recognition of his refugee status does not therefore make him a refugee but declares him to be one. He does not become a refugee because of recognition, but is recognised because he is a refugee.[48]

As Hathaway and Foster say, refugee status 'inheres by virtue of facts rather than formalities'.[49] The point has been accepted in multiple jurisdictions and multiple legal instruments.[50] A person outside their country of origin

---

[48] UNHCR (1979) *Handbook and Guidelines on Procedures and Criteria for Determining Refugee Status under the 1951 Convention and the 1967 Protocol Relating to the Status of Refugees* (re-issued 2011) [28].

[49] Hathaway, J. and Foster, M. (2014) *The Law of Refugee Status* (2nd edn), Cambridge: Cambridge University Press, p 1.

[50] See for example *Hoxha v Secretary of State for the Home Department* [2005] UKHL 19, [2005] WLR 1063 [60]; *G v G* [2021] UKSC 9 [81–82]; *Minister for Immigration and Multicultural*

may therefore, for example, become what is known as a *sur place* refugee due to a change in their individual circumstances or due to events in their country of origin.[51] The Refugee Convention is also silent on where a refugee may or must claim asylum; there is no obligation to claim asylum in the first safe country a refugee may reach nor any prohibition on crossing multiple borders. Sadly, though, this is seldom how refugee receiving states in the Global North treat newly arrived putative refugees in practice. This is where the weaknesses of the protection regime become evident. The convention specifies no minimum standards for ensuring that the determination of refugee status is timely or fair, for example. It has been suggested that an omission to determine refugee status individually should be interpreted as *prima facie* acceptance that a person or group is or are entitled to the benefits of the Refugee Convention.[52] But there is no legal requirement or legal presumption that this is so. There is no right of entry for the purpose of claiming asylum, as is discussed further in Chapter 7, only a right not to be exposed to persecution. Most fundamentally, the Refugee Convention is not backed by any effective enforcement mechanism whereby an 'International Court of Refugees' could find a signatory state in breach of the convention or forced it to comply with its provisions. Refugees rely on state parties adhering to their international law obligations in good faith. The only enforcement mechanism written into the convention is an inter-state one, and it has never been invoked.[53] As discussed in Chapter 1, regional courts such as the Court of Justice of the European Union and the Inter-American Court of Human Rights have begun to address issues of asylum and *non-refoulement*, to some extent addressing this deficit. Nevertheless, the lacunae in the international regime have encouraged and enabled some state parties to effectively evade their obligations to refugees while maintaining the pretence of adherence to the terms of the Refugee Convention.

A 'well-founded-fear of being persecuted' for a convention reason is the key to refugee status but the convention does not require that this be the main or sole reason for a refugee leaving or refusing to return to their

---

and *Indigenous Affairs v QAAH* [2006] HCA 53 (Aus HC) [96] (Kirby J); *Németh v Canada (Minister of Justice)* [2010] 3 SCR 281 [50]; *Pacheco Tineo Family v Bolivia*, Inter-American Court of Human Rights, Series C No. 272, 25 November 2013 [147]; Qualification Directive 2011/95/EU, Preamble [21].

[51] See further Chapter 2.
[52] UNHCR (1979) *Handbook and Guidelines on Procedures and Criteria for Determining Refugee Status under the 1951 Convention and the 1967 Protocol Relating to the Status of Refugees* (re-issued 2011) [44]; Goodwin-Gill, G. (1983) *The Refugee in International Law*, Oxford: Oxford University Press, p 45.
[53] Convention Relating to the Status of Refugees 1951, Article 38.

country of origin. If a person fulfils the criteria for refugee status, they are a refugee no matter what other motives they may have had for reaching their country of refuge. Thus a person who crosses a border purely for family, social or economic reasons may not be likely to meet the criteria for refugee status but nor are they excluded from it. The language used in the news and media to discuss the movement of people across borders labels some as 'migrants' and others as 'refugees' as if these were mutually exclusive categories. Under the terms of the Refugee Convention, it is possible for a refugee to move partly for economic or other reasons but still to qualify for refugee status. A Syrian stuck for months or years in a refugee camp in Jordan may decide to move to another country in the hope of a better future for themselves and their family; if that Syrian still fulfils the criteria in Article 1A(2) of the Refugee Convention in relation to their county of nationality, they are therefore under international law a refugee no matter where they move to or how many borders they cross.

Purpose of the Refugee Convention

Article 31 of the Vienna Convention on the Law of Treaties begins by stating: 'A treaty shall be interpreted in good faith in accordance with the ordinary meaning to be given to the terms of the treaty in their context and in the light of its object and purpose.'[54] The purpose of the Refugee Convention is therefore important when seeking to understand and interpret it. Divining the purpose of the convention is not entirely straightforward, however, and involves a certain degree of positivist pretence that a single intent can be discerned from the disparate motives behind the actors who drafted, amended and voted on it.[55] As Lord Lloyd noted of the convention in one of the early landmark United Kingdom refugee law cases, *ex p Adan*, 'the final text will have been the product of a long period of negotiation and compromise'.[56] The language employed would, therefore, as with many other treaties, be expected to be somewhat imprecise. Lord Lloyd went on to say that:

> one is more likely to arrive at the true construction of article 1A(2) by seeking a meaning which makes sense in the light of the Convention

---

[54] Vienna Convention on the Law of Treaties 1969, Article 31(1). While the treaty came after the Refugee Convention of 1951 and is not formally retroactive, it is considered to constitute customary international law.

[55] See for example Chimni, B.S. (1998) 'The Geopolitics of Refugee Studies: View from the South', *Journal of Refugee Studies*, 11(4): 350–374.

[56] [1999] AC 293 (UK HL).

as a whole, and the purposes which the framers of the Convention were seeking to achieve, rather than by concentrating exclusively on the language. A broad approach is what is needed, rather than a narrow linguistic approach.[57]

The courts have emphasized that the Refugee Convention 'must be interpreted as an international instrument, not a domestic statute', meaning that the normal rules of interpretation for domestic statutes should give way before the principles of the Vienna Convention on the Law of Treaties.[58] But with 149 state parties to the convention, there is clearly a risk that different jurisdictions might conclude differently on purpose and interpretation. Despite the danger of divergence, a remarkable degree of convergence has been brought about by two influences, both discussed further in Chapter 1. The first is that of the UN High Commissioner for Refugees, who is charged by Article 35 of the Refugee Convention with a duty of 'supervising the application of the provisions of this Convention' and with whom state parties are obliged to cooperate. The second, and perhaps even more important, influence has been what has been described as a 'transnational judicial dialog' across jurisdictions.[59]

Judges and jurists agree that the purpose of the Refugee Convention is not simply to save or rescue people: it is not merely or exclusively a humanitarian instrument. At least, if that were the convention's purpose, it is self-evidently not very good at fulfilling it given the range of those in dire humanitarian need who are excluded from its protection. The drafters sought to balance what has been said to be the 'competing interests' of the humane treatment of victims of oppression and the wish of sovereign states to exercise control over those entering their territory.[60] The Refugee Convention is generally regarded as a backup or failsafe available to those to whom national protection is unavailable. Goodwin-Gill has written that 'it is the lack of protection by their own government which distinguishes

---

[57] *R v Secretary of State for the Home Department, ex p Adan* [1999] 1 AC 293 (UK HL). See also *Applicant A v Minister for Immigration and Ethnic Affairs* [1997] HCA 4 (Aus HC) (Brennan CJ).

[58] See for example *Applicant A v Minister for Immigration and Ethnic Affairs* [1997] HCA 4 (Aus HC), *ex p Adan and Aitsegur* [2001] 2 AC 477 (UK HL), *Januzi v Secretary of State for the Home Department* [2006] UKHL 5, [2006] 2 AC 426 [4], *R v Afsaw* [2008] UKHL 31, [2008] 1 AC 1061 [125].

[59] Hathaway, J. and Foster, M. (2014) *The Law of Refugee Status* (2nd edn), Cambridge: Cambridge University Press, pp 4–5.

[60] *R (European Roma Rights Centre) v Immigration Officer at Prague Airport* [2004] UKHL 55, [2005] 2 AC 1 [15] (Lord Bingham). See also *Applicant A v Minister for Immigration and Ethnic Affairs* [1997] HCA 4 (Aus HC); *Rodriguez v United States* (1987) 480 US 522 525–526 (US SC).

refugees from ordinary aliens'.⁶¹ The idea that a refugee is a person who needs international protection because the protection of their home country is unavailable to them is supported by the way in which international refugee law definitions emerged and then evolved from the 1920s onwards, as we saw previously. In one of the earliest United Kingdom refugee law cases, the essential purpose of the Refugee Convention was said to be 'to afford protection and fair treatment to those for whom neither is available in their own country'.⁶² This proposition was later memorably encapsulated by Hathaway in his aphorism that the Refugee Convention offers 'surrogate or substitute protection'.⁶³ Drawing explicitly on this analysis, La Forest J held in the landmark Canadian case of *Ward*: 'International refugee law was formulated to serve as a back-up to the protection one expects from the State of which an individual is a national. It was meant to come into play only in situations when that protection is unavailable, and then only in certain situations.'⁶⁴ Courts in Australia, New Zealand and the United Kingdom have explicitly adopted the same approach.⁶⁵ On this view, 'the failure of state protection is central to the whole system' because '[t]he general purpose of the Convention is to enable the person who no longer has the benefit of protection against persecution for a Convention reason in his own country to turn for protection to the international community'.⁶⁶ The notion of surrogacy has been criticized, however. Elevating the notion of surrogacy from a shorthand description of the broad function of the Refugee Convention to its conceptual basis has been argued to encourage a focus on the performance of the state from which the refugee comes rather than on the situation of the individual refugee (see further Chapter 4).⁶⁷

The near unanimity in the jurisprudence is largely shared by philosophers and ethicists, although many have been explicitly or implicitly critical of the convention's limitations. For Arendt, refugees lack 'the right to have rights' and are cast adrift as 'the scum of the earth' in a system of sovereign nation-states.⁶⁸ But for those to whom asylum is offered, it can act as 'a

---

61 Goodwin-Gill, G. (1983) *The Refugee in International Law*, Oxford: Oxford University Press, p 6.
62 *R (on the application of Sivakumuran) v Secretary of State for the Home Department* [1988] AC 958, 992H-993A (UK HL).
63 Hathaway, J. (1991) *The Law of Refugee Status*, Toronto: Butterworths Canada, p 135.
64 *Canada (Attorney-General) v Ward* (1993) 103 DLR (4th) 1 [12] (Can SC).
65 *Applicant A v Minister for Immigration and Ethnic Affairs* [1997] HCA 4 (Aus HC) (Dawson J); *Butler v Attorney-General* [1999] NZAR 205 (NZ CA) [47] (Keith J), *Horvath v Secretary of State for the Home Department* [2000] AC 489 (UK HL).
66 *Horvath v Secretary of State for the Home Department* [2000] AC 489 (UK HL) (Lord Hope).
67 Goodwin-Gill, G. and McAdam, J. (2021) *The Refugee in International Law* (4th edn), Oxford: Oxford University Press, pp 7–9.
68 Arendt, H. (2017) *The Origins of Totalitarianism*, London: Penguin, pp 388, 349.

genuine substitute for national law'.[69] Haddad goes further and asserts that refugees are 'an inevitable if unintended consequence of the international states system ... They are the human reminder of the failings of modern international society'.[70] The refugee is both a victim and ward of this international society. She proposes an alternative definition of a refugee as 'an individual who has been forced, in significant degree, outside the domestic political community indefinitely'. In his influential essay 'Who Is a Refugee?', Shacknove argues from a humanitarian and ethical perspective that it is 'absence of state protection which constitutes the full and complete negation of society and the basis of refugeehood'.[71] He concludes that the Refugee Convention does not go far enough in compensating for failure of state protection, though. States can and do fail their citizens within their own borders and, while persecution might be a sufficient condition to show state failure, it should not be a necessary condition. For Shacknove, a refugee is a person 'whose government fails to protect their basic needs, who have no remaining recourse other than to seek international restitution of these needs, and who are so situated that international assistance is possible'. Gibney pragmatically accepts the need for alienage but otherwise takes a similar view and argues that what distinguishes a refugee from other 'foreigners in need' is that 'he or she is in need of the protection afforded by short or long-term asylum (i.e. residence in a new state) because there is no reasonable prospect of that person finding protection any other way'.[72] Emphasizing the political dimension of a grant of asylum, Price argues that asylum 'responds to the distinctive situation of persecuted people, who have been expelled from their political communities, by expressing condemnation of persecutory regimes and by providing a remedy – surrogate membership abroad – that matches the social harm they have suffered'.[73] Owen defines refugees as 'persons whose basic rights are unprotected by their state and can only be protected through recourse to the international order of states acting *in loco civitatis*'.[74] In a rare dissent, Betts and Collier condemn the Refugee Convention as an antiquated and Eurocentric product of the Cold War intended primarily to permit victims of Soviet state persecution to relocate

---

[69] Arendt, H. (2017) *The Origins of Totalitarianism*, London: Penguin, p 386.
[70] Haddad, E. (2008) *The Refugee in International Society*, Cambridge: Cambridge University Press, pp 1, 3.
[71] Shacknove, A.E. (1985) 'Who Is a Refugee?', *Ethics*, 95(2): 274–284.
[72] Gibney, M. (2004) *The Ethics and Politics of Asylum: Liberal Democracy and the Response to Refugees*, Oxford: Oxford University Press, p 8.
[73] Price, M. (2009) *Rethinking Asylum: History, Purpose, and Limits*, Cambridge: Cambridge University Press, p 13.
[74] Owen, D. (2020) *What Do We Owe to Refugees?*, Cambridge: Polity, p 50.

to the West.⁷⁵ They prefer a purely humanitarian conception of the refugee based on the moral duty of rescue and the need to restore autonomy to the refugee. Observing that the de facto international response to a refugee crisis is the pitching of tents, they eschew a theory of surrogacy or debate about principled international legal solutions which are often ignored in practice. They propose instead that wealthy countries should, of their own volition, motivated partly by moral duty and partly by self-interest, fund regional solutions more proximate to refugee-producing countries which provide jobs through private enterprise and 'development areas'.

The interpretation of all aspects of the refugee definition has been influenced by the prevalent surrogacy approach, with the divined purpose of the Refugee Convention being considered relevant to determining the standard of proof, the level of risk of harm, the meaning of the words 'being persecuted', the interpretation and role of the convention grounds and the understanding of what is meant by 'protection'. Broad agreement on the purpose of the Refugee Convention does not inexorably lead to agreement on the interpretation of these different words and concepts, however. In *Horvath*, for example, the case in which the United Kingdom's House of Lords adopted the language of surrogate protection, Lord Lloyd accepted the analysis of the majority on the purpose of the Refugee Convention but nevertheless dissented on the meaning of the word 'persecution'.⁷⁶ Even the meaning of 'protection' has been contested. Fortin agrees that the Refugee Convention offers surrogate protection but argues that the protection of which a refugee must be unable or unwilling to avail themselves is the diplomatic protection of their country of nationality.⁷⁷ While this view has not gained much traction in case law, it illustrates the potential for divergent views.⁷⁸

Criticisms of the Refugee Convention

The Refugee Convention has been criticized by some scholars and politicians as a Eurocentric product of the Cold War which fails refugees because it is outdated and ill-suited to modern refugee crises.⁷⁹ Some argue

---

⁷⁵ Betts, A. and Collier, P. (2017) *Refuge: Transforming a Broken Refugee System*, London: Penguin, pp 6–7.

⁷⁶ [2001] AC 489 (UK HL) (Lord Lloyd).

⁷⁷ Fortin, A. (2000) 'The Meaning of "Protection" in the Refugee Definition', *International Journal of Refugee Law*, 12(4): 548–576.

⁷⁸ It was cited with approval in *Minister for Immigration and Multicultural Affairs v Khawar* [2002] HCA 14 (Aus HC) by Gleeson CJ at paragraph 21 and McHugh and Gummow JJ at paragraph 73.

⁷⁹ See for example Betts, A. and Collier, P. (2018) *Refuge: Transforming a Broken Refugee System*, St. Ives: Penguin. In reply, see White, B. (2019) '"Refuge" and History: A Critical Reading of a Polemic', *Migration and Society: Advances in Research*, 2(1): 107–118.

that the convention needs to be strengthened through new mechanisms of enforcement and mandatory sharing of financial burdens and responsibility for refugees. Others suggest the convention, by permitting but not facilitating refugee mobility, rewards only those refugees who are able to travel, not necessarily the most vulnerable refugees most in need of assistance. They argue the convention should be sidelined and replaced with tailored national or regional solutions. Those advocating for change often seek to appropriate the concept of compassion to support their position, for example arguing that refugees should be prevented from undertaking dangerous journeys or falling into the hands of people smugglers by deterring them from setting out on such journeys in the first place.[80] Others respond that it is these supposedly compassionate policies of *non-entrée* and deterrence which cause the journeys to be dangerous and that safe and legal routes to claim asylum would be a more humane response.

It is hard to argue that the Refugee Convention does not have Eurocentric origins. As we have seen, the legal definition of a 'refugee' emerged in Europe in the interwar period in response to events in Europe. Earlier conventions and the Refugee Convention itself were negotiated and agreed at a time when many states in the Global South had no seat at the table because they remained under colonial rule. The delegates to the Conference of Plenipotentiaries that finalized the text of the Refugee Convention were predominantly from Western European states, although countries including Colombia, Egypt, Turkey, Venezuela and Yugoslavia (the only Soviet country present) were represented. The version of the convention agreed in 1951 included an option for a state party to limit the definition of a refugee to events arising in Europe.[81] This undoubtedly and understandably gives the impression of Eurocentrism. Only a handful of European state parties exercised the option to limit the scope of the definition, though; it was more commonly adopted outside Europe.[82] In the initial drafts of the refugee definition, the limitation to events in Europe was an inherent part of the definition and it was European powers, namely the United Kingdom and France, that first pushed for a universal refugee definition (although France later reversed its position). Newly independent India and Pakistan engaged enthusiastically with the early drafting process but grew disillusioned by the proposed limitation to Europe, the otherwise narrow nature of the definition and the profound lack of international interest in or material aid for the

---

[80] See analysis in Sirriyeh, A. (2018) *The Politics of Compassion: Immigration and Asylum Policy*, Bristol: Bristol University Press.

[81] Refugee Convention, Article 1B.

[82] Bem, K. (2004) 'The Coming of a "Blank Cheque" – Europe, the 1951 Convention, and the 1967 Protocol', *International Journal of Refugee Law*, 16(4): 626 n 77.

massive movement of population caused by the partition of British India.[83] Neither state ratified the new convention, and by 1961 only 27 states had done so, most of which were European. The abandonment of the temporal and geographical limitations to the Refugee Convention in 1967 was too little and too late to placate many defiant states.[84] Today, several significant refugee host countries still have not ratified the Refugee Convention, including Bangladesh, India, Iraq, Jordan, Lebanon, Malaysia and Pakistan. The nature of the institutions in charge of refugee protection has also been said to be 'intrinsically Eurocentric' and the regime's 'grandiose aspirations of universalism' have been argued to 'present an illusory picture of accessible protection and humanitarianism, which makes all other forms of alternate histories, conceptions, locations of practice and discourses optional and relevant only as critiques to this larger hegemonic framework'.[85] Even international law itself, of which the Refugee Convention is part, has been criticized as a colonial, Eurocentric paradigm.[86]

The origins of the Refugee Convention are therefore undoubtedly European and were seen as such from the outset. It does not necessarily follow that the key principles of the convention are not universal. Examination of state practice in South Asia, for example, reveals respect for the principle of *non-refoulement* and other protection norms despite none of these countries ratifying the Refugee Convention.[87] The principle of *non-refoulement* is so widely accepted, even by states which have not ratified the convention, that it has been argued by some to have attained the status of customary international law.[88] Those who suggest the Refugee Convention is not suited to modern, large, spontaneous flows of unauthorized refugees appear to forget that this was exactly the historical context of the emergence of the refugee in international law in the interwar period. The 1951 convention was negotiated and drafted in the immediate aftermath of truly

---

[83] Oberoi, P. (2001) 'South Asia and the Creation of the International Refugee Regime', *Refuge*, 19(5): 36–45.

[84] Hamlin, R. (2021) *Crossing: How We Label and React to People on the Move*, Stanford: Stanford University Press, pp 96–99.

[85] Ramasubramanyam, J. (2018) 'Subcontinental Defiance to the Global Refugee Regime: Global Leadership or Regional Exceptionalism?', *Asian Yearbook of International Law*, 24: 60, 78–79.

[86] Anghie, A. (2006) 'The Evolution of International Law: Colonial and Postcolonial Realities', *Third World Quarterly*, 27: 739.

[87] Ramasubramanyam, J. (2021) 'Regional Regimes: South Asia', in Costello, C., Foster, M. and McAdam, J. (eds) *The Oxford Handbook of International Refugee Law*, Oxford: Oxford University Press.

[88] See for example Costello, C. and Foster, M. (2016) 'Non-refoulement as Custom and Jus Cogens? Putting the Prohibition to the Test', *Netherlands Yearbook of International Law*, 46: 273.

massive population displacement and large, unauthorized movement of refugees was at the forefront of the minds of the drafters of the convention. Similarly, the suggestion that the 'new asylum seekers' originating in the Global South from the 1980s onwards were somehow radically different from the invented idea of the 'normal' refugee who was 'white, male and anti-communist – which clashed sharply with individuals fleeing the Third World' has been criticized.[89] This retrospective reimagining of refugees, described by leading international refugee law scholar B.S. Chimni as the 'myth of difference', ignores the evolution of the refugee definition from the 1920s onwards and the reality of refugee flows during the Cold War itself. There were millions of refugees in Europe in the interwar and Second World War period, millions of refugees fled conflict in China between 1949 and 1950 and from the Korean War of 1950 to 1953, the Hungarian crisis of 1956 gave rise to an estimated 200,000 refugees and the conflicts in South East Asia caused as many as three million refugees to flee in the late 1970s and 1980s.[90] Few of these refugees, who came from many walks of life and fled for many reasons, would have matched the imagined picture of the 'normal' Cold War refugee.

The Cold War hypothesis can be traced back to arguments advanced by Soviet delegates to the United Nations in the immediate post-war years. During the debate on the creation of the office of High Commissioner for Refugees in 1950, for example, the Russian delegate asserted that the new organization was 'intended to perpetuate the bondage of refugees and displaced persons and to doom them to hunger and the privation of rights'.[91] He went on to argue, unironically underlining the whole point of refugee status, that those who 'refuse to accept assistance from the government of the country of which they are nationals and refuse to co-operate with their own people in the reconstruction of their country new and democratic foundations' should not be considered refugees.[92] Likewise, the Polish delegate opined that refusal to repatriate Soviet citizens amounted to a policy of 'acquisition of cheap labour' by the United States and the United Kingdom.[93] The accusations were not completely fanciful. Under the

---

[89] Chimni, B.S. (1998) 'The Geopolitics of Refugee Studies: View from the South', *Journal of Refugee Studies*, 11(4): 350–374.

[90] Mayblin, L. (2014) 'Colonialism, Decolonisation, and the Right to be Human: Britain and the 1951 Geneva Convention on the Status of Refugees', *Journal of Historical Sociology*, 27(3): 423–441.

[91] Mr Soldatov of Russia, General Assembly Official Records, 5th Session, A/PV.325 at 73 (14 December 1950).

[92] Mr Soldatov of Russia, General Assembly Official Records, 5th Session, A/PV.325 at 77 (14 December 1950).

[93] Mr Drohojowski of Poland, General Assembly Official Records, 5th Session, A/PV.325 at 111 (14 December 1950).

auspices of the European Volunteer Worker scheme, the United Kingdom did in fact recruit an estimated 91,000 displaced people from the Baltics, Balkans and central and eastern Europe as workers in the post-war years under circumstances that involved a significant degree of compulsion.[94] However, refugees could return to their own countries voluntarily should they wish to, and the fact the workers were refugees and therefore could not be *forced* to leave if they fell sick or were judged unsuitable was considered by British officials a disadvantage. Terje Einarsen, in a detailed consideration of the drafting history, concludes that the refugee definition was, 'contrary to common belief, not influenced much by the Cold War'.[95] The United States did not, after all, ratify the resulting convention and only ratified the protocol in 1968. There was if anything more disagreement among Western powers on aspects of the refugee definition than between the West and the rest. Similarly, Matthew Price concedes that the refugee definition was used for political ends during the Cold War but, tracing its deep historical and philosophical origins, he argues that the granting of asylum has always expressed political values and communicated condemnation of persecuting regimes.[96]

Global Compact on Refugees

There has been no real change to the fundamentals of the international law framework protecting refugees since the 1967 protocol removed the temporal and geographical limitations to the 1951 Refugee Convention. An attempt to enshrine a right of access to asylum in international law began with the Declaration on Territorial Asylum of 1967 but ended with failure to agree a full and binding convention ten years later. The prospect of legally binding and enforceable positive reforms to enhance the protection provided by the Refugee Convention now seems remote. This is not to say that refugee law itself has stood still, as the following chapters will show. But positive reforms to enhance the protection of refugees now appears to depend on shifting norms, regional protection arrangements and on other areas of international law.

---

[94] Kay, D. and Miles, R. (1988) 'Refugees or Migrant Workers? The Case of the European Volunteer Workers in Britain (1946–1951)', *Journal of Refugee Studies*, 1(3–4): 214–236, 223.

[95] Einarsen, T. (2011) 'Drafting History of the 1951 Convention and the 1967 Protocol', in Zimmermann, A. (ed.) *The 1951 Convention Relating to the Status of Refugees and Its 1967 Protocol: A Commentary*, Oxford: Oxford University Press, p 67.

[96] Price, M. (2009) *Rethinking Asylum: History, Purpose, and Limits*, Cambridge: Cambridge University Press, pp 7, 57.

The United Nations General Assembly's New York Declaration for Refugees and Migrants of 2016 is a case in point.[97] This non-binding and unenforceable statement of principles and exhortations led to the adoption of the equally non-binding and unenforceable Global Compact on Refugees of 2018.[98] The objectives of the latter document are stated to be to ease pressures on host countries, enhance refugee self-reliance, expand access to third-country solutions and support conditions in countries of origin for return in safety and dignity.[99] Essentially, the hope is that better immediate refugee reception arrangements can be made when a refugee crisis arises, the burden of hosting refugees can be more widely shared and that durable solutions can be found for refugees, namely voluntary return to their country of origin, resettlement away from first countries of asylum or integration into the economy and society of whichever country they reside. Member states of the United Nations committed to convening a Global Refugee Forum every four years and the agenda at such meetings is intended to be set by the objectives of the Global Compact. One of the principles underpinning the agreement is the adoption of a 'multi-stakeholder and partnership approach' whereby actors other than central governments are engaged in responses and solutions for refugees. This includes humanitarian and development actors, the World Bank, national parliaments, local government, cities and municipalities, civil society organizations, faith-based groups, the private sector and academics. Without specifically referencing the rights afforded to refugees by the Refugee Convention, the Global Compact encourages focus on providing refugees with education, jobs and livelihoods, health care, decent living circumstances, food security, civil and birth registration and addressing the specific needs of women and children.

The Global Compact on Refugees has politely been described by Alexander Betts as 'relatively modest in scope and ambition' and somewhat less politely by James Hathaway as the 'Global Cop-Out on Refugees'.[100] It was accompanied by the Global Compact for Migration, which sets out 23 also non-binding and unenforceable objectives. Many of them are relevant to refugees.[101] For example, Objective 8 is to '[s]ave lives and establish coordinated international efforts on missing migrants' and clearly applies to putative but as yet unrecognized refugees in flight. It is too early

---

[97] UN General Assembly (2015) *New York Declaration for Refugees and Migrants* (UN Doc A/RES/71/1).
[98] Global Compact on Refugees (UN Doc A/73/12 (Part II)) (2 August 2018).
[99] Global Compact on Refugees (UN Doc A/73/12 (Part II)) (2 August 2018) [7].
[100] See 'Special Edition: The 2018 Global Compacts on Refugees and Migration', *International Journal of Refugee Law*, 30(4), December 2018.
[101] Global Compact for Safe, Orderly and Regular Migration (UN Doc A/RES/73/195) (19 December 2018).

to assess the impact of the compacts, if any, but we will return to the issue in the Conclusion.

Structure of the book

As intimated earlier, the structure of this book broadly follows the structure of the Refugee Convention. Chapter 1 examines the outline of the legal structure of international refugee protection. The Refugee Convention is the single most important legal instrument but it is not alone. It sits alongside other international legal instruments, which can add context, interpretative value and complementary forms of protection. Regional and domestic legal regimes add further interpretation and sometimes substance to the text of the convention. In countries that have not ratified the Refugee Convention, these other forms of protection – variously referred to as alternative, complementary, humanitarian, subsidiary or supplementary protection – may be the only forms of asylum available. Jurisprudence at international, regional and national levels has elucidated the meaning of the words and concepts of the convention and other legal instruments, and an international community of refugee law has influenced the evolution of common understanding in many countries. By their nature, regional and domestic interpretative aides and understandings have led to a certain amount of divergence, however, and, against that, UNHCR provides guidance intended to act as a centripetal force to prevent excessive fragmentation. While this book focuses principally on refugees as defined by the Refugee Convention, other forms of asylum and international protection, including under human rights instruments, anti-statelessness and anti-trafficking conventions are also considered.

Chapter 2 examines the role, importance and interpretation of the words in the refugee definition 'well-founded fear'. These words have become central to the refugee status determination process in many countries; arguably too central. They also influence the approach to asylum in other international legal instruments. This chapter considers the ways in which the words have been analyzed and understood in refugee law literature and case law. Many maintain that literal subjective 'fear' is required of a refugee although in reality it is rarely considered necessary in practice – and with good reason. The burden of proof in refugee cases is generally considered to rest with refugees. To ameliorate the effect, the standard of proof is considered to be a low one. Nevertheless, evaluation of the truthfulness or 'credibility' of a refugee and their narrative of their past experiences remains highly problematic in the refugee status determination process. Proper focus on future risk is sometimes lost. So-called bad faith claims to refugee status are considered as are *sur place* claims where the person becomes a refugee while already physically present in another country, for example, due to events in their country of origin. The chapter ends by looking at the relevance of dual nationality and the words 'country of his former habitual residence'.

Chapter 3 turns to the question, 'well-founded fear of what?' The Refugee Convention states that the fear must be of 'being persecuted' but does not expand on or elucidate what this means. Different approaches have been adopted at different times (and sometimes at the same time). A linguistic approach of applying the dictionary definition of the word 'persecute' is no longer generally preferred, although it is universally accepted that the harm feared must be serious in nature to qualify. Instead, the word is usually understood through the framework of international and/or regional human rights laws. This human rights approach to understanding persecution is often cited, but in reality, rarely applied in a meaningful way in practice.

Understanding the full concept of 'being persecuted' requires consideration of other elements of the definition of a refugee. Chapter 4 considers two other related requirements. The first of these is the need to show that protection is not available in the country of origin. While some of the later words of the definition appear to address this issue separately, the absence of state protection has become an integral part of the concept of being persecuted in many jurisdictions. This approach flows from the sometimes controversial idea that the Refugee Convention offers what has been called surrogate international protection, to which a refugee is only entitled if their own country has failed to provide it. The necessary level and effectiveness of the protection available is disputed, at least in theory, with the concept of 'sufficient' protection emerging in jurisprudence in the United Kingdom. Also flowing from the idea of surrogate protection is the argument that a refugee does not need protection abroad if they can safely relocate within their own country. Variously called internal protection, internal relocation or the 'internal flight alternative', this approach is now embedded in many jurisdictions despite not being an explicit requirement of the convention itself. This approach requires new questions to be asked, such as whether a dangerous journey must be undertaken and whether the existence of a safe but remote desert or mountainous location in a country precludes refugee status.

Chapter 5 looks at what are often called the 'convention reasons' or 'convention grounds' (and sometimes capitalized). These are the reasons which must be behind the well-founded fear of being persecuted. The role of the convention grounds in refugee law is more significant than may first appear from the text of Article 1A(2). They differentiate the Refugee Convention from more universalist human rights instruments, for example, excluding some who may experience extreme suffering if returned to their country of origin and determining whether ill-treatment is sufficiently serious so as to amount to being persecuted. The chapter considers the meaning, interpretation and extent of the five grounds of race, religion, nationality, membership of a particular social group or political opinion, and the significance of the common thread that runs through them: discrimination. The causal relationship between the convention ground and the persecution experienced is considered along with the concept of imputed or attributed convention grounds in which the persecutor thinks or believes the refugee has a quality which in truth they do not.

Chapter 6 ventures beyond the refugee definition at Article 1A to consider the loss of and exclusion from refugee status. Article 1C of the convention, sometimes referred to as the cessation clause (or clauses because of its subclauses), sets out the circumstances in which refugee status can be lost. These include voluntary reavailment of the protection of the country of origin, voluntary re-establishment in the country of origin and an end to the circumstances which gave rise to the claim to refugee status. While formal recognition of refugee status in the Global North often leads to settlement, this is not a right conferred on refugees by the Refugee Convention itself. Some individuals are excluded by Article 1F of the convention from becoming refugees at all because of their actions outside the country of refuge. The meaning and extent of these exclusion clauses, which cite crimes against peace, war crimes, crimes against humanity, serious non-political crimes and acts contrary to the purposes and principles of the United Nations, are considered. Those who commit serious crimes in the country of refuge and who are regarded as a danger to the security or community of the country concerned can, under Article 33(2) of the convention, be denied the benefits of refugee status in some circumstances. The governments of refugee hosting countries have tended to interpret these concepts expansively with the effect that more refugees are excluded from the protection of the convention. The effect has been to generate high-level case law in several jurisdictions on the level of personal responsibility and seriousness of the conduct that is needed to engage these exclusion clauses.

The rights of refugees conferred – or not – by the Refugee Convention are the subject of Chapter 7. The most important of these is the right of *non-refoulement*, meaning the right of a refugee not to be returned to their country of origin either directly or indirectly. The convention also sets out rights to work, self-employment, freedom of association, freedom of religion, public housing, education, social security and more. There is a scheme to these rights based on the level of attachment of the refugee to the host country, and the rights are not all conferred in absolute terms. There is no explicit right to family unity in the convention itself, with the result that some refugees struggle to reunite themselves with family members left behind in the country of origin. There is also no explicit right to enter a country of refuge or to have one's claim to fulfil the definition of a refugee determined swiftly or indeed at all. The closest the convention itself comes to protecting refugees who are in flight is the non-penalization clause, which in some circumstances prevents state parties from imposing penalties on a refugee for their illegal entry or presence. The absence of explicit procedural protection for putative refugees has enabled some countries to explore 'offshore processing' whereby refugees are intercepted and redirected before arrival or even simply removed to another country to have their claims decided there instead.

Chapter 8 turns to the process of refugee status determination, with the process in the United Kingdom being used as an example. While there is no formal process mandated by the convention, some norms have developed in the Global North, as have some trends in the treatment and processing of refugees. These include securitization of borders, policies of deterrence, denial of mainstream welfare benefits and accommodation, use of detention and a sceptical and sometimes even cynical approach to determining whether refugees are telling the truth about their experiences. This chapter also looks at what can happen in practice to refugees after their status has been recognized.

Finally, the conclusion briefly considers the successes and failures of the protection regime represented by the Refugee Convention and the issue of durable solutions for the vast majority of refugees who remain outside the Global North. The book ends by looking to the future with the issue of climate change and the UN Global Compact on Refugees.

Suggested further reading

Bem, K. (2004) 'The Coming of a "Blank Cheque" – Europe, the 1951 Convention, and the 1967 Protocol', *International Journal of Refugee Law*, 16(4): 626.

Betts, A. (2013) *Survival Migration: Failed Governance and the Crisis of Displacement*, New York: Cornell University Press, Chapter 1.

Cantor, D. (2016) 'Defining Refugees: Persecution, Surrogacy and the Human Rights Paradigm', in Cantor, D. and Burson, B. (eds) *Human Rights and the Refugee Definition: Comparative Legal Practice and Theory*, Leiden: Brill.

Chimni, B.S. (1998) 'The Geopolitics of Refugee Studies: View from the South', *Journal of Refugee Studies*, 11(4): 350–374.

Crawley, H. and Skleparis, D. (2018) 'Refugees, Migrants, Neither, Both: Categorical Fetishism and the Politics of Bounding in Europe's "Migration crisis"', *Journal of Ethnic and Migration Studies*, 44(1): 48–64.

Einarsen, T. (2011) 'Drafting History of the 1951 Convention and the 1967 Protocol', in Zimmermann, A. (ed.) *The 1951 Convention Relating to the Status of Refugees and Its 1967 Protocol: A Commentary*, Oxford: Oxford University Press.

Goodwin-Gill, G. (2021) 'International Refugee Law in the Early Years', in Costello, C., Foster, M. and McAdam, J. (eds) *The Oxford Handbook of International Refugee Law*, Oxford: Oxford University Press.

Hathaway, J. (1984) 'The Evolution of Refugee Status in International Law: 1920–1950', *International and Comparative Law Quarterly*, 33(2): 348–380.

Hathaway, J. and Foster, M. (2014) *The Law of Refugee Status* (2nd edn), Cambridge: Cambridge University Press, Introduction.

Loescher, G. (2021) *Refugees: A Very Short Introduction*, Oxford: Oxford University Press.

Oberoi, P. (2001) 'South Asia and the Creation of the International Refugee Regime', *Refuge*, 19(5): 36–45.

1

Legal Framework

At the time the Refugee Convention was negotiated and agreed, international human rights law was in its infancy. The Universal Declaration of Human Rights had been agreed in 1948 and included in Article 14 a right to seek (but not necessarily be *granted*) asylum: 'Everyone has the right to seek and to enjoy in other countries asylum from persecution.' The Refugee Convention embodies that right although, as is discussed in Chapter 7, it falls short of providing a right of entry for the purpose of seeking asylum. In turn, the Refugee Convention cites the Universal Declaration of Human Rights as well as the Charter of the United Nations. International human rights law has expanded and evolved considerably since 1951 and the Refugee Convention now sits alongside a developing, sometimes overlapping system of protection. It has even been argued that human rights law, with its centralized institutions and enforcement mechanisms, has become '*the* primary source of refugee protection', with the Refugee Convention playing 'a complementary and secondary role'.[1] Others retort that the decentralized regime of refugee law has led the way in protection from *refoulement* and has 'its own progressive dynamic which leads human rights law just as much, if not more, than it follows human rights law'.[2] The situation of specific groups like trafficking victims and stateless persons has been addressed with new international agreements, a right of *non-refoulement* has been recognized in human rights law, regional legal instruments addressing the situation of refugees have been adopted and various states have either or both incorporated a constitutional right to asylum or passed their own laws delineating access to and the content

---

[1] Chetail, V. (2014) 'Are Refugee Rights Human Rights? An Unorthodox Questioning of the Relations between Refugee Law and Human Rights Law', in Rubio-Martin, R. (ed) *Human Rights and Immigration*, Oxford: Oxford University Press, pp 19–72, 22 (emphasis in original).
[2] Costello, C. (2016) 'The Search for the Outer Edges of Non-Refoulement in Europe', in Cantor, D. and Burson, B. (eds) *Human Rights and the Refugee Definition: Comparative Legal Practice and Theory*, Leiden: Brill, pp 180–209, 208–209.

of refugee status. These developments have not been spontaneous, isolated events; they have taken place in the context of an ongoing dialogue between a range of international actors. The voices of refugees themselves played an important role at the time of the framing of the Refugee Convention but have too often been absent from the ongoing conversation.[3] This chapter addresses the interplay between international human rights law and refugee law, other aspects of the international protection system than the Refugee Convention itself and, briefly, some examples of national laws applying to refugees. A comprehensive survey of domestic national laws on refugee status would be an enormous undertaking and is beyond the scope of this book.

International community of refugee law and practice

Institutions, agencies, non-governmental organizations, civil servants, academics, judges, lawyers and campaigners from a range of countries have conversed with one another in a variety of ways since the early 1990s, giving rise to a remarkable degree of international consensus on the interpretation of the Refugee Convention and the norms of refugee protection. These actors collectively constitute what might be described as an international community of law, 'a partially insulated sphere in which legal actors interact based on common interests and values, protected from direct political interference'.[4] As the number of asylum claims grew rapidly in the Global North in the 1990s, these various newly emerging actors needed to acquire knowledge and understanding of a rapidly growing area of legal practice. Reference to international authority could also serve to legitimate decisions, an important consideration given the politically contentious nature of those decisions. Small in number in their own jurisdiction, they turned to others in a like situation elsewhere. What has since been described as a 'transnational judicial dialogue' took place between judges and others in different jurisdictions, and it is possible to trace the emergence, spread, modification and re-seeding of ideas in reported cases and, sometimes, in legislation.[5] Initially, this was carried out indirectly by means of the simple expedient of reading academic works and law reports from one another's countries. Literal conversations, or at least attendance at seminars and lectures, took place directly through international conferences run by organizations such as the European Council on Refugees and Exiles, courses run by institutions and

---

[3] Harley, T. (2020) 'Refugee Participation Revisited: The Contributions of Refugees to Early International Refugee Law and Policy', *Refugee Survey Quarterly*, 40(1): 58–81.
[4] Helfer, L.R. and Slaughter, A. (1997) 'Toward a Theory of Effective Supranational Adjudication', *Yale Law Journal*, 107: 273–391.
[5] Hathaway, J. and Foster, M. (2014) *The Law of Refugee Status* (2nd edn), Cambridge: Cambridge University Press, p 4.

law schools like the Refugee Studies Centre at the University of Oxford, the law school of the University of Michigan, the Kaldor Centre for International Refugee Law at the University of New South Wales and the Refugee Law Initiative at the University of London and events held by networks such as the International Association of Refugee and Migration Judges.[6] Exchange of ideas was facilitated by emerging internet resources, the development of free-to-access national case law databases run by various national legal information institutes and others and the creation of the Reflaw database compiled and managed by UNHCR.[7] In the absence of an international court of adjudication for the Refugee Convention, national judges have acted as the main arbiters of refugee law. As a matter of judicial policy, justified by reference to the Vienna Convention on the Law of Treaties and the international nature of the Refugee Convention, senior judges have chosen to refer to carefully reasoned authorities from other jurisdictions and the works of key academics.[8] A relatively small number of judges have decided some of the key leading cases and several of their names repeatedly recur in the law reports. As Audrey Macklin has observed, refugee law is replete with examples of positions advocated for or devised by prominent legal scholars, which have subsequently found favour within national jurisprudence.[9] Some of these ideas have even found legislative expression: the European Union's Qualification Directive, whose very purpose was to harmonize divergent approaches, shows clear signs of being heavily influenced by the transnational judicial conversation, for example.[10]

Today, refugee law is certainly international in scope and character. There is, however, a marked bias towards knowledge produced in the

---

[6] Hathaway, J. (2003) 'A Forum for the Transnational Development of Refugee Law: The IARLJ's Advanced Refugee Law Workshop', *International Journal of Refugee Law*, 15(3): 418–421.

[7] These include the Australasian Legal Information Institute (AustLII), the British and Irish Legal Information Institute (BAILII), the Canadian Legal Information Institute (CanLII) and the New Zealand Legal Information Institute (NZLII), all of which run a free-to-access case law database which is invaluable for accessing judgments and determinations both nationally and internationally. See also the JUSTIA database of United States case law and the CURIA database for the Court of Justice of the European Union.

[8] Hélène Lambert notes that reference to foreign law occurs exclusively at a senior level and cross referencing of foreign language decisions is almost unheard of even within the shared jurisdiction of the Common European Asylum System: Lambert, H. (2009) 'Transnational Judicial Dialogue, Harmonisation and the Common European Asylum System', *International and Comparative Law Quarterly*, 58(3): 519–543.

[9] Macklin, A. (2017) 'Book Review of James C Hathaway and Michelle Foster, The Law of Refugee Status', *Human Rights Quarterly*, 39: 220.

[10] Kneebone, S. (2014) 'Refugees as Objects of Surrogate Protection: Shifting Identities', in Kneebone, S., Stevens, D. and Baldassar, L. (eds) *Refugee Protection and the Role of Law: Conflicting Identities*, Abingdon: Routledge.

Global North. This book forms no exception and much of the case law cited comes not just from countries in the Global North but also from Anglophone countries in the Global North with common law systems of law. As Catherine Dauvergne has commented, Global South decisions 'have not attained that odd legal status of "leading"'.[11] Highlighting this disparity, B.S. Chimni has called for 'scholarship that questions the assumptions that inform dominant strands of Northern thinking with regard to the causes and solutions of refugee flows, and to advance alternative viable models of responsibility sharing and humanitarian assistance'.[12]

While there are differences between national jurisdictions, there is nevertheless a remarkable degree of convergence on basic but once-contentious issues such as the perceived purpose of the Refugee Convention, the standard of proof, the threshold of harm for establishing persecution, the proposition that persecution can be carried out by non-state actors, the need to show failure of state protection and the meaning of the words 'membership of a particular social group'. Consensus can also be read as conformity, however. The boundaries between the actors constituting this community of law are highly permeable and the field is highly networked.[13] Many individuals perform multiple roles simultaneously, for example as lawyer and judge or scholar and campaigner. Many others move between different roles during their careers. The author, for example, has worked for non-governmental organizations, as an employed and self-employed lawyer, has written books and articles, has taught students and lawyers and has campaigned on refugee protection issues. Those who work in the field often feel a 'dual imperative' to perform their designated role according to professional standards and expectations but also to advance the protection of refugees.[14] The availability of funding, the political environment and established institutional interests mandate certain ways of working and encourage a focus on certain issues. As a result, there is pressure to adhere to established norms in thinking and an echo-chamber effect. Some reactions to the publication of *Refuge: Transforming a Broken Refugee System* by Alexander Betts and Paul Collier in 2017 might arguably be a case in point. There is

---

[11] Dauvergne, C. (2021) 'Women in Refugee Jurisprudence', in Costello, C., Foster, M. and McAdam, J. (eds) *The Oxford Handbook of International Refugee Law*, Oxford: Oxford University Press, p 731.

[12] Chimni, B.S. (2009) 'The Birth of a "Discipline": From Refugee to Forced Migration Studies', *Journal of Refugee Studies*, 22(1): 16–17.

[13] Crisp, J. (2018) 'A Global Academic Network on Refugees: Some Unanswered Questions', *International Journal of Refugee Law*, 30(4): 641.

[14] See Byrne, R. and Gammeltoft-Hansen, T. (2020) 'International Refugee Law between Scholarship and Practice', *International Journal of Refugee Law*, 32(2): 181–199.

a risk of narrow, stale thinking and missed opportunities to enhance the protection of refugees.

Similar sharing of ideas has occurred between governments, as the work of Daniel Ghezelbash and others has shown.[15] Pushbacks, maritime interdiction and extraterritorial (or 'off-shore') processing of asylum claims are policies developed cooperatively between governments to achieve common goals and legitimate policies at home. They are also in part competitive, used to gain a perceived advantage over other countries in a race to the bottom to deter so-called 'forum shopping' or 'asylum shopping' by refugees, whereby a refugee supposedly selects a country of sanctuary based on a comparative evaluation of their prospects of gaining status.[16] Some of this interaction is done directly through closed-door intergovernmental meetings and some more openly through the Executive Committee of UNHCR and the IOM.

Role of UNHCR

The obligation of state parties to the Refugee Convention to cooperate with UNHCR and 'facilitate its duty of supervising the application of the provisions of this Convention' has empowered UNHCR to offer guidance on the interpretation and application of the convention and obliged state parties to pay attention.[17] There is, however, no means by which UNHCR can enforce compliance with the Refugee Convention. The convention was only the second to be negotiated and adopted by the United Nations and the supervision mechanism has been described as 'innovative at the time' but 'to suffer the drawbacks of being one of the first external supervisory mechanisms in that it is of a rather rudimentary nature'.[18] UNHCR's independence is also, as discussed earlier, compromised by its reliance on voluntary financial contributions and state cooperation. Later human rights treaties include reporting obligations, an independent supervisory body, complaints mechanisms and other means of enforcement.

These constraints have not prevented UNHCR from largely successfully entrenching norms of refugee protection and socializing newly independent countries to these norms over the course of the second half of the 20th

---

[15] Ghezelbash, D. (2018) *Refuge Lost: Asylum Law in an Interdependent World*, Cambridge: Cambridge University Press, Chapter 7.
[16] See for example *NS and Others* (C-411/10 and C-493/10) [79].
[17] Refugee Convention, Preamble and Article 35 and 1967 Protocol, Article 2.
[18] Zieck, M. (2011) 'Executory and Transitory Provisions, Article 35 of the 1951 Convention/ Article II of the 1967 Protocol', in Zimmermann, A. (ed) *The 1951 Convention Relating to the Status of Refugees and Its 1967 Protocol: A Commentary*, Oxford: Oxford University Press, p 1508.

century.[19] In the sphere of refugee law and the interpretation of the terms of the refugee definition, UNHCR's *Handbook on Procedures and Criteria for Determining Refugee Status* was first published in 1979 and has been highly influential.[20] The Handbook has variously been described by the United States Supreme Court as offering 'significant guidance', Canada's Supreme Court as 'a highly relevant authority' and the United Kingdom's House of Lords as having 'high persuasive authority', for example.[21] While it has undoubtedly been influential and instructive, it is not binding and does not have force of law. It is also now somewhat outdated given it does not refer to or incorporate any legal developments occurring since 1979. A series of authoritative UNHCR Executive Committee ('ExCom') Conclusions and, latterly, Guidelines on International Protection have provided further guidance on all aspects of the interpretation and application of modern refugee law. UNHCR has also intervened in key legal cases as *amicus curiae*. Behind the scenes it has influenced governmental actors through consultations and lobbying and non-governmental actors through funding, training, provision of resources like the Reflaw database and involvement in the International Journal of Refugee Law and other publications. UNHCR has not made law in a strictly formal sense but, as Goodwin-Gill has argued, its activities 'can and do generate relevant practice and, in turn, lead to the emergence of *opinio juris*'.[22]

Arguably, though, all varieties of UNHCR guidance today play a less significant role in the contemporary legal landscape than in previous years. Following the surge in the quantity and quality of case law and academic writing interpreting and interrogating the Refugee Convention in the two decades following the mid-1980s – a sort of refugee law equivalent to the Cambrian explosion of life on Earth – there are now mature bodies of law which act as authority both within and between jurisdictions; UNHCR is no longer the only show in town. It has been argued that the sheer volume of UNHCR guidance, and inevitable ensuing inconsistency,

---

[19] Loescher, G. (2001) *The UNHCR and World Politics: A Perilous Path*, Oxford: Oxford University Press, pp 5–6.

[20] UNHCR (1979) *Handbook and Guidelines on Procedures and Criteria for Determining Refugee Status under the 1951 Convention and the 1967 Protocol Relating to the Status of Refugees* (re-issued 2011). See Vienna Convention Article 31(3)(b) and, for example, *R v Secretary of State for the Home Department, ex p Adan and Aitsegeur* [1999] Imm AR 521 (Eng CA) (Laws LJ).

[21] *Immigration and Naturalization Service v Cardoza-Fonesca* (1987) 480 US 421 (US SC) [439]; *Chan v Canada* [1995] 3 SCR 593 (Can SC) [46]; *R v Secretary of State for the Home Department, ex p Adan and Aitsegeur* [2001] 2 AC 477 (UK HL) (Lord Steyn).

[22] Goodwin-Gill, G. (2020) 'The Office of the United Nations High Commissioner for Refugees and the Sources of International Refugee Law', *International and Comparative Law Quarterly*, 69: 1–41, 40.

has also lessened its clarity and impact.[23] Goodwin-Gill, while implicitly recognizing the reality of reduced influence, proposes that far more weight should be attached to recent guidance from UNHCR given the mandate and role of the body and that the guidance itself is both authoritative and up-to-date.[24]

Academic works

It is impossible to overstate the influence of academic works addressing the Refugee Convention, a role acknowledged by Lord Lloyd when he wrote that 'it is academic writers who provide the best hope of reaching international consensus on the meaning of the Convention'.[25] Two in particular stand out: Guy Goodwin-Gill, formerly of Oxford University and University of New South Wales and James Hathaway of the Michigan Law School. Goodwin-Gill's *The Refugee in International Law*, first published in 1983 and now in its fourth edition, and Hathaway's *The Law of Refugee Status*, first published in 1991 and now in its second edition, are both seminal texts and have been cited in numerous judgments. Goodwin-Gill analyzed the Refugee Convention through the prism of international human rights law throughout his book and Hathaway has been highly influential in his analysis of the Refugee Convention as offering surrogate or substitute protection available only where there has been a failure of state protection in the refugee's country of origin. Both have also been key figures in the international community of law. Goodwin-Gill was the founding editor of the International Journal of Refugee Law, for example, and Hathaway, as well as speaking at innumerable conferences and events, convened a series of international round-table events giving rise to the influential 'Michigan Guidelines', which served to consolidate understanding of the emerging body of refugee law.[26] Hathaway's subsequent *The Rights of Refugees in International Law*, which examines the contents of the Refugee Convention beyond Article 1, was first published in 2005 and entered its second edition in 2021. Hathaway and Goodwin-Gill built on the work

---

[23] See for example Hathaway, J. (2021) *The Rights of Refugees under International Law* (2nd edn), Cambridge: Cambridge University Press, pp 63–67.

[24] Goodwin-Gill, G. (2020) 'The Office of the United Nations High Commissioner for Refugees and the Sources of International Refugee Law', *International and Comparative Law Quarterly*, 69: 1–41, 21.

[25] *R v Secretary of State for the Home Department, ex p Adan* [1999] 1 AC 293 (UK HL) (Lord Lloyd).

[26] For repository of full series of Michigan Guidelines see http://www.mjilonline.org/jdforum/digital-scholarship/opinio-juris-2/michigan-guidelines/ [last accessed 14 September 2021].

of earlier scholars, in particular Atle Grahl-Madsen, author of *The Status of Refugees in International Law* in 1966, Nehemiah Robinson and Paul Weis. Numerous other scholars have followed, including Michelle Foster and Jane McAdam, who collaborated with Goodwin-Gill and Hathaway on later editions of their works. In the United Kingdom, *Asylum Law and Practice* by Mark Symes and Peter Jorro offers an invaluable and comprehensive compendium of case law and procedure. Meanwhile, the International Journal of Refugee Law and other journals offer widely-read fora for the elucidation, development and sharing of ideas. The Global Compact on Refugees of 2018 called for the creation of a 'global academic network on refugee, other forced displacement, and statelessness issues ... involving universities, academic alliances, and research institutions, together with UNHCR and other relevant stakeholders' but it remains to be seen whether this is entirely aspirational in nature.[27]

Judicial dialogue

International refugee law bears the imprint of transnational judicial dialogue. Certain key cases, sometimes referred to as leading cases, have been highly influential not just in their own jurisdictions but beyond. As noted earlier, these cases are invariably decided in the Global North. Some of the most prominent and widely cited include the United States case of *Cardoza-Fonseca* in 1987, the Canadian case of *Ward* in 1993, the United Kingdom cases of *R v Immigration Appeal Tribunal, ex p Shah* in 1999 and *Horvath* in 2000, and the Australian cases of *Applicant A* in 1997 and *Appellant S395/2002* in 2003.[28] These examples are all from the supreme court of the relevant jurisdiction, but other less exalted judgments have also been cited on the international stage. The United States Board of Immigration Appeals interim decision in *In re Acosta* proved to be hugely influential internationally after being identified and championed by James Hathaway in 1991 in *The Law of Refugee Status* on the interpretation of 'membership of a particular social group'. The evidence of cross-fertilization of ideas and concepts is plainly recorded in the law reports, with the major refugee law decisions routinely citing not just domestic but international authorities. This is justified by referring to the desirability of an international treaty being interpreted in

---

[27] Global Compact on Refugees (UN Doc A/73/12) (2 August 2018) [43].
[28] *Immigration and Naturalization Service v Cardoza-Fonseca* 480 US 421 (1987) (US SC); *Attorney General of Canada v Ward* [1993] 2 SCR 689 (Can SC); *R v Immigration Appeal Tribunal, ex p Shah* [1999] 2 AC 629 (UK HL); *Horvath v Secretary of State for the Home Department* [2001] AC 489 (UK HL); *Applicant A v Minister for Immigration and Ethnic Affairs* [1997] HCA 4 (Aus HC); *Appellant S395/2002 v Minister for Immigration and Multicultural Affairs* [2003] HCA 71 (Aus HC).

the same way wherever it is applied: 'the general rule is that international treaties should, so far as possible, be construed uniformly by the national courts of all states'.[29]

How the judges came to know about international cases is not quite so self-evident. The lawyers advocating on behalf of their clients no doubt played a role, which begs the question of where they obtained their knowledge. Law reporters played a part, with some series like the Immigration and Nationality Law Reports in the United Kingdom making a conscious effort to report interesting international case law. Academics including Goodwin-Gill and Hathaway and the editors and contributors to the International Journal of Refugee Law performed a significant role. So too did the International Association of Refugee Law Judges, founded in the mid-1990s (now named the International Association of Refugee and Migration Judges). As with the waning influence of UNHCR, the maturation of refugee law perhaps means that international influences are less obvious today than in previous years. This can be regarded as a sign of success of earlier endeavours: a broad international consensus on the meaning and interpretation of the Refugee Convention is so deeply embedded that it has become unremarkable. That is not to say there is no future role for further international dialogue. The rights of refugees are particularly contentious in contemporary debate. There is room for the further evolution of refugee law around, for example, human rights standards, newly appreciated forms of harm for particular groups, emerging rights such as the right of conscientious objection and how movement across borders caused by climate change can or should be addressed.

Regional and domestic refugee definitions

As well as the Refugee Convention, three main regional legal instruments adopt their own expanded or adjusted refugee definition and numerous countries have incorporated their own version of refugee definition into their domestic law. The existence of multiple definitions risks fragmentation in understanding of who qualifies for refugee status and might also be thought to motivate what has sometimes been termed 'forum shopping', as discussed earlier. These concerns are allayed by the express provision in regional definitions that they complement the Refugee Convention, combined with the reality that the countries that have adopted more expansive definitions applying to a wider range of individuals tend to be in refugee-producing regions.

---

[29] *Horvath v Secretary of State for the Home Department* [2001] AC 489 (UK HL) (Lord Hope).

Africa

The earliest of the regional refugee definitions is found in the Organization of African Unity's Convention Governing the Specific Aspects of Refugee Problems in Africa of 1969, or 'African Refugee Convention'. This convention is now ratified by 47 of the 55 member states of what has become the African Union.[30] The process of drafting began in 1964 and was prompted by two key concerns.[31] Firstly, members of the Organization of African Unity sought to extend international refugee law to their region: at that time the dateline of the unmodified Refugee Convention rendered it inapplicable in contemporary Africa because it applied only to 'events occurring before 1 January 1951'. Secondly, even if the Refugee Convention were applicable, newly independent African countries were concerned that freedom fighters against colonial rule were excised from protection by the exclusion clause affecting those who committed serious crimes (see further Chapter 6). In response to the negotiations, UNHCR accelerated efforts to coordinate an agreement to remove the dateline from the Refugee Convention. UNHCR were anxious that the Refugee Convention (and therefore UNHCR) retain primacy and the resulting protocol of 1967 heavily influenced the final draft of the African Refugee Convention. The final version explicitly recognizes in its preamble that the 1951 Refugee Convention 'constitutes the basic and universal instrument relating to the status of refugees'. The definition of a refugee replicates that of the Refugee Convention, minus the dateline, but then goes on:

> The term 'refugee' shall also apply to every person who, owing to external aggression, occupation, foreign domination or events seriously disturbing public order in either part or the whole of his country of origin or nationality, is compelled to leave his place of habitual residence in order to seek refuge in another place outside his country of origin or nationality.[32]

The apparently wider complementary route to refugee status appears to meet many of the objections made by critics of the definition in the main Refugee Convention. The reference to 'external aggression, occupation, foreign domination' originates in the concern of the drafters to offer

---

[30] Cantor, D. and Chikwanha, F. (2019) 'Reconsidering African Refugee Law', *International Journal of Refugee Law*, 31(2): 182–260, 190.

[31] See Sharpe, M. (2018) *The Regional Law of Refugee Protection in Africa*, Oxford: Oxford University Press, Chapter 2.

[32] African Refugee Convention, Article I(2).

sanctuary to those resisting colonial or white minority rule. The words have an autonomous meaning, though, and must today be interpreted in contemporary terms. The ordinary meaning of the phrase 'events seriously disturbing public order' would seem to include events domestically as well as with an international dimension. The concept of public order does not have a constant meaning or usage in international law. It appears not only in the Refugee Convention but also in the International Covenant on Civil and Political Rights and elsewhere. For example, a refugee is under a duty to conform to measures 'taken for the maintenance of public order' and may be expelled on 'grounds of national security or public order'.[33] Public order is one of the potential justifications for interference with certain qualified rights in international human rights law.[34] This all suggests the term should therefore be understood to be a wide one. It has even been persuasively argued that 'events seriously disturbing public order' need not be generated by human activity and might extend to environmental events or disasters such as drought, earthquakes or floods.[35]

Moving on to other elements of the definition, a person does not need to experience or be at real risk of being persecuted in order to qualify for status. Instead they can show they were compelled to leave their normal home for one of the broadly specified reasons often known to generate significant numbers of refugees as the word is popularly understood. There is no need to demonstrate failure of state protection over and above the specified reasons that might give rise to a claim for refugee status. Further, the words 'in either part or the whole of his country of origin or nationality' limits the scope to deny refugee status on the basis of the variously named doctrine of internal relocation or internal protection discussed in Chapter 4. In contrast to the individualized assessment implicitly required by the wording of the Refugee Convention definition, the thrust and tenor of the African Refugee Convention definition is more readily enabling of rapid *prima facie* refugee status recognition for large numbers of refugees on the basis of readily apparent, objective circumstances in the country of origin.[36] Cessation and exclusion clauses broadly similar to those of the Refugee Convention are included.

---

[33] Refugee Convention, Articles 2 and 32.

[34] See for example International Covenant on Civil and Political Rights, Article 12 (freedom of movement), Article 19 (right to hold opinions), Article 21 (freedom of association) and certain other rights.

[35] Wood, T. (2019) 'Who Is a Refugee in Africa? A Principled Framework for Interpreting and Applying Africa's Expanded Refugee Definition', *International Journal of Refugee Law*, 31(2/3): 290–320, 307.

[36] See UNHCR, *Guidelines on International Protection No. 11: Prima Facie Recognition of Refugee Status*, HCR/GIP/15/11, 5 June 2015.

The complementary refugee definition in the African Refugee Convention has been widely considered to be more generous than that of the Refugee Convention. A careful reading of the text combined with analysis of how it is applied in practice reveals that the definition does extend protection but is less expansive than might at first be thought.[37] The words 'owing to' and 'compelled to leave' imply a causal nexus between the events that might give rise to refugee status and the person's departure from their country, for example. Unless the events that may give rise to refugee status affect the whole of the applicant's country, this reading of the definition suggests that an individual assessment of an asylum applicant's circumstances is required, or at least justified, under the African Refugee Convention. The 'compelled to leave' requirement might conceivably be read as precluding *sur place* refugee status claims, although UNHCR guidance urges otherwise.[38] The reference to a 'place of habitual residence' might be interpreted as introducing a form of internal relocation requirement, at least in some situations. In one case, for example, a man who was originally from Kinshasa was denied refugee status because he had moved to Bukavu, over 2,000 km away, for four years and then fled violence there. The South African Refugee Appeal Board held that the man's place of habitual residence was Kinshasa and he could safely return there.[39]

The African Refugee Convention includes several other novel features beyond the refugee definition itself. By sitting alongside the global Refugee Convention, it operates to extend internationally agreed refugee rights to a wider class of individuals. It specifically provides that 'the Contracting State of Asylum shall determine whether an applicant is a refugee', thus explicitly eliminating the possibility of what has become known euphemistically as 'offshore processing'.[40] It does not quite go so far as to remedy the omission of a right to enter a country for asylum, which is absent from the Refugee Convention, but does provide that states 'shall use their best endeavours consistent with their respective legislations to receive refugees and to secure the settlement of those refugees who, for well-founded reasons, are unable or unwilling to return to their country of origin or nationality'.[41] State

---

[37] Sharpe, M. (2018) *The Regional Law of Refugee Protection in Africa*, Oxford: Oxford University Press, pp 54–60.

[38] UNHCR, *Guidelines on International Protection No. 12: Claims for Refugee Status Related to Situations of Armed Conflict and Violence under Article 1A(2) of the 1951 Convention and/or 1967 Protocol Relating to the Status of Refugees and the Regional Refugee Definitions*, HCR/GIP/16/12, 2 December 2016.

[39] Cited in Schreier, T. (2014) 'The Expanded Refugee Definition', in Khan, F. and Schreier, T., *Refugee Law in South Africa*, Cape Town: Juta & Co Ltd.

[40] African Refugee Convention, Article I(6).

[41] African Refugee Convention, Article II(1).

parties are encouraged to 'in the spirit of African solidarity and international co-operation take appropriate measures to lighten the burden' of other state parties requesting assistance.[42] In an attempt to depoliticize the act of granting asylum, recognition of refugee status is specified to be 'a peaceful and humanitarian act and shall not be regarded as an unfriendly act by any Member State'.[43] The African Refugee Convention explicitly draws a distinction between a refugee 'who seeks a peaceful and normal life' and 'a person fleeing his country for the sole purpose of fomenting subversion from outside'.[44] Nevertheless, the latter is not excluded from refugee status or the duty of *non-refoulement*. Subversive activities by refugees are prohibited and, perhaps more to the point, state parties are required to prohibit such activities.[45] This provision goes well beyond the very limited exhortation in the Refugee Convention that refugees conform to the laws of the country of refuge as well as 'measures taken for the maintenance of public order'.[46] What has sometimes been described as the 'exilic' approach to refugee status is clearly and explicitly stated in the African Refugee Convention, in contrast to the Refugee Convention: '[t]he essentially voluntary character of repatriation shall be respected in all cases and no refugee shall be repatriated against his will'.[47] The prohibition on *non-refoulement* in the African Refugee Convention appears wider than that in the Refugee Convention because it explicitly applies to 'rejection at the frontier', but close analysis shows that the two duties broadly run in parallel.[48]

Legal innovation in refugee rights and protection in Africa is not limited to the African Refugee Convention. The convention sits within or alongside the African Union's regional framework of human rights instruments and protection mechanisms including the African Charter on Human and Peoples' Rights (African Charter), the African Commission on Human and Peoples' Rights (African Commission) and the African Court on Human and Peoples' Rights (African Court).[49] The rights set out in the African Charter apply to 'every individual' and an explicit protection from discrimination applies to 'national and social origin … or any other status', therefore applying the enunciated rights to refugees as well as citizens. The

---

[42] African Refugee Convention, Article II(4).
[43] African Refugee Convention, Article II(2).
[44] African Refugee Convention, Preamble.
[45] African Refugee Convention, Article III.
[46] Refugee Convention, Article 2.
[47] African Refugee Convention, Article V(1).
[48] African Refugee Convention, Article II(3); Sharpe, M. (2018) *The Regional Law of Refugee Protection in Africa*, Oxford: Oxford University Press, p 74.
[49] See Sharpe, M. (2018) *The Regional Law of Refugee Protection in Africa*, Oxford: Oxford University Press, Chapters 5 and 7.

African Charter goes on to enshrine a right for every individual 'when persecuted, to seek *and obtain* asylum in other countries in accordance with the law of those countries and international conventions' (emphasis added).[50] The 'clawback' wording at the end of this provision means that it falls short of an absolute right to asylum but this nevertheless goes beyond international refugee and human rights law. Procedural rights for refugees are protected by prohibitions on mass expulsion of non-nationals and on expulsion of a non-nationally legally admitted to a country – which will often be the case with *prima facie* recognized refugees – other than 'by virtue of a decision taken in accordance with the law'.[51] The African Commission began operating in 1987 as a supervisory body for the African Charter with a promotional mandate to advance a culture of respect for human rights and a protective mandate to hear and investigate individual complaints and communicate decisions. Decisions are widely ignored, however. Their legal status is disputed, the commission's authority to order remedies is also disputed, there is little monitoring of compliance and there is little political engagement within the African Union.[52] This deficiency was in theory remedied by a later amendment to the African Charter to create the African Court, which became operational in 2004 and whose decisions are binding.

In practice, this legal framework does little to protect refugee rights on the ground. The African Refugee Convention definitions of a refugee are incorporated into domestic law directly or by reference in many African states.[53] Implementation in individual cases is questionable, however. Studies of refugee status determinations and appeals in South Africa and Kenya have suggested that the expanded protection envisaged by the African Refugee Convention definition is seldom realized.[54] In contrast, the definition does appear to be referenced in *prima facie* status determination and, importantly, is considered to accord *prima facie* refugees the same rights as other refugees,

---

[50] African Charter on Human and People's Rights, Article 12(3).
[51] African Charter on Human and People's Rights, Article 12(4) and (5).
[52] Viljoen, F. and Louw, L. (2004) 'The Status of the Findings of the African Commission: From Moral Persuasion to Legal Obligation', *Journal of African Law*, 48(1): 1–22; Murray, R. and Long, D. (2015) *The Implementation of the Findings of the African Commission on Human and Peoples' Rights*, Cambridge: Cambridge University Press.
[53] See survey in Cantor, D. and Chikwanha, F. (2019) 'Reconsidering African Refugee Law', *International Journal of Refugee Law*, 31(2): 182–260.
[54] Amit, R. (2011) 'No Refuge: Flawed Status Determination and the Failures of South Africa's Refugee System to Provide Protection', *International Journal of Refugee Law*, 23(3): 458, 473; Wood, T. (2014) 'Expanding Protection in Africa? Case Studies of the Implementation of the 1969 African Refugee Convention's Expanded Refugee Definition', *International Journal of Refugee Law*, 26(4): 555–580, 564, 574.

at least in theory.⁵⁵ Jeff Crisp has argued that the reality on the ground for many refugees in Africa is that the 'golden age' of prevalent – but by no means universal – humane and generous treatment of refugees in Africa of the 1960s to 1980s has ended.⁵⁶ Instead, Crisp suggests, the continent's refugees increasingly find that by crossing an international border, they exchange one form and degree of vulnerability for another. Marina Sharpe writes that while governments and courts have recognized the binding nature of the principle of *non-refoulement*, 'in Africa non-refoulement is often honoured in the breach'.⁵⁷ Similarly, involuntary repatriation of refugees may be prohibited by the African Refugee Convention but it undoubtedly occurs in practice. Refugee camps are increasingly dangerous places, sometimes owing to direct attack by the foreign states from which the refugees fled in the first place and sometimes because of violence, coercion, intimidation and criminal activity. This worsening of refugee rights and protection coincides with more widespread adoption by African countries of national refugee laws.⁵⁸ Both trends might be explained as responses to rising numbers of refugees and displaced people in Africa, but troubling questions of causation and correlation arise. The introduction of refugee laws to restrict refugee rights in the face of greater need for asylum is a path already well-trodden in the Global North, after all. In the face of these widespread violations of refugee rights, the African Commission's record of engagement 'has not produced systemic success'.⁵⁹ Meanwhile, the African Court has never adjudicated a refugee rights case on its merits.

Perhaps ironically, given its arguably limited contemporary impact in contemporary Africa, the African Refugee Convention has been conceptually influential far beyond its direct reach. It is explicitly cited as an inspiration in the Cartagena Declaration in South America and Sharpe argues it has clearly influenced the League of Arab States' Arab Convention on Regulating Status of Refugees in the Arab Countries (not in force at the time of writing and therefore not otherwise addressed in this book), the gradual expansion of the UNHCR mandate beyond those

---

[55] Sharpe, M. (2018) *The Regional Law of Refugee Protection in Africa*, Oxford: Oxford University Press, p 70; Cantor, D. and Chikwanha, F. (2019) 'Reconsidering African Refugee Law', *International Journal of Refugee Law*, 31(2): 182–260, 237.

[56] Crisp, J. (2010) 'Forced Displacement in Africa: Dimensions, Difficulties, and Policy Directions', *Refugee Survey Quarterly*, 29(3): 1–27, 3.

[57] Sharpe, M. (2018) *The Regional Law of Refugee Protection in Africa*, Oxford: Oxford University Press, p 74.

[58] Cantor, D. and Chikwanha, F. (2019) 'Reconsidering African Refugee Law', *International Journal of Refugee Law*, 31(2): 182–260, 188.

[59] Sharpe, M. (2018) *The Regional Law of Refugee Protection in Africa*, Oxford: Oxford University Press, p 218.

strictly defined as refugees and the gradual spread of the concept of forms of protection complementary to refugee status.[60] Looking to the future, the recognition in the African Refugee Convention that 'events seriously disturbing public order' might generate refugees may have implications for the protection of so-called 'climate refugees', an issue to which we return in the Conclusion.

Latin America

There is a long tradition of political asylum in Latin America, in which political asylees ('asilado político') were envisaged to be a small number of self-supporting individuals fleeing direct political persecution.[61] The Montevideo Treaty on International Penal Law 1889, for example, refers to territorial asylum (on the territory) and diplomatic asylum (at an embassy or at sea).[62] A series of later conventions addressed political asylum either in part or in full, culminating in the Caracas Conventions on Territorial and Diplomatic Asylum 1954. These instruments were primarily concerned with relationships between the states concerned and were not widely ratified. The political asylee regime proved to be inadequate to address the mass refugee flows that began in South and Central America from the 1970s onwards. A series of high-level meetings organized by UNHCR beginning in 1981 led to the adoption by the Organization of American States of what has become known as the Cartagena Declaration on Refugees of 1984, usually referred to as just the 'Cartagena Declaration'. The impetus for the declaration derived from the increasing numbers of refugees, non-ratification of the Refugee Convention by key countries including Mexico and Honduras, the paucity of national legal frameworks or refugee status determination procedures across the region and by the success of the regional approach pioneered by the African Refugee Convention.[63]

The Cartagena Declaration placed the Refugee Convention and UNHCR centre stage in Latin America, effectively abandoning the pre-existing regional concept of political asylum. The declaration goes further, encouraging countries in the region to extend refugee status to: 'persons

---

[60] Sharpe, M. (2018) *The Regional Law of Refugee Protection in Africa*, Oxford: Oxford University Press, pp 37–38.

[61] Fischel de Andrade, J. (2019) 'The 1984 Cartagena Declaration: A Critical Review of Some Aspects of Its Emergence and Relevance', *Refugee Survey Quarterly*, 38(4): 341–362.

[62] Treaty on International Penal Law, adopted by the First South American Congress on Private International Law in Montevideo on 23 January 1889.

[63] See for example Reed-Hurtado, M. (2013) 'The Cartagena Declaration on Refugees and the Protection of People Fleeing Armed Conflict and Other Situations of Violence in Latin America', *UNHCR Legal and Protection Policy Research Series*, PPLA/2013/03.

who have fled their country because their lives, security or freedom have been threatened by generalized violence, foreign aggression, internal conflicts, massive violation of human rights or other circumstances which have seriously disturbed public order'.[64]

The declaration also reaffirms the 'peaceful, non-political and exclusively humanitarian nature of grant of asylum', the principle that recognition of a refugee should not be interpreted as 'an unfriendly act towards the country of origin of refugees' and 'the importance and meaning of the principle of *non-refoulement* (including the prohibition of rejection at the frontier) as a cornerstone of the international protection of refugees'.[65]

The Cartagena Declaration can be characterized as a 'soft law' instrument: it is not a treaty and has no binding legal effect unless incorporated into national law. Cantor and Trimiño Mora observe that the Vienna Convention on the Law of Treaties therefore does not apply and argue that the language of the document should not be interpreted in an overly legalistic or literal way, as if it had been drafted with a similar degree of precision to that of a treaty.[66] They suggest that the exhortatory nature of the Cartagena Declaration is better understood if greater emphasis than usual is placed on the purpose and context of the agreement. Looking at the extended refugee definition, this interpretative approach helps to make sense of the use of the plural rather than singular ('persons' and 'their'), the lack of precision in the 'threatened by' language, the considerable overlap between the potential causes of refugee flight and the difficulty in mapping these potential causes to established concepts of international human rights law. As with the African Refugee Convention, the Cartagena Declaration extended definition is more amenable to use in *prima facie* status assessments in instances of mass influx of refugees. The use of the plural and the fact the potential causes of refugee flight lend themselves to objective determination on the basis of verifiable information both point in this direction. While it is arguable that 'events seriously disturbing public order' might apply to those fleeing climate-related disasters, state practice does not suggest this interpretation is applied on the ground in Latin America. Climate and disaster migration tends to be addressed within the region as an immigration law issue rather

---

[64] Cartagena Declaration on Refugees, adopted by the Colloquium on the International Protection of Refugees in Central America, Mexico and Panama, Cartagena de Indias, Colombia, 22 November 1984, Conclusion 3.

[65] Cartagena Declaration, Conclusions 4 and 5.

[66] Cantor, D. and Trimiño Mora, D. (2014) 'A Simple Solution to War Refugees? The Latin American Expanded Definition and Its Relationship to International Human Rights Law', in Cantor, D. and Durieux, J.-F. (eds) *Refuge from Inhumanity? War Refugees and International Humanitarian Law*, Leiden: Brill, pp 204–224.

than as one of international protection.[67] Unlike the African Refugee Convention, there is no explicit 'part of country' wording in the extended Cartagena refugee definition ruling out the application of internal relocation as a potential ground for refusing refugee status. However, it has been argued that 'the logic of applying the Cartagena refugee definition per se or on a situation- or group-basis precludes the possibility of analysing internal relocation alternatives'.[68] The words 'threatened by' are capable of being read as requiring a subjective assessment of individual cases and has been equated with the 'well-founded fear' requirement of the Refugee Convention.[69] Cantor and Timiño Mora argue that 'the very concept of "threat" clearly implies that it not have been consummated' and go on to observe that the extended definition does not require the same element of individual discrimination as the Refugee Convention definition.[70] The words are therefore better understood in context as referring to large groups of refugees.

Whether despite or because of its lack of legal force, the Cartagena Declaration has proven to be highly influential, at least in theory. Ratification of the Refugee Convention was successfully promoted in Latin America and the regional political asylee regime was abandoned in favour of an expanded version of the international refugee regime. Adoption, or at least adaptation, of the extended refugee definition in national asylum laws is very widespread in Latin American countries.[71] Ten-year anniversary conferences held in 1994, 2004 and 2014 to evaluate the region's needs, adopt follow-up plans and involve additional countries have garnered increasing levels of regional

---

[67] Cantor, D. (2021) 'Environment, Mobility, and International Law: A New Approach in the Americas', *Chicago Journal of International Law*, 21(2): 263–322.

[68] UNHCR, Summary Conclusions on the Interpretation of the Extended Refugee Definition in the 1984 Cartagena Declaration; roundtable 15 and 16 October 2013, Montevideo, Uruguay, 7 July 2014, Available from: https://www.refworld.org/docid/53c52e7d4.html [last accessed 17 March 2021].

[69] Fortin, A. (2005) 'Doctrinal Review of the Broader Refugee Definition Contained in the Cartagena Declaration', *Memoir of the Twentieth Anniversary of the Cartagena Declaration on Refugees 1984–2004*, Editorama, p 279.

[70] Cantor, D. and Trimiño Mora, D. (2014) 'A Simple Solution to War Refugees? The Latin American Expanded Definition and Its Relationship to International Human Rights Law', in Cantor, D. and Durieux, J.-F. (eds) *Refuge from Inhumanity? War Refugees and International Humanitarian Law*, Leiden: Brill, p 221.

[71] Reed-Hurtado, M. (2013) 'The Cartagena Declaration on Refugees and the Protection of People Fleeing Armed Conflict and Other Situations of Violence in Latin America', *UNHCR Legal and Protection Policy Research Series*, PPLA/2013/03; Jubilut, L., Espinoza, M. and Mezzanotti, G. (2019) 'The Cartagena Declaration at 35 and Refugee Protection in Latin America', *E-International Relations*, Available from: https://www.e-ir.info/2019/11/22/the-cartagena-declaration-at-35-and-refugee-protection-in-latin-america/ [last accessed 24 May 2021].

engagement. In practice, the impact of the extended refugee definition of the Cartagena Declaration is less clear. As with the African Refugee Convention equivalent, the Cartagena Declaration extended definition is seldom applied in individual refugee status determinations.[72] While the political process surrounding the Cartagena Declaration may perhaps have fostered a more welcoming approach to refugees in the region than would otherwise have been the case, the counterfactual of what would have happened without it is unknowable. Arguably the biggest challenge faced by the regional regime has been the Venezuelan refugee crisis beginning in 2014, which by the end of 2020 had caused an estimated 5.4 million Venezuelans to leave their country.[73] Despite widespread international condemnation of widespread human rights abuses in Venezuela and the self-evident fact that public order has been 'serious disturbed', very few Venezuelans fleeing their country have been recognized as refugees. Alternative forms of status have been offered instead, few Venezuelans are reported to have actively applied for refugee status on their own initiative and host countries appear to be wary of committing to offering the full set of rights that would accompany formal refugee status.[74] Of the two main host countries, Peru imposed a visa requirement on Venezuelans in 2019 and Colombia avoids calling Venezuelans refugees, instead referring to them as 'nuestros hermanos venezolanos' (our Venezuelan sisters and brothers).[75] Treading carefully for political reasons, UNHCR side-steps the issue by describing Venezuelans abroad variously as 'Venzuelans displaced abroad' or as 'refugees, migrants and asylum-seekers'.[76] The Cartagena Declaration might therefore be thought to have failed its ultimate test. More realistically, any rights-based refugee law framework would likely be incapable of responding to such a large influx of refugees, at least without mandatory burden and responsibility sharing built into it. Formal application of the Cartagena Declaration extended definition may have in effect been abandoned, but the single most important right for any refugee, that of *non-refoulement*, appears to have been respected and Venezuelans have not been subject to forced repatriation. This is despite chronic under-funding of the

---

[72] Reed-Hurtado, M. (2013) 'The Cartagena Declaration on Refugees and the Protection of People Fleeing Armed Conflict and Other Situations of Violence in Latin America', *UNHCR Legal and Protection Policy Research Series*, PPLA/2013/03, pp 18–29.

[73] UNHCR (2021) *Global Trends 2020*, Brussels: UNHCR.

[74] Blouin, C., Berganza, I. and Freier, L. (2020) 'The Spirit of Cartagena? Applying the Extended Refugee Definition to Venezuelans in Latin America', *Forced Migration Review*, 63: 64–66.

[75] Hamlin, R. (2021) *Crossing: How We Label and React to People on the Move*, Stanford: Stanford University Press, pp 111–115.

[76] UNHCR (2021) *Global Trends 2020*, Brussels: UNHCR, pp 2–3.

response to the refugee crisis by the international community compared to other contemporary refugee situations, with less than one-tenth as much being spent per person from Venezuela compared to per person from Syria.[77] Fischel de Andrade concludes that with the passage of time, the practical, political and legal relevance of the Cartagena Declaration has become obsolete but that nevertheless, the 'Spirit of Cartagena is still very much alive and palpable in the region's resolve not to be stuck in the past, but rather to face and address both the changing nature of forced migration movements and the protection needs of their victims'.[78]

International human rights instruments have also played a role in Latin American treatment of refugees, although their practical import is doubtful. The most relevant regional instruments are the American Declaration of the Rights and Duties of Man 1948 (American Declaration) and the American Convention on Human Rights 1969 (American Convention). Both are widely ratified in Latin America. The American Declaration, which is not binding, enshrines a right 'to seek *and receive* asylum' (emphasis added) and the American Convention, which is binding, includes a right 'to seek *and be granted* asylum' (emphasis added).[79] These are the only major international or regional instruments to incorporate a right to asylum, although both are qualified by 'claw back' clauses to the effect that this must be in accordance with the laws of each country and with international agreements. The American Convention also incorporates a right of *non-refoulement* as well as procedural protections.[80] The Organization of American States has established two bodies intended to implement the legal framework of the American Declaration and the American Convention. The first of these is the Inter-American Commission on Human Rights (Inter-American Commission), created in 1959 and based in Washington DC. Its reports and recommendations are not binding, but it has addressed refugee and related human rights issues on a number of occasions. The most famous of these is perhaps a North American rather than Latin American case, the *Haitian Interdiction Case*, in which the United States Supreme Court was held to have misinterpreted the *non-refoulement* protection of the Refugee Convention and the United States government to have breached the right to asylum, the right to life, liberty and the security of the person, the right to equality

---

[77] Behar, D. and Dooley, M. (2019) 'Venezuela Refugee Crisis to Become the Largest and Most Underfunded in Modern History', *Brookings Institute*, 9 December 2019.

[78] Fischel de Andrade, J. (2019) 'The 1984 Cartagena Declaration: A Critical Review of Some Aspects of Its Emergence and Relevance', *Refugee Survey Quarterly*, 38(4): 341–362, 362.

[79] American Declaration of the Rights and Duties of Man 1948, Article 27; American Convention on Human Rights 1969, Article 22(7).

[80] American Convention on Human Rights 1969, Article 22(8).

before the law and the right to a fair trial.[81] The response of the United States government was simply to ignore the commission's conclusions. The second institution is the Inter-American Court of Human Rights (Inter-American Court), created in 1979 and based in San José in Costa Rica. The jurisdiction of this court is primarily adjudicatory or advisory: direct complaints must be directed instead to the Inter-American Commission, which can then refer cases to the court. The Inter-American Court has directly addressed the right to asylum twice, one on referral from the Inter-American Commission, in *Pacheco Tineo Family v Bolivia*, and on the other occasion on the request for an advisory opinion from Ecuador.[82] Both decisions serve to establish legal minimum standards for the assessment of applications for asylum. Given there is no mechanism to enforce compliance with decisions, the minimum standards established by the court can therefore be seen as somewhat hypothetical.[83]

KEY CASE

Pacheo Tineo Family v Bolivia was the first time the Inter-American Court of Human Rights directly addressed the rights to seek and receive asylum and of *non-refoulement*. A Peruvian couple had been detained in a notorious prison in Peru on suspicion of membership of a terrorist organization. After they were released they fled to Bolivia, where they were recognized as refugees in 1995. They later moved to Chile, where they were again recognized as refugees. They briefly returned to Peru before fleeing again to Bolivia with their children and claiming asylum again in 2001. They were arrested and returned to Peru on the basis of their illegal entry and a summary refusal of their request for asylum.

The court held that the right to asylum had been breached because of the failure properly to consider the asylum application by verifying the facts of the case and applying the relevant law. No interview or hearing had been conducted, the family had no opportunity to submit evidence, no analysis at all had been undertaken of the asylum claim and no reasons were recorded. The prohibition on *refoulement* had

---

[81] *Haitian Centre for Human Rights et al v United States*, Case 10.675, Inter-American Commission on Human Rights, 13 March 1997 [157], [163], [167], [169], [170], [177]-[178], [180].
[82] *Pacheco Tineo Family v Bolivia*, Inter-American Court of Human Rights, Series C No. 272, 25 November 2013; *The Institution of Asylum and Its Recognition as a Human Right in the Inter-American System of Protection (Interpretation and Scope of Articles 5, 22.7 and 22.8 in relation to Article 1(1) of the American Convention on Human Rights)*, Inter-American Court of Human Rights, Advisory Opinion OC-25/18, 30 May 2018.
[83] Beduschi, A. (2015) 'The Contribution of the Inter-American Court of Human Rights to the Protection of Irregular Immigrants' Rights: Opportunities and Challenges', *Refugee Survey Quarterly*, 34: 45–74, 68–71.

also been breached because there had been no determination of whether the family would face danger if returned to Peru. Similarly, the rights to a fair trial and judicial protection had been breached because the family was removed the same morning they were notified of the decision and no domestic remedy at all had been made available to the family. The right to physical, mental and moral integrity was breached by the anguish and fear caused to the family when they were detained unexpectedly and without notice. Finally, the treatment of the family also breached the rights of the child and rights of the family because the children were not given an opportunity to be heard and there was no record of the interests of the children being considered.

The court ordered that damages be paid and that Bolivia implement training for its officials in the handling of applications for asylum, although it is not clear that Bolivia fully complied with this order.

The decision by Ecuador to grant diplomatic asylum to Julian Assange in 2012 showed that the Latin American tradition of diplomatic asylum had not entirely died following the Cartagena Declaration. The episode also highlighted notable flaws in the tradition. Assange was accused of a serious non-political crime – rape. While Ecuador was a signatory to the Caracas Convention on Diplomatic Asylum 1954, the country in which the relevant Ecuadorian embassy was based, the United Kingdom, was not and would not agree to safe passage out of its territory. While Assange was resident at its embassy, Ecuador sought an opinion from the Inter-American Court on the nature of the international and regional asylum regime. The court concluded in the resulting *Advisory Opinion OC-25/18* that the American Declaration and American Convention right to seek and receive asylum did not extend to diplomatic asylum but, nevertheless, states 'have the power to grant diplomatic asylum as an expression of their sovereignty, which is in line with the logic of the so-called "Latin American tradition of asylum"'.[84] The court also reaffirmed that the principle of *non-refoulement* applies in any situation where a state exercises control over a person and involves the minimum procedural protections outlined in the earlier *Pacheo Tineo Family v Bolivia* case. In short, the court held there is no individual right to diplomatic asylum and a decision to grant this status was purely a matter of discretion. But if a country does grant diplomatic asylum, that country is obliged to at least interview the person and carry

---

[84] *The Institution of Asylum and Its Recognition as a Human Right in the Inter-American System of Protection (Interpretation and Scope of Articles 5, 22.7 and 22.8 in relation to Article 1(1) of the American Convention on Human Rights)*, Inter-American Court of Human Rights, Advisory Opinion OC-25/18, 30 May 2018 [156] and [163].

out a preliminary assessment in order to determine whether there is a risk of serious harm if the person is removed. Assange was evicted from the Ecuadorian embassy the following year.

European Union

The breakup of the former Yugoslavia in the early 1990s and ensuing conflicts generated a considerable flow of refugees into the European Union. The influx coincided with the process of abolition of internal borders by some European Union countries following the Schengen Agreement of 1985, which has been described as the 'primary driving force' of the adoption of what became known as the Common European Asylum System.[85] The purpose of abolishing checks at internal frontiers might have been to promote ease of movement of citizens, but it inevitably also facilitated the movement of third country nationals. For policy makers, this was an unfortunate by-product which required mitigation. The Dublin Convention of 1990, which came into force in 1997, allocated responsibility between signatory countries for the examination of asylum applications.[86] From the outset, the core principle was that the country by which an asylum applicant enters the European Union should normally be responsible for hosting that asylum applicant and examining their application. Where an applicant for asylum moved between participating countries, the person would normally be transferred back to the country of entry. The system was predicated on the assumption that parties to the convention applied equivalent standards and protection. This premise was clearly unfounded in 1990, when different countries applied different interpretations of the Refugee Convention. It remains highly questionable today given marked variation in asylum acceptance rates between some European countries.[87] Principled concerns about inconsistent treatment of refugees were matched by more pragmatic concerns about so-called 'forum shopping' by refugees supposedly seeking the most favourable conditions of asylum. The Treaty of Amsterdam of 1997 subsumed the Schengen arrangements into European Union law and enabled the adoption of European Union laws on asylum over which the Court of Justice of the European Union would have

---

[85] Chetail, V. (2016) 'The Common European Asylum System: Bric-à-Brac or System?', in Chetail, V., De Bruycker, P. and Maiani, F. (eds) *Reforming the Common European Asylum System: The New European Refugee Law*, Boston: Brill Nijhoff, p 4.
[86] Convention Determining the State Responsible for Examining Applications for Asylum Lodged in One of the Member States of the European Communities ('Dublin Convention'), 15 June 1990.
[87] Batsaikhan, U., Darvas, Z. and Raposo, I.G. (2018) *People on the Move: Migration and Mobility in the European Union*, Bruegel Blueprint Series 28, 22 January 2018, Chapter 3.

competence. Following the adoption of the Tampere Conclusions in 1999, legislators set about creating a Common European Asylum System with the objective of standardizing interpretation of the Refugee Convention, the rights of refugees and the processing of asylum claims.[88] The Dublin system of allocation of responsibility between states for deciding applicants for asylum was, like Schengen, subsumed into European Union law. The initial phase of introducing common minimum standards was completed by 2005 with the introduction of several key directives and regulations. A second phase of amendment and revision took place between 2008 and 2013. Since then, following a substantial growth in the number of applicants for asylum arriving in Europe from 2015 onwards, further negotiations have repeatedly foundered on the issue of sharing of responsibility for refugees.

At the time of writing, the legal framework for the Dublin system is now in its third iteration.[89] Some exceptions to the general principle that the country of entry is normally responsible for examination of an asylum claim have been built into the amended system. Where an unaccompanied child is found to have close family in another European Union country, for example, the child can be transferred to that country. Importantly, it is now recognized that the asylum applicant is entitled to challenge a transfer decision.[90] The system is underpinned by the Eurodac database of fingerprints and photographs of applicants for asylum which can be accessed and searched by all European Union member states.[91] The global distribution of wealth combined with the geography of Europe means that applicants for asylum usually arrive at southern and eastern member states such as Greece, Hungary, Italy and Spain. The huge numbers of Syrians fleeing the conflict in their

---

[88] European Council, *Tampere European Council 15 and 16 October 1999*, Presidency Conclusions.

[89] Regulation EU No. 604/2013 of the European Parliament and of the Council of 26 June 2013 establishing the criteria and mechanisms for determining the Member State responsible for examining an application for international protection lodged in one of the Member States by a third-country national or a stateless person (recast), sometimes referred to as 'Dublin III' or 'the Dublin system'.

[90] See Case C-63/16 *Ghezelbash v Netherlands* [51] and Case C-670/16 *Mengesteab v Germany* [48].

[91] Regulation (EU) No. 603/2013 of the European Parliament and of the Council of 26 June 2013 on the establishment of 'Eurodac' for the comparison of fingerprints for the effective application of Regulation (EU) No. 604/2013 establishing the criteria and mechanisms for determining the Member State responsible for examining an application for international protection lodged in one of the Member States by a third-country national or a stateless person and on requests for the comparison with Eurodac data by Member States' law enforcement authorities and Europol for law enforcement purposes, and amending Regulation (EU) No. 1077/2011 establishing a European Agency for the operational management of large-scale IT systems in the area of freedom, security and justice (recast).

own country from 2015 onwards and travelling the European Union via these countries caused the collapse of the Dublin system, at least in the short term, as entry states were administratively overwhelmed.

KEY CASE

NS v United Kingdom and ME v Ireland was a decision of the Court of Justice of the European Union on the meaning and application of the Dublin II Regulation, in force between 2006 and 2013.[92] The cases were brought by asylum applicants who had entered the European Union via Greece and then travelled onwards to the United Kingdom and Ireland respectively. They sought to avoid transfer back to Greece on the basis that the asylum system there was failing to comply with European Union law minimum standards.

The court held that the Dublin system is founded on a system of 'mutual confidence' and a 'presumption of compliance' with European Union law and fundamental rights. A transferring country can therefore presume that the receiving country will adhere to the required minimum standards of treatment. However, this presumption might be rebutted 'if there are substantial grounds for believing that there are systemic flaws in the asylum procedure and reception conditions for asylum applicants in the Member State responsible, resulting in inhuman or degrading treatment'. A transfer in such circumstances would breach the Charter of Fundamental Rights of the European Union and Article 6 of the Treaty on European Union, which in effect incorporates the European Convention on Human Rights into European Union law. Following and applying the earlier European Court of Human Rights case of *MSS v Belgium*, the court held that transfer to Greece was therefore unlawful because of the inhuman and degrading conditions experienced by asylum seekers in Greece contrary to the requirements of European Union law.[93]

Transfers to Greece under the Dublin system remained suspended until a European Commission recommendation in 2016 that they might safely resume.[94] Despite this, at the time of writing, relatively few transfers to Greece had taken place in practice due to restraint by transferring countries given the very high number of asylum applications made in Greece over the course of the Syrian refugee influx or, failing that, refusal by the Greek authorities to accept requests.[95]

---

[92] Joined Cases C-411/10 and C-493/10.
[93] Application No. 30696/09.
[94] European Union Commission, *Recommendation of 8 December 2016 addressed to the Member States on the resumption of transfers to Greece under Regulation (EU) No. 604/2013*.
[95] Alper, L., *Greece Is Not Safe for Asylum Seekers and Refugees to Be Sent Back to* (18 April 2019), Available from: https://www.freemovement.org.uk/returns-to-greece/. [last accessed 9 August 2021].

The most relevant European Union legislation on international refugee law is a directive usually referred to as the Qualification Directive. This sets out 'minimum standards for the qualification and status of third-country nationals or stateless persons as refugees or as persons who otherwise need international protection and the content of the protection granted'.[96] The first version of this directive was adopted in 2004 and an amended (or 'recast') version was adopted in 2011.[97] Prior to Brexit taking full legal effect on 31 December 2020, the United Kingdom had been party to the original version but had opted out of the recast version. As with the African Refugee Convention and Cartagena Declaration, the Qualification Directive is framed as being complementary to the Refugee Convention, with the Refugee Convention acknowledged to be 'the cornerstone of the international legal regime for the protection of refugees'.[98] Where a person is excluded from refugee status under EU law that person can still retain refugee status under the Refugee Convention but will lose the additional benefits conferred by EU law.[99]

The Qualification Directive establishes common rules of interpretation. By adding to the language of the Refugee Convention, these provisions modify it slightly, although broadly in line with modern interpretation of the Refugee Convention in the major common law jurisdictions. A very slightly modernized version of the definition of a refugee used in Article 1A(2) of the Refugee Convention is adopted (using more gender-neutral language and the word 'stateless'). The directive then goes on to elucidate the terms used in that definition, including provisions defining, among other things, actors of persecution, actors of protection, internal protection, acts of persecution and reasons for persecution.[100] The directive includes exclusion clauses which are based upon but arguably wider than the exclusion clauses of the Refugee Convention itself. It provides for withdrawal of refugee status itself on the basis of those exclusion clauses, not just withdrawal of protection from *refoulement*. These elucidations on – or perhaps modifications to – the Refugee Convention are addressed in the relevant chapters of this book.

More radically, the Qualification Directive also creates a separate form of asylum labelled somewhat unromantically 'subsidiary protection' (known

---

[96] Directive 2011/95/2011, Preamble [1].
[97] Directive 2004/83/EU and Directive 2011/95/EU respectively.
[98] Directive 2004/83/EU, Preamble (3) and Directive 2011/95/EU, Preamble (4).
[99] Joined Cases C-391/16, C-77/17 and C-78/17 *M v Czech Republic and others* [100] and [111].
[100] Directive 2011/95/2011. Refugee is defined at Article 2(c), actors of persecution at Article 6, internal protection at Article 8, acts of persecution at Article 9 and reasons for persecution at Article 10.

as 'humanitarian protection' in the United Kingdom). Unlike under the African Refugee Convention or Cartagena Declaration, those entitled to this complementary protection are not considered or labelled refugees as such, and indeed the qualifying criteria for this protection are simultaneously wider and narrower than might be associated with popular conceptions of refugeehood. A person is entitled to this supplementary form of protection where they face a real risk of one of three forms of serious harm: (1) the death penalty or execution, (2) torture or inhuman or degrading treatment or punishment or (3) 'serious and individual threat to a civilian's life or person by reason of indiscriminate violence in situations of international or internal armed conflict'.[101] Subsidiary protection thus primarily builds upon the very limited obligations imposed on states by human rights laws, the limitations of which are discussed in what follows, but it also potentially goes beyond those obligations. The strength of subsidiary protection compared to bare human rights law is that, where engaged, it offers more than mere protection from *refoulement*. The Qualification Directive obliges states to offer a person qualifying for subsidiary protection a form of immigration status broadly equivalent to refugee status, including family reunion rights, a travel document, to engage in employed or self-employed activities, access to social assistance and health care and more.[102]

The first two qualifying criteria for subsidiary protection are rooted in the European Convention on Human Rights, discussed immediately in what follows and in Chapter 3.[103] These provisions will in some circumstances offer protection to persons in a refugee-like situation. A police informant facing very serious harm from a criminal gang from which their home state offers insufficient protection is in a refugee-like situation but would not usually qualify as a refugee under the Refugee Convention because of the absence of a connection to a convention ground. Such a person might qualify for subsidiary protection, as might a person fleeing civil war or famine, who if returned would face very serious harm. Not every person protected from *refoulement* is entitled to subsidiary protection, however. Exclusion clauses apply to subsidiary protection as well as refugee status, meaning that a person who has committed a very serious crime and faces the death penalty if extradited is not entitled to the benefits of formal subsidiary protection, even if, as discussed in a moment, they cannot be extradited owing to the effect of Article 3 of the European Convention on Human

---

[101] Directive 2011/95/EU, Article 15(a), 15(b) and 15(c) respectively.
[102] Directive 2011/95/EU, Articles 23–34.
[103] European Convention for the Protection of Human Rights and Fundamental Freedoms, Article 2 and Protocol 13 on the death penalty and Article 3 on torture, inhuman or degrading treatment or punishment.

Rights. Similarly, a person who faces deterioration in their health because of unavailability of medical treatment is protected against *refoulement* by the European Convention on Human rights and by the European Union Charter of Fundamental Rights but will not qualify for subsidiary protection unless that person is intentionally deprived of health care.[104]

The protection available to those who would suffer a serious and individual threat to their life or person by reason of indiscriminate violence in situations of international or internal armed conflict has no explicit foundation in human rights law. It is broadly humanitarian in nature, more closely akin to (but undoubtedly narrower than) the expansion of the refugee definition in the African Refugee Convention and Cartagena Declaration. The apparent humanitarian intent is undermined by the formulation of language employed: to require proof of 'individual' threat due to 'indiscriminate' violence appears contradictory and self-defeating. Addressing this issue, the Court of Justice of the European Union concluded that a person need not show they have been specifically targeted. Rather, the provision applies where 'substantial grounds are shown for believing that a civilian, returned to the relevant country or, as the case may be, to the relevant region, would, solely on account of his presence on the territory of that country or region, face a real risk of being subject to [serious and individual threat to the life or person]'.[105] It is not immediately obvious that this wording improves the clarity of the original. Slightly more meaningfully, the court went on to hold that 'the more the applicant is able to show that he is specifically affected by reason of factors particular to his personal circumstances, the lower the level of indiscriminate violence required for him to be eligible for subsidiary protection'. The provision has been interpreted as giving legal effect to a previous policy of, for 'reasons on common humanity', not returning unsuccessful asylum seekers to 'war zones or situations of armed anarchy'.[106] In reality, it seems to add little additional protection to that which should already be provided by the Refugee Convention and human rights law.

Unlike the Refugee Convention, the Common European Asylum System, including the Qualification Directive, is backed by an established and active enforcement regime: the European Union. This includes the EU law doctrine of direct effect, whereby national courts can enforce rights conferred by European Union legal instruments, the European Union's Commission and, ultimately, the Court of Justice of the European Union. The combination of the primacy given in European Union law to

---

[104] Case C-562/13 *Belgium v Abdida*; Case C-542/13 *Mohamed M'Bodj v Belgium*.
[105] Case C-465/07 *Elgafaji v Netherlands*.
[106] *QD (Iraq) v Secretary of State for the Home Department* [2009] EWCA Civ 620, [2011] 1 WLR 689.

the Refugee Convention and the interpretative function of the Court of Justice of the European Union created what Roland Bank has described as 'a grand potential' for the shaping of international refugee law.[107] In practice, Bank suggests the court has failed to deliver on this promise owing to a combination of reticence to refer cases by national courts, the way the standard-setting role of the court encourages judicial caution and the tendency of Advocates General and the judges to refer principally to European Union law as a self-contained legal system isolated from international law. The paucity of reference to or reasoning regarding the Refugee Convention has diminished the role the court's judgments might otherwise have played on the international law stage.

Domestic definitions

In states with a monist system of law, ratification of the Refugee Convention incorporates its provisions into national law. In common law dualist countries, national implementing legislation is required. Around 35 per cent of countries have explicitly incorporated a right to asylum into their constitution in some shape or form while others have adopted their own definition of a refugee in sub-constitutional national law.[108] Given the dependency of the international refugee protection regime on voluntary national compliance, these domestic definitions can enhance or reduce protection for refugees compared to the Refugee Convention.

In theory, a constitutional right to asylum would appear self-evidently helpful to those seeking asylum. Potentially, such a right might not only serve to establish or reinforce a legal norm but might enable a constitutional court to override national laws interfering with that right. Constitutional rights tend to be more durable and less easily amended than national laws. The content of the constitutional right is significant, though. Some constitutions confer a right of asylum on individuals, but others make the right conditional on domestic legislation or frame the right as that of the state, to be exercised at its discretion.[109] In practice, examples of reliance on a constitutional right to asylum are rare. In Ecuador, a presidential decree severely curtailing access to asylum by imposing strict time limits on making a

---

[107] Bank, R. (2015) 'The Potential and the Limitations of the Court of Justice of the European Union in Shaping International Refugee Law', *International Journal of Refugee Law*, 27(2): 213–244, 241.

[108] Kowalczyk, L. and Versteeg, M. (2017) 'The Political Economy of the Constitutional Right to Asylum', *Cornell Law Review* 102(5): 1219–1318, 1224.

[109] Foster, M. and Klaaren, J. (2012) 'Asylum and Refugees', in Tushnet, M., Fleiner, T. and Saunders, C. (eds) *Routledge Handbook on Constitutional Law*, Abingdon: Routledge, pp 416–417.

claim or lodging an appeal was declared unconstitutional in 2014. In Mexico a similar challenge was ultimately unsuccessful.[110] India is not a signatory to the Refugee Convention and, although the country has a high degree of engagement with UNHCR and participates in its executive committee, it lacks an explicit constitutional right to asylum or comprehensive national legislation on asylum.[111] Tibetan, Bangladeshi and Sri Lankan refugees have been treated quite differently from one another. Nevertheless, an implicit right to asylum was recognized by the Indian Supreme Court in 1996 when the court held that the Indian constitution's protection of life and liberty included a right of *non-refoulement*.[112]

Domestic definitions of a refugee in national law are often derived from the Refugee Convention but may be subtly different. A full survey is beyond the scope of this book but we can see variation even between countries sharing a common law heritage. In Australia, the term 'refugee' is defined in the Migration Act 1958 across multiple sections and subsections, which among other things elaborate on 'well-founded fear', 'persecution', 'effective protection' and 'reasonable steps to modify ... behaviour'.[113] This was at one time thought to have caused Australian law to diverge from the autonomous meaning of the Refugee Convention, with the domestic statutory definition being described as a 'manifestation of a statutory intent to define persecution, and therefore serious harm, in strict and perhaps narrower terms than an unqualified reading of [Art 1A(2)] might otherwise require'.[114] Later more definitive case law has suggested that the domestic statutory definitions merely 'restore' the autonomous meaning from earlier arguably divergent cases.[115] In Canada, the Immigration and Refugee Protection Act 2001 defines a 'Convention refugee' in similar but not identical terms to the Refugee Convention.[116] New Zealand has incorporated the Refugee Convention directly into domestic law in the Immigration Act 1987 and

---

[110] Sentencia N 002-14-Sin-CC, Case No. 0056-12-IN y 0003-12-IA 14 August 2014 and Amparo en Revisión 353/2019 16 October 2019 (Ministro José Fernando Franco González Salas), cited by Meili, S. (2021) 'National Constitutions and the Right to Asylum', in Costello, C., Foster, M. and McAdam, J. (eds) *The Oxford Handbook of International Refugee Law*, Oxford: Oxford University Press.

[111] Ramasubramanyam, J. (2021) 'Regional Regimes: South Asia', in Costello, C., Foster, M. and McAdam, J. (eds) *The Oxford Handbook of International Refugee Law*, Oxford: Oxford University Press.

[112] *National Human Rights Commission v State of Arunachal Pradesh* 1996 SCC (1) 742 (India SC).

[113] See ss 5H–5M.

[114] *VBAO v Minister for Immigration, Multicultural and Indigenous Affairs* [2006] HCA 60 (Aus) (Callinan and Heydon JJ) [49].

[115] *Minister for Immigration and Border Protection v WZAPN* [2015] HCA 22 [87].

[116] See s 96.

defines 'refugee' straightforwardly as 'within the meaning of the Refugee Convention'.[117] The United Kingdom was, until Brexit took effect at the end of 2020, bound by the refugee definition incorporated into European Union law discussed earlier. Since then, a refugee has not been defined in primary legislation, only in forms of secondary legislation.[118] This was set to change at the time of writing, as the Nationality and Borders Bill 2021 was expected to define or elaborate on key refugee law concepts including well-founded fear, persecution, protection and internal relocation when it became law. In the United States, the Refugee Act 1980 inserted a definition of the term 'refugee' into the Immigration and Nationality Act 1952, which is based closely on the Refugee Convention but which is structured differently and includes an additional exclusion clause in the definition itself.[119]

International human rights law

The preamble to the Refugee Convention begins by noting that state parties have, in agreeing to be bound by its terms, considered the Charter of the United Nations and the Universal Declaration of Human Rights and 'affirmed the principle that human beings shall enjoy fundamental rights and freedoms without discrimination'. These introductory words have been argued to embed the Refugee Convention within the post-war system of international human rights law.[120] Others have suggested that the words of the preamble are a 'poor hook' on which to hang interpretation of the Refugee Convention according to the tenets of human rights law.[121] Even if the justification and approach are somewhat contested, though, the relevance of human rights law to the interpretation of the Refugee Convention is not seriously disputed.

International human rights law has evolved considerably since the Universal Declaration of Human Rights of 1948 in its content, scope and depth. The International Covenants on Civil and Political Rights (ICCPR) and on Economic, Social and Cultural Rights (ICESCR) implement as binding law and expand upon the Universal Declaration of Human Rights. The

---

[117] See Schedule 6 and s 129F(1).
[118] Immigration Rules HC 395, Part 11; Protection Regulations (Refugee or Person in Need of International Protection (Qualification) Regulations 2006 SI 2006/2525) (which became retained European Union law under section 2 of the European Union (Withdrawal) Act 2018).
[119] 8 USC 1101(a)(42).
[120] Hathaway, J. (1991) *The Law of Refugee Status*, Toronto: Butterworths Canada.
[121] Cantor, D. (2016) 'Defining Refugees: Persecution, Surrogacy and the Human Rights Paradigm', in Cantor, D. and Burson, B. (eds) *Human Rights and the Refugee Definition: Comparative Legal Practice and Theory*, Leiden: Brill, p 376.

covenants were agreed in 1966, came into effect in 1976 and have been very widely ratified. The three instruments are sometimes collectively referred to as the International Bill of Human Rights. A range of treaties has been agreed which add depth, context and understanding to these human rights, such as the International Convention on the Elimination of All Forms of Racial Discrimination (ICERD), the Convention on the Elimination of All Forms of Discrimination Against Women (CEDAW), the Convention on the Rights of the Child (CRC) and the Convention on the Rights of Persons with Disabilities (CRPD).[122] Other treaties have been agreed which focus on very specific aspects of human rights, such as the Convention Against Torture (CAT) and the Palermo Protocol on human trafficking.[123] In some cases, the treaties feature optional enforcement mechanisms, including committees to adjudicate upon and interpret the meaning of the words of the treaties. To take the preamble of the Refugee Convention at face value and have regard only to the Universal Declaration of Human Rights itself and disregard what has since been done to realize its ideals would be perverse. More prosaically, it would also be to ignore the Vienna Convention on the Law of Treaties.[124] As Lord Bingham recognized in *Sepet*, 'the reach of an international human rights convention is not forever determined by the intentions of those who originally framed it'.[125]

Meanwhile, regional human rights instruments coexist with the global instruments. These include the European Convention on Human Rights and Fundamental Freedoms of 1950, the American Convention on Human Rights of 1967 and the African Charter on Human and Peoples' Rights of 1981. Reference to these regional instruments, which inevitably vary in emphasis and enforceability, carries a hypothetical risk of fragmentation of understanding. In reality, the regional and global treaties for the most part sit happily alongside one another without incompatibility. The regional instruments both influence and reflect the key international instruments and can be characterized as implementing and enforcing broadly similar standards.

---

[122] Convention on the Elimination of All Forms of Discrimination Against Women 1979, United Nations, Treaty Series, Vol. 1249, p 13; Convention on the Rights of the Child 1989, United Nations, Treaty Series, Vol. 1577, p 3; Convention on the Rights of Persons with Disabilities 2007 (UN Doc A/RES/61/106).

[123] Convention Against Torture and Other Cruel, Inhuman or Degrading Treatment or Punishment, United Nations, Treaty Series, Vol. 1465, p 85; Protocol to Prevent, Suppress and Punish Trafficking in Persons, Especially Women and Children, Supplementing the United Nations Convention against Transnational Organised Crime 2003 (UN Doc A/RES/55/25).

[124] Vienna Convention on the Law of Treaties 1969, Articles 31 and 32.

[125] *Sepet v Secretary of State for the Home Department* [2003] UKHL 15, [2003] 3 All ER 304 [11] (Lord Bingham). The House of Lords concluded that a right to refuse to undertake military service on grounds of conscience had not yet become internationally recognized.

All these other legal instruments can aid the interpretation of key terms and concepts within the Refugee Convention. Sometimes they can also, by their differences, reveal the purpose, meaning and extent of the Refugee Convention. The traffic is not all one way: refugee law has influenced key aspects of human rights law, including the right of *non-refoulement*. As we will see, this cross-fertilization does not always necessarily favour improved protection for refugees and other forced migrants.

Interpretation and interplay

It has long been recognized that international human rights law should be considered relevant to understanding the words 'being persecuted' in Article 1A(2) of the Refugee Convention. Goodwin-Gill wrote in 1983 that 'comprehensive analysis requires the general notion [of persecution] to be related to developments within the broad field of human rights'.[126] In 1991, Professor James Hathaway proposed a more structured relationship between the concepts, arguing that 'persecution may be defined as the sustained or systemic violation of basic human rights demonstrative of a failure of state protection'.[127] Discussed in more depth in Chapter 3, the more formalized linkage between persecution and human rights law has become so widely adopted that it has been described as 'the most important paradigm shift in refugee jurisprudence to have occurred since the publication of the 1979 United Nations High Commissioner for Refugees (UNHCR) Handbook'.[128] International human rights law is now widely referenced as a guide to assessing the level of seriousness of harm necessary to amount to persecution. The framework of international human rights law provides a set of standards, which by their nature are internationally agreed: they potentially offer a ready-made yardstick for determining the point at which harm tips over into becoming persecution. Without an objective standard of this nature, there is a clear risk of variation in standards between asylum assessors within and between jurisdictions. As Michelle Foster has written, the risk of subjectivity is 'particularly acute in cases involving gender-related persecution, where decision-makers in many jurisdictions have shown a greater propensity to dismiss claims based on the view that

---

[126] Goodwin-Gill, G. (1983) *The Refugee in International Law*, Oxford: Oxford University Press, p 38.

[127] Hathaway, J. (1991) *The Law of Refugee Status*, Toronto: Butterworths Canada, pp 104–105.

[128] Storey, H. (2012) 'Armed Conflict in Asylum Law: The "War-Flaw"', *Refugee Survey Quarterly*, 31(2): 1–32. See also Foster, M. (2007) *International Refugee Law and Socio-Economic Rights: Refuge from Deprivation*, Cambridge: Cambridge University Press, pp 27–33.

discrimination against women is justified by culture, religion or social norms'.[129] While all, or at least most, agree that international human rights law therefore can and should provide the applicable standards, there is no clearly stated consensus on the question of what kinds of human rights violations might cross the threshold of persecution and in what circumstances.

Where there appears to be divergence in international understanding as to what is or is not internationally recognized as a human right, decision makers have to make a judgment. This was the situation in the case of *Sepet*, where the applicants argued that a right to conscientious objection from military service had emerged in recent years. The judges assessed a considerable weight of international and academic material on this question and eventually concluded that there was at that time no 'clear international recognition' of the asserted right, while acknowledging that the applicant's arguments 'may well reflect the international consensus of tomorrow'.[130] No clear test was proposed in *Sepet* for how the emergence of a new right might be recognized in future. Only eight years later, the European Court of Human Rights held that 'already a virtually general consensus on the question in Europe and beyond' that the right to conscientious objection is protected by the right to freedom of thought, conscience and religion.[131]

For good or ill, international human rights law has also been invoked as guidance as to the degree of failure of state protection required before a person at risk of serious harm becomes eligible for refugee status. There is a positive obligation in human rights law to protect against harm, for example by 'putting in place effective criminal law provisions to deter the commission of offences against the person backed up by law enforcement machinery for the prevention, suppression and sanctioning of breaches of such provisions'.[132] But this obligation to protect is not absolute, nor does it require the state to reduce the probability of harm below a certain level, such as real risk or well-founded fear. The notion of state accountability was explicitly referenced by Lord Clyde in the refugee law case of *Horvath*: 'account should be taken of the operational responsibilities and the constraints on the provision of police protection and accordingly the obligation to protect must not be so interpreted as to impose an impossible

---

[129] Foster, M. (2007) *International Refugee Law and Socio-Economic Rights: Refuge from Deprivation*, Cambridge: Cambridge University Press, pp 38–39.

[130] *Sepet v Secretary of State for the Home Department* [2003] UKHL 15, [2003] 3 All ER 304 (Lord Bingham).

[131] *Batayan v Armenia* [2011] ECHR 1095 [108]. See also *Yeo-Bum Yoon and Myung-Jin Choi v Republic of Korea*, CCPR/C/88/D/1321-1322/2004, UN Human Rights Committee, 23 January 2007.

[132] *Osman v United Kingdom* [1998] ECHR 101 [115].

or disproportionate burden upon the authorities'.[133] Parallels have also been drawn in academic work, with Goodwin-Gill and McAdam arguing that the notion of lack of protection 'invites attention to the general issue of a State's duty to protect and promote human rights'.[134] In the context of protection, though, the contentious question is not merely of benchmarking but whether it is appropriate to reference human rights standards in refugee law at all. Hathaway and Foster forcefully argue that the doctrine of state accountability, derived from international human rights law, has no place in refugee law because it invites inappropriate focus on state responsibility, wrongly conflates willingness to provide protection with the ability to provide protection, is primarily retrospective in outlook rather than, like the Refugee Convention, prospective, and interferes with what ought to be the real question, which is whether the protection is sufficiently effective so as to mean there is no well-founded fear of being persecuted.[135]

Although there is potential for interplay, which we have seen is contested in some contexts, there are key conceptual differences between the Refugee Convention and international human rights law. The framing of the Refugee Convention as a series of obligations on state parties is a reminder that it emerged from an earlier era of international law. For example, Article 26 of the Refugee Convention on freedom of movement begins by stating that '[e]ach Contracting State shall accord to refugees lawfully in its territory the right to choose their place of residence to move freely within its territory ...'. In contrast, Article 12 of the International Covenant on Civil and Political Rights boldly proclaims the innate existence of the same right: '[e]veryone lawfully within the territory of a State shall, within that territory, have the right to liberty of movement and freedom to choose his residence'. The most significant departure point is that while the Refugee Convention is a humanitarian instrument, it is somewhat morally selective rather than applying equally to all. By means of the limitations in the refugee definition and the exclusion clauses discussed in Chapter 6, the framers of the Refugee Convention deliberately withheld its protection from some groups or individuals, including those who behave in reprehensible ways. In contrast, the foundational principle of the concept of human rights is that they are inalienable, applying equally to all humans irrespective of behaviour

---

[133] *Horvath v Secretary of State for the Home Department* [2001] AC 489 (UK HL) (Lord Clyde). The linkage was cemented and made more explicit in the later case of *R (on the application of Bagdanavicius) v Secretary of State for the Home Department* [2005] UKHL 38, [2005] 2 AC 668.

[134] Goodwin-Gill, G. and McAdam, J. (2021) *The Refugee in International Law* (4th edn), Oxford: Oxford University Press, p 157.

[135] Hathaway, J. and Foster, M. (2014) *The Law of Refugee Status* (2nd edn), Cambridge: Cambridge University Press, pp 308–315.

or conduct.[136] While under the Refugee Convention a person who has committed a crime against peace, a war crime or a crime against humanity can be sent back to their country of origin to face persecution, human rights instruments impose an absolute bar on exposing any person to torture.

Non-refoulement in human rights cases

A further important point of difference between the Refugee Convention and the principal international human rights instruments is that many of the latter do not feature an explicit prohibition on *refoulement* to prevent future breaches of human rights by a party outside the jurisdiction of a given state party.[137] Sometimes labelled foreign cases, they are to be distinguished from domestic cases in which it is alleged that the relevant state party will itself breach a person's human rights directly by removing a person.[138] A considerable body of jurisprudence has developed around the right to a private and family life in domestic breach cases, but this falls outside the scope of this book.[139] Even without express provision, core human rights instruments have come to be regarded as imposing a duty of *non-refoulement* in foreign breach cases, at least in some circumstances. In this respect, the European Court of Human Rights has been described as the 'vanguard institution on *non-refoulement*', which not only pioneered *non-refoulement* in human rights law but then went on substantively to lead further development of the concept.[140]

Article 3 of the European Convention on Human Rights is an absolute right from which no derogation can be made, stating simply '[n]o one shall be subjected to torture or to inhuman or degrading treatment or punishment'. Similar rights are enshrined in other regional instruments, including at Article 5 of the American Convention on Human Rights and Article 5 of the African Charter on Human and Peoples' Rights. These echo the language of Article 5 of the Universal Declaration of Human Rights and Article 7 of the ICCPR.

---

[136] See for example Universal Declaration of Human Rights, Preamble and Articles 1 and 2.

[137] An explicit right of *non-refoulement* is included in the American Convention on Human Rights at Article 22(8), the United Nations Convention against Torture at Article 3, the International Convention for the Protection of All Persons from Enforced Disappearance at Article 16 and the European Union Charter of Fundamental Rights at Article 19(2).

[138] *R (Ullah and Do) v Special Adjudicator* [2004] 2 AC 323, [2004] UKHL 26 [7] and [9].

[139] In the context of the right to private and family life set out at Article 8 of the European Convention on Human Rights, see for example *Boultif v Switzerland* (2001) 33 EHRR 50, *Uner v Netherlands* (2006) 45 EHRR 14 and *Maslov v Austria* [2008] ECHR 546.

[140] Çalı, B., Costello, C. and Cunningham, S. (2020) 'Hard Protection through Soft Courts? Non-Refoulement before the United Nations Treaty Bodies', *German Law Journal*, 21: 355–384, 357.

KEY CASE

In the landmark case of *Soering v United Kingdom* in 1989, the European Court of Human Rights held that extradition of a person to a country where there was a real risk they would face inhuman or degrading treatment would breach Article 3 of the European Convention on Human Rights.[141] *Soering* involved a request to extradite a double murder suspect to the state of Virginia in the United States, where, if convicted, there were 'substantial grounds for believing' he would face the death penalty, preceded by being held for a prolonged period in what the court described as 'extreme conditions' awaiting execution. The formulation of 'substantial grounds for believing' is considered to amount to the same standard of proof as 'well-founded fear' under the Refugee Convention. The term 'real risk' is often deployed as a synonym.[142] The majority judgment turned on the prohibition on inhuman or degrading treatment or punishment, not on the right to life. Article 2 of the European Convention on Human Rights includes an exception for the death penalty 'in the execution of a sentence of a court following his conviction of a crime for which this penalty is provided by law'. This exception was later removed in 2002.[143] The United Kingdom was the state party to the case but was not responsible for acts carried out by another government outside the jurisdiction of the United Kingdom. The double murder in question involved a frenzied killing and was obviously a very serious matter; it was important that if Mr Soering was guilty he be held to account. But it was not clear that Mr Soering would be convicted, if he would be sentenced to death or, if he was, how long he would await execution. The court cut through the issues of state responsibility and chain of causation with the 'substantial grounds for believing' formulation, which requires a fact-finder to make some level of prediction of future events.

Following the case, the state of Virginia gave assurances that the death penalty would not be sought. Mr Soering was duly extradited and, in 1990, tried, convicted and sentenced to life imprisonment. The prohibition on *refoulement* had worked, in the sense that extradition had eventually proceeded but only after the risk of inhuman or degrading treatment or punishment had been eliminated.

---

[141] App. No. 14038/88 [1989] ECHR 14 [88].

[142] See for example Directive 2011/EU/95, Articles 4(4), 5 and 8; *R (on the application of Sivakumuran) v Secretary of State for the Home Department* [1988] AC 958 (UK HL) (Lords Keith and Goff); *Demirkaya v Secretary of State for the Home Department* [1999] Imm AR 498 (EW CA) [16]; *Chahal v United Kingdom* App. No. 70/1995/576/662 [1996] 23 EHRR 413 [74], [96], [97], [107]; *D v United Kingdom* App. No. 30240/96 [1997] ECHR 25 [50].

[143] Protocol No. 13 to the Convention for the Protection of Human Rights and Fundamental Freedoms, concerning the abolition of the death penalty in all circumstances (ETS No. 187).

Soering was followed in 1996 by the case of *Chahal v United Kingdom*, in which the European Court of Human Rights reiterated that the prohibition on torture or inhuman or degrading treatment was absolute.[144] Even in a case involving national security, the court held there was no room 'for balancing the risk of ill-treatment against the reasons for expulsion'. Soon after that, the case of *D v United Kingdom* came before the court. The applicant was at the critical stage of a terminal illness (HIV/AIDS). He was receiving palliative care in the host country but would have no access at all to medical treatment or other care after his removal.[145] The result of removal in these circumstances would be that his condition would rapidly deteriorate and he would die experiencing 'acute mental and physical suffering', which the court considered would amount to inhuman treatment. Having earlier proclaimed that the prohibition on torture or inhuman or degrading treatment or punishment 'enshrines one of the most fundamental values of democratic society' it seemed logical that *refoulement* was therefore prohibited. However, the court emphasized the exceptional nature of the facts of the case. Further litigation followed, with the European Court of Human Rights at first seeming to strictly limit the scope of the earlier judgment in the case of *N v United Kingdom* in 2008 and then later somewhat relaxing its previous approach in *Paposhvili v Belgium* in 2016.[146] The test remains a strict one. Although the person need not demonstrate an imminent risk of death, the obligation of *non-refoulement* only arises in medical treatment cases where 'on account of the absence of appropriate treatment in the receiving country or the lack of access to such treatment' the person concerned can show 'a serious, rapid and irreversible decline in his or her state of health resulting in intense suffering or to a significant reduction in life expectancy'. The cases all involved very seriously ill individuals, with the applicant in *N v United Kingdom* being reported to die shortly after her removal to her country of origin and the applicant in *Paposhvili* dying before the court reached judgment in his case. The applicability of the principle of *non-refoulement* where a

---

[144] *Chahal v United Kingdom* App. No. 70/1995/576/662 [1996] 23 EHRR 413. See also United Nations Committee against Torture, *General Comment No. 4 (2017) on the Implementation of Article 3 of the Convention in the Context of Article 22*, CAT/C/GC/4, 4 September 2018 [9].

[145] *D v United Kingdom* App. No. 30240/96 [1997] ECHR 25 [50].

[146] *N v United Kingdom* App. No. 26565/05 [2008] ECHR 453; *Paposhvili v Belgium* App. No. 41738/10 [2016] ECHR 1113. See also United Kingdom domestic cases of *N v Secretary of State for the Home Department* [2005] UKHL 31, [2005] 2 AC 296 and *AM (Zimbabwe) v Secretary of State for the Home Department* [2020] UKSC 17, [2020] 3 All ER 1003.

person's health will be very seriously affected has also been recognized by the Inter-American Court.[147]

A further, distinct line of authority has developed around severe social and economic deprivation. In *MSS v Belgium and Greece* the European Court of Human Rights held that transfer of an asylum seeker by Belgium to Greece under the Dublin system would breach the prohibition on inhuman and degrading treatment because of the 'extreme material poverty' experienced by asylum seekers in Greece.[148] This was a notably lower threshold of suffering than had been developed in the medical treatment cases. The court based this new approach on the legal duty imposed on Greece by European Union law to provide for asylum seekers and the special situation of vulnerability of asylum seekers. The divergence in approach was underlined by the subsequent judgment in *Sufi and Elmi v United Kingdom* concerning deportation to Somalia.[149] The court held that same approach as in the medical treatment cases would be applied in cases involving dire humanitarian conditions caused by simple poverty or a state's lack of resources but where those conditions were caused directly or indirectly by parties to a conflict, the lower threshold of *MSS v Belgium and Greece* would be applicable. As Costello has observed, the distinction between lack of resources and deliberate harm is not a straightforward one to apply in practice and tends to undermine protection from *non-refoulement* in cases involving non-state actors.[150]

The right of *non-refoulement* in situations that would breach the right to life or the right to freedom from torture or cruel, inhuman or degrading treatment or punishment is now very widely recognized and has been argued by some to have reached the status of customary international law.[151] The United Nations Human Rights Committee concluded in 1992 that states parties 'must not expose individuals to the danger of torture or cruel,

---

[147] Advisory Opinion OC-21/14, 'Rights and Guarantees of Children in the Context of Migration and/or in Need of International Protection', OC-21/14, Inter-American Court of Human Rights, 19 August 2014 [229].

[148] *MSS v Belgium and Greece* (2011) 53 EHRR 2 [252].

[149] *Sufi and Elmi v United Kingdom* (2012) 54 EHRR 9.

[150] Costello, C. (2016) 'The Search for the Outer Edges of Non-Refoulement in Europe', in Cantor, D. and Burson, B. (eds) *Human Rights and the Refugee Definition: Comparative Legal Practice and Theory*, Leiden: Brill, pp 180–209, 194.

[151] Lauterpacht, E. and Bethlehem, D. (2003) 'The Scope and Content of the Principle of Non-refoulement', in Feller, E., Türk, V. and Nicholson, F. (eds) *Refugee Protection in International Law*, Cambridge: Cambridge University Press; *R v Immigration Officer at Prague Airport, ex p European Roma Rights Centre* [2004] UKHL 55, [2005] 2 AC 1 [26]; Goodwin-Gill, G. and McAdam, J. (2021) *The Refugee in International Law* (4th edn), Oxford: Oxford University Press, pp 300–306; but *contra* see Hathaway, J. (2021) *The Rights of Refugees under International Law* (2nd edn), Cambridge: Cambridge University Press, pp 435–459.

inhuman or degrading treatment or punishment upon return to another country by way of their extradition, expulsion or refoulement'.[152] The same committee reiterated and expanded the point in 2004, concluding that the ICCPR 'entails an obligation not to extradite, deport, expel or otherwise remove a person from their territory, where there are substantial grounds for believing that there is a real risk of irreparable harm ... either in the country to which removal is to be effected or in any country to which the person may subsequently be removed'.[153] The Committee Against Torture has affirmed the absolute nature of the prohibition on *refoulement* in cases of torture and the Committee on the Rights of the Child has done so if there is a 'real risk of irreparable harm to the child'.[154] The Inter-American Court adopts a similar line.[155]

Both the European Court of Human Rights and the Inter-American Court have found that the right of *non-refoulement* includes implicit procedural safeguards. In *Hirsi v Italy*, the European Court held the complainants 'had no access to a procedure to identify them and to assess their personal circumstances before they were returned' and therefore that the right to an effective remedy had been breached.[156] The Inter-American Court considers that a state 'must at least interview the person and carry out a prior or preliminary assessment'.[157] A similar approach has been adopted by the United Nations Committee against Torture:

> Each case should be examined individually, impartially and independently by the State party through competent administrative and/or judicial authorities, in conformity with essential procedural safeguards, notably the guarantee of a prompt and transparent process, a review of the deportation decision and a suspensive effect of the

---

[152] United Nations Human Rights Committee, *General Comment No. 20: Article 7 (Prohibition of Torture, or Other Cruel, Inhuman or Degrading Treatment or Punishment)*, HRI/GEN/1/Rev.9 (Vol. I), 10 March 1992 [9].

[153] United Nations Human Rights Committee, *General Comment No. 31: The Nature of the General Legal Obligation Imposed on States Parties to the Covenant*, CCPR/C/21/Rev.1/Add.13, 26 May 2004 [12].

[154] United Nations Committee against Torture, *General Comment No. 4 (2017) on the Implementation of Article 3 of the Convention in the Context of Article 22*, CAT/C/GC/4, 4 September 2018 [9]; United Nations Committee on the Rights of the Child, *General Comment No. 6: Treatment of Unaccompanied and Separated Children Outside their Country of Origin*, CRC/GC/2005/6, 1 September 2005 [27].

[155] *Pacheco Tineo Family v Bolivia*, Inter-American Court of Human Rights, Series C No. 272, 25 November 2013; *Advisory Opinion OC-25/18*, Inter-American Court of Human Rights, 30 May 2018.

[156] *Hirsi v Italy* App. No. 27765/09 (ECHR, 23 February 2012) [202]-[205].

[157] *Pacheco Tineo Family v Bolivia*, Inter-American Court of Human Rights, Series C No. 272, 25 November 2013 [196].

appeal. In each case, the person concerned should be informed of the intended deportation in a timely manner. Collective deportation, without an objective examination of the individual cases with regard to personal risk, should be considered as a violation of the principle of non-refoulement.[158]

Other human rights obligations have been held to give rise to an independent right of *non-refoulement*, albeit in very narrow – perhaps even illusory – circumstances. In the United Kingdom, the House of Lords held in the case of *Ullah and Do* in 2004 that other rights protected by the European Convention on Human Rights aside from the prohibition on torture or inhuman or degrading treatment or punishment could, in theory, be breached by removal, albeit a 'very strong case' would need to be presented showing that the future breaches would amount to a 'fragrant denial' of the right in question.[159] At the time of that judgment, there were no concrete findings from the European Court of Human Rights confirming that the principles of *Soering* might also apply to other rights, although several judgments had allowed for the possibility.[160] In a later case, involving two Christians from Pakistan, the court stated that it 'shares the view of the House of Lords in the *Ullah* case that it would be difficult to visualize a case in which a sufficiently flagrant violation of Article 9 [freedom of religion] would not also involve treatment in violation of Article 3 [freedom from torture or inhuman or degrading treatment] of the Convention'.[161] One possible example of *non-refoulement* outside the scope of torture or inhuman or degrading treatment arose in a United Kingdom case in 2011, in which the House of Lords held that the removal of a mother and child together to another country where they would then be separated met the flagrant denial test in the context of the right to a private and family life, with the effect that *refoulement* was therefore prohibited under human rights law.[162] The court did not make findings on whether the future harm of family separation might also amount to inhuman or degrading treatment or being persecuted because those questions had fallen away earlier in the proceedings. A further example arose

---

[158] United Nations Committee against Torture, *General Comment No. 4 (2017) on the Implementation of Article 3 of the Convention in the Context of Article 22*, CAT/C/GC/4, 4 September 2018 [13].

[159] [2004] UKHL 26, [2004] 2 AC 323.

[160] For example see dissenting opinions in *Mamatkulov and Askarov v Turkey* App. No 46827/99, 46951/99 [2003] ECHR 68 and authorities surveyed in *R (Ullah and Do) v Special Adjudicator* [2004] UKHL 26, [2004] 2 AC 323 and later in *EM (Lebanon) v Secretary of State for the Home Department* [2008] UKHL 64, [2009] 1 AC 1198.

[161] *Z & T v United Kingdom* App. No. 27034/05 (ECHR, 28 February 2006).

[162] *EM (Lebanon) v Secretary of State for the Home Department* [2008] UKHL 64, [2009] 1 AC 1198.

in 2012 in the case of *Othman* when the court held in the context of the right to a fair trial that the duty of *non-refoulement* would be triggered by a 'flagrant denial of justice', which was 'so fundamental as to amount to a nullification, or destruction of the very essence, of the right'.[163] The court held that the admission of evidence obtained by torture in Mr Othman's trial *in absentia* did reach this stringent threshold. Even in this case, though, it was not clear that the flagrant denial would have been sufficient in and of itself to bar *refoulement* without other serious consequences; it was common ground that a substantial period of imprisonment awaited Mr Othman if he was removed to the country in question.[164]

Whether a 'flagrant denial' of a right other than the prohibition on torture or cruel, inhuman or degrading treatment or punishment will always in any event breach the latter right is therefore as yet unclear. But these other human rights, and the mature yet ever-evolving jurisprudence which surrounds them, can help to inform as to whether a particular form of harm might amount to inhuman or degrading treatment or being persecuted within the meaning of the Refugee Convention. For example, the Court of Justice of the European Union has, in a case involving the right to freedom of religion, found that prohibition on worship would amount to persecution if the person concerned 'will, *inter alia*, be prosecuted or subject to inhuman or degrading punishment'.[165] The wording makes clear that inhuman or degrading punishment is not the relevant test as such, but the overlap between human rights law and refugee law is nevertheless underlined.

Jurisdiction and international human rights law

The right of *non-refoulement* is widely considered to apply to any person under the jurisdiction of a state and to carry with it procedural protections. A state's jurisdiction for this purpose is broadly understood in human rights law. In *Banković v Belgium* the European Court of Human Rights held that a state's jurisdiction is 'primarily territorial' but can also arise where a state exercises 'physical power and control over the person in question'.[166] A similar formula has been adopted by the United Nations Human Rights Committee.[167] This principle was applied to interdiction at sea in the case

---

[163] *Othman v United Kingdom* App. No. 8139/09 [2012] 55 EHRR 1 [260].
[164] *Othman v United Kingdom* App. No. 8139/09 [2012] 55 EHRR 1 [262].
[165] Joined Cases C-71/11 and C-99/11 *Y and Z v Germany* [69].
[166] *Banković v Belgium* [2001] ECHR 890 [59]; *Al-Skeini v United Kingdom* [2011] ECHR 1093 [136].
[167] United Nations Human Rights Committee, *General Comment No 31: The Nature of the General Legal Obligation Imposed on States Parties to the Covenant* (UN Doc CCPR/C/21/Rev.1/Add.13) (26 May 2004) [10].

of *Hirsi v Italy*, in which the European Court of Human Rights held that a refugee rescued or intercepted at sea is under the continuous and exclusive *de jure* and de facto control of the relevant authorities and therefore within the jurisdiction of those authorities for the purposes of human rights law.[168] A state's jurisdiction is also engaged where a person remains on their own vessel but under 'full and exclusive control' of the state concerned.[169] The Inter-American Court has likewise held that 'the principle of *non-refoulement* can be invoked by any alien over whom the State in question is exercising authority or who is under its control, regardless of whether she or he is on the land, rivers, or sea or in the air space of the State'.[170] The legal position in the United States is notably different, with the Supreme Court holding in a much-criticized decision that interception of a boat of Haitians in international waters and return to their country of origin without assessment of their claims to refugee status did not breach the Refugee Convention because the convention does not apply to the actions of a state party outside its own territory.[171] While the Inter-American Commission disagreed in a later decision on similar facts, decisions by the commission have only moral force.[172]

Rights and status under international human rights law

In refugee law, the negative duty of *non-refoulement* may be the single most important aspect of refugee protection, but it is accompanied by other positive duties of refugee assistance. In contrast, human rights law does not make explicit provision for immigration status or other corollary rights for a person who is protected from *refoulement*. In some circumstances a state party is required by human rights law not to expose a person to a real risk of a future breach of their human rights; it is unclear in what circumstances, if at all, the state party is obliged to grant the person lawful status, a right to work and similar. This is not a surprise as it is doubtful that the framers of the core treaties anticipated that a duty of *non-refoulement* would arise at all. In any event, it does not necessarily

---

[168] *Hirsi v Italy* App. No. 27765/09 (ECHR, 23 February 2012) [81]-[82].
[169] *Medvedyev v France* App. No. 3394/03 (ECHR, 29 March 2010) [67].
[170] Advisory Opinion OC-21/14, 'Rights and Guarantees of Children in the Context of Migration and/or in Need of International Protection', Inter-American Court of Human Rights, 19 August 2014 [219]; see also *Pacheco Tineo Family v Bolivia*, Inter-American Court of Human Rights, Series C No. 272, 25 November 2013 [177] and [187]-[188].
[171] *Sale v Haitian Centers Council* 509 US 153 (21 June 1993) (US SC).
[172] Case 10.675, *Haitian Centre for Human Rights et al v United States*, Inter-American Commission on Human Rights, 13 March 1997.

follow that not exposing a person to torture also requires that the person be afforded additional rights over and above not being exposed to torture. For this reason, where there arises an issue of continued reliance on human rights laws as protection against *refoulement*, the burden continues to rest with the person resisting *refoulement* to show ongoing protection needs. This contrasts with the position under the Refugee Convention, where the onus shifts to the host state to show that cessation can be justified.[173] Ultimately, the human rights treaties were not created for the purpose of providing surrogate international protection.

That said, a state might be obliged by human rights laws to offer some sort of security of status, or at least the means by which to survive. This is not because to do otherwise might force the person to leave the host country and therefore amount to indirect *refoulement*. Rather, it is because human rights laws include positive as well as negative obligations.[174] To leave a person with no legal status and therefore unable to access social assistance or employment would be in effect to force the person into destitution, which could itself amount to inhuman or degrading treatment or punishment.[175] Denial of resolution of status for a prolonged period might also amount to a breach of a person's private life and their right to an effective remedy.[176] The Inter-American Court has held that this form of 'complementary protection' constitutes 'a normative development that is consistent with the principle of non-refoulement, by means of which States safeguard the rights of those who do not qualify as refugee or under any other migratory status but who cannot be returned'.[177] While the basic human rights of the person concerned must be respected, a state 'may limit the exercise of certain rights when granting this protection, provided that this is based on sound and objective reasons and does not violate the principle of non-discrimination'. Even provision of temporary renewable legal status – with an accompanying right to access social assistance or work – might eventually be considered to breach the right to a private and family life if sufficiently prolonged.[178]

---

[173] *Secretary of State for the Home Department v MM (Zimbabwe)* [2017] EWCA Civ 797. See further Chapter 7 in respect of cessation of refugee status.

[174] *Pretty v United Kingdom* App. No. 2346/02 [2002] ECHR 427.

[175] *R (on the application of Limbuela) v Secretary of State for the Home Department* [2005] UKHL 66, [2006] 1 AC 396.

[176] *B.A.C. v Greece* App. No. 11981/15 [2016] ECHR 883.

[177] Advisory Opinion OC-21/14, 'Rights and Guarantees of Children in the Context of Migration and/or in Need of International Protection', Inter-American Court of Human Rights, 19 August 2014 [240].

[178] *Mendizabal v France* App. No. 51431/99 [2006] ECHR 34; *Hoti v Croatia* App. No. 63311/14 (ECHR, 26 April 2018).

Trafficking victims

A relatively recent and still-developing arena of international protection applies to victims of human trafficking, at least in some countries. Slavery, servitude and forced labour have long been recognized as serious breaches of human rights, as recognized in the principal international human rights treaties.[179] Trafficking of human beings for the purposes of exploiting them has been recognized as a particular form of breach of this core human right and international attention has gradually come to bear on addressing the issue.[180] However, the primary purpose of the existing international framework of laws on human trafficking is law enforcement and prevention, not the protection of those who have already fallen victim. While there is some hypothetical recognition that successful detention and prosecution of traffickers requires the provision of safety and sanctuary to the victims, in practice this tends to be undermined by the desire of national authorities to enforce immigration laws.[181]

To coordinate and promote international efforts to combat trafficking, an agreement referred to as the Palermo Protocol was adopted by the UN General Assembly in 2000.[182] Trafficking in human beings is defined at Article 3 as:

> the recruitment, transportation, transfer, harbouring or receipt of persons, by means of the threat or use of force or other forms of coercion, of abduction, of fraud, of deception, of the abuse of power or of a position of vulnerability or of the giving or receiving of payments or benefits to achieve the consent of a person having control over another person, for the purpose of exploitation.

'Exploitation' is then defined as including, at a minimum: 'the exploitation of the prostitution of others or other forms of sexual exploitation, forced labour or services, slavery or practices similar to slavery, servitude or the removal of organs'. Trafficking is theoretically distinct from smuggling. Trafficking is by definition non-consensual and involves exploitation. Smuggling can be characterized as voluntary: it involves payment in return for a service,

---

[179] See for example Universal Declaration of Human Rights, Article 4; European Convention on Human Rights, Article 4; International Covenant of Civil and Political Rights, Article 8; International Covenant on Economic, Social and Cultural Rights, Articles 6 and 7.
[180] For example at Article 7(1)(c) of the Statute of the International Criminal Court 1998; *Siliadin v France* App. No. 73316/01 [2005] ECHR 545 [120] and [129] and *Rantsev v Cyprus and Russia* App. No. 25965/04 (ECHR, 10 October 2010) [282].
[181] See for example Kenway, E. (2021) *The Truth about Modern Slavery*, London: Pluto Press.
[182] United Nations, *Treaty Series*, Vol. 2237, p 319; UN Doc A/55/383.

albeit one that is illegal and may well involve considerable risk to the smuggled person. In practice, it is not always straightforward to distinguish clearly between the two.[183] The objectives of the protocol were to prevent trafficking, protect victims from traffickers and promote cooperation between states to achieve these goals. State parties agreed to 'consider implementing measures to provide for the physical, psychological and social recovery of victims of trafficking' and 'consider adopting legislative or other appropriate measures that permit victims of trafficking in persons to remain in its territory, temporarily or permanently, in appropriate cases'.[184] It can immediately be seen that these are extremely weak obligations. Although the protocol explicitly states that nothing in it shall affect the rights or responsibilities under international law, including the Refugee Convention, it does not give rise to any new or additional enforceable 'right' to asylum or protection status for victims.[185]

The Council of Europe followed the Palermo Protocol with a new Convention on Action against Trafficking in Human Beings in 2005.[186] The definitions of trafficking and exploitation under this convention are the same as under the earlier protocol, but the obligations are more concrete. While the focus of the convention is on detecting and prosecuting the traffickers, states are also required to 'assist victims in their physical, psychological and social recovery' by providing secure accommodation, psychological and material assistance, access to emergency medical treatment, translation and interpretation services where needed, counselling and information on their legal rights and services available to them, assistance in protecting their interests and rights in criminal proceedings against offenders and access to education for children.[187] The identification of victims is effectively broken into a two-stage process. If the national authorities have 'reasonable grounds to believe that a person has been victim of trafficking' then the person must not be removed from the territory while a full decision is made and must be provided with the assistance described earlier.[188] The convention also provides for a 'recovery and reflection period' of at least 30 days once a potential victim of trafficking is identified, during which time no expulsion should normally be enforced.[189] Where a final decision has been made that a person

---

[183] See for example Plambech, S. (2016) 'Becky Is Dead', *Open Democracy*, Available from: https://www.opendemocracy.net/en/beyond-trafficking-and-slavery/becky-is-dead/ [last accessed 21 September 2021].
[184] Palermo Protocol, Articles 6(3) and 7(1) respectively.
[185] Palermo Protocol, Article 14.
[186] Council of Europe Treaty Series No. 197.
[187] Convention on Action against Trafficking in Human Beings, Article 12.
[188] Convention on Action against Trafficking in Human Beings, Article 10(2).
[189] Convention on Action against Trafficking in Human Beings, Article 13.

is indeed a victim of trafficking, a renewable residence permit should be issued to the person where either or both the national authorities consider the victim's stay 'is necessary owing to their personal situation' or is necessary for the purpose of cooperation in investigation or criminal proceedings.[190] There is no specific provision made for the victim to remain long-term, although the short-term residence is stated to be 'without prejudice to the right to seek and enjoy asylum'. Where repatriation is pursued by the host state, the convention states that it shall 'preferably' be voluntary, very much leaving open the possibility of enforced returns.[191]

In the United Kingdom, the convention was signed in 2007 and ratified in 2008. Legislation to consolidate the relevant criminal offences and impose legal duties and obligations for the identification of victims was later introduced in the form of the Modern Slavery Act 2015. Implementation has from the start been led by the immigration directorate of the Home Office rather than a police agency, which has not assuaged concerns that immigration enforcement might potentially interfere with the protection of victims.[192] The institutions and processes set up to comply with the convention's requirements are plagued by opaque titles, acronyms and capital letters. A National Referral Mechanism (NRM) was created in 2009 in order to centralize the process by which trafficking victims are identified. Under this process, a 'reasonable grounds' decision is made first, after which a person becomes eligible for initial support. A period of at least 45 days then follows in order to provide a rest and recovery period, followed by a 'conclusive grounds' decision. A negative conclusive grounds decision can be reviewed on request or an application for judicial review of the decision can be made. A positive conclusive grounds decision may lead to a grant of a renewable residence permit and can be of considerable assistance in pursuing an asylum claim under the Refugee Convention.[193] Trafficking victims have been recognized as potentially being members of a particular social group and a positive finding discloses at least a potential risk of future harm from the original traffickers or through re-trafficking by others.[194] Initially, both stages of the decision on identifying victims were made by

---

[190] Convention on Action against Trafficking in Human Beings, Article 14.
[191] Convention on Action against Trafficking in Human Beings, Article 16.
[192] Balch, A. and Geddes, A. (2011) 'Opportunity from Crisis? Organisational Responses to Human Trafficking in the UK', *British Journal of Politics and International Relations*, 13(1): 26–41.
[193] Convention on Action against Trafficking in Human Beings, Article 14(1).
[194] *SB (PSG – Protection Regulations – Reg 6) Moldova CG* [2008] UKAIT 00002. But the tribunal determining the asylum claim is not bound by positive or negative findings made within the National Referral Mechanism: *MS (Pakistan) v Secretary of State for the Home Department* [2020] UKSC 9, [2020] 3 All ER 733.

multiple agencies, but in 2019 a Single Competent Authority was created, based at the Home Office. Belying this name, it was joined in 2021 by a new Immigration Enforcement Competent Authority. Only designated 'first responder' organizations can make a referral into the NRM, including police forces, immigration officials, local authorities, the Gangmasters and Labour Abuse Authority and certain specified charities.

As with human rights laws, trafficking prevention laws offer some additional limited relief to those whose rights have been breached. In practice, long-term sanctuary and security will often depend on making out a claim to refugee status or a form of complementary protection. It is therefore beneficial to use anti-trafficking laws and best practice to inform and interpret refugee law. For example, being a victim of trafficking may well impact a person's ability to give an account of their experiences and thus be relevant to determining the well-foundedness of fear. As UNHCR argue, 'the evolution of international law in criminalizing trafficking can help decision makers determine the persecutory nature of the various acts associated with trafficking'.[195] Effective compliance by a state with international minimum standards for combatting trafficking and the protection and care of victims of trafficking might well be considered relevant to the issue of state protection. Trafficking victims may potentially be members of a particular social group. These issues are discussed further in Chapters 2, 3, 4 and 5 respectively.

Statelessness

A stateless person is 'a person who is not considered as a national by any State under the operation of its law'.[196] As discussed in the Introduction, statelessness and refugeehood are related, in that one of the major problems faced by a refugee is that they are de facto (effectively) stateless. A refugee is, by definition, outside their country of origin and has lost the protection of that country, leaving them without 'the right to have rights' in a system of sovereign nation-states.[197] But, formally, a refugee will often retain the nationality of their country of origin. Some refugees may also be *de jure* (in law) stateless, as is recognized in the refugee definition itself in the reference to a person 'who, not having a nationality and being outside the country of his former habitual residence'. However, it is not necessary for a refugee to also be stateless. As the preamble to the Convention Relating to the Status

---

[195] UNHCR, *Guidelines on International Protection No. 7: The Application of Article 1A(2) of the 1951 Convention and/or 1967 Protocol Relating to the Status of Refugees to Victims of Trafficking and Persons at Risk of Being Trafficked*, HCR/GIP/06/07, 7 April 2006 [15].

[196] UN Convention Relating to the Status of Stateless Persons 1954, Article 1(1).

[197] Arendt, H. (2017) *The Origins of Totalitarianism*, London: Penguin, p 388.

of Stateless Persons 1954 ('Stateless Persons Convention') observes, there are many stateless persons who are not refugees. Indeed, many are stateless within the country in which they were born and still reside.

The Stateless Persons Convention, which was originally drafted in parallel with and as a protocol to the Refugee Convention, defines a stateless person and imparts to that person certain rights aimed at ameliorating their situation. These rights are similar to those of the Refugee Convention, with the notable exception of there being no right of *non-refoulement*. As with the Refugee Convention, different rights are assigned to a person at different states of attachment to the state in question, such as within the jurisdiction of a state, physically present and lawfully present (see Chapter 7 in respect of the rights of refugees). Again mirroring the Refugee Convention, the Stateless Persons Convention does not explicitly provide for or require a status determination procedure. Logically, one must be necessary if those who are stateless are to be identified and to be afforded the rights conferred by the convention. Since the mandate of UNHCR was extended to include stateless persons, efforts have been made to encourage countries to adopt such a procedure, identify stateless persons in their territories and afford them their rights under the Stateless Persons Convention.[198] This includes granting them lawful residence and, ultimately, facilitating their naturalization as citizens.[199]

The United Kingdom has, at the behest of UNHCR, adopted a set of rules and policies addressed to the situation of stateless persons. The rules adopt the 1954 Convention definition of statelessness and set out criteria for the grant of temporary then permanent residence permits.[200] These include showing that the person concerned is not admissible as a permanent resident to another country and that the person 'has sought and failed to obtain or re-establish their nationality with the appropriate authorities of the relevant country'. Which is the 'relevant' country depends on the person's situation and is not further defined; this is often the heart of the issue in statelessness cases because it can be very challenging for a person to prove a negative; that is to say, that they are not a national of any country. UNHCR suggests that the same standard of proof should apply in statelessness cases to that in refugee cases: to require only a 'reasonable degree' of proof.[201] The courts have not so far concurred, preferring to apply the more exacting balance

---

[198] See for example General Assembly resolution 50/152 (UN Doc A/RES/50/152).
[199] UNHCR (2014) *Handbook on Protection of Stateless Persons under the 1954 Convention Relating to the Status of Stateless Persons* [148]; Stateless Persons Convention 1954, Article 32 on naturalization.
[200] At the time of writing, at Part 14 of the Immigration Rules HC395.
[201] UNHCR (2014) *Handbook on Protection of Stateless Persons under the 1954 Convention Relating to the Status of Stateless Persons* [91].

of probabilities approach.²⁰² However, where the person concerned appears to be making genuine efforts but is struggling, officials are encouraged in departmental guidance to assist by conducting research or, as long as there is no asylum claim pending, contacting the relevant national authorities. Where a residence permit is granted, this carries with it the rights conferred by the 1954 Convention such as the right to work, access to social security and issue of a travel document.²⁰³ In addition, a faster route by which stateless children born in the United Kingdom can be registered as British is provided requiring five years of residence from birth rather than the normal ten years.²⁰⁴

The Stateless Persons Convention is supplemented by the Convention on the Reduction of Statelessness 1961, which entered into force in 1975. This later convention is not intended to assist those who are already stateless but rather to prevent statelessness arising in the first place, for example by requiring state parties to reform their nationality laws to grant nationality to those born in their territory or born abroad to their nationals who would otherwise be stateless and by limiting automatic or discretionary loss or deprivation of nationality.

As with human rights and anti-trafficking laws, international law on statelessness can add its own form of status protection to some individuals. It should not be regarded solely as a separate and compartmentalized regime, though. Understanding of statelessness and the fact it has been singled out by the international community as a particular problem can help to inform and interpret both human rights and refugee law.²⁰⁵ The European Court of Human Rights has found that failure by a state to provide 'an effective and accessible procedure or a combination of procedures' to assist a long-term resident stateless person might eventually amount to a breach of the right to a private life.²⁰⁶ As discussed in Chapters 3, 4 and 5 respectively, denial of nationality has been found to amount to being persecuted, could be highly relevant to the question of state protection and stateless individuals may well form a particular social group in a country depending on context.

Suggested further reading
Balch, A. and Geddes, A. (2011) 'Opportunity from Crisis? Organisational Responses to Human Trafficking in the UK', *British Journal of Politics and International Relations*, 13(1): 26–41.

---

[202] *AS (Guinea) v Secretary of State for the Home Department* [2018] EWCA Civ 2234 [59].
[203] 1954 Stateless Persons Convention, Articles 17, 18, 19, 23, 24 and 28.
[204] British Nationality Act 1981, Schedule 2, paragraph 3.
[205] See for example UNHCR, *Guidelines on Statelessness No. 5: Loss and Deprivation of Nationality under Articles 5–9 of the 1961 Convention on the Reduction of Statelessness*, HCR/GS/20/05, May 2020.
[206] *Hoti v Croatia* App. No. 63311/14 (ECHR, 26 April 2018) [141].

Byrne, R. and Gammeltoft-Hansen, T. (2020) 'International Refugee Law between Scholarship and Practice', *International Journal of Refugee Law*, 32(2): 181–199.

Cantor, D. and Chikwanha, F. (2019) 'Reconsidering African Refugee Law', *International Journal of Refugee Law*, 31(2): 182–260.

Chetail, V. (2016) 'The Common European Asylum System: Bric-à-Brac or System?', in Chetail, V., De Bruycker, P. and Maiani, F. (eds) *Reforming the Common European Asylum System: The New European Refugee Law*, Boston, MA: Brill Nijhoff.

Chetail, V. (2014) 'Are Refugee Rights Human Rights? An Unorthodox Questioning of the Relations between Refugee Law and Human Rights Law', in Rubio-Martin, R. (ed) *Human Rights and Immigration*, Oxford: Oxford University Press.

Costello, C. (2016) 'The Search for the Outer Edges of Non-Refoulement in Europe', in Cantor, D. and Burson, B. (eds) *Human Rights and the Refugee Definition: Comparative Legal Practice and Theory*, Leiden: Brill.

Gallagher, A. (2010) *The International Law of Human Trafficking*, Cambridge: Cambridge University Press.

Milner, J. and Ramasubramanyam, J. (2021) 'The Office of the United Nations High Commissioner for Refugees', in Costello, C., Foster, M. and McAdam, J. (eds) *The Oxford Handbook of International Refugee Law*, Oxford: Oxford University Press.

Reed-Hurtado, M. (2013) 'The Cartagena Declaration on Refugees and the Protection of People Fleeing Armed Conflict and Other Situations of Violence in Latin America', *UNHCR Legal and Protection Policy Research Series*, PPLA/2013/03.

Sharpe, M. (2018) *The Regional Law of Refugee Protection in Africa*, Oxford: Oxford University Press, Chapters 2 and 3.

UNHCR, *Guidelines on International Protection No. 7: The Application of Article 1A(2) of the 1951 Convention and/or 1967 Protocol Relating to the Status of Refugees to Victims of Trafficking and Persons at Risk of Being Trafficked*, HCR/GIP/06/07, 7 April 2006.

Wood, T. (2021) 'The International and Regional Refugee Definitions Compared', in Costello, C., Foster, M. and McAdam, J. (eds) *The Oxford Handbook of International Refugee Law*, Oxford: Oxford University Press, pp 625–642.

2

Well-founded Fear

The refugee status determination process is often, rightly or wrongly, fixated on the first words of the definition of a refugee: a person who has a 'well-founded fear'. These simple words do not have a precise, legal meaning. They are capable of being understood in different ways, as the literature and jurisprudence on refugee status have amply established. Many have argued, with considerable weight of authority to support them, that the phrase connotes both a subjective and an objective element to the definition of a refugee. UNHCR argues, for example, that 'it is not only the frame of mind of the person concerned that determines his refugee status, but that this frame of mind must be supported by an objective situation'.[1] While superficially appealing and certainly consistent with the natural meaning of the words, this distinction between subjective and objective can, at least in theory, deny refugee status to some of the most vulnerable individuals in the world most in need of protection. It has also arguably led to an unnecessary focus on evaluating the 'credibility' of claimants to refugee status, a process that has developed something of a mythology to it. Ultimately, in practice, the words have come to be almost universally understood as requiring in refugee cases, firstly, a low standard of proof and, secondly, an inquiry into future risk. As McHugh and Kirkby JJ held in a landmark and internationally influential Australian case, 'in all asylum cases there is ultimately but a single question to be asked: is there a serious risk that on return the applicant would be persecuted for a Convention reason? If there is, then he is entitled to asylum'.[2]

---

[1] UNHCR, *Handbook on Procedures and Criteria for Determining Refugee Status and Guidelines on International Protection under the 1951 Convention and the 1967 Protocol Relating to the Status of Refugees*, HCR/1P/4/ENG/REV.4 (1979, reissued 2019) [37].
[2] *Appellant S395/2002 v Minister for Immigration and Multicultural Affairs* [2003] HCA 71 (Aus HC) [42].

Burden of proof

The general rule in adversarial litigation is that the person asserting a fact must prove it. There are several reasons why this principle might not be considered to be fully applicable in the refugee status determination process. The adversarial model, in which two parties advocate their own version of events before an impartial, independent judge, is not the only one available. Many legal systems are inquisitorial in nature, in which a judge is empowered to conduct their own investigation. In any event, a claim for asylum is not litigation but rather is a plea for help to the authorities of a host country which is a signatory state to the Refugee Convention and therefore does not, as a matter of principle, have an interest in denying asylum to a person who is a refugee. Finally, it is very difficult for a vulnerable refugee in a strange country far from their own, often with few if any resources, to prove anything. In contrast, the authorities from which the refugee seeks asylum may have plentiful resources available.

It has been suggested that while it is ultimately for the asylum applicant to prove their case, the burden for establishing the relevant facts is a shared one between the applicant and the assessor. In some cases it may be for the assessor 'to use all the means at his disposal to produce the necessary evidence in support of the application'.[3] At the very least, it is said, where an applicant has done what they can and appears to be truthful, they should be given the 'benefit of the doubt'.[4] In practice, state parties to the Refugee Convention often do little to shoulder this shared burden of proof and it is doubtful that the application of 'benefit of the doubt' adds anything to the internationally acknowledged already-low threshold of well-founded fear.[5] Asylum countries will provide their decision makers with reports about the human rights situation in a relevant country.[6] These country reports, which can and should inform asylum assessors on both the plausibility of claimed past events and the likelihood of future risk, are discussed later.

---

[3] UNHCR, *Handbook on Procedures and Criteria for Determining Refugee Status and Guidelines on International Protection under the 1951 Convention and the 1967 Protocol Relating to the Status of Refugees*, HCR/1P/4/ENG/REV.4 (1979, reissued 2019) [196].

[4] UNHCR, *Handbook on Procedures and Criteria for Determining Refugee Status and Guidelines on International Protection under the 1951 Convention and the 1967 Protocol Relating to the Status of Refugees*, HCR/1P/4/ENG/REV.4 (1979, reissued 2019) [196], [203], [204]. For an example of this being embedded in law, see EU Directive 2004/83/EC ('the Qualification Directive') at Article 4(5).

[5] Hathaway, J. and Foster, M. (2014) *The Law of Refugee Status* (2nd edn), Cambridge: Cambridge University Press, p 120. See also discussion and review of authorities in *KS (benefit of the doubt)* [2014] UKUT 00552 (IAC).

[6] European Union countries are indeed obliged to provide decision makers with such reports, by Directive 2005/85/EC ('the Procedures Directive') at Article 8(2)(b).

Active investigation or verification of previous events narrated by the refugee or even documents presented by the refugee is unusual, though. Where a document is presented by a refugee it is usually considered necessary for the refugee to prove the veracity of the document rather than for the asylum assessor to prove that it is fraudulent.[7]

Standard of proof

The words 'well-founded' at the very beginning of the refugee definition indicate that the risk to a refugee must be objectively established and must be more than merely perceived or fanciful. This much is universally agreed. Quite how 'well-founded' the risk must be has proven controversial as the words do not directly translate to any conventional standard of proof.

A legal adjudication process normally requires a notional 'standard of proof' which states the probability threshold for establishing claimed facts. If the jury or judge considers that the threshold is reached, then the fact is considered to be 'proven' and the person or party seeking to prove the fact succeeds. The concept of a standard of proof has been described as 'a pragmatic legal fiction' but it is one which is useful for establishing a winner and loser in a zero-sum, adversarial legal dispute.[8] In criminal cases, the standard of proof is set at a high level because the conviction and sentencing of an innocent person is considered to be highly undesirable; a magistrate or jury can only convict a person of a criminal offence if the facts are proven 'beyond reasonable doubt'. In civil cases such as contract or family law disputes, where there is no risk of criminal sanction, the standard of proof is said to be the 'balance of probabilities', meaning that the person or party will succeed if they can produce evidence that shows it is more probable than not that the facts are as they claim. Not all legal disputes are necessarily zero-sum, however, and not all legal proceedings need to be adversarial. Refugee status determination might be considered one such example, and indeed the conventional common law standard of proof approach has been called into question.

In a refugee status claim, there are three very strong, practical reasons why it would be undesirable to require facts to be established to a high degree of probability. Firstly, most refugees would find it impossible to produce

---

[7] *Tanveer Ahmed* [2002] UKIAT 00439 is the leading reference case on this issue in the United Kingdom. Although not a Refugee Convention case, see *Singh v Belgium* App. No. 33210/2011 (ECHR, 2 January 2013) for an example of a court overturning refusal of an international protection claim for failure to attempt to verify documents from an international organization that should have been easily verifiable.

[8] *Karanakaran v Secretary of State for the Home Department* [2000] 3 All ER 449 (EWCA) [16] (Sedley LJ).

documentary, photographic, independent witness or other evidence to show that they are telling the truth about what happened to them in the past. Persecutors rarely document their persecutory acts and even more rarely make such documentation available to those they persecute. Even if they did, a refugee fleeing such persecution may not have the foresight, time or resources to stop and collect any such documents. Secondly, it is famously impossible to prove that a future event will definitely take place; it is very hard even to show a high degree of probability that particular actions will be applied to a particular person. To try to establish a future personal risk to themselves a refugee might point to how some individuals with similar characteristics to themselves are being treated. There may well be other like individuals who are not, however, and it would be undesirable to return a refugee to face possible persecution based on a mathematical calculation of what proportion of at-risk individuals are actively suffering persecution.[9] Thirdly and finally, the same reasoning that gives rise to the high standard of proof in criminal cases applies in reverse to refugee cases. The degree of consequence of an incorrect, mistaken decision is very high in both situations. It is undesirable for an innocent person to be convicted. It is perhaps even more undesirable for a genuine refugee to be returned to face persecution and perhaps death. To repurpose Blackstone's famous idiom about letting the guilty go free rather than punishing the innocent, it is surely better that ten non-refugees are granted asylum than one genuine refugee is persecuted.[10]

There are two complementary strands of thinking that have emerged in response to these considerations, at least in common law jurisdictions. One is that the standard of proof in refugee cases is a low one, said to be variously 'reasonable degree of likelihood', 'a reasonable chance', 'substantial grounds for thinking', 'a serious possibility', 'real and substantial risk', 'real risk', 'real chance', 'reasonable possibility' or 'substantial risk'.[11] These various formulae all denote a level of probability which is lower than the 49:51 'balance of probabilities' or 'more probable than not' standard that applies in civil cases (and much lower than the 'beyond reasonable doubt' that applies in criminal ones). But the precise meaning of the words remains

---

[9] This has not prevented such calculations being deployed from time to time, unfortunately sometimes featuring basic statistical errors. See *AS (Afghanistan) v Secretary of State for the Home Department* [2019] EWCA Civ 873, criticizing the tribunal below for misstating risk by a factor of ten.

[10] The original: 'It is better that ten guilty persons escape than that one innocent suffer.' Blackstone, *Commentaries on the Laws of England*.

[11] The first five formulations were all approved in *R (on the application of Sivakumuran) v Secretary of State for the Home Department* [1988] AC 958 (UK HL). See also *Immigration and Naturalization Service v Cardoza-Fonseca* 480 US 421 (1987) (US SC), *Chan v Minister for Immigration and Ethnic Affairs* [1989] HCA 62 (Aus HC) and *Chan v Canada* [1995] 3 SCR 593 (Can SC).

ambiguous. This appears a matter of deliberate judicial policy; more precise articulation of levels of risk required has generally been eschewed, with the notable exception of an analogy drawn by Lord Justice Sedley: 'If a type of car has a defect which causes one vehicle in ten to crash, most people would say that it presents a real risk to anyone who drives it, albeit crashes are not generally or consistently happening'.[12] The constructive lack of precision empowers the individual judge with discretion to interpret and apply the threshold in individual cases. The other strand of thinking is that the whole notion of a standard of proof probability threshold is unhelpful in refugee status determination. Instead, a decision-making authority should evaluate all of the evidence and 'must not exclude any matters from its consideration ... unless it feels that it can safely discard them because it has no real doubt that they did not in fact occur'.[13] Or, as another judge put it in the same case, '[n]o probabilistic cut-off operates here: everything capable of having a bearing has to be given the weight, great or little, due to it'.[14]

There was some early jurisprudential debate whether the same or different standards of proof applied to the evaluation of past facts and future risk. This is the approach adopted in the United States and at the time of writing the United Kingdom was poised to legislate to follow suit.[15] Given the holistic nature of the refugee definition, it is generally considered undesirable as well as being impractical to apply differing standards within the same claim.

Meaning of 'fear'

On a literal, linguistic analysis of the phrase 'a person with a well-founded fear', 'fear' might be interpreted as meaning 'terror', 'dread' or – more neutrally – 'trepidation' in a personal, subjective and emotional sense. If so, a person who cannot experience literal fear would appear to be excluded from refugee status. It seems unlikely, however, that the framers of the Refugee Convention intended to exclude from its protection young children or those who lack mental capacity, or even those who stoically claim not to be

---

[12] *Batayav v Secretary of State for the Home Department* [2003] EWCA Civ 1489 [38], quoted with approval by Lord Walker in *HJ (Iran) v Secretary of State for the Home Department* [2010] UKSC 31, [2011] 1 AC 596.

[13] *Karanakaran v Secretary of State for the Home Department* [2000] 3 All ER 449 (EWCA) [102] (Brook LJ).

[14] *Karanakaran v Secretary of State for the Home Department* [2000] 3 All ER 449 (EWCA) [18] (Sedley LJ).

[15] *Immigration and Naturalization Service v Cardoza-Fonseca* 480 US 421 (1987) (US SC). Nationality and Borders Bill 2021. At the time of writing the issue had never been decided by the UK Supreme Court: see *MA (Somalia) v Secretary of State for the Home Department* [2010] UKSC 49 [20].

afraid. Such an interpretation would undermine the capacity of the Refugee Convention to 'afford protection and fair treatment to those for whom neither is available in their own country'.[16] Nevertheless, some judges have adopted a literal approach. The UNHCR Handbook lends them support, stating that:

> Since fear is subjective, the definition involves a subjective element in the person applying for recognition as a refugee. Determination of refugee status will therefore primarily require an evaluation of the applicant's statements rather than a judgement on the situation prevailing in his country of origin.[17]

Perhaps unsurprisingly, given the international coordinating function of UNHCR, this analysis has been influential. For example, the US Supreme Court held in one early case '[t]hat the fear must be "well-founded" does not alter the obvious focus on the individual's subjective beliefs'.[18] Similar pronouncements can be found in early high-level jurisprudence in Canada and Australia.[19] A judge of the United Kingdom Supreme Court opined that the Convention 'directs attention to the state of mind of the individual. It is the fear that person has which must be examined and shown to be well-founded'.[20] It is possible sometimes to sidestep the obvious problem the approach creates for children by suggesting that fear for a child can be imputed from a parent.[21] As Pobjoy observes, this may assist in some cases but it reduces the child to an adjunct of the parent and in some situations the parent may be unable or even unwilling to demonstrate subjective fear, leaving the child at objective risk of being persecuted.[22] It does nothing to assist the older child or adult who for whatever reason is unaware of or indifferent to dangers that await.

---

[16] *R (on the application of Sivakumuran) v Secretary of State for the Home Department* [1988] AC 958 (UK HL) (Lord Keith).

[17] UNHCR, *Handbook on Procedures and Criteria for Determining Refugee Status and Guidelines on International Protection under the 1951 Convention and the 1967 Protocol Relating to the Status of Refugees*, HCR/1P/4/ENG/REV.4 (1979, reissued 2019) [37].

[18] *Immigration and Naturalization Service v Cardoza-Fonseca* 480 US 421 (1987) (US SC).

[19] *Attorney General of Canada v Ward* [1993] 2 SCR 689 (Can SC) [64]; *Re Minister for Immigration and Multicultural Affairs, ex p Miah* [2001] HCA 22 (Aus HC) [62].

[20] *HJ (Iran) v Secretary of State for the Home Department* [2010] UKSC 31, [2011] 1 AC 596 [17] (Lord Hope).

[21] *Chen Shi Hai v Minister for Immigration and Multicultural Affairs* [2000] HCA 19 (Aus HC).

[22] Pobjoy, J. (2017) *The Child in International Refugee Law*, Cambridge: Cambridge University Press, pp 84–89; Hathaway, J. (2021) *The Rights of Refugees under International Law* (2nd edn), Cambridge: Cambridge University Press, p 92; *HJ (Iran) v Secretary of State for the Home Department* [2010] UKSC 31, [2011] 1 AC 596 and *Immigration and Naturalization Service v Cardoza Fonesca* (1987) 480 US 421 (US SC).

The imposition of a subjective as well as objective element to the refugee definition is not without its critics. Rejecting the proposition that refugee status should be denied to an applicant for refugee status who did not display 'reasonable courage', Lord Keith pointed out in the case of *Sivakumaran* that 'it might be by no means easy to decide what degree of courage a person of ordinary fortitude might be expected to display'.[23] Hathaway argues that what he calls the 'bipartite' analysis of well-founded fear is 'neither historically defensible nor practically meaningful' and that it is 'unprincipled'.[24] Instead, the concept of well-founded fear is 'inherently objective' in that it 'denies protection to persons unable to demonstrate a real chance of present or prospective persecution, but does not in any sense condition refugee status on the ability to show subjective fear'.[25] Hathaway and Foster propose that in the context of the full phrase 'well-founded fear', 'fear' should be read as a somewhat old-fashioned way of saying 'apprehension', 'anticipation' or 'expectation', in the sense of an understanding that something might come to pass in the future; 'I fear it may rain' or similar. Rather than requiring an enquiry into the state of mind or beliefs of the refugee, the focus should be entirely on whether there is a real risk of future persecution. This analysis is at least not contradicted by the French language version of the phrase ('*craignant avec raison*'), which can also be read as meaning trepidation or forward-looking expectation.

In practice, despite some statements in high-level jurisprudence suggesting otherwise, experience suggests that refugee status determination rarely if ever turns on the subjective beliefs of the refugee. Decision makers tend to focus on future risk, subject to the discussion later on the issue of asylum seeker 'credibility'. It is preferable for conceptual clarity and to fulfil the underlying purpose of the Refugee Convention to read the words 'well-founded fear' as 'well-founded future risk'. The key questions are often who must prove what and how.

Credibility and truthfulness

Whether a refugee is telling the truth about past events often becomes the central issue in many asylum claims. Sometimes this is appropriate. Whether an asylum seeker will face a real risk of being persecuted in future does in

---

[23] *R (on the application of Sivakumuran) v Secretary of State for the Home Department* [1988] AC 958 (UK HL) (Lord Keith).

[24] Hathaway, J. (1991) *The Law of Refugee Status*, Toronto: Butterworths Canada, p 65 and Hathaway, J. and Foster, M. (2014) *The Law of Refugee Status* (2nd edn), Cambridge: Cambridge University Press, p 95.

[25] Hathaway, J. and Foster, M. (2014) *The Law of Refugee Status* (2nd edn), Cambridge: Cambridge University Press, p 92.

some cases turn on the truth or otherwise of key elements of the asylum seeker's account of past events. If an asylum seeker is lying about being a political activist, for example, but claims future risk of being persecuted because of their past and perhaps future political activities, it will usually (but not always, as we will see in a moment) be necessary to consider whether the asylum seeker is telling the truth about their past history. Not infrequently, though, the refugee status determination process degenerates into unfocused consideration of the general 'credibility' of the asylum seeker. Some asylum assessors show signs of evolving their own distinct subculture around the meaning and interpretation of this word:

> The term 'credibility' is used a good deal in the context both of asylum appeals and of decisions whether a person is a victim of trafficking, and we have detected a tendency to treat it as having some special technical meaning. But in truth it connotes no more than whether the applicant's account is to be believed.[26]

A nebulous notion of the general 'credibility' of the refugee as a person can become a distraction from the real issue under the Refugee Convention: whether there is a real future risk of being persecuted. Decision makers tend to compare the account given in an asylum claim against a stock narrative delivered by a notional and unconsciously idealized model refugee.[27] This idealized refugee would finely judge the level of risk and attempt to relocate within their own country before departing, would claim asylum at the first opportunity in the first safe country reached and stay there, remember exactly what happened to them and when, be able and willing immediately on arrival to describe events chronologically and in detail, will also present as the assessor preconceives that a vulnerable and traumatized person will present, will always tell the truth about everything and will generally behave according to the expectations of the assessor. Many of these assumptions about refugee behaviour are derived from culture-specific stereotypes, have no objective basis in reality and, in any event, are conflicting or even mutually exclusive. Over 30 years ago, Walter Kälin observed that many refugees will struggle to express themselves:

---

[26] *MN v Secretary of State for the Home Department* [2020] EWCA Civ 1746 [127] (Underhill LJ).

[27] See for example Vogl, A. (2013) 'Telling Stories from Start to Finish: Exploring the Demand for Narrative in Refugee Testimony', *Griffith Law Review*, 22(1): 63–86. Some of these considerations are, regrettably, incorporated into law in the United Kingdom: see Asylum and Immigration (Treatment of Claimants for example) Act 2004, s 8.

Especially in the case of refugees from Third World countries, the experience of culture shock obviously can gravely impair the applicant's ability to make a forceful statement: Such an asylum seeker may speak in a confused, nervous, fragmented and unconvincing manner not because he or she is lying but because of the anxiety and insecurity caused by the difficulties of life in an entirely new social and cultural environment.[28]

The process of experiencing, remembering, recounting and recording events in writing is a complex one where 'what has actually happened to the refugee ("life as lived") might ultimately bear little resemblance to the written claim ("life as text")'.[29] Refugees struggling to transition from an old sense of self to a new one may well understand or interpret past events in different ways at different times.[30] There is no research on refugee decision-making which suggests that the place or timing of a claim for asylum is in any way relevant to the well-foundedness of the case to be a refugee as defined in Article 1A(2) of the Refugee Convention. There is plentiful research, though, showing that a traumatized individual is less, not more, able to recount past events accurately, particularly traumatic events.[31] One of the key measures for 'credibility' is consistency, yet one of the characteristics of a traumatized refugee may actually be inconsistency. Even the underlying premise of the whole concept of 'credibility' – that a person who lies about one thing may well lie about other things – may well be of limited usefulness in asylum claims made by desperate, vulnerable individuals. As Lord Dyson has commented: 'The consequences of failure for those whose cases are genuine are usually grave. It is not, therefore, surprising that appellants frequently give fabricated evidence in order to bolster their cases'.[32] An analogy has been drawn with the 'Lucas direction' sometimes given by judges to juries in criminal trials in the United Kingdom: 'people sometimes lie, for example, in an attempt to bolster up a just cause, or out of shame or out of a wish to conceal disgraceful behaviour from their family'.[33] While the analogy is not exactly in asylum

---

[28] Kälin, W. (1986) 'Troubled Communication: Cross-Cultural Misunderstandings in the Asylum-Hearing', *International Migration Review*, 20: 230, 232.

[29] Zambelli, P. (2017) 'Hearing Differently: Knowledge-Based Approaches to Assessment of Refugee Narrative', *International Journal of Refugee Law*, 29(1): 10–41.

[30] Shuman, A. and Bohmer, C. (2004) 'Representing Trauma: Political Asylum Narrative', *Journal of American Folklore*, 117: 394.

[31] See for example UNHCR (2013) *Beyond Proof: Credibility Assessment in EU Asylum Systems*;

[32] *MA (Somalia) v Secretary of State for the Home Department* [2010] UKSC 49 [21] (Lord Dyson).

[33] *MA (Somalia) v Secretary of State for the Home Department* [2010] UKSC 49 [32] (Lord Dyson) citing *R v Lucas* [1981] QB 720.

cases, it is surely true that 'the significance of lies will vary from case to case'.[34] A similar direction by a judge to a jury is recommended in rape cases where relevant:

> Experience has shown that inconsistencies in accounts can happen whether a person is telling the truth or not. This is because if someone has a traumatic experience such as the kind alleged in this case, their memory may be affected in different ways. It may affect that person's ability to take in and later recall the experience. Also, some people may go over an event afterwards in their minds many times and their memory may become clearer or can develop over time. But other people may try to avoid thinking about an event at all, and they may then have difficulty in recalling the event accurately.[35]

Asylum assessors who approach their task reliant on unfounded assumptions based on the generalized notion of 'credibility' are therefore liable to adopt a sceptical and even cynical mindset when deciding claims. This has been described as a 'culture of disbelief'.[36]

Nonetheless, assessors do usually have to make decisions on whether refugees are telling the truth or not about past events. The tools available for conducting this exercise fairly and appropriately are flawed and limited, but, ultimately, a determination of status must be made.

Plausibility

An asylum applicant who relies on claims about events which seem to the assessor to be implausible or unlikely may struggle to establish they have a well-founded fear. Firstly, the assessor may consider that the applicant is not telling the truth. Secondly, irrespective of whether the applicant is telling the truth, the assessor may conclude that there is no sufficient risk of repetition in future, as discussed later. The reasons for refusal of an asylum claim will often include assertions that the applicant or a third party acted in an improbable way which is therefore considered to be unbelievable, for example. Great care must be taken with this notion of plausibility, for it is axiomatic that the experiences of refugees will usually be very profoundly different to those of their assessors:

---

[34] *MA (Somalia) v Secretary of State for the Home Department* [2010] UKSC 49 [33] (Lord Dyson).
[35] Judicial College, *Crown Court Compendium: Part I: Jury and Trial Management and Summing Up*, August 2021 [20–7].
[36] Asylum Aid (1999) *Still No Reason At All: Home Office Decisions on Asylum Claims*, London: Asylum Aid.

> Inherent probability, which may be helpful in many domestic cases, can be a dangerous, even a wholly inappropriate, factor to rely on in some asylum cases. Much of the evidence will be referable to societies with customs and circumstances which are very different from those of which the members of the fact-finding tribunal have any (even second-hand) experience. Indeed, it is likely that the country which an asylum-seeker has left will be suffering from the sort of problems and dislocations with which the overwhelming majority of residents of this country will be wholly unfamiliar.[37]

The words of Thomas Bingham, later to become President of the UK Supreme Court, in an article from 1985 remain famous in this context in the United Kingdom:

> No judge worth his salt could possibl[y] assume that men of different nationalities, educations, trades, experience, creeds and temperaments would act as he might think he would have done or even – which may be quite different – in accordance with his concept of what a reasonable man would have done.[38]

The distinction drawn between probability and plausibility is an important one. It may be improbable that when two dice are thrown the outcome will be a double six; it is perfectly plausible, however, as improbable things happen all the time. It is therefore vital that assessors take steps to inform themselves using country information and expert evidence so that the applicant's narrative can be evaluated against an informed understanding of what goes on in the country concerned.[39] The assessor 'must look through the spectacles provided by the information he has about conditions in the country in question'; or, more prosaically, information about the relevant country can offer 'a factual context in which it may be necessary for the fact-finder to survey the allegations placed before him; and such context may prove a crucial aid to the decision whether or not to accept the truth of them'.[40]

---

[37] *HK v Secretary of State for the Home Department* [2006] EWCA Civ 1037 [29].

[38] Bingham, T. (1985) 'The Judge as Juror: the Judicial Determination of Factual Issues', *Current Legal Problems*, 38(1): 1–27, cited in *Kasolo v Secretary of State for the Home Department* (13190) and later, for example, in *Y v Secretary of State for the Home Department* [2006] EWCA Civ 1223.

[39] *Y v Secretary of State for the Home Department* [2006] EWCA Civ 1223 [25] (Keene LJ).

[40] Respectively *Y v Secretary of State for the Home Department* [2006] EWCA Civ 1223 [27] (Keene LJ) and *Mibanga v Secretary of State for the Home Department* [2005] EWCA Civ 367 [24] (Wilson LJ).

Referred to variously as 'country reports', 'country of origin information' or sometimes rather inaccurately as 'objective evidence' (all such reports are selective and the selection process inevitably introduced bias of some sort), this material might typically consist of compilations and distillations of sources by governmental or non-governmental organizations such as the US Department of State, UK Home Office, Amnesty International or Human Rights Watch; press reports from national and international media organizations; specially commissioned reports from experts on the country concerned; journal articles; more esoteric sources such as social media or websites. Standards have emerged for the production and evaluation of country information, the key criteria being relevance, reliability and balance, accuracy and currency, and transparency and traceability.[41] Even where a source does not meet these standards it should not necessarily be disregarded; a polemical and old website report might offer some corroboration that a political rally took place at a particular time and place, for example.

Corroboration

Refugees are rarely able to offer corroboration for their own personal testimony of what happened to them in the past: '[i]n most cases a person fleeing from persecution will have arrived with the barest necessities and very frequently even without personal documents'.[42] There is, consequently, no formal requirement for corroboration in asylum claims, and statutory rules in the European Union and the United States both broadly provide that where an account is generally 'credible' then corroboration is unnecessary.[43] As we have already seen, credibility is a problematic concept in asylum applications. Common sense suggests that attempting to corroborate an asylum claim is wise given that success will place the applicant in a stronger position than would otherwise be the case.

Reliance is sometimes placed on documentary evidence such as arrest warrants, court documents or written death threats, either brought with the applicant on their journey or sent from the country of origin by friends, family or other acquaintances. The reliability and veracity of such documents are often doubted by assessors, in which case further levels of corroboration

---

[41] See for example Austrian Centre for Country of Origin and Asylum Research and Documentation (ACCORD), *Researching Country of Origin Information Training Manual* (2nd edn).

[42] UNHCR, *Handbook on Procedures and Criteria for Determining Refugee Status and Guidelines on International Protection under the 1951 Convention and the 1967 Protocol Relating to the Status of Refugees*, HCR/1P/4/ENG/REV.4 (1979, reissued 2019) [196].

[43] Respectively Directive 2011/95/EU, Article 4(5) and 8 USC § 1158(b)(1)(B)(ii) (2006).

to confirm the authenticity of the documents may be attempted. An expert can be asked to compare a document against others of its kind, for example, or a lawyer or some other reputable individual or organization can be asked to confirm evidence. Corroborating witness testimony from friends, family members or other individuals known to the applicant personally can be sought and adduced. This type of supporting testimony is sometimes dismissed as 'self-serving' and therefore carrying little weight, whether given from the country of asylum or the country of origin.[44] As has been said in the United States, though, '[t]he testimony of every applicant for asylum for asylum is self-serving. This does not make it untrue'.[45] Notwithstanding the limited weight attached to these forms of corroboration when they are produced, their absence is sometimes cited as a reason for refusing a claim.

Medical evidence, whether of physical or mental health, is sometimes deployed to act as a form of corroboration in asylum claims. Where a person claims to have been tortured, for example, their body may bear the physical scars of their suffering. Their mind may bear the mental scars. A scale of certainty has been developed to state the confidence of association between a physical wound or scar (a 'lesion') with the claimed cause, ranging from 'not consistent' to 'diagnostic of'.[46] In this context 'decision-makers can legitimately receive assistance, often valuable, from medical experts who feel able, within their expertise, to offer an opinion about the consistency of their findings with the asylum seeker's account of the circumstances in which the scarring was sustained, not limited to the mechanism by which it was sustained'.[47] Some assessors have been reluctant to, as they see it, surrender a significant part of their discretion over fact-finding to an expert witness.[48] This resistance has been most marked in cases involving psychological or psychiatric evidence and in cases where the doctor states an opinion as to the truthfulness of the assertions made by the applicant.[49] Other assessors have proven too eager to delegate their function to experts, sometimes with questionable levels of expertise. As the Court of Justice of the European

---

[44] For example in *R (on the application of SS) v Secretary of State for the Home Department ("self-serving" statements)* [2017] UKUT 164 (IAC).

[45] *El Moraghy v Ashcroft* 331 F3d 195 (1st Cir 2003), 205.

[46] See *Manual on the Effective Investigation and Documentation of Torture and Other Cruel, Inhuman or Degrading Treatment or Punishment* (usually known as the 'Istanbul Protocol') [187].

[47] *KV (Sri Lanka) v Secretary of State for the Home Department* [2019] UKSC 10 [20] (Lord Wilson).

[48] Redmayne, M. (2001) *Expert Evidence and Criminal Justice*, Oxford: Oxford University Press, Chapter 6; Good, A. (2007) *Anthropology and Expertise in the Asylum Courts*, Abingdon: Routledge, Chapter 9.

[49] See discussion in *MN v Secretary of State for the Home Department* [2020] EWCA Civ 1746 [102]-[124].

Union puts it, 'the determining authority cannot base its decision solely on the conclusions of an expert's report and that that authority cannot, a fortiori, be bound by those conclusions when assessing the statements made by an applicant'.[50] A holistic assessment of all of the relevant evidence should be made.

Evidence relied on by governments against asylum applicants has sometimes raised questions of probative value and human dignity. Some asylum authorities have commissioned and sought to rely on linguistic analysis evidence which purports to pinpoint the geographical origins of an applicant for asylum. Such evidence may be relevant where there is some doubt that an applicant for asylum really comes from the country or part of the country they claim, for example. While this evidence may be useful in principle, care must be taken that the evidence conforms to high standards of impartiality and genuine expertise and that the evidence is not considered determinative.[51] The Court of Justice of the European Union considers that 'certain forms of expert reports may prove useful for the assessment of the facts and circumstances and may be prepared without prejudicing the fundamental rights of that applicant'.[52] But medical tests purporting to establish a person's sexuality have been held to, by their nature, infringe human dignity and thus be unlawful.[53] For the same reason, detailed questioning as to sexual practices should not be carried out and applicants for asylum should not be permitted to perform sexual acts or present filmed evidence of sexual acts to establish their sexual orientation. Similarly, expert psychological reports on sexuality based on projective personality tests have been held to amount to unjustifiable and disproportionate interference with an asylum applicant's right to respect for private life.[54]

Quality of narrative

One of the principal tools employed by asylum assessors to divine whether or not an applicant is telling the truth about past events is the quality of the narrative the applicant provides. The assessor may variously consider the level of detail provided by the applicant, the coherency and consistency of the narrative, the demeanour of the applicant – for example, their level of distress while recounting traumatic events – and their level of knowledge or understanding. Self-evidently, judgments on these issues

---

[50] Case C-473/16 *F v Hungary* [42].
[51] *Secretary of State for the Home Department v MN and KY* [2014] UKSC 30.
[52] Case C-473/16 *F v Hungary* [37].
[53] Joined Cases C-148/13–C-150/13 *A, B and C v Netherlands*.
[54] Case C-473/16 *F v Hungary*.

are not sound foundations for determining the truth or otherwise of key parts of an asylum claim by a person from a very different culture with very different life experiences to the assessor where the person concerned may be deeply traumatized. Worse, though, research suggests that these supposed indicators of deceit can be evidence of a truthful rather than untruthful account of past events. The UNHCR publication *Beyond Proof: Credibility Assessment in EU Asylum Systems* sets out extensive references to academic studies showing not just that these assumptions are fallacious but that they may be diametrically opposed to reality.[55] Memories are imperfectly recorded at the time of events, are imperfectly stored over time and are imperfectly recalled under questioning. Once a certain level of emotion is experienced, a person becomes significantly disabled from being able accurately to recall the details of events. Victims of terrible, humiliating personal trauma such as rape and torture are, understandably, reluctant freely to discuss the details of what happened to them, particularly with a stranger who is also an authority figure in a context where the power relationships clearly favour the interrogator. The asylum applicant is summoned to an interview, attends the workplace of the interviewer, may be searched on arrival, is often kept waiting, sits where instructed by the interviewer, is asked countless questions, some of which will seem irrelevant and even insulting, must wait while the interviewer records questions and the whole interview process is controlled by the interviewer. The environment and way in which questions are asked can alter a person's narrative in important ways. All of these issues then impact upon the ability of the asylum applicant to narrate a consistent account of past facts: events are recalled differently on different occasions, some events may be forgotten or elided together and additional detail may be provided in response to different questions in a more comfortable setting. In fact, inconsistency might properly be understood as an indicator of the truth of past trauma, as has been recognized by the UN Committee against Torture:

> The State party has pointed to contradictions and inconsistencies in the author's story, but the Committee considers that complete accuracy is seldom to be expected by victims of torture and that such inconsistencies as may exist in the author's presentation of the facts are not material and do not raise doubts about the general veracity of the author's claims.[56]

---

[55] UNHCR (2013) *Beyond Proof: Credibility Assessment in EU Asylum Systems*, Brussels: UNHCR. See Chapter 3 in particular.

[56] *Alan v Switzerland* (Committee against Torture, 8 May 1996) (CAT/C/16/D/21/1995).

Consistency might instead be interpreted as the hallmark of rote-learned testimony. A person may show dissociation, emotional numbness, apparent indifference or even culturally incongruous reactions such as laughter or smiling when recalling traumatic past events rather than outwardly visible emotional distress. Demeanour is therefore a particularly unreliable way of assessing truthfulness, a consideration which calls into question the evident anxiety of judges (and lawyers) in common law jurisdictions to preserve the tradition of direct, in-person oral testimony in response to cross-examination.[57] Even the knowledge of the applicant for asylum, which may at first appear a relatively objective means by which to assess truthfulness in some cases, turns out on closer consideration to be all too fallible. People may convert from one religion to another or support a political party for reasons of emotion, loyalty and identity, for example, and can seldom name specific theological texts or otherwise obscure party functionaries beyond the leader. In one case in which a religious conversion was doubted, the judge observed that evidence of church attendance provided a more solid foundation for assessing the claim:

> It is a dangerous thing for anyone, and perhaps especially a judge, to peer into what some call a man or woman's soul to assess whether a professed faith is genuinely held, and especially not when it was and is agreed that she was and is a frequent participant in church services. It is a type of judicial exercise very popular some centuries ago in some fora, but rather rarely exercised today. I am also uneasy when a judge, even with the knowledge one gains judicially in a city as diverse as Manchester, is bold enough to seek to reach firm conclusions about a professed conversion, made by a woman raised in another culture, from the version of Islam practised therein, to an evangelical church in Bolton within one strand of Christianity. I am at a loss to understand how that is to be tested by anything other than considering whether she is an active participant in the new church.[58]

This example provides a practical illustration of how other evidence might at least in some cases form a better, more reliable – but admittedly not infallible – means for assessing truthfulness.

---

[57] See for example *Nare (evidence by electronic means) Zimbabwe* [2011] UKUT 00443 (IAC): '… the usual model in the common-law system is for direct oral evidence to be given in the courtroom. Departures from that model are likely to reduce the quality of evidence, the ability of the parties to test it, and the ability of the judge to assess it, particularly where it has to be assessed against other oral evidence.'

[58] *R (SA (Iran)) v Secretary of State for the Home Department* [2012] EWHC 2575 (Admin) [24] (HHJ Gilbert).

Ultimately, a person may well have a well-founded fear of being persecuted yet their account may lack detail, may be inconsistent and incoherent, may be narrated with no outward sign of emotion and the person may know and understand little. The refugee status determination process nevertheless tends to be structured to encourage the qualitative approach that has repeatedly been called into question by both experience and research. Applicants are repeatedly required to give an account of past events, for example on arrival or initial application, then in more detail to the asylum authorities and then, if initially refused asylum, in a pre-prepared witness statement and again in oral evidence to a court or tribunal. In the absence of corroborating evidence from documents or witnesses, the very existence of these different accounts encourages their careful examination; often there is no other evidence on which a decision might be based. The involvement of lawyers and judges in the status determination process also militates in favour of evaluation of the quality of witness testimony given that this plays a key role in legal training and contentious court cases in other areas of legal practice.

The persistence of these assumptions on what makes a 'good quality' narrative despite the considerable research and guidance to the contrary partly reflects widespread social and cultural misconceptions which are not specific to asylum claims of how memory and recall work. From a legal perspective, little of the voluminous guidance and research is reflected in reported case law, unlike the occasional (but useful) judicial commentary on plausibility and context. This is perhaps because assessment of truthfulness is generally considered a matter of judicial discretion, which is therefore not easily amenable to an appeal to the higher courts; there is therefore little opportunity for these matters, as important as they are, to be commented upon in reported case law. Alternatively, it may be the case that judges do quietly rely on these flawed tools in their internalized decision-making yet do not say so in their publicly expressed reasons. They may instead find other less contentious reasoning on which to rely as the apparent justification for their decisions.

Future risk

The well-founded fear requirement is forward-facing in the sense that it only operates to offer refugee status as protection from future harm, not as solace for past suffering. Attempts have been made to argue that the 'owing to ... is outside ...' wording of the refugee definition means that a historic fear of being persecuted is sufficient if that is the reason the person fled their country and the reason they remain outside it. This interpretation has been definitively rejected in favour of applying 'well-founded fear' in the present tense: 'This is not to say that historic fear may not be relevant. It may well provide evidence to establish present fear. But it is the existence, or otherwise, of present fear which is determinative.'[59] In this respect, the 1951 Refugee Convention represents a departure from previous legal instruments protecting refugees, which conferred refugee status on the basis of past events. It had been proposed during the drafting of the Refugee Convention that the words 'who has had, or has, well-founded fear of being the victim of persecution' be used but the option was ultimately rejected in favour of focusing on present and future risk.[60] Similarly, the argument that the text of Article 1C(5) of the Refugee Convention, which states that cessation does not apply to a person 'who is able to invoke compelling reasons arising out of previous persecution for refusing to avail himself of the protection of the country of nationality', means that refugee status is retained in some cases even through a person no longer has a well-founded fear has been rejected. Those words are considered to be applicable only to historic refugees recognized under prior legal instruments in existence before the 1951 Refugee Convention was adopted.[61]

Relevance of past events

Past events may be relevant to the risk of future harm. It is not that past persecution or truth-telling are necessary preconditions to establishing a well-founded fear. Rather, where a person can show past persecution this may be an indicator that there may be a risk of the same things happening again in future for the same reasons as before. This is a principle reflected in academic writing, jurisprudence and rules. After quoting a passage from Professor Hathaway to like effect, for example, Lord Justice Stuart-Smith held in the case of *Demirkaya* that 'evidence of individualized past persecution is generally a sufficient, though not a mandatory, means of establishing prospective risks'.[62] In the United Kingdom, this principle is reflected in the immigration rules relating to asylum, and in the European Union, it finds expression in a key directive.[63] There are important provisos to emphasize, though. Firstly, it is in no way necessary to show past persecution. In some cases, for example, where past events are undiscoverable or irrelevant, this

---

[59] *R v Secretary of State for the Home Department, ex p Adan* [1999] 1 AC 293 (UK HL) (Lord Lloyd).

[60] Economic and Social Council, *Official Records*, 11th session, 3 July–16 August 1950, Annexes, Agenda item 32, p 22.

[61] Refugee Convention, Article 1A(1) and *Hoxha v Secretary of State for the Home Department* [2005] UKHL 19, [2005] WLR 1063. Article 11(3) of the EU Qualification Directive 2011/95/EU goes beyond the Refugee Convention by applying the 'compelling reasons' proviso to all refugees, as does Canadian statute.

[62] *Demirkaya v Secretary of State for the Home Department* [1999] Imm AR 498 (EW CA).

[63] Immigration Rules HC 395 paragraph 339K and Directive 2011/95/EU Article 4(4).

issue can prove to be a distraction. This may be the case where there is evidence of future risk irrespective of what took place in the past, as in a *sur place* refugee claim. Secondly, even where past persecution is demonstrated to the necessary standard, this is not necessarily decisive of a claim. Situations on the ground can be fluid and change rapidly, either for the worse or better. International intervention, change of government, change of policy and sometimes the simple passage of time since the events which caused the refugee to flee can all reduce or increase the future risk of harm.

Identifying risk

Some refugee status claims are based on the applicant being personally singled out because of their own personal actions or beliefs. A refugee may be a prominent politician, journalist, activist or preacher, for example, and have been personally singled out and targeted. It is undoubtedly helpful to show such personalized risk, not least because, for the reasons already explored, where a person has suffered persecution in the past this suggests that, absent a change of circumstances, they are at risk of similar persecution in the future. It is not necessary for a refugee to show singling out, however: 'they, like the Jews in Nazi-occupied lands, need not prove they will be individually targeted to establish a well-founded fear of future persecution'.[64] To deny asylum on the basis that the fear is as a member of a persecuted group rather than as a singled out individual has quite properly been criticized as a 'startling proposition' and 'dismal distinction' which has no bearing upon whether the individual has a well-founded fear of being persecuted.[65] Indeed, it is very common for an asylum application to be founded on one or more characteristics shared with others – sometimes many others – in a class or group. In *Adan* Lord Lloyd observed that 'generalised oppression may indeed give rise to refugee status'.[66] The refugee might be a member of a political party, an adherent of a religion or a member of a racial group in a country where some members of that group are targeted because of their membership. Clearly, in a claim specifically for refugee status the group would need to be one which can be identified with race, religion, nationality, political opinion or membership of a particular social group, as discussed further in Chapter 5.

In practice, many refugee status and international protection claims are based on a combination of these considerations: the applicant belongs to a

---

[64] *Knezevic v Ashcroft* 367 F3d 1206 (9th Cir 2004).
[65] *R v Secretary of State for the Home Department, ex p Jeyakumaran* [1994] Imm AR 45 (EW HC).
[66] *R v Secretary of State for the Home Department, ex p Adan* [1999] 1 AC 293 (UK HL).

group which it is asserted is generally at risk, but the person also has personal characteristics or personal history that mean they are at enhanced risk over and above other members of the group. In some instances, the range of circumstances which suggest risk or otherwise have been labelled 'risk factors', an approach which can be instructive but which can also bring its own complications to the refugee status determination process.[67] Separate risk factors might include, for example, ethnicity, family background, membership of a political party, personal history such as previous interest by the authorities, means of departure and time spent abroad. In some circumstances, a single 'risk factor' might be sufficient on its own to disclose a well-founded fear but in other cases, it might take a combination or two or more such risk factors. It is undoubtedly helpful to regard risk cumulatively and assess future risk on the basis of the interaction of a variety of different considerations, circumstances and personal characteristics or qualities. However, danger lies in an identified list of risk factors being regarded as effectively definitive in all cases, no matter the exhortations to the contrary of more senior judges. They may morph into a pre-determined set of asylum criteria. Such an approach risks undermining individual assessment and also might encourage artificial straightjacketing of asylum claims by applicants, lawyers and judges whereby aspects of the case not falling within the risk factors are ignored and aspects that do being given greater prominence than in truth they deserve. Where a list of risk factors becomes established, it also risks becoming entrenched in the face of evidence of changing circumstances in the country concerned. In the context of a human rights claim, the European Court of Human Rights accepted that it is 'in principle legitimate, when assessing the individual risk to returnees, to carry out that assessment based on the list of "risk factors"' but, presumably for these reasons, warned that it is important to be 'careful to avoid the impression that these risk factors were a "check list" or exhaustive'.[68]

The other form of risk sometimes identified in asylum applications aside from deliberate targeting of individuals or groups are more 'generic' risks which arise incidentally or accidentally. These are really a form of group risk case, albeit a very widely defined group which will often fall outside the Refugee Convention because it lacks connection to one of the five convention grounds of race, religion, nationality, political opinion or membership of a particular social group. Examples might include where a person claims to be at risk of serious harm because of general prison

---

[67] In the United Kingdom, this approach rose to prominence in *LP (LTTE area – Tamils – Colombo – risk?) Sri Lanka CG* [2007] UKAIT 00076.

[68] *NA v United Kingdom* App. No. 25904/07 (ECHR, 17 July 2008).

conditions in a given country or to be at risk of serious harm because of extremely poor general humanitarian conditions. Where the serious harm is experienced by some but not all of a widely defined group such as 'all prisoners' or 'all internally displaced persons' it can be challenging for an individual who faces such risks to show a real risk of experiencing the harm feared. Some cases have appeared to elaborate on the normal standard of proof of 'real risk' by suggesting that a 'consistent pattern' of the serious harm must be demonstrated.[69] As Lord Justice Sedley has said, though '[g]reat care must be taken with such epithets. They are intended to elucidate the jurisprudential concept of risk, not to replace it'.

Future activities

A claim to refugee status may potentially be founded on an assertion that a person will behave in future in a way which creates a risk of being persecuted which would not otherwise have arisen. For example, a political activist may claim that they will, if returned to their country of origin, attend demonstrations or carry out political campaigning work; a religious adherent may claim they will attend a place of worship or attempt to proselytize; a gay man may claim he will be open about his sexuality. There was early resistance to such claims, with one judge finding that it was 'going much too far' to suggest that 'that if a person has to refrain from political activity in order to avoid persecution he should qualify for political asylum'.[70] A more pragmatic position emerged in later cases whereby it became a matter of fact for a judge to determine whether a person would or would not act in such a way to place themselves in danger on their return.[71] If they would place themselves in danger, they were entitled to refugee status. If they would not place themselves in danger, they were not.

Acknowledgement that refugee status might be founded on future behaviour was undoubtedly a step forward but recognition as a refugee was restricted only to those who it was believed would act in such a way as to place themselves in danger. Ultimately, this pragmatic approach unravelled on the issue of sexuality and sexual identity. In an Australian case involving two gay men from Bangladesh, McHugh and Kirby JJ held that 'persecution does not cease to be persecution for the purpose of the Convention because those persecuted can eliminate the harm by taking avoiding action within

---

[69] *Hariri v Secretary of State for the Home Department* [2003] EWCA Civ 807.

[70] In *R v Immigration Appeal Tribunal, ex p Jonah* [1985] Imm AR 7 (EW HC) [12] (Nolan J).

[71] *Secretary of State for the Home Department v Iftikhar Ahmed* [1999] EWCA Civ 3003, [2000] INLR 1.

the country of nationality'.⁷² Not only that but where a person has modified or will modify their natural behaviour or expression of their core identity (as protected by a convention ground) because of the risk of persecution, that person may be a refugee: '[i]t is the threat of serious harm with its menacing implications that constitutes the persecutory conduct'.⁷³ In the United Kingdom, this line of jurisprudence was somehow for a time interpreted as meaning that an applicant for asylum could be expected to live discreetly in their country of origin and this would only constitute being persecuted if such discretion was 'something that the appellant could reasonably be expected to tolerate'.⁷⁴ On this approach, refugees were effectively held responsible for bringing persecution down on their own heads by the boldness of their beliefs or behaviour. Asylum assessors were faced with somehow determining what each individual might reasonably be expected to tolerate, an impossible and demeaning endeavour for applicant and assessor alike. This doctrine, under which LGBTQ+ individuals were returned to countries where they would have to suppress their sexual identity in order to avoid persecution, ended in the United Kingdom with the Supreme Court decision usually referred to in shorthand as *HJ (Iran)*.⁷⁵

KEY CASE

HJ (Iran) and HT (Cameroon) v Secretary of State for the Home Department involved two separate appeals by gay men linked together so that the courts could address the issues arising from asylum claims based on sexuality. One of the appellants was from Iran. He had a number of gay relationships in Iran. His family and some close friends knew that he was gay but he behaved very discreetly in public for fear of the consequences. In contrast, he was able to live openly and without fear in the United Kingdom. The other appellant was from Cameroon and had two gay relationships before leaving. One of these had been discovered, leading to a serious attack, and he fled the country.

The lower courts had dismissed both appeals on the basis that the appellants could return to their countries and continue to have gay relationships as long as they were discreet. Those decisions were overturned in the Supreme Court. Lord Dyson commented:

---

[72] *S395/2002 v Minister for Immigration and Multicultural Affairs* [2003] HCA 71 (Aus HC) [40].
[73] *S395/2002 v Minister for Immigration and Multicultural Affairs* [2003] HCA 71 (Aus HC) [43].
[74] *J v Secretary of State for the Home Department* [2006] EWCA Civ 1238, [2007] Imm AR 73. The appellant in this case was the same appellant as in *HJ (Iran)*, in what follows.
[75] *HJ (Iran) v Secretary of State for the Home Department* [2010] UKSC 31, [2011] 1 AC 596.

> If the price that a person must pay in order to avoid persecution is that he must conceal his race, religion, nationality, membership of a social group or political opinion, then he is being required to surrender the very protection that the Convention is intended to secure for him.

Decisively rejecting the 'reasonable toleration' line of authority, Lord Rodger observed in his judgment:

> Where would the tribunal find the yardstick to measure the level of suffering which a gay man – far less, the particular applicant – would find reasonably tolerable? How would the tribunal measure the equivalent level for a straight man asked to suppress his sexual identity indefinitely? The answer surely is that there is no relevant standard since it is something which no one should have to endure.

> Instead, where an applicant has established that they are gay, that gay men are persecuted in the relevant country and that the applicant would behave discreetly in order to avoid being persecuted (even if only partly for this reason), then the applicant is a refugee.

Logically, moving elsewhere in the country (see Chapter 4) cannot alleviate the risk of persecution in such a case if the risk of persecution extends to the whole country. If there is an area where the person will not be forced to be discreet in order to remain safe and to which the person can reasonably relocate, this will defeat the claim to refugee status.[76]

The same reasoning applies to other characteristics protected by the Refugee Convention, such as political opinion and religion. In principle, an applicant can advance a claim to refugee status on the basis of intended future activities which will expose them to persecution. An assertion that an applicant for asylum will place themselves in harm's way is more likely to be considered believable where the applicant can establish they have behaved that way previously, whether in the country from which they fled or in the country of asylum. This may arise in cases where the person has converted from one religion to another or has experienced a political awakening in the country of asylum, perhaps through contact with an expatriate community. In practice, without establishing past or present similar conduct an assessor is likely 'to regard such an assertion as intrinsically self-serving and to examine it with a considerable degree of scepticism'.[77] This widespread anxiety

---

[76] *YD (Algeria) v Secretary of State for the Home Department* [2020] EWCA Civ 1683 [57]–[66]; *MB (Internal relocation – burden of proof) Albania* [2019] UKUT 392 (IAC).

[77] *Secretary of State for the Home Department v Iftikhar Ahmed* [1999] EWCA Civ 3003 [2000] INLR 1.

not to grant refugee status unnecessarily lies behind controversial lines of questioning by assessors intended to identify the pretended gay man, the opportunistic religious convert and the artificial activist.

Refugees sur place

Future risk need not always arise from past experiences in the country of origin. Something may change, either in the country of origin or with the individual and their relationship with that country, which might create or give rise to a new risk which was not present at the time the applicant left their own country. As UNHCR puts it, '[a] person who was not a refugee when he left his country, but who becomes a refugee at a later date, is called a refugee *"sur place"*'.[78] The paradigm *sur place* claim arises where a revolution or coup d'etat in the country of origin places the refugee at risk if they return, for example because they were closely associated with the overthrown regime. More subtly, the individual may have known or suspected there were problems when they departed but the situation may have deteriorated since their departure. A *sur place* claim may also arise where something is discovered about the person by the authorities of the country of origin while he or she is outside the country. Or a person 'may become a refugee *"sur place"* as a result of his own actions, such as associating with refugees already recognized, or expressing his political views in his country of residence'.[79] The same principle also applies to religious conversion or coming out as LGBTQ+. Asylum claims are sometimes made by individuals claiming to have become involved with opposition politics among the diaspora community of their home country, for example, or to have attended meetings or demonstrations outside embassies. There is no legal rule preventing such a claim from succeeding but asylum assessors will often approach such cases with a somewhat sceptical mindset. They will assume that some applicants making such assertions are opportunists seeking to manufacture an asylum claim which would not otherwise exist. Such claims are often referred to as 'bad faith' claims, as discussed in a moment.

A variation on or specific form of a *sur place* claim may arise where the applicant for asylum asserts that they will be in danger on their return irrespective of the truth of their account of past and present activities. This

---

[78] UNHCR, *Handbook on Procedures and Criteria for Determining Refugee Status and Guidelines on International Protection under the 1951 Convention and the 1967 Protocol Relating to the Status of Refugees*, HCR/1P/4/ENG/REV.4 (1979, reissued 2019) [94].

[79] UNHCR, *Handbook on Procedures and Criteria for Determining Refugee Status and Guidelines on International Protection under the 1951 Convention and the 1967 Protocol Relating to the Status of Refugees*, HCR/1P/4/ENG/REV.4 (1979, reissued 2019) [96].

may arise, for example, where it is asserted that an illegal departure from a country would be punished by persecutory treatment on the person's return or where a test of loyalty to the governing party or regime might be applied on return, failure to pass which would expose the person to serious harm.[80] It has sometimes been argued that the authorities of even very repressive regimes are nevertheless realistic, are aware that their citizens sometimes go abroad for economic reasons and are not interested in wasting time persecuting mere 'hangers-on' who have been to a few demonstrations but are not genuine activists or leaders. As has repeatedly been found, it is unwise to credit repressive regimes with logical, rational behaviour.[81] Where there is clear evidence a government represses political opposition, affirmative evidence will not necessarily be required that the intelligence services of such a government photograph and film those demonstrating outside its embassy or monitor the internet for information about political opponents.[82]

Where an applicant for asylum would be placed in danger by a forced return but could safely make a voluntary return to their country of origin, that person is not a refugee because he or she is not outside his or her country of origin for reason of a well-founded fear of being persecuted.[83]

Bad faith claims

The possibility of being able to claim asylum based on one's activities in the asylum state opens the possibility that a cynical individual might engage in such activities in bad faith purely for the purpose of artificially manufacturing an asylum claim that would not otherwise exist. While this will seem unattractive to some, there is no basis in the Refugee Convention on which the motivation behind activities might exclude a person from protection unless the exclusion clauses of the convention are engaged (see Chapter 6). The important question is whether there is a well-founded fear of being persecuted for a convention reason.[84] The principle is now embedded in European Union law, with Directive 2011/95/EU stating that an assessor

---

[80] See *MO (illegal exit – risk on return) Eritrea CG* [2011] UKUT 00190 (IAC) for an example of the former and *RT (Zimbabwe) v Secretary of State for the Home Department* [2012] UKSC 38 for an example of the latter.

[81] See for example *Suleyman* (16242) (UK IAT, 11 February 1998) and *KS (Burma) v Secretary of State for the Home Department* [2013] EWCA Civ 67.

[82] *YB (Eritrea) v Secretary of State for the Home Department* [2008] EWCA Civ 360.

[83] *AA and LK v Secretary of State for the Home Department* [2006] EWCA Civ 401.

[84] *Danian v Secretary of State for the Home Department* [2000] Imm AR 96 (EW CA); *Li v Canada (Citizenship and Immigration)* 2012 FC 998 [24]; *Bastanipour v Immigration and Naturalisation Service* 980 F2d 1129 (7th Cir 1992); *YLs v Refugee and Protection Officer* [2017] NZCA 582 [60].

must take into account 'whether the applicant's activities since leaving the country of origin were engaged in for the sole or main purpose of creating the necessary conditions for applying for international protection' but going on to provide that the assessor must still 'assess whether those activities would expose the applicant to persecution or serious harm if returned to that country'.[85] Nevertheless, a person found to be lying in this way is likely to struggle to prove a risk on return: 'Where the appellant has given a totally incredible account of the relevant facts, the tribunal must decide what weight to give to the lie, as well as to all the other evidence in the case, including the general evidence.'[86] The exception to this general approach is Australia, where domestic legislation goes behind the plain effect of the Refugee Convention by requiring that assessors disregard conduct by the applicant that the applicant cannot show was carried out in good faith.[87]

Suggested further reading

Goodwin-Gill, G. and McAdam, J. (2021) *The Refugee in International Law* (4th edn), Oxford: Oxford University Press, Chapter 3.

Hathaway, J. and Foster, M. (2014) *The Law of Refugee Status* (2nd edn), Cambridge: Cambridge University Press, Chapter 2.

Kälin, W. (1986) 'Troubled Communication: Cross-Cultural Misunderstandings in the Asylum-Hearing', *International Migration Review*, 20: 230.

Noll, G. (2021) 'Credibility, Reliability, and Evidential Assessment', in Costello, C., Foster, M. and McAdam, J. (eds) *The Oxford Handbook of International Refugee Law*, Oxford: Oxford University Press, pp 607–622.

UNHCR, *Handbook on Procedures and Criteria for Determining Refugee Status and Guidelines on International Protection under the 1951 Convention and the 1967 Protocol Relating to the Status of Refugees*, HCR/1P/4/ENG/REV.4 (1979, reissued 2019), [37]-[50], [94]-[96] and [189]-[219].

Vogl, A. (2013) 'Telling Stories from Start to Finish: Exploring the Demand for Narrative in Refugee Testimony', *Griffith Law Review*, 22(1): 63–86.

Zambelli, P. (2017) 'Hearing Differently: Knowledge-Based Approaches to Assessment of Refugee Narrative', *International Journal of Refugee Law*, 29(1): 10–41.

---

[85] Article 4(3)(d) of Directive 2011/95/EU.

[86] *MA (Somalia) v Secretary of State for the Home Department* [2010] UKSC 49 [32] (Lord Dyson).

[87] Migration Act 1958, s 5J(6) and *Minister for Immigration and Citizenship v SZJGV; Minister for Immigration and Citizenship v SZJXO* [2009] HCA 40.

3

Being Persecuted

The Refugee Convention protects certain individuals and groups from 'being persecuted'. No further direct definition is offered in the text of the convention and the question of what might constitute 'being persecuted' has proven to be a challenging one to answer. The ambiguity can be regarded as constructive in nature: from the *travaux préparatoires*, we know that the drafters of the Refugee Convention had in mind that 'being persecuted' involved a high level of harm, but they declined to lay down a more precise meaning. As an early scholar of refugee law, Grahl-Madsen, put it, '[i]t seems as if the drafters have wanted to introduce a flexible concept which might be applied to circumstances as they might arise; or, in other words, that they capitulated before the inventiveness of humanity to think up new ways of persecuting fellow men'.[1] Goodwin-Gill makes the same point, saying '[t]here being no limits to the perverse side of human imagination, little purpose is served by attempting to list all known measures of persecution'.[2] Enumeration of the various horrible acts that might amount to 'being persecuted' – or those slightly less horrible acts that might not – becomes self-evidently undesirable when seen in this light. A list may be simple and easily comprehended, but it is too rigid, in that it fails to allow for context and is incapable of evolving over time. In 1979, the UNHCR Handbook stated that '[t]here is no universally accepted definition of "persecution", and various attempts to formulate such a definition have met with little

---

[1] Grahl-Madsen, A. (1966) *The Status of Refugees in International Law (Vol. I)*, Cambridge: Cambridge University Press.
[2] Goodwin-Gill, G. (1983) *The Refugee in International Law*, Oxford: Oxford University Press, p 40.

success'.³ This passage is perhaps no longer as true as it once was. A broad consensus has emerged based on international human rights law standards, albeit the approach applied by asylum examiners in practice is not necessarily as principled as may first appear.

Individual impact

One of the earliest attempts in reported case law to attribute meaning to 'being persecuted' resorted to the expedient of looking it up in a dictionary. In *Jonah*, the judge turned to the Shorter Oxford Dictionary definitions of 'persecute': firstly, 'To pursue, hunt, drive' and, secondly, 'To pursue with malignancy or injurious action; esp. to oppress for holding a heretical opinion or belief'.⁴ While simple and consistent with the legal interpretation principle of applying ordinary meaning, this approach does not contextualize the term 'being persecuted' within the Refugee Convention. Article 31(1) of the Vienna Convention on the Law of Treaties tells us that a treaty must be interpreted 'in good faith in accordance with the ordinary meaning to be given to the terms of the treaty in their context and in the light of its object and purpose'. More prosaically, resorting to one's dictionary of choice tells us nothing of the level of seriousness required for harm to amount to being persecuted and fails to capture the importance of the use of the passive voice in those words.⁵ The passive phrasing has been said to convey 'a compound notion, concerned both with the conduct of the persecutor and the effect that conduct has on the person being persecuted'.⁶ Discussion of the refugee definition often – as in this book – deploys the noun 'persecution' for the sake of convenience. Taken alone and out of context, the noun 'persecution' seems to imply an active course of conduct. The danger is that the mind of the decision maker is incorrectly directed to the intention of the persecutor instead of the effect on the persecuted. Hathaway and Pobjoy argue that the Refugee Convention 'is concerned with protection against a predicament or condition' and therefore 'consideration must be given to both the nature of the risk and the nature of the state response (if

---

³ UNHCR, *Handbook on Procedures and Criteria for Determining Refugee Status and Guidelines on International Protection under the 1951 Convention and the 1967 Protocol Relating to the Status of Refugees*, HCR/1P/4/ENG/REV.4 (1979, reissued 2019) [52].
⁴ *R v Immigration Appeal Tribunal, ex p Jonah* [1985] Imm AR 7 (EW HC) [13] (Nolan J). See also *Applicant A v Minister for Immigration and Ethnic Affairs* [1997] HCA 4 (Aus HC) (Gummow J).
⁵ *Refugee Appeal No. 71427/1999* (NZ RSAA, 16 August 2000) (Rodger Haines QC); *Minister for Immigration and Multicultural Affairs v Khawar* [2002] HCA 14 (Aus HC) [35] (Kirby J).
⁶ *Minister for Immigration, Multicultural and Indigenous Affairs v Kord* [2002] FCAFC 390 (Aus) [2].

any) since it is the combination of the two that gives rise to the predicament of "being persecuted"'.[7]

The UNHCR Handbook endorses this personalized approach to judging what amounts to being persecuted:

> The subjective character of fear of persecution requires an evaluation of the opinions and feelings of the person concerned. It is also in the light of such opinions and feelings that any actual or anticipated measures against him must necessarily be viewed. Due to variations in the psychological make-up of individuals and in the circumstances of each case, interpretations of what amounts to persecution are bound to vary.[8]

The sex, age, state of health and other personal characteristics of the victim may well affect the seriousness of any ill-treatment meted out to them: '[a]n activity which would not amount to persecution if done to some people may amount to persecution if done to others'.[9] In the United States, the courts have adopted a subjective, potentially flexible definition of persecution, understanding the words to mean 'the infliction of suffering or harm upon those who differ (in race, religion or political opinion) in a way regarded as offensive'.[10] In Australia, a landmark judgment suggested that treatment would only amount to persecution 'if, by reason of its intensity or duration, the person cannot reasonably be expected to tolerate it'.[11] This 'know-it-when-I-see-it' approach to identifying persecution appeals to common sense and will often prove to be harmless in its application; experience suggests that in practice few refugee status determinations really turn on the question of where exactly to situate the threshold of persecutory treatment.

Requiring a decision maker to make a subjective judgment about the impact on another person from a very different environment and culture is inherently dangerous, though. It not only risks inconsistency and undermines

---

[7] Hathaway, J. and Pobjoy, J. (2011) 'Queer Cases Make Bad Law', *New York University Journal of International Law and Politics*, 44(2): 315–88 at 320. See also *Refugee Appeal No. 72635/01* (NZ RSAA) (6 September 2002); [2003] INLR 629 [168].

[8] UNHCR, *Handbook on Procedures and Criteria for Determining Refugee Status and Guidelines on International Protection under the 1951 Convention and the 1967 Protocol Relating to the Status of Refugees*, HCR/1P/4/ENG/REV.4 (1979, reissued 2019) [52].

[9] *Katrinak v Secretary of State for the Home Department* [2001] EWCA Civ 832 [21] (Schiemann LJ).

[10] *Korablina v Immigration and Naturalization Service* (1998) 158 F3d 1038 (9th Cir, 23 October 1998). The approach originated with *Kovac v Immigration and Naturalization Service* (1968) 407 F2d 102 (9th Cir).

[11] *Appellant S395/2002 v Minister for Immigration and Multicultural Affairs* [2003] HCA 71 (Aus HC) [40] (McHugh and Kirby JJ).

the principle that treaties should be interpreted uniformly but also leaves decision makers faced with an impossible task. Asked to find that police brutality did not amount to persecution because it did not attain a notional minimum level of severity, Lord Justice Sedley responded '[s]peaking for myself, I do not know what a minimum level of brutality is'.[12] Several years later, decisively rejecting the subjective 'reasonable toleration' approach to defining persecution, Lord Rodger asked in the same vein '[w]here would the tribunal find the yardstick to measure the level of suffering which a gay man – far less, the particular applicant – would find reasonably tolerable?'[13] There is another definition of 'being persecuted' available, though, which allows for a principled rather than subjective consideration of individual impact.

The bifurcated approach

In 1991 James Hathaway proposed that 'persecution may be defined as the sustained or systemic violation of basic human rights demonstrative of a failure of state protection'.[14] This formulation has since been described as the 'bifurcated approach' because it comprises two elements.[15] The first is harm which is serious in nature as judged against international human rights standards. The second is the failure of the person's own state to protect them from that harm. This approach has been very widely adopted in the intervening years. Perhaps most strikingly, Lord Hoffman succinctly held in the case of *R v Immigration Appeal Tribunal, ex p Shah* in 1999 that

Persecution = Serious Harm + The Failure of State Protection.[16]

'Serious harm' is a useful, readily intelligible working definition of what level of harm is required but it begs the question of against what standard or scale of seriousness the harm might be judged. Lord Hoffman did not in this particular passage specifically tie 'serious harm' to violations of human rights but he does so implicitly throughout his judgment, as discussed later. The following year, in 2000, the House of Lords consciously and explicitly adopted the Hathaway formulation in the case of *Horvath*.[17] The Canadian

---

[12] *Svazas v Secretary of State for the Home Department* [2002] EWCA Civ 74, [2002] WLR 1891 [38] (Sedley LJ).
[13] *HJ (Iran) v Secretary of State for the Home Department* [2010] UKSC 31, [2011] 1 AC 596 [80] (Lord Rodger).
[14] Hathaway, J. (1991) *The Law of Refugee Status*, Toronto: Butterworths Canada, pp 104–105.
[15] Hathaway, J. and Foster, M. (2014) *The Law of Refugee Status* (2nd edn), Cambridge: Cambridge University Press, p 183.
[16] *R v Immigration Appeal Tribunal, ex p Shah* [1999] 2 AC 629 (UK HL), attributed to Refugee Women's Legal Group (1988) *Gender Guidelines for the Determination of Asylum Claims in the UK*.
[17] *Horvath v Secretary of State for the Home Department* [2001] AC 489 (UK HL).

Supreme Court had already done so in 1993 in *Ward*, the New Zealand Refugee Status Appeals Authority in 1996 in *Re MN Refugee Appeal No 2039/93* and the High Court of Australia followed (in part at least) in 2002 with *Khawar*.[18] A similar approach is implicit in the structure of the European Union's Qualification Directive, the first version of which passed into law in 2004.[19] The only major common law jurisdiction not to follow suit has been the United States.

By tying the threshold for persecution to international human rights standards, the bifurcated approach offers an objective and principled definition which remains flexible and has evolved over time. Because of the structure and sequence of Article 1A(2) of the Refugee Convention ('well-founded fear of being persecuted *for reasons of* ...' emphasis added) the bifurcated approach also has the virtue of offering protection from discriminatory treatment by a state in its failure to provide protection against non-state actors. If failure of protection is decoupled from persecution, it is hard to see how the five convention grounds might be relevant in such cases. Understanding the failure of state protection as part of the meaning of persecution has been said to provide 'the bridge between persecution by the state and persecution by non-state agents which is necessary in the interests of the consistency of the whole scheme'.[20] In *R v Immigration Appeal Tribunal, ex p Shah* Lord Hoffman justified and explained his 'Persecution = Serious Harm + The Failure of State Protection' formula by asking the reader to imagine themselves in Germany in 1935 and to 'suppose that the Nazi government in those early days did not actively organize violence against Jews, but pursued a policy of not giving any protection to Jews subjected to violence by neighbours'. He went on:

> A Jewish shopkeeper is attacked by a gang organised by an Aryan competitor who smash his shop, beat him up and threaten to do it again if he remains in business. The competitor and his gang are motivated by business rivalry and a desire to settle old personal scores, but they would not have done what they did unless they knew that the authorities would allow them to act with impunity. And the ground upon which they enjoyed impunity was that the victim was a Jew. Is

---

[18] *Canada (Attorney General) v Ward* [1993] 2 SCR 689 at 733 (La Forest J), *Re MN Refugee Appeal No. 2039/93* (NZ RSAA, 12 February 1996) (Rodger Haines QC), *Minister for Immigration and Multicultural Affairs v Khawar* [2002] HCA 14 (Aus HC) [37] (Kirby J).

[19] Council Directive 2004/83/EC of 29 April 2004 on minimum standards for the qualification and status of third-country nationals or stateless persons as refugees or as persons who otherwise need international protection and the content of the protection granted at Articles 6, 7 and 9. See also Case C-255/19, *United Kingdom v OA* [56].

[20] *Horvath v Secretary of State for the Home Department* [2001] AC 489 (UK HL) (Lord Hope).

he being persecuted on grounds of race? Again, in my opinion, he is. An essential element in the persecution, the failure of the authorities to provide protection, is based upon race. It is true that one answer to the question 'Why was he attacked?' would be 'because a competitor wanted to drive him out of business'. But another answer, and in my view the right answer in the context of the Convention, would be 'he was attacked by a competitor who knew that he would receive no protection because he was a Jew'.[21]

While Lord Hoffman here referred to race, the context of *R v Immigration Appeal Tribunal, ex p Shah* itself was oppressed women. The linkage established by the bifurcated approach between protection and discrimination on Convention grounds has proven to be important in asylum claims based on non-state persecution, notably in claims based on gender and sexuality.[22]

The bifurcated approach has its sceptics, however.[23] As part and parcel of the conception of the Refugee Convention as an instrument of surrogate international protection, the approach is subject to the same criticisms of that analysis considered in Chapter 4. It is possible to define 'being persecuted' by reference to human rights standards without also requiring demonstration of a failure of state protection. Doing so need not necessarily prejudice those targeted by non-state persecution, given modern understanding of societal and structural discrimination. Where a person suffers serious human rights abuses, a significant causal element may well lie in the fact the person is perceived as possessing a characteristic protected from discrimination. As Lord Hutton put it in one case involving targeting of young Tamil men by the Sri Lankan security services, 'the fact of excessive and arbitrary punishment may, in the circumstances of a particular case, give rise to the factual inference that a reason for that punishment was the race or membership of a particular social group or political opinion of the victim'.[24] Nor does the bifurcated approach to understanding 'persecution' sit easily with the plain text of the definition of a refugee. The definition begins by requiring that a refugee have a well-founded fear of being persecuted for one of five grounds and be

---

[21] *R v Immigration Appeal Tribunal, ex p Shah* [1999] 2 AC 629 (UK HL) (Lord Hoffman).
[22] On the problems arising in gender-based claims, see for example *Matter of R-A-22 I. & N. Dec. 906* (BIA 1999), discussed in Musalo, K. (2010) 'A Short History of Gender Asylum in the United States: Resistance and Ambivalence May Very Slowly be Inching Towards Recognition of Women's Claims', *Refugee Survey Quarterly*, 29(2): 46.
[23] See for example Cantor, D. (2016) 'Defining Refugees: Persecution, Surrogacy and the Human Rights Paradigm', in Cantor, D. and Burson, B. (eds) *Human Rights and the Refugee Definition*, Leiden: Brill, pp 349–395.
[24] *R (on the application of Sivakumar) v Secretary of State for the Home Department* [2003] UKHL 14, [2003] 2 All ER 1097 [30].

outside their country of nationality. The text of Article 1A(2) then goes on to state that the refugee must be 'unable or, owing to such fear ... unwilling to avail himself of the protection of that country'.[25] It might be thought that to read a requirement of absence of state protection into two separate parts of the refugee definition involves unnecessary repetition and therefore offends against the statutory interpretation rule of surplusage.[26] Three solutions have been proposed. Hathaway and Foster argue that 'protection of that country' in the second part of the definition should be read as a reference to internal protection elsewhere within the country of origin, an issue addressed in Chapter 4.[27] Alternatively, the reference to protection in the second part of the definition can be understood as diplomatic or consular protection extended abroad by a country to its nationals, thereby attributing different meanings to 'protection' in the two parts of the definition.[28] It is highly likely this was the intended meaning of those who drafted the Refugee Convention, but it is generally accepted that there has since then been a shift in understanding.[29] The third approach is a pragmatic one: to ignore this issue. In the United Kingdom, the House of Lords declined to adopt either the internal protection or the diplomatic protection analyses on the basis that the refugee definition should be read as a whole and therefore no impermissible repetition arises because the different elements of the definition all inform one another.[30]

Actors of persecution

If the purpose of the Refugee Convention is to act as surrogate international protection, it would seem to follow that the precise source of harm is of little consequence. What matters is, firstly, whether the treatment feared is sufficiently serious and, secondly, whether the home state has failed to

---

[25] Refugee Convention Article 1A. In respect of those who are stateless Article 1A(2) provides '... or who, not having a nationality and being outside the country of his former habitual residence as a result of such events, is unable or, owing to such fear, is unwilling to return to it'.

[26] In short, where one reading would make part of the statute redundant and a second reading would avoid the redundancy, the second reading is preferred.

[27] Hathaway, J. and Foster, M. (2014) *The Law of Refugee Status* (2nd edn), Cambridge: Cambridge University Press, p 332.

[28] *Minister for Immigration and Multicultural Affairs v Khawar* [2002] HCA 14 (Aus HC) [21], [62] (Gleeson CJ). See Fortin, A. (2000) 'The Meaning of "Protection" in the Refugee Definition', *International Journal of Refugee Law*, 12(4): 548–576.

[29] In *Januzi v Secretary of State for the Home Department* [2006] UKHL 5, [2006] 2 AC 426 (Lord Carswell).

[30] See *Horvath v Secretary of State for the Home Department* [2001] AC 489 (UK HL) and *Januzi v Secretary of State for the Home Department* [2006] UKHL 5, [2006] 2 AC 426.

provide protection. There have previously been some jurisdictions in which an 'accountability' analysis of the Refugee Convention was followed, in which refugee status was available only where persecution was attributable, directly or indirectly, to the state. Broadly, this might arise where persecutory acts were carried out by the state itself or where persecution could be shown to be tolerated or encouraged by the state, or where the state was unwilling as a matter of policy to offer protection against it.[31] France and Germany had adopted versions of this approach but the advent of the European Union's Qualification Directive in 2004 ended this divergence in thinking.[32] It is now very widely accepted, for example, under the African Refugee Convention and Cartagena Declaration and in Australia, Canada, the European Union, New Zealand, the United Kingdom and the United States, that acts of persecution can in principle, subject to other requirements of the Refugee Convention, be carried out by any person, whether a state actor or otherwise.[33]

While there is no principle that by its nature the persecution must emanate from the state, whether the state is the source of persecution is often highly relevant in a claim to refugee status from a practical perspective. For example, where it is the state that carries out the persecution feared there will usually be little question as to whether protection is available or whether internal relocation is possible: see further Chapter 4. Further, acts perpetrated by state officials (or others in a position of trust) 'can be particularly sinister, pernicious and invasive above and beyond the nature of non-state persecution' and could arguably more readily amount to being persecuted.[34]

Concept of serious harm

As we have seen, the threshold of harm for establishing what amounts to being persecuted has been described as 'serious harm' and 'the sustained or systemic violation of basic human rights demonstrative of a failure of state

---

[31] See discussion in *R (on the application of Adan and Aitsegur) v SSHD* [2001] 2 AC 477 (UK HL).

[32] See Directive 2004/83/EC at Article 6.

[33] Australia: *Minister for Immigration and Multicultural Affairs v Khawar* [2002] HCA 14 (Aus HC); Canada: *Canada (Attorney General) v Ward* [1993] 2 SCR 689; New Zealand: *Butler v Attorney-General* [1997] NZCA 309; United Kingdom: *R v Secretary of State for the Home Department, ex p Adan* [1999] 1 AC 293 (UK HL); United States: *INS v Elias-Zacarias* (1992) 502 US 478 (US SC).

[34] Yeo, C. (2002) 'Agents of State: When Is an Official of the State an Agent of the State?', *International Journal of Refugee Law*, 14(4): 509–533 at 515; McGlynn, C. (2009) 'Rape, Torture and the European Convention on Human Rights', *International and Comparative Law Quarterly*, 58(3): 565–595 at 574, 576–578.

protection'.[35] Questions arise as to which human rights are the 'basic' ones, whether persecution must be sustained over a period or whether single acts might qualify and the role of discrimination and the Convention grounds in defining persecution. We turn now to explore these questions on the qualities that might turn harm into serious harm. Understanding of the answers is now largely shared across multiple jurisdictions, although that understanding proves to be a somewhat hazy one on close inspection.

Role of human rights standards

If human rights standards act as a guide to the meaning of persecution, this begs the question of *which* human rights. When proposing the adoption of human rights law as the measure of persecution, Hathaway referred to 'sustained or systemic violation' of 'basic human rights' or 'one of the core entitlements which has been recognized by the international community'.[36] As discussed in Chapter 1, there is now a range of international human rights instruments which are very widely ratified. They therefore offer an internationally agreed set of standards by which serious harm may be judged and as to whether a law or cultural practice in a country is persecutory. In *R v Immigration Appeal Tribunal, ex p Shah*, for example, one of the judges had at an early stage in the legal proceedings said that the evidence of discrimination against women in Pakistan contained 'overt and implicit criticisms of Pakistani society and the position of women in that and other Islamic states. We do not think that the purpose of the Convention is to award refugee status because of a disapproval of social mores or conventions in non-western societies'.[37] Lord Hoffman disposed of this peculiar reasoning by reference to both national and international standards. He observed that the constitution of Pakistan prohibited discrimination on the basis of sex, as did various international legal instruments, and that Pakistan had ratified the Convention on the Elimination of All Forms of Discrimination against Women. This is not, however, to say that a country must have acceded to key international human rights instruments before they can usefully be deployed to analyze the conduct of actors of persecution in that country. Rather, it underlines that international standards can and should be used as a benchmark.

---

[35] *R v Immigration Appeal Tribunal, ex p Shah* [1999] 2 AC 629 (UK HL) (Lord Hoffman) and Hathaway, J. (1991) *The Law of Refugee Status*, Toronto: Butterworths Canada, pp 104–105 respectively.

[36] Hathaway, J. (1991) *The Law of Refugee Status*, Toronto: Butterworths Canada, pp 104–105 and 112.

[37] Cited with disapproval by Lord Hoffman in his own judgment *R v Immigration Appeal Tribunal, ex p Shah* [1999] 2 AC 629 (UK HL).

Nevertheless, it is widely and intuitively felt that breaches of some human rights are more serious than breaches of others. In the context of international protection claims, decision makers and judges might consider that, for example, a breach of the prohibition on torture is more serious – and therefore likely to amount to being persecuted – than a breach of the right to freedom of speech or right to a private life. The working definition of 'being persecuted' is often taken to be *serious* harm, after all. Lord Millet said in a dissenting judgment in *R v Immigration Appeal Tribunal, ex p Shah* that '[t]he denial of human rights ... is not the same as persecution, which involves the infliction of serious harm'.[38] Lord Dyson has said that 'persecution is more than a breach of human rights'.[39] Similarly, McHugh J has commented that '[t]orture, beatings or unjustifiable imprisonment, if carried out for a Convention reason, will invariably constitute persecution for the purpose of the Convention. But the infliction of many forms of economic harm and the interference with many civil rights may not reach the standard of persecution'.[40] Most emphatically, French CJ and the majority in the Australian High Court case of *WZAPN* held that persecution does not arise from 'the demonstration of any breach, or apprehended breach, of human rights'.[41] Even in judgments acknowledging a vital role for human rights in delineating persecution, it is not said that breaches of all human rights might constitute persecution so much as breaches specifically of 'fundamental' human rights.[42]

This instinctive sense that human rights are not necessarily all equal has led to a search for a means to differentiate between variously expressed 'basic', 'core' or 'fundamental' rights and other allegedly less significant rights. One such schema was proposed by Hathaway in *The Law of Refugee Status* in 1991.[43] This approach was proselytized by UNHCR and others, featured in United Kingdom jurisprudence and was later partially endorsed in a qualified way by the European Union in its Qualification Directive (see further in what follows).[44] Hathaway's original methodology, from which

---

[38] *R v Immigration Appeal Tribunal, ex p Shah* [1999] 2 AC 629 (UK HL) (Lord Millet).

[39] *RT (Zimbabwe) v Secretary of State for the Home Department* [2012] UKSC 38, [2013] 1 AC 152 [50].

[40] *Minister for Immigration and Multicultural Affairs v Haji Ibrahim* [2000] HCA 55 [55] (McHugh J).

[41] *Minister for Immigration and Border Protection v WZAPN* [2015] HCA 22 [71]. Subsequently cited with approval in *BRF038 v The Republic of Nauru* [2017] HCA 44 [43]–[44].

[42] *Fornah v Secretary of State for the Home Department* [2007] AC 412 [13] (Lord Bingham).

[43] Hathaway, J. (1991) *The Law of Refugee Status*, Toronto: Butterworths Canada, pp 108–112.

[44] *Gashi v Secretary of State for the Home Department* [1997] INLR 96 (IAT); Symes, M. and Jorro, P. (2010) *Asylum Law and Practice* (2nd edn), Chippenham: Bloomsbury Professional, pp 128–131; Directive 2004/83/EC Article 9(1).

he has since resiled, began by differentiating rights based on 'derogability', the right in international human rights law of states to restrict or suspend some human rights in times of emergency. Some rights may never be derogated from, such as protection from torture or cruel, inhuman or degrading treatment or punishment. Derogation can be made from some other rights in times of emergency, such as freedom from arbitrary arrest or detention or the right to a fair trial. But different human rights instruments permit derogation from different rights and whether a state may or may not derogate from a right does not reduce the impact of interference on the person concerned. Hathaway proposed further differentiation with reference to the nature of the obligation imposed on states by various rights, some of which are framed as requiring immediate respect – often civil and political rights – and others of which are framed as requiring progressive implementation – often economic, social and cultural rights. But these distinctions were not intended to signal that some rights were more important than others, only that some rights would take longer to realize than others. Ultimately, as Michelle Foster has argued, the problem with these attempts at grading rights is that neither the Universal Declaration of Human Rights nor other later international human instruments present rights in a discernible or principled hierarchy of importance.[45] Indeed, the absence of a hierarchy of rights is an internationally recognized feature of human rights law: '[all] human rights are universal, indivisible and interdependent and interrelated. The international community must treat human rights globally in a fair and equal manner, on the same footing, and with the same emphasis'.[46] Hathaway has in response revised his position and with Foster wrote in 2014 that there is 'no convincing conceptual framework that is capable of distinguishing on an absolute basis between those rights that are "basic", "fundamental", or "important" and those that are not'.[47] Similarly, the New Zealand the Immigration and Protection Tribunal has rejected 'the notion that international human rights law is to be approached from a hierarchical perspective in which civil and political rights take precedence over, or are a superior form of rights, to their economic, social and cultural counterparts'.[48]

---

[45] Foster, M. (2007) *International Refugee Law and Socio-Economic Rights: Refuge from Deprivation*, Cambridge: Cambridge University Press, Chapter 4.
[46] United Nations, Vienna Declaration and Programme of Action (UN Doc A/CONF.157/23) (12 July 1993).
[47] Hathaway, J. and Foster, M. (2014) *The Law of Refugee Status* (2nd edn), Cambridge: Cambridge University Press, p 204.
[48] *BG (Fiji)* [2012] NZIPT 800091 [90]. See also *DS (Iran)* [2016] NZIPT 800788.

Hathaway and Foster now together argue that no additional framework of hierarchy is possible in principle and nor is one needed in practice.[49] Human rights law recognizes that not all acts which infringe on a right will breach the obligation imposed by that right. For example, an act which amounts to torture will always breach the obligation imposed by Article 7 of the International Covenant on Civil and Political Rights (ICCPR) because that is framed in absolute terms which allow for no exception in any circumstances: 'No one shall be subjected to torture or to cruel, inhuman or degrading treatment or punishment. In particular, no one shall be subjected without his free consent to medical or scientific experimentation'. An act which amounts to an interference with freedom of thought, conscience or religion will not always breach the obligation imposed by ICCPR Article 18 because clause (3) of that article recognizes the right may be subject 'to such limitations as are prescribed by law and are necessary to protect public safety, order, health, or morals or the fundamental rights and freedoms of others'. It is important to distinguish between an interference and a breach in this context. Similarly, some rights may, as already noted, be derogated from in times of emergency, such as the right to liberty and security of the person protected by ICCPR Article 9. Without having to classify rights as more or less valuable in some way, an asylum assessor may legitimately take derogability into account in deciding whether infringements of rights might amount to being persecuted in the context of the country concerned. As long ago as the case of *Sivakumaran*, for example, a context of civil disorder and civil war was recognized as being relevant to whether infringement of rights amounted to persecution.[50] New Zealand case law has adopted a similar approach, clearly drawing on Foster's work, and focusing instead on the 'minimum core obligation' of a given right which cannot legitimately be derogated from or qualified.[51] This is, as Jason Pobjoy puts it, 'simply to take international human rights law on its own terms'.[52]

It is questionable whether this approach adequately addresses oft-expressed judicial concern that breaches of some very widely recognized human rights will not attain the minimum level of severity to amount to being persecuted.

---

[49] Hathaway, J. and Foster, M. (2014) *The Law of Refugee Status* (2nd edn), Cambridge: Cambridge University Press, p 204.

[50] *R (on the application of Sivakumuran) v Secretary of State for the Home Department* [1988] AC 958 (UK HL) per Lord Keith.

[51] *DS (Iran)* [2016] NZIPT 800788 [184]–[202]. See Foster, M. (2007) *International Refugee Law and Socio-Economic Rights: Refuge from Deprivation*, Cambridge: Cambridge University Press, Chapter 4 generally and particularly pp 195–201.

[52] Pobjoy, J. (2017) *The Child in International Refugee Law*, Cambridge: Cambridge University Press, p 107.

Hathaway and Foster acknowledge there will be 'occasional' cases of breaches of a human right in which 'the threat is so far at the margins of a rights violation as to amount to a *de minimus* harm'. They argue such a situation involves only a non-cognizable harm which therefore does not amount to being persecuted within the meaning of the Refugee Convention.[53] This is undoubtedly a principled and well-argued position to adopt, but, given the weight of authority cited earlier, it is perhaps advocacy for what the law should be rather than a statement of international legal consensus as it stands today.

This may prove to be a circular argument which ends where it first began: with non-derogable human rights representing the benchmark for treatment that amounts to being persecuted. As discussed in Chapter 1, the duty of *non-refoulement* in human rights law currently only arises in two situations. Firstly, a person cannot be sent abroad to face torture or inhuman or degrading treatment or punishment. For other human rights, the test for *non-refoulement* is whether there will be a 'flagrant denial' of that other right 'which is so fundamental as to amount to a nullification, or destruction of the very essence, of the right guaranteed by that article'.[54] Actual cases are vanishingly rare. Even where a flagrant denial of a right has been found, *refoulement* may only be prohibited where there will also be serious consequences which would amount to torture or cruel, inhuman or degrading treatment or punishment.[55] Both the House of Lords and the European Court of Human Rights have commented that it is 'hard to visualise' a case in which a sufficiently flagrant violation of the right to freedom of religion would not also involve violation of the right to freedom from inhuman or degrading treatment.[56] A similar approach has been adopted by the Court of Justice of the European Union.[57]

This is not to say that human rights and refugee law do not add anything to one another. The fact that rights such as to freedom of religion and private and family life have been enunciated and endorsed by the international community gives valuable guidance as to contemporary understanding

---

[53] Hathaway, J. and Foster, M. (2014) *The Law of Refugee Status* (2nd edn), Cambridge: Cambridge University Press, p 206.

[54] *EM (Lebanon) v Secretary of State for the Home Department* [2008] UKHL 64, [2009] 1 AC 1198 [3]-[4] (Lord Hope); *Othman v United Kingdom* App. No. 8139/09 [2012] 55 EHRR 1 [260].

[55] *Othman v United Kingdom* App. No. 8139/09 [2012] 55 EHRR 1 [262].

[56] *R (on the application of Ullah) v Special Adjudicator* [2004] UKHL 26, [2004] 2 AC 323 [67] (Lord Carswell); *EM (Lebanon) v Secretary of State for the Home Department* [2008] UKHL 64, [2009] 1 AC 1198 [12] and [16] (Lord Hope); *Z and T v United Kingdom* App. No. 27034/05 (ECHR, 28 February 2006) p 7.

[57] Joined Cases C-71/11 and C-99/11 *Y and Z v Germany* [67] and [69].

of what it means to be human. As Matthew Gibney has written, human rights are not luxuries or a utopian wish list of desires but rather 'the basic minimum that each individual has to have in order to live a human (rather than inhuman) existence'.[58] Denial of those basic minimums of human existence may well in some circumstances be inhuman and degrading, and that is a useful standard when it comes to judging what amounts to serious harm for the purpose of the Refugee Convention.

The evident concern shared by state parties and some judges not to extend the protection of the Refugee Convention too widely can to some extent be assuaged by considering and applying two further elements widely considered to be necessary for breaches of human rights to amount to persecution. One is that breaches must be 'sustained or systemic', as discussed in what follows. The other is that the Refugee Convention itself explicitly imposes further limits on the extent to which harm or breaches of rights might lead to recognition as a refugee: the convention grounds operate as a further filter, as discussed in Chapter 5.

Nature or repetition

On a simple reading of the human rights analysis of persecution, it might be thought that breaches of human rights have to occur on multiple occasions or over a substantial period of time. Hathaway deploys the words 'sustained or systemic' and the word 'persistent' has also been used and widely cited.[59] In fact, it is well established that single incidents of very serious future harm will constitute persecution: 'conduct may be so extreme that one instance is sufficient'.[60] This is implicitly recognized in the European Union's Qualification Directive, which provides that to amount to persecution, harm must 'be sufficiently serious by its nature or repetition as to constitute a severe violation of basic human rights' and goes on to state that 'an accumulation of various measures' might potentially reach that standard.[61] 'Sustained' is perhaps better understood in the sense

---

[58] Gibney, M. (2008) *International Human Rights Law: Returning to Universal Principles*, Lanham, MD: Rowman & Littlefield, p 4.

[59] Hathaway, J. (1991) *The Law of Refugee Status*, Toronto: Butterworths Canada, pp 104–105 and 112 and *Ravichandran and Sandralingham v Secretary of State for the Home Department* [1996] Imm AR 97 (UK CA) at 114 (Staughton LJ).

[60] *Demirkaya v Secretary of State for the Home Department* [1999] Imm AR 498 (EW CA) [18] (Stuart-Smith LJ), *Chan v Minister for Immigration and Ethnic Affairs* [1989] HCA 62 (Aus HC) [36] (Dawson J). See also for example *Minister for Immigration and Multicultural Affairs v Haji Ibrahim* [2000] HCA 55 (Kirby J): 'the notion of "systematic" conduct is a possible, but not a necessary element, in the idea of "persecution"'.

[61] Directive 2004/83/EC, Article 9(1)(a).

of 'ongoing' and 'systemic' in the sense of 'endemic to the political or social system'.[62] If there is no risk of future harm, the asylum applicant will be found to have no well-founded fear.

Some forms of harm will always therefore be sufficiently serious so as to amount to persecutory harm, such as torture or rape, although even then they may not be persecution for reasons of a Convention ground.[63] Other forms of harm will only conditionally amount to persecution. One such transformative condition might be persistence or repetition or, to put it another way, the cumulative impact. Cumulative impact might arise from repetition of the same form of harm persistently or repeatedly or from an accumulation of different measures. It is well established that persecution might arise from a variety of forms of harm which taken singly one by one are not in themselves so serious as to amount to persecution.[64]

Discrimination

Since the publication of Hathaway's *The Law of Refugee Status* in 1991, the focal point of academic and legal discussion of the refugee definition has tended to be the persecution component of the refugee definition.[65] Being persecuted is but one element of Article 1A(2) of the Refugee Convention, though. Discrimination has been said to be 'central to an understanding of the Convention'.[66] Such discrimination must be for one of five grounds, referred to as the Convention grounds or reasons: race, religion, nationality, membership of a particular social group or political opinion (see Chapter 5). David Cantor has argued that the refugee definition can and should be read with this concept of discrimination at its heart.[67] He advocates in favour of a model in which 'persecution is instead viewed as an exacerbated form of discrimination that follows from the making of unjust distinctions recognized by the Convention grounds'.

---

[62] Hathaway, J. and Foster, M. (2014) *The Law of Refugee Status* (2nd edn), Cambridge: Cambridge University Press, p 195.

[63] *Sepet v Secretary of State for the Home Department* [2001] EWCA Civ 681, [2001] Imm AR 452 [63] (Laws LJ).

[64] UNHCR, *Handbook on Procedures and Criteria for Determining Refugee Status and Guidelines on International Protection under the 1951 Convention and the 1967 Protocol Relating to the Status of Refugees*, HCR/1P/4/ENG/REV.4 (1979, reissued 2019) [53] and [55].

[65] Hathaway, J. (1991) *The Law of Refugee Status*, Toronto: Butterworths Canada.

[66] *R v Immigration Appeal Tribunal, ex p Shah* [1999] 2 AC 629 (UK HL) (Lord Hoffman).

[67] Cantor, D. (2016) 'Defining Refugees: Persecution, Surrogacy and the Human Rights Paradigm', in Cantor, D. and Burson, B. (eds) *Human Rights and the Refugee Definition: Comparative Legal Practice and Theory*, Leiden: Brill, p 391.

The requirement for discrimination on one of the five convention grounds acts to exclude many from refugee status but to include others. It excludes because even where a person fears harm that may be very serious, that person may not meet the criteria for protection:

> [n]o matter how devastating may be the epidemic, natural disaster or famine, a person fleeing them is not a refugee within the terms of the Convention. And by incorporating the five Convention reasons the Convention plainly contemplates that there will even be persons fearing persecution who will not be able to gain asylum as refugees.[68]

Discrimination on convention grounds may also operate to include, for example by transforming conduct from non-persecutory serious harm into persecution. Where a person faces imprisonment, for example, this may amount to being persecuted if done for a convention reason, whereas in other circumstances it may not.[69] The European Union's Qualification Directive recognizes the role of discrimination in defining some acts of persecution. Examples of conduct that might potentially amount to persecution include 'legal, administrative, police, and/or judicial measures which are in themselves discriminatory or which are implemented in a discriminatory manner', 'prosecution or punishment which is disproportionate or discriminatory' and 'denial of judicial redress resulting in a disproportionate or discriminatory punishment'.[70]

Discrimination is therefore perhaps best seen not so much as a potential form of 'being persecuted', as is suggested in the UNHCR Handbook but as a defining feature of, or at least an essential ingredient of, persecution.[71] Just as breaches of some human rights might become persecutory in nature if sustained or systemic, so breaches of human rights might become persecutory if done based on a convention ground. For example, even persistent denial of a trading licence or a professional practising certificate because of capriciousness or failure to pay a bribe is unlikely to amount to harm sufficiently serious to amount to persecution. But it might possibly do so if done because of the person's race, religion or other protected characteristic, particularly if combined with other discriminatory measures.

---

[68] *Applicant A v Minister for Immigration and Ethnic Affairs* [1997] HCA 4 (Aus HC) (Dawson J).
[69] See further Chapter 5 and *Sepet v Secretary of State for the Home Department* [2001] EWCA Civ 681, [2001] Imm AR 452 (Laws LJ).
[70] Directive 2011/95/EU, Article 9(2).
[71] UNHCR (1979) *Handbook and Guidelines on Procedures and Criteria for Determining Refugee Status under the 1951 Convention and the 1967 Protocol Relating to the Status of Refugees* (re-issued 2011) [54]-[55].

European Union Qualification Directive definition

The European Union's Qualification Directive definition of 'acts of persecution' successfully and concisely encapsulates many of the concepts elucidated over many years of jurisprudence in multiple jurisdictions. It has even been held out as 'a template for a universal working definition' of persecution.[72] One of its strengths arguably lies in the way it repeatedly appears to offer a clear, concise but also seemingly rigid definition before then going on to offer more malleable alternatives. This offers clarity but allows for flexibility. Where the directive does risk divergence from international comity, as for example in the way it defines 'membership of a particular social group' (see Chapter 5) and perhaps also 'acts of persecution', this is regrettable but not necessarily fatal given that it does not replace but adds to Refugee Convention obligations.[73] At the time of writing, most of this definition remained adopted into domestic legislation in the United Kingdom despite the departure from the European Union.[74]

The definition of 'acts of persecution' begins by stating such an act must 'be sufficiently serious by its nature or repetition as to constitute a severe violation of basic human rights, in particular, the rights from which derogation cannot be made under … the European Convention for the Protection of Human Rights and Fundamental Freedoms'.[75] The first words capture the universally recognized need for persecution to meet a certain level of seriousness. The definition immediately moves on to note that this might be through one-off acts or by repeated acts before then tying persecution firmly to the human rights standards. Problematically, though, it specifies that violations of human rights must be 'severe' (as well as being 'sufficiently serious by nature or repetition') and the rights in question must be the 'basic' ones; these requirements appear to require the kind of subdivision of what ought to be indivisible human rights discussed earlier in this chapter. This part of the definition cites 'in particular' the human rights from which derogation cannot be made under the European Convention on Human Rights (ECHR); this may not be ideal given that the ECHR is

---

[72] Storey, H. (2014) 'What Constitutes Persecution? Toward a Working Definition', *International Journal of Refugee Law*, 26(2): 272–285.

[73] Directive 2011/95/EC, Preamble [4] and [17] and Article 3 on more favourable standards; Joined Cases C-391/16, C-77/17 and C-78/17 *M v Czech Republic and others*.

[74] Refugee or Person in Need of International Protection (Qualification) Regulations 2006 (SI 2006/2525) (transposing the original not recast Directive 2004/83/EC), set at the time of writing to be replaced with broadly equivalent but slightly amended definitions by the Nationality and Borders Bill 2021.

[75] Directive 2011/95/EU, Article 9(1)(a).

regional, not international, but the use of the words 'in particular' can be read as offering these by way of illustration.

The next part of the definition states that in the alternative ('or') persecution might 'be an accumulation of various measures, including violations of human rights which is sufficiently severe as to affect an individual in a similar manner' as previously described.[76] This clause usefully makes explicit that persecution can be cumulative in nature while also, by using the word 'including', offering potential flexibility in the recognition of other forms of serious harm.

A list of examples of forms of harm that might amount to persecution is then offered.[77] As a closed list this would be objectionable, but it is not held out as exhaustive. The definition states that persecution 'can, *inter alia*, take the form of ...'. As illustrative examples, the list is a useful one and tends to expand rather than restrict understanding of what might amount to persecution. As well as physical violence, mental and sexual violence are specifically cited, as are 'acts of a gender-specific or child-specific nature'.[78] Examples of state action which might potentially amount to persecution are offered: 'legal, administrative, police, and/or judicial measures which are in themselves discriminatory or which are implemented in a discriminatory manner', 'prosecution or punishment which is disproportionate or discriminatory' and 'denial of judicial redress resulting in a disproportionate or discriminatory punishment'. The difficult issue of asylum claims based on refusal to perform military service is also addressed: 'prosecution or punishment for refusal to perform military service in a conflict, where performing military service would include crimes or acts falling within the scope of the grounds for exclusion'.

Finally, the definition ends by making clear that there must be a connection between either the acts of persecution as described or 'the absence of protection against such acts' and the Convention grounds, which are elucidated elsewhere in the directive.[79]

Examples of persecution

Having set out some of the differing approaches to identifying sufficiently serious harm – and therefore persecution – in principle, it is useful to examine how those principles have been applied in practice. What follows does not purport to define or delimit the concept of persecution, only to

---

[76] Directive 2011/95/EU, Article 9(1)(b).
[77] Directive 2011/95/EU, Article 9(2)(a)–(f).
[78] This last element was never explicitly transposed into United Kingdom law.
[79] Directive 2011/95/EU, Article 9(3).

describe ways in which the law has been stated or applied in the senior courts of some jurisdictions, generally in the Global North. There are also other reasons this exercise should not be regarded as a comprehensive one.

Firstly, the judgments of senior courts may not reflect the reality of how asylum assessors making the vast majority of refugee status determination decisions understand the concept of persecution. While the meaning of 'being persecuted' is a legal question and might therefore potentially be the subject of an appeal to a senior court on an error of law, there are numerous barriers to such appeals being brought. As well as procedural barriers, legal costs and the difficulties in accessing high-quality legal representation, the inherent flexibility of the concept of being persecuted imparts a degree of discretion to asylum assessors which serves to insulate their decisions from appeal. The issue may therefore not reach the senior courts for decision as often as might otherwise be expected. Similarly, though, the dearth of modern reported case law on certain key propositions of refugee law may well reflect the fact that these propositions are now considered uncontroversial. It takes two parties to make a court case, and state parties to the Refugee Convention may not on their domestic plane be contesting findings of what amounts to being persecuted.

Secondly, even where the senior courts have been able and willing to pronounce on the nature of persecution, there is a notable disjunct between what judges are willing to say in theory when the issue is not necessarily decisive in the instant case (referred to as '*obiter dicta*' or just '*obiter*') and what they are willing to find in practice when the issue becomes determinative of the outcome ('*ratio decidendi*' or just 'the *ratio*'). For example, in the early Australian case of *Chan*, McHugh J said that 'the denial of access to employment, to the professions and education or the imposition of restrictions on the freedoms traditionally guaranteed in a democratic society such as freedom of speech, assembly, worship or movement may constitute persecution if imposed for a Convention reason'.[80] This was one judgment of several in the case and the facts actually involved a risk of interrogation, detention and internal exile. Later reported cases in which denial of access to employment have been found to amount to being persecuted are, at best, rare. In another Australian case, *Chen*, the majority held that 'denial of access to food, shelter, medical treatment and, in the case of children, denial of an opportunity to obtain an education involve such a significant departure from the standards of the civilized world as to constitute persecution'.[81] The case has been cited for the proposition that denial of education may amount to being persecuted. But on the facts, the impact on the particular

---

[80] *Chan v Minister for Immigration and Ethnic Affairs* [1989] HCA 62 (Aus HC) [36].
[81] *Chen Shi Hai v Minister for Immigration and Multicultural Affairs* [2000] HCA 19 (Aus HC) [29].

child concerned appeared life-threatening. The comments on education can be read as *obiter* and therefore not setting a precedent. Again, it is unusual to find this principle applied in reported cases. The pattern of theory not being reflected in practice is a recurrent one when it comes to human rights standards. Cantor suggests that intuitive understanding of persecution continues *sotto voce* among many asylum assessors and that 'one can almost hear the old dictionary definitions ("pursue with malignancy" etc) echoing between the lines of judgments as decision makers strive to draw the dividing line on whether a particular form of human rights abuse constitutes persecution'.[82]

Returning to the brief survey exercise, the forms of harm that have been acknowledged as – or at least argued to potentially amount to – persecution are split here into direct physical harm, loss of liberty or freedom and infringement of personal autonomy or dignity. This classification is largely arbitrary, but some structure is needed here for pedagogical purposes. Further, it is a mistake to gradate forms of persecution because the degree of persecution is irrelevant to the refugee status enquiry. As Lord Justice Sedley has said, '[t]o say that particular ill-treatment falls towards the bottom end of the scale of what amounts to persecution is not, therefore, to say anything that matters legally'. Broadly speaking, direct serious physical harm will almost always amount to being persecuted, although it will not attract the protection of the Refugee Convention unless linked to a convention ground. Serious or sustained infringement of liberty and freedom will generally amount to persecution where it is linked to a convention ground. Serious or sustained infringement of personal autonomy or identity may amount to persecution where the consequences to the affected individual are grave and done for a convention reason. In reality, as discussed earlier in this chapter, the consequences will generally have to be so grave as to amount to inhuman or degrading treatment.

Physical harm

Arbitrary loss of life, the 'supreme right', will always be capable of amounting to persecution.[83] This is evident from the text of the Refugee Convention itself, which refers to a threat to 'life or freedom' at both Articles 31 and 33. Any person who can show a well-founded fear of being murdered or killed

---

[82] Cantor, D. (2016) 'Defining Refugees: Persecution, Surrogacy and the Human Rights Paradigm', in Cantor, D. and Burson, B. (eds) *Human Rights and the Refugee Definition: Comparative Legal Practice and Theory*, Leiden: Brill, pp 387, 395.

[83] Human Rights Committee (2019) *General Comment No. 36 on Article 6 of the International Covenant on Civil and Political Rights, on the Right to Life* (UN Doc CCPR/C/GC/36).

for a convention reason has therefore established a risk of being persecuted. This might arise where the state directly targets a person to kill or 'disappear' them or where non-state actors such as paramilitaries or private individuals do so in cases of political assassination, family murder, genocide and the infinite other descriptors for dealing death.

Where a person faces the death penalty pursuant to a final judgment made by a competent court, the situation may be more ambiguous. Article 6 of the ICCPR explicitly permits states to retain the death penalty for the most serious crimes. In Europe, 44 states have ratified or acceded to a protocol to the ECHR which abolishes the death penalty.[84] However, there is no widely agreed international consensus that imposition of the death penalty contravenes 'a right commanding international recognition'.[85] It cannot, therefore, be said that imposition of the death penalty of itself amounts to persecution. Imposition of the death penalty following a conviction for contravention of the law may lack the necessary connection to one of the convention grounds. As discussed in Chapter 5, this is because a person prosecuted, convicted and sentenced for committing a crime has not been targeted for reasons of their race, religion, nationality, membership of a particular social group or political opinion but because they broke the law. Such a case may turn on whether the law in question is one that conforms to international human rights law: a sentence of death for a minor political offence or contravention of a law prohibiting homosexuality or practice of a religion would amount to persecution whereas a sentence of death for committing a politically inspired murder would not.

Similarly, a well-founded fear of death due to very poor social and economic conditions will reach the threshold of serious harm but a causal link to a convention ground is required before the Refugee Convention is engaged. Whether the same is true where conditions are not so serious as to risk death but are argued to prevent the person from living an adequate life is contested, as discussed later. Similarly, exposure to an ongoing armed conflict will reach the threshold of serious harm but will only amount to persecution if there is a connection to a convention ground. In *Adan*, the House of Lords held that where a state of civil war exists and 'every group seems to be fighting some other groups or groups', a person must show a 'differential impact' for a convention reason over and above the general risks of the conflict.[86] The scope of this decision is controversial, however.[87]

---

[84] Protocol 13 on the death penalty and Article 3 on torture, inhuman or degrading treatment or punishment.

[85] *Sepet v Secretary of State for the Home Department* [2003] UKHL 15, [2003] 3 All ER 304 [18] (Lord Bingham).

[86] *R v Secretary of State for the Home Department, ex p Adan* [1999] 1 AC 293 (UK HL).

[87] See for example UNHCR, *Guidelines on International Protection No. 12 on Claims for Refugee Status Related to Situations of Armed Conflict and Violence under Article 1A(2) of the 1951*

The judgment arose from the situation in Somalia in the 1990s after the total collapse of the central government and the descent of the country into an anarchic clan-based conflict. Jurists have questioned whether the reasoning applies to a person who, if returned, would be a civilian targeted by combatants on an actual or perceived convention ground.[88] In a civil war where a central government retains some authority, it is hard to rationalize how members of a population group who are targeted for a convention reason, such as a racial or ethnic group, would not satisfy the criteria for refugee status. In the case of *Knezevic* in the United States, an appeals court drew a distinction between indiscriminate Luftwaffe bombing of London, which would not ground a claim to refugee status by a Londoner, and deliberate targeting of Jewish neighbourhoods on the Eastern Front, which would ground a claim to refugee status by a Jew.[89] Canadian jurisprudence accepts that a claim to refugee status may succeed based on even a generalized risk felt by all civilians, as long as it is linked to a convention ground and is not simply of indiscriminate violence.[90]

It is universally accepted that torture will always be sufficiently serious so as to be capable of being persecuted. Unlike the right to life, the right not to be subjected to torture or cruel, inhuman or degrading treatment or punishment (the formula of words used in the ICCPR) is absolute and unqualified. Torture is defined in the CAT as

> any act by which severe pain or suffering, whether physical or mental, is intentionally inflicted on a person for such purposes as obtaining from him or a third person information or a confession, punishing him for an act he or a third person has committed or is suspected of having committed, or intimidating or coercing him or a third person, or for any reason based on discrimination of any kind …[91]

The definition goes on to state that such an act must be inflicted 'by or at the instigation of or with the consent or acquiescence of a public official or other person acting in an official capacity' and that pain or suffering arising from lawful sanctions are excluded. However, neither of these provisos feature in the ICCPR or the ECHR and therefore should not be considered required

---

Convention and/or 1967 Protocol Relating to the Status of Refugees and the Regional Refugee Definitions, 2 December 2016, HCR/GIP/16/12 [23].

[88] See for example Symes, M. and Jorro, P. (2010) *Asylum Law and Practice* (2nd edn), Chippenham: Bloomsbury Professional, pp 155–159 and notes.

[89] *Knezevic v Ashcroft* 367 F3d 1206 (9th Cir 2004).

[90] *Saliban v Minister of Employment and Immigration* (Can FCA, 24 May 1990).

[91] UN Convention against Torture and Other Cruel, Inhuman or Degrading Treatment or Punishment, Article 1.

elements of torture. A special stigma is attached to torture as deliberate inhuman treatment causing very serious and cruel suffering.[92] While this can be very important in holding those responsible to account, in shifting norms of behaviour and offering some comfort or vindication to some victims, the distinction between torture and inhuman or degrading treatment or punishment matters little in refugee status claims. All these forms of harm are prohibited, all are considered to reach the threshold necessary to amount to serious harm and the Refugee Convention is not concerned with the culpability of the persecutor so much as the security of the persecuted.

A 'minimum level of severity' is necessary for harm to amount to torture or inhuman or degrading treatment or punishment and whether this threshold is reached 'depends on all the circumstances of the case, such as the duration of the treatment, its physical or mental effects and, in some cases, the sex, age and state of health of the victim, etc.'.[93] Although state responsibility is irrelevant to the refugee status enquiry, as discussed earlier, it is arguable that acts perpetrated by state officials (or others in a position of trust) have a more serious and pernicious character than acts carried out by non-state actors.[94] Warning against minimizing the effects of some forms of harm, Lord Justice Sedley has commented that 'brutality on the part of police officers is always unacceptable, and its repetition can amount to persecution'.[95] Similarly, physical harm inflicted on a detained person may, because of the person's vulnerable situation, have a more severe impact on a person than the same treatment meted out in a different context.[96] Physical assaults may amount to persecution, but this will depend on the severity, frequency and context, including the characteristics of the person affected. A single beating, unless it was particularly vicious or injurious, may not be considered sufficiently serious so as to qualify as being persecuted (although it might be said that it would be unusual for a future risk of a single, isolated beating to arise on the facts of a case).[97] It has sometimes been said that 'harassment' will amount to persecution, but other than suggesting an element of persistency of conduct this term is not especially revealing as to the type of harm

---

[92] *Aydin v Turkey* (1998) 25 EHRR 251 [82].

[93] *Ireland v United Kingdom* (1979–80) 2 EHRR 25 [162]; *Selmouni v France* (2000) 29 EHRR 403 [100].

[94] Yeo, C. (2002) 'Agents of State: When Is an Official of the State an Agent of the State?', *International Journal of Refugee Law*, 14(4): 509–533; McGlynn, C. (2009) 'Rape, Torture and the European Convention on Human Rights', *International and Comparative Law Quarterly*, 58(3): 565–595 at 574, 576–578.

[95] *Svazas v Secretary of State for the Home Department* [2002] EWCA Civ 74, [2002] WLR 1891 [38] (Sedley LJ).

[96] *Ribitsch v Austria* App. No. 18896/91, 4 December 1995 [36].

[97] *Demirkaya v Secretary of State for the Home Department* [1999] Imm AR 498 (EW CA) [19] (Stuart-Smith LJ).

involved.[98] 'Domestic violence' (violence within the home often inflicted by men on women or children) may also meet the threshold of severity for persecution.[99]

Rape, which has been defined for international law purposes as 'a physical invasion of a sexual nature, committed on a person under circumstances which are coercive', has been recognized as torture.[100] Without a doubt rape is also persecution.[101] Female genital mutilation has been recognized as a form of being persecuted, albeit somewhat belatedly in some jurisdictions.[102] Forced sterilization or forced abortion also amount to persecution, as might other forced medical procedures.[103] It has been widely acknowledged that other gender-specific forms of harm such as forced marriage may be persecutory.[104] It is more straightforward to analyze forced marriage as persecution where it is induced by actual or threatened violence and consent is thereby clearly and completely vitiated but a forced marriage induced by social or familial pressure may also potentially amount to persecution.

Threats of harm may constitute being persecuted, for example where the threats suggest there is a real risk of their being carried out in future or where the threats themselves are 'something extraordinarily ominous' or cause serious psychological harm.[105] This may be more likely to arise for vulnerable individuals or in cases of 'indirect persecution' or 'persecution by proxy' involving threats against a loved one or family member.[106]

Liberty and freedom

Loss or infringement of liberty or freedom may, depending on the circumstances, amount to being persecuted. The Refugee Convention

---

[98] See for example *Chan v Minister for Immigration and Ethnic Affairs* [1989] HCA 62 (Aus HC) [11] (Mason CJ).
[99] *R v Immigration Appeal Tribunal, ex p Shah* [1999] 2 AC 629 (UK HL).
[100] Case No. ICTR–96-4-T, *Prosecutor v Jean-Paul Akayesu* (2 September 1998) [597]–[598]. See also *Aydin v Turkey* (1998) 25 EHRR 251 [86].
[101] *Hoxha v Secretary of State for the Home Department* [2005] UKHL 19, [2005] WLR 1063 [36] (Baroness Hale); *Fornah v Secretary of State for the Home Department* [2006] UKHL 46, [2007] 1 AC 412 [87] (Baroness Hale).
[102] *In re Kasinga* (1996) 21 I & N Dec 357; *Fornah v Secretary of State for the Home Department* [2006] UKHL 46, [2007] 1 AC 412; *IAM (on behalf of KYM) v Denmark* Communication No. 3/2016 (UN Doc CRC/C/77/D/3/2016), 25 January 2018.
[103] See for example *Chan v Canada* [1995] 3 SCR 593 (Can SC) and *Applicant A v Minister for Immigration and Ethnic Affairs* [1997] HCA 4 (Aus HC).
[104] *AM and BM (Trafficked women) Albania CG* [2010] UKUT 80 (IAC) [171] and Hathaway, J. and Foster, M. (2014) *The Law of Refugee Status* (2nd edn), Cambridge: Cambridge University Press, pp 221–224 and notes.
[105] *Pathmakanthan v Holder* (2010) 612 F3d 618.
[106] *Katrinak v Secretary of State for the Home Department* [2001] EWCA Civ 832 [22] and [23].

specifically cites a threat to 'life or freedom' as examples of harm a refugee might have fled.[107] The convention grounds have a particularly important role to play in this context, as further discussed in Chapter 5. In short, not all interferences with liberty or freedom are inherently persecutory. A sentence of imprisonment following a fair trial and conviction for committing an internationally recognized criminal offence is not persecution, for example. In some cases, whether the loss of liberty is carried out in accordance with the law will indicate whether it is persecutory in nature. Where the law in question does not comply with international human rights law standards – for example where laws discriminate on convention grounds against a race, religion or other protected group – then loss of liberty in accordance with such a law may well be persecutory. Prosecution and persecution are not mutually exclusive: if the harm is for reasons of one of the convention grounds then this can have what Lord Justice Laws described as a transformative effect and render such treatment persecutory.[108] Detention can be sufficiently serious so as to amount to persecution but even where a convention ground is engaged this depends on the circumstances. A loss of liberty so severe as to amount to 'a catastrophic destruction of ... autonomy as a human being' will reach the threshold but is not required for that threshold to be crossed.[109] Short periods of detention for the purpose of preventing or dealing with terrorism – a purpose for which derogation from the right to liberty and security of the person is permissible – may not, however.[110] Hathaway and Foster argue that a formal state derogation on grounds of national emergency from the relevant rights should be necessary if such conduct is not to amount to being persecuted, but this is not currently the prevalent approach in case law.[111] Instead, the courts prefer to apply a qualitative judgment, which will include 'an evaluation of the nature and gravity of the loss of liberty' and the impact on the individual, taking into account that individual's personal characteristics and any particular vulnerabilities.[112] In practice, loss of liberty may also be accompanied by a risk of other forms of harm. Where country information

---

[107] Refugee Convention, Articles 31 and 33.
[108] *Sepet v Secretary of State for the Home Department* [2001] EWCA Civ 681, [2001] Imm AR 452 [65].
[109] *Minister for Immigration and Border Protection v WZAPN* [2015] HCA 22 [44]. The case arose in the specific context of interpreting the Australian domestic statutory definition of 'serious harm' in the Migration Act 1958 but is probably of wider application.
[110] *Velluppillai v Canada (Minister of Citizenship and Immigration)* [2000] FCJ No. 301; *R (on the application of Sivakumuran) v Secretary of State for the Home Department* [1988] AC 958 (UK HL); *Pathmakanthan v Holder* (2010) 612 F3d 618.
[111] Hathaway, J. and Foster, M. (2014) *The Law of Refugee Status* (2nd edn), Cambridge: Cambridge University Press, pp 241–243.
[112] *Minister for Immigration and Border Protection v WZAPN* [2015] HCA 22 (Aus HC) [45].

suggests a real risk of detainees or detained suspects as a class being subjected to police brutality, torture or very poor detention conditions, this will amount to being persecuted.[113] Internal exile to a remote location at pain of imprisonment for escape has been found to constitute persecution when done for a convention reason.[114]

All stages of the normal criminal justice process of investigation, arrest, detention, interrogation, prosecution, conviction and sentence might singly or collectively amount to being persecuted. Again, this depends on whether there is a link to a convention ground and on the circumstances. Repeated arrests pursuant to a law forbidding the practice of a given religion which have the effect of preventing collective worship be a form of persecution, for example.[115] Occasional arrest and release without charge for attending political demonstrations might not, at least without more.

It is not just arrest and detention which might negate a person's liberty. Slavery and servitude in all their forms are potentially persecutory, including forced or compulsory labour and trafficking for the purpose of exploitation (see Chapter 1 in relation to trafficking). This is an absolute right from which derogation in times of emergency cannot be made, although some forms of mandated activity such as military service and prison labour are excluded from its scope. Slavery is defined in the Slavery Convention 1926 as 'the status or condition of a person over whom any or all of the powers attaching to the right of ownership are exercised' and this definition has been adopted and applied in modern case law.[116] Servitude has been defined as 'an obligation to provide one's services that is imposed by the use of coercion, and is to be linked with the concept of slavery'.[117] A person forced to perform domestic service for 15 hours a day with no time off or pay for several years has been found to be in a condition of servitude, for example.[118] The question of exercise of control in the context of domestic servitude 'involves a complex set of dynamics, involving both overt and more subtle forms of coercion, to force compliance'.[119] Similarly, a worker will not be considered to be offering to work voluntarily 'where an employer abuses his power or takes advantage of the vulnerability of his workers in order to exploit

---

[113] For example *Thirunavukkarasu Canada (Minister of Employment and Immigration)* [1994] 1 FC 589.

[114] *Chan v Minister for Immigration and Ethnic Affairs* [1989] HCA 62 (Aus HC).

[115] For example *Pathmakanthan v Holder* (2010) 612 F3d 618 [11]-[12].

[116] *Siliadin v France* (2006) 43 EHRR 16 [122].

[117] *Seguin v France* App. No. 42400/98 (ECHR, 7 March 2000); *Siliadin v France* (2006) 43 EHRR 16 [124].

[118] *Siliadin v France* (2006) 43 EHRR 16.

[119] *CN v United Kingdom* App. No. 4239/08 (ECHR, 13 November 2012) [80].

them' and 'the prior consent of the victim is not sufficient to exclude the characterisation of work as forced labour'.[120]

Dignity and autonomy

There is a broad and long-standing theoretical consensus that violation of human dignity amounts to, or at least is capable of amounting to, persecution. Paul Weis proposed in 1960 that 'other measures in disregard of human dignity may also constitute persecution'.[121] Goodwin-Gill surveyed the refugee law landscape in 1983 and wrote that 'the notion of individual integrity and human dignity' has to be considered alongside 'the manner and degree to which they stand to be injured'.[122] Hathaway argued in 1991 that 'refugee law ought to concern itself with actions which deny human dignity in any key way, and that the sustained or systemic denial of human rights is the appropriate standard'.[123] Similar formulations can be found in key cases internationally. Baroness Hale has referred to 'cumulative denial of human dignity which to my mind is quite capable of amounting to persecution'.[124] Lord Collins held that 'an affront to internationally accepted human rights norms, and in particular the core values of privacy, equality and dignity' will amount to persecution.[125] Lord Dyson, citing earlier cases, said that '[t]he right to dignity is the foundation of all the freedoms protected by the Convention'.[126] McHugh J found that conduct 'which constitutes an interference with the basic human rights or dignity of that person or the persons in the group' and 'which is so oppressive or likely to be repeated or maintained that the person threatened cannot be expected to tolerate it' constitutes persecution.[127] Human rights and the idea of human dignity are intimately related, with Article 1 of the Universal Declaration of Human Rights declaring 'All human beings are born free and equal in dignity and rights'. There is, however, no consensus in practice on what amounts to

---

[120] *Chowdury and Others v Greece* App. No. 21884/15 (ECHR, 30 March 2017) [96].
[121] Weiss, P. (1960) 'The Concept of Refugee in International Law', *Journal du Droit International*, 4: 928–1001, HCR/INF/49, cited by various.
[122] Goodwin-Gill, G. (1983) *The Refugee in International Law*, Oxford: Oxford University Press, p 40.
[123] Hathaway, J. (1991) *The Law of Refugee Status*, Toronto: Butterworths Canada, p 108.
[124] *Fornah v Secretary of State for the Home Department* [2006] UKHL 46, [2007] 1 AC 412 [36].
[125] *HJ (Iran) v Secretary of State for the Home Department* [2010] UKSC 31, [2011] 1 AC 596 [101].
[126] *RT (Zimbabwe) v Secretary of State for the Home Department* [2012] UKSC 38, [2013] 1 AC 152 [39].
[127] *Minister for Immigration and Multicultural Affairs v Haji Ibrahim* [2000] HCA 55 (Aus HC) [65].

a sufficiently serious violation of human dignity. Here we see reach the contested limits of the linkage between human rights and persecution.

The right to hold and express a political opinion and the right of association are protected in international human rights law.[128] For many, the archetypical refugee is a political refugee, a person who flees their home country because their political activities have endangered them with the ruling regime. The Refugee Convention specifically cites political opinion as one of the potential grounds for refugee status. It is therefore consistent with the purpose of the Refugee Convention and with international human rights law to conclude that a breach of the right to hold or express a political opinion (or to hold or express no political opinion) will amount to being persecuted.[129] If a person is arrested and imprisoned under a law prohibiting membership of a political party, this would generally be considered an example of being persecuted, for example. There is no clear authority to the effect that a breach of this right short of a threat of physical harm or loss of liberty would amount to being persecuted for example by closing down meetings, closing down printing presses or websites or other means by which political views might be expressed.[130] Criminalization alone is not considered to amount to persecution without some sort of enforcement.[131] In reality, such interference will usually have to be carried out by means of physical force, meaning the hypothetical question rarely if ever arises.

Like political opinion, the right to freedom of thought, conscience and religion is protected by international human rights law and specifically cited by the Refugee Convention as one of the protected grounds. And as with political opinion, there is no clear authority to the effect that breach of this right amounts to persecution without there also being a threat of physical harm or loss of liberty. Interferences with expressions of opinion which might lead to public violence might be justified by reference to the maintenance of public order, for example, and might therefore not amount to persecution.[132] In practice, most religious persecution cases do involve restrictions on religious freedom enforced by imprisonment and by violence. Thus, restrictions on the practice of Falun Gong enforced violently

---

[128] See for example Universal Declaration of Human Rights, Articles 18 and 19; International Covenant on Civil and Political Rights, Articles 18 and 19; European Convention on Human Rights, Articles 9 and 10.

[129] On political opinion including the right to apathy, see *RT (Zimbabwe) v Secretary of State for the Home Department* [2012] UKSC 38.

[130] *RT (Zimbabwe) v Secretary of State for the Home Department* [2012] UKSC 38, [2013] 1 AC 152 [50]; *WA (Pakistan) v Secretary of State for the Home Department* [2019] EWCA Civ 302 [48].

[131] Joined Cases C-199/12, C-200/12, and C-201/12 *Netherlands v X, Y and Z*.

[132] *WA (Pakistan) v Secretary of State for the Home Department* [2019] EWCA Civ 302 [47].

by local officials in China, measures pursued against Christian converts or Baha'i enforced by central government in Iran and prevention of Ahmadi proselytizing in Pakistan enforced by a combination of legal sanctions backed by imprisonment or death and unofficial but state-sanctioned violence have all been held to amount to persecution.[133] Judges have been reluctant to go further. The United Kingdom's immigration tribunal has stated that it did not accept 'that there can be acts which are so restrictive of the practice of religion that the intrinsic severity of the restriction itself is enough to amount to persecution regardless of the consequences'.[134] Examples can nevertheless be found of cases in which it has been said in passing that imprisonment or physical violence are not requisite.[135] The Court of Justice of the European Union judgment in *Y and Z*, concerning the treatment of Ahmadis in Pakistan, is more typical.[136] The court accepted in theory that interference with freedom of religion could amount to persecution (paragraph 57) but went on to hold that only a 'severe violation' having 'significant effect' on the person concerned would do so (paragraph 59), determined by 'the severity of the measures and sanctions adopted or liable to be adopted against the person concerned' (paragraph 66). Ultimately, the court concluded that 'where an applicant for asylum, as a result of exercising that freedom in his country of origin, runs a genuine risk of, *inter alia*, being prosecuted or subject to inhuman or degrading treatment or punishment' (paragraph 67). The use of the words '*inter alia*' preserves the possibility that breaches of freedom of religion might themselves amount to persecution, but the court clearly envisages and encourages focus on consequences of prosecution or violence, or at least treatment that is so bad that it would in any event amount to inhuman or degrading treatment or punishment. The approach corresponds with that of the United Kingdom's House of Lords and the European Court of Human Rights on the issue of human rights and *refoulement*.[137]

---

[133] *L (China) v Secretary of State for the Home Department* [2004] EWCA Civ 1441 [33]; *PS (Christianity – risk) Iran CG* [2020] UKUT 46 (IAC); *SH (Baha'is) Iran CG* [2006] UKAIT 00041; *MN and others (Ahmadis – country conditions – risk) Pakistan CG* [2012] UKUT 389 (IAC).

[134] *MN and others (Ahmadis – country conditions – risk) Pakistan CG* [2012] UKUT 389 (IAC) [99].

[135] *Bucur* (USCA, 7th Cir, 1997); *Wang v Minister for Immigration and Multicultural Affairs* [2000] FCA 1599; *Kazatkine v Canada (Minister of Citizenship and Immigration)* (1996) 111 FTR 127.

[136] Joined Cases C-71/11 and C-99/11 *Germany v Y and Z*.

[137] See further Chapter 1 and *Ullah and Do* 2 AC 323, [2004] UKHL 26; *EM (Lebanon) v Secretary of State for the Home Department* [2008] UKHL 64, [2009] 1 AC 1198; *Othman v United Kingdom* App. No. 8139/09 [2012] 55 EHRR 1.

Denial of the right to work or earn a livelihood offers a further example.[138] Such cases might potentially be analyzed through the lens of human rights. The International Covenant of Economic, Social and Cultural Rights protects 'the right to work, which includes the right of everyone to the opportunity to gain his living by work'.[139] A single incidence of denial of a particular form of work or loss of a particular job is unlikely to amount to being persecuted but ongoing, persistent and serious denial of that right might cross the threshold. Thus, total economic proscription or blacklisting 'so severe as to deprive a person of all means of earning a livelihood' is likely to amount to being persecuted, although findings of fact to this effect are vanishingly rare in refugee law jurisprudence.[140] Other lesser forms of interference with the right to earn a livelihood could potentially amount to being persecuted. The UNHCR Handbook suggests that 'serious restrictions on [a person's] right to earn his livelihood' might amount to persecution, for example, and advocates taking a cumulative view of such measures.[141] In some early refugee law cases, discriminatory denial of access to certain forms of employment was been found to constitute persecution where it left the person concerned reliant on demeaning work or at least on unskilled work when the person is highly qualified.[142] Michelle Foster observes that issues of class bias on the part of asylum assessors may arise in this context.[143]

Cases involving other issues of fundamental identity, such as sexuality, offer a possible but ambiguous glimpse of breaches of human rights amounting to persecution without the threat of physical harm or loss of liberty. It is widely agreed that where a person will be forced to suppress or conceal their sexual identity for fear of being persecuted, the person is a refugee.[144]

---

[138] *Xie v Canada (Minister of Employment and Immigration)* (1994) 75 FTR 125; *Chan v Minister for Immigration and Ethnic Affairs* [1989] HCA 62 (Aus HC) [36] (McHugh J); see further Hathaway, J. and Foster, M. (2014) *The Law of Refugee Status* (2nd edn), Cambridge: Cambridge University Press, pp 252–260 and Symes, M. and Jorro, P. (2010) *Asylum Law and Practice* (2nd edn), Chippenham: Bloomsbury Professional, p 150 n 2 for reviews of what authorities there are.

[139] Article 6(1).

[140] Grahl-Madsen, A. (1966) *The Status of Refugees in International Law (Vol. I)*, Cambridge: Cambridge University Press, p 208.

[141] UNHCR, *Handbook on Procedures and Criteria for Determining Refugee Status and Guidelines on International Protection under the 1951 Convention and the 1967 Protocol Relating to the Status of Refugees*, HCR/1P/4/ENG/REV.4 (1979, reissued 2019) [53]-[55].

[142] *Prahastono* (Aus FC 1997); *Ye Hong v Minister for Immigration and Multicultural Affairs* [1998] FCA 1356; *He v Canada (Minister of Employment and Immigration)* (1994) 78 FTR 313.

[143] Foster, M. (2007) *International Refugee Law and Socio-Economic Rights: Refuge from Deprivation*, Cambridge: Cambridge University Press, p 102.

[144] *Appellant S395/2002 v Minister for Immigration and Multicultural Affairs* [2003] HCA 71 (Aus HC); *HJ (Iran) v Secretary of State for the Home Department* [2010] UKSC 31, [2011] 1 AC 596.

On one analysis, it is the suppression or concealment which itself constitutes the persecution, a form of 'self-oppression'.[145] This can be held out as an example of the human rights analysis of persecution in action if it rests on breaches of the protected rights to privacy and equality from which the state is unable or unwilling to protect the person concerned.[146] But it may instead be analyzed as self-oppression amounting to inhuman and degrading treatment. Or, on yet another analysis, the claim to refugee status may succeed because there is an independent risk of external persecution, such as prosecution, harassment or violence, and the person concerned has a well-founded fear of that persecution for reasons of their identity and who they are.[147] The different approaches lead to the same point but by different paths.

Two further examples of breaches of human rights widely considered to amount to being persecuted offer an illustration in practice of how the apparently different approaches are in truth synchronized. It is widely accepted that deprivation of nationality can amount to persecution. This has been framed as the loss of 'the right to have rights' and with reference to international human rights instruments protecting the right not to be arbitrarily deprived of nationality.[148] Discriminatory denial of education to a child also appears to be widely considered to amount to being persecuted, although clear findings to that effect in individual cases are unusual, as discussed earlier. It seems likely that arbitrary deprivation of nationality or discriminatory denial of education would both be considered to amount to inhuman and degrading treatment or punishment. But this misses the point: the fact these rights are enshrined in international human rights law offers a guide as to what is considered inhuman and degrading. It is not that treatment must reach some independent threshold of inhuman or degrading treatment but rather that breaches of protected human rights may well be inhuman and degrading.

Suggested further reading

Cantor, D. (2016) 'Defining Refugees: Persecution, Surrogacy and the Human Rights Paradigm', in Cantor, D. and Burson, B. (eds) *Human Rights and the Refugee Definition: Comparative Legal Practice and Theory*, Leiden: Brill.

---

[145] *National Coalition for Gay and Lesbian Equality v Minister of Justice* 1999 (1) SA 6 [130] (Sachs J).

[146] See *Refugee Appeal No: 74665* [2004] NZRSAA 228 [113]–[115].

[147] See *Appellant S395/2002 v Minister for Immigration and Multicultural Affairs* [2003] HCA 71 (Aus HC) [53] (McHugh and Kirby JJ) and [83] (Gummow and Hayne JJ); *HJ (Iran) v Secretary of State for the Home Department* [2010] UKSC 31, [2011] 1 AC 596 [82] (Lord Rodger).

[148] *EB (Ethiopia) v Secretary of State for the Home Department* [2007] EWCA Civ 809, [2009] QB 1.

Foster, M. (2007) *International Refugee Law and Socio-Economic Rights: Refuge from Deprivation*, Cambridge: Cambridge University Press, Chapters 3 and 4.

Goodwin-Gill, G. and McAdam, J. (2021) *The Refugee in International Law* (4th edn), Oxford: Oxford University Press, Chapter 3.

Hathaway, J. and Foster, M. (2014) *The Law of Refugee Status* (2nd edn), Cambridge: Cambridge University Press, Chapter 3.

UNHCR, *Handbook on Procedures and Criteria for Determining Refugee Status and Guidelines on International Protection under the 1951 Convention and the 1967 Protocol Relating to the Status of Refugees*, HCR/1P/4/ENG/REV.4 (1979, reissued 2019), [51]-[65].

Chan v Minister for Immigration and Ethnic Affairs [1989] HCA 62 (Aus HC).

R v Immigration Appeal Tribunal, ex p Shah [1999] 2 AC 629 (UK HL).

Horvath v Secretary of State for the Home Department [2001] AC 489 (UK HL).

4

Protection and Relocation

Refugees have long been regarded as 'unprotected persons'. In the interwar period, absence of national protection was considered the key defining characteristic of a refugee in international law.[1] Even as other qualifying requirements for refugee status began to emerge before, during and immediately after the Second World War, the absence of protection remained central to the various refugee definitions. It was only when the Refugee Convention was agreed that the issue of protection was, on the face of it, relegated to the second part of the definition of a refugee in Article 1A(1):

> … and is unable or owing to such fear, is unwilling to avail himself of the protection of that country; or who, not having a nationality and being outside the country of his former habitual residence is unable or, owing to such fear, unwilling to return to it.

For a stateless refugee, though, it can be seen that refugee status is about inability or unwillingness to return, not the absence of protection as such. The language of protection also arises in the cessation clauses at Article 1C. Where a person voluntarily avails themselves of the protection of their country of nationality or acquires a new nationality and enjoys the protection of that country, then a person ceases to be a refugee.[2] Similarly, a person loses his refugee status if he 'can no longer, because the circumstances in connexion with which he has been recognized as a refugee have ceased to exist, continue to refuse to avail himself of the protection of the country of his nationality'.[3] As with Article 1A(1), for a stateless person, cessation of status turns on re-establishment in the country the person left or is outside or where circumstances have changed and they are able to return.[4]

---

[1] See Introduction.
[2] Refugee Convention, Article 1C(1) and (3) respectively.
[3] Refugee Convention, Article 1C(5).
[4] Refugee Convention, Article 1C(4) and (6) respectively.

The alternative wordings applicable to stateless refugees, who must show inability or unwillingness to return, seems to disrupt the idea that modern refugee status is all about protection: there is no explicit reference in the definition to protection for a stateless refugee. This might therefore be considered to call into question the conceptualization of the Refugee Convention as an instrument of international surrogate protection triggered by a failure of national protection.[5] Three distinct but potentially overlapping routes to reconciling the text of the convention with the near-universal acknowledgement that absence of protection is a defining feature of refugeehood. One is to regard the concept of persecution from the first part of the refugee definition as incorporating not only a notion of serious harm but also a failure of state protection.[6] Another is to interpret the word 'protection' in Article 1A(2) as meaning external diplomatic or consular protection abroad rather than internal protection within the country concerned, something which is self-evidently unavailable to a stateless person.[7] The last is to read the effectiveness of protection into the requirement that a fear be well-founded.[8] A number of issues arise from these rationalizations: what does 'protection' mean, who might provide the protection in question, what are the implications for non-state persecution, what degree of failure of protection is necessary before the Refugee Convention is engaged and whether protection might be considered to be available elsewhere in the country concerned. Unlike the broad (if hazy) degree of unanimity on the degree of serious harm considered necessary to reach the threshold of 'being persecuted', answers to questions of protection and relocation significantly differ between national jurisdictions.

Dual and multiple nationality

The second paragraph of Article 1A(2) of the Refugee Convention states:

> In the case of a person who has more than one nationality, the term 'the country of his nationality' shall mean each of the countries of

---

[5] Cantor, D. (2016) 'Defining Refugees: Persecution, Surrogacy and the Human Rights Paradigm', in Cantor, D. and Burson, B. (eds) *Human Rights and the Refugee Definition: Comparative Legal Practice and Theory*, Leiden: Brill.
[6] See preceding chapter and Lord Hoffman's famous dictum in *R v Immigration Appeal Tribunal, ex p Shah*: Persecution = Serious Harm + Failure of State Protection.
[7] Fortin, A. (2000) 'The Meaning of "Protection" in the Refugee Definition', *International Journal of Refugee Law*, 12(4): 548–576.
[8] Wilsher, D. (2003) 'Non-State Actors and the Definition of a Refugee in the United Kingdom: Protection, Accountability or Culpability?', *International Journal of Refugee Law*, 15(1): 68–112.

which he is a national, and a person shall not be deemed to be lacking the protection of the country of his nationality if, without any valid reason based on well-founded fear, he has not availed himself of the protection of one of the countries of which he is a national.

The meaning appears clear: where a person is persecuted in one country and holds the nationality of one or more other countries, the person is not entitled to refugee status in a third country unless the person can show a well-founded fear of being persecuted there as well. They have no need of the surrogate protection of the international community. As UNHCR put it, '[w]herever available, national protection takes precedence over international protection'.[9] The provision is framed in the present tense and applies only to the nationality of an internationally recognized country.[10]

Difficulties can arise in cases where it is not clear whether a person does or does not hold a relevant nationality. This question is to be determined by the laws of the country of which nationality is asserted. However, the meaning and effect of these laws may not be straightforward to decipher in practice. A court will have to form a judgment based on expert evidence and, if necessary, its own reading of the relevant foreign law.[11] In some cases, it may be abundantly clear that a person holds a given nationality, for example where they hold or held a valid passport for the relevant country or are otherwise clearly and expressly accepted to be a national by the country concerned. In other situations, the nationality laws of the country may be unclear or may appear to render the person a national but this interpretation may not be accepted by the country concerned. A risk might then arise that the person could be sent to the country of supposed nationality but then *refouled* to the country in which they were persecuted.[12] A person may not hold the nationality of a country at the present time but be eligible to claim that nationality as of right, a situation sometimes described as 'inchoate' nationality. Or a person may not hold the nationality of a country but might be eligible to make a discretionary application, meaning an application which might be refused at the discretion of the country concerned.

As a matter of plain language and plain law, a person who could apply for a nationality but has not yet done so is not a national of a

---

[9] UNHCR, *Handbook on Procedures and Criteria for Determining Refugee Status and Guidelines on International Protection under the 1951 Convention and the 1967 Protocol Relating to the Status of Refugees*, HCR/1P/4/ENG/REV.4 (1979, reissued 2019) [106].
[10] *Tjhe Kwet Koe v Minister for Immigration* [1997] FCA 912; *Saber v Secretary of State for the Home Department* [2003] ScotCS 360, [2004] INLR 222.
[11] *Pham v Secretary of State for the Home Department* [2015] UKSC 19, [2015] 1 WLR 1591.
[12] *Jong Kim Koe v Minister for Immigration* [1997] FCA 306.

country.¹³ This is irrespective of whether an application is as of right or discretionary but is particularly important where the application is a discretionary one which might be refused.¹⁴ Nevertheless, case law to the contrary has developed in some countries, particularly Canada.¹⁵ It has also been suggested that a nationality must be 'effective' for refugee status to be refused on the basis a person can turn to another country for protection.¹⁶ While this would be a useful protection and is consistent with the Refugee Convention acting as surrogate international protection, there is no real basis for this approach in nationality law nor on the face of the Refugee Convention.

Internal or external protection

A refugee must be unable or, owing to their well-founded fear of being persecuted, unwilling to avail themselves of the protection of their country of nationality or, in the case of a stateless person, return to their country of former habitual residence. Despite the fact that for the stateless refugee the issue is one of return, this has sometimes been characterized as the 'protection test'. The different wording applicable to refugees with and without a nationality hints at what today seems an esoteric meaning to the word 'protection' in Article 1A(2): diplomatic or consular protection. This is sometimes referred to as 'external protection', in contrast to 'internal protection' within the country of origin. It refers to the enforcement of individual rights in the country of refuge through the medium of the assistance of the country of nationality. Refugees were first defined by reference to the absence of this external protection by international agreements in the interwar years.¹⁷ International law concerned relations between states; indeed it was often referred to as the law of nations. In an era before the idea even emerged of universal human rights derived from international conventions enforceable by individuals, a person was considered to derive their rights from their relationship with their country of nationality.

---

[13] *Secretary of State for the Home Department v Al-Jedda* [2013] UKSC 62, [2014] AC 253. See also Fripp, E. (2016) *Nationality and Statelessness in the International Law of Refugee Status*, London: Hart, pp 198–205.
[14] *Katkova v Minister of Citizenship and Immigration* (1997) 130 FTR 192 concerning the Israeli law of right of return.
[15] See *Minister of Citizenship and Immigration v Williams* [2005] FCA 126.
[16] UNHCR, *Handbook on Procedures and Criteria for Determining Refugee Status and Guidelines on International Protection under the 1951 Convention and the 1967 Protocol Relating to the Status of Refugees*, HCR/1P/4/ENG/REV.4 (1979, reissued 2019) [107].
[17] Skran, C. (1995) *Refugees in Inter-War Europe: The Emergence of a Regime*, Oxford: Oxford University Press, pp 109–110.

Solutions to the condition of a refugee, therefore, focused on their lack of these juridical rights, such as the right to a passport to enable travel or recognition of marriage, wills, property rights and similar, because their country of origin refused to assist them abroad. The Refugee Convention built upon pre-war understanding and, as one of the first treaties agreed under the emerging post-war international law regime, was transitional. One foot of the refugee definition rests in the past, but the other stepped somewhat hesitantly forward into the new era. The reference to protection in Article 1A(2) of the Refugee Convention was therefore very likely to have been understood by the drafters and signatories to be to external protection.[18] In a modern context, this seems a strange determinant of refugee status, particularly given that a repressive state might be willing to extend consular services to a person while they remain abroad and yet wish to persecute them if they were to return to the country concerned.

The rules of treaty interpretation provide that 'a special meaning shall be given to a term if it is established that the parties so intended'.[19] While the drafters and early signatories of the Refugee Convention may have *assumed* that the word 'protection' meant 'external protection', it is far from clear that they *intended* the meaning to be forever limited in this way. Treaties must also be interpreted 'in accordance with the ordinary meaning to be given to the terms of the treaty in their context and in the light of its object and purpose' and 'subsequent practice in the application of the treaty' should also be considered.[20] As discussed in the Introduction, the Refugee Convention is widely perceived today as being an instrument of surrogate international protection which becomes available to a person only if protection within their own country of origin is unavailable. Further, the Refugee Convention is regarded as a 'living instrument in the sense that while its meaning does not change over time its application will'.[21] It is now almost universally accepted by academic commentators and in international case law that the concept of protection in the Refugee Convention includes internal protection within the country of origin of the refugee as well as, or even instead of, external protection.[22] There is disagreement about precisely how this reading of the

---

[18] Fortin, A. (2000) 'The Meaning of "Protection" in the Refugee Definition', *International Journal of Refugee Law*, 12(4): 548–576; Kälin, W. (2001) 'Non-State Agents of Persecution and the Inability of the State to Protect', *Georgetown Immigration Law Journal*, 15(3): 415–431.

[19] Vienna Convention on the Law of Treaties 1969, Article 31(4).

[20] Vienna Convention on the Law of Treaties 1969, Article 31(1) and (2)(b).

[21] *Sepet v Secretary of State for the Home Department* [2003] UKHL 15, [2003] 3 All ER 304 (Lord Bingham) [6].

[22] Hathaway, J. and Foster, M. (2014) *The Law of Refugee Status* (2nd edn), Cambridge: Cambridge University Press, pp 332–335; Goodwin-Gill, G. and McAdam, J. (2021) *The*

convention is achieved, though. The methodology matters because it can have important real-world consequences for those seeking asylum.

One potential drawback of the more modern, inclusive interpretation of protection is that, on a literal reading of the Refugee Convention, the issue of protection may potentially recur in the first and second parts of the refugee definition. Availability of protection can be factored into consideration of whether fear of persecution is well-founded. In short, if there is effective state protection available, then the fear might be said not to be well-founded because the risk of the harm occurring is reduced. This approach has the advantage of using the Refugee Convention's own well-founded fear standard to establish the adequacy or effectiveness of the protection.[23] Another way forward is to understand the concept of being persecuted as including a failure of state protection, the bifurcated approach advocated by Hathaway and adopted in cases including *Horvath* in the United Kingdom.[24] This analysis has sometimes led to focus on the issue of state responsibility and even to the expropriation from human rights law of the standard of due diligence, a concept otherwise alien to refugee law.[25] If either of these approaches is adopted then, at least for a refugee who is not stateless, the issue of availability of protection appears to arise again, separately, in the second part of the definition with the reference to unwillingness or inability to avail oneself of the protection of one's own country. One solution is to read this second part of the refugee definition as referring to internal protection, in the sense of 'protection elsewhere' within the country of origin.[26] The Australian High Court had adopted another way forward but one which potentially causes a more serious problem than it purports to solve. In *Khawar*, persecution was understood as including the absence of internal state protection and the second part of the refugee definition was interpreted as referring to external protection.[27] A fear of non-state persecution is, however, unlikely ever to cause a person to be unable or unwilling to seek diplomatic assistance from the relevant state. On

---

Refugee in International Law (4th edn), Oxford: Oxford University Press, pp 8, 28; *Horvath v Secretary of State for the Home Department* [2001] AC 489 (UK HL).

[23] Wilsher, D. (2003) 'Non-State Actors and the Definition of a Refugee in the United Kingdom: Protection, Accountability or Culpability?', *International Journal of Refugee Law*, 15(1): 68–112; see also *Refugee Appeal No. 71427/99* [2000] NZRSAA 337 [62]-[67].

[24] *Horvath v Secretary of State for the Home Department* [2001] AC 489 (UKHL).

[25] Goodwin-Gill, G. and McAdam, J. (2021) *The Refugee in International Law* (4th edn), Oxford: Oxford University Press, pp 7–9; Hathaway, J. and Foster, M. (2014) *The Law of Refugee Status* (2nd edn), Cambridge: Cambridge University Press, pp 307–319.

[26] Hathaway, J. and Foster, M. (2014) *The Law of Refugee Status* (2nd edn), Cambridge: Cambridge University Press, pp 332–335.

[27] *Minister for Immigration v Khawar* [2002] HCA 14 (Aus HC) (Gleeson CJ and McHugh and Gummow JJ).

this analysis, the second part of the refugee definition would seemingly rule out claims to refugee status based on non-state persecution. In an attempt to resolve the issue, it has been argued that a person who has experienced non-state persecution from which their country of origin was unwilling to protect them cannot be expected to accept diplomatic assistance from that country because to do so would trigger the cessation clauses and lead to the refugee being returned.[28] The argument is logically unappealing given that it renders the second part of the refugee definition redundant.

The Gordian Knot can be severed by ignoring the problems caused by a literal interpretation and instead adopting the purposive approach proper to an international treaty. The refugee definition can be understood as posing a 'single composite question' with it being 'a mistake to isolate the elements of the definition, interpret them, and then ask whether the facts of the instant case are covered by the sum of those individual interpretations'.[29] On this approach, issues of repetition may simply be disregarded. While this may not be the most intellectually satisfying outcome, it is consistent with the role of the Refugee Convention as an instrument of surrogate international protection. Refugee status should be understood to hinge on a need to establish a well-founded fear of being persecuted for one of the convention grounds and also a need to establish failure by the state to provide adequate protection within the country.

Unwilling or unable

The text of the convention seemingly provides two different routes to satisfy the second part of the refugee definition: inability or unwillingness. During the drafting of the Refugee Convention, one of the early preparatory documents suggested that '"unable" refers primarily to stateless refugees but includes refugees possessing a nationality who are refused passports or other protection by their own Government'. In contrast, '"[u]nwilling" refers to refugees who refuse to accept the protection of the government of their nationality'.[30] Despite the drafting history and the text referring to the actions of the person seeking asylum, discussion around protection, ability and willingness typically defaults to whether the country of origin

---

[28] Fortin, A. (2000) 'The Meaning of "Protection" in the Refugee Definition', *International Journal of Refugee Law*, 12(4): 548–576, 576.

[29] *Ravichandran and Sandralingham v Secretary of State for the Home Department* [1996] Imm AR 97 (UK CA) (Simon Brown LJ); *Applicant A v Minister for Immigration and Ethnic Affairs* [1997] HCA 4 (Aus HC) (McHugh J).

[30] Ad Hoc Committee on Statelessness and Related Problems (1950) *Report of the Ad Hoc Committee on Statelessness and Related Problems, Lake Success, New York, 16 January to 16 February 1950* (UN Docs E/1618 and E/AC.32/5), p 39.

is able or willing to provide protection. Where it is recognized that the wording refers to the putative refugee, the jurisprudence on protection overwhelmingly focuses on inability. The notion that a person might be able to avail themselves of protection or return, but be unwilling to do so and thereby qualify for refugee status, is exotic. Refugee status is not considered to be a voluntary condition.

This raises the question of the circumstances in which refugee status might be gained because a refugee is unwilling to seek protection. The answer is usually considered to lie in the qualifying words 'owing to such fear', which are read as meaning that 'the applicant's fear must be a well-founded fear of being persecuted for availing himself of the state's protection'.[31] The requirement for a well-founded fear of persecution arises twice within the refugee definition. Firstly, the person must be outside their country of origin owing to such fear. Secondly, the person must also be unwilling to return to that country for the same well-founded fear of being persecuted.[32] On this understanding, a person who fears persecutory treatment at the hands of non-state actors will qualify for refugee status if they will face persecution for seeking state protection. This approach is not so intuitive as to be universally accepted, however, and appears to add nothing to the 'inability' route, contrary to normal rules of treaty interpretation. It has in the past been suggested that there might be some special circumstances, undefined but likely few in number, where a person might be able but unwilling to avail themselves of protection.[33]

Agents of the state

Where the source of persecution is the state itself, issues of protection would usually be considered not to arise. As Lord Clyde said in *Horvath*, '[a]ctive persecution by the state is the very reverse of protection'.[34] The European Union's recast Qualification Directive partially endorses this reasoning in its preamble, which states that '[w]here the State or agents of the State are the actors of persecution or serious harm, there should be a presumption that effective protection is not available'.[35] Such a presumption seems

---

[31] *Horvath v Secretary of State for the Home Department* [2001] AC 489 (UK HL) (Lord Hope, giving the leading judgment).
[32] Zimmermann, A. and Mahler, C. (2011) 'Part Two General Provisions, Article 1 A, para. 2', in Zimmermann, A. (ed.) *The 1951 Convention Relating to the Status of Refugees and Its 1967 Protocol: A Commentary*, Oxford: Oxford University Press, p 443.
[33] *Horvath v Secretary of State for the Home Department* [2001] AC 489 (UK HL) (Lord Lloyd, dissenting judgment).
[34] *Horvath v Secretary of State for the Home Department* [2001] AC 489 (UK HL) (Lord Clyde).
[35] Directive 2011/95/EC, Preamble [27].

unobjectionable as a matter of common sense but if elevated to a legal rule it becomes problematic and can distort the refugee status determination process. Firstly, it is wrong in principle to investigate state responsibility because it is not relevant to refugee status. To make factual findings that a state is or is not responsible for persecution exacerbates the politicization of refugee claims. It would be ahistorical and naive to think that the recognition of a refugee is not in part a political act but adding fuel to the fire is unhelpful to those in need of protection and therefore undermines the humanitarian purpose of the convention.[36] As we saw in Chapter 1, both the African Refugee Convention and Cartagena Declaration attempt to depoliticize recognition of refugees for this reason. Secondly, treating state and non-state persecution cases differently by imposing a protection test in one but not the other incentivizes refugees to attempt to prove state responsibility in their cases, thereby avoiding the need also to prove absence of protection. Differing approaches to state and non-state persecution cases may be unavoidable to some degree, but a rule or formal presumption that a protection test does not apply in state persecution cases will tend to increase rather than decrease the risk of becoming distracted by a question which is ultimately a sterile one. Thirdly and finally, attempting to determine state responsibility is fraught with severe philosophical and practical difficulties. Lawyers may be accustomed to the language of responsibility, liability and accountability – these being foundational concepts in law, after all – but deciding when an official or a private person is acting on behalf of or as an emanation of the state will often be not just undesirable but impossible in refugee status claims. An official, declared state policy of persecution of a minority group carried out by the military or police would be the clearest paradigm example of state persecution in which no issue of protection would arise. Most states are rarely so forthcoming about their persecutory intentions, however. Instead, the state may unofficially encourage, sanction or tolerate persecutory conduct by state officials, such as the police, or actors closely linked to the state, such as paramilitaries. In *Horvath*, for example, Lord Hope referred to 'the state or its own agents' and in *S152/2003* Kirby J referred to 'the state and its agencies and officials'.[37] But what of rogue officials who from time to time abuse their authority with impunity? In other cases, the state may want to prevent abuses by state officials but be unable to do so in practice and therefore fail to intervene to prevent, investigate or punish such persecutory conduct.

---

[36] On asylum as a political act, see Price, M. (2009) *Rethinking Asylum: History, Purpose, and Limits*, Cambridge: Cambridge University Press.

[37] *Horvath v Secretary of State for the Home Department* [2001] AC 489 (UK HL); *Minister for Immigration and Multicultural Affairs v Respondents S152/2003* [2004] HCA 18 (Aus HC).

Rather than attempting to draw an otherwise pointless bright line between state and non-state agents or persecution it is preferable to focus on the more pertinent question of whether the state will, in future, be able to protect the person against the harm in question, whatever its origin. In the case of *Svazas*, Lord Justice Simon Brown suggested there is 'a spectrum of cases between on the one extreme those where the only ill-treatment is by non-state agents and on the other extreme those where the state itself is wholly complicit in the ill-treatment'.[38] He went on to suggest that the more senior the officers of the state concerned, and the more closely involved they are in the refugee's ill-treatment, the easier it will be to show that state protection has failed. This pragmatic approach avoids the need to investigate state responsibility by focusing instead on individual circumstances and future risk.

Source of protection

If the Refugee Convention exists to provide surrogate protection where a person's own home state has failed to protect them, it would seem logical that the protection which has failed must be that provided by the state itself. The language of the convention, which on the face of it refers to 'the protection of that country' in the sense of a country capable of granting nationality, supports this conclusion. If the reference in the refugee definition to 'the protection of that country' is understood to be a reference to external diplomatic or consular protection, which can only be provided by a state authority, the point becomes all the stronger.[39] Nevertheless, the principle that protection must be state protection has been called into question in some situations in which private actors, groups or quasi-state bodies have been considered capable of providing the required protection, leading to rejection of claims to refugee status. This approach risks return of refugees to unstable situations in which internationally unaccountable bodies in control of shifting territories become responsible for the safety of those living under their *de facto* control. A series of cases in the United Kingdom have found explicitly or implicitly that protection can be provided by majority clans in Somalia, for example.[40] The United Nations Interim Administration Mission in

---

[38] *Svazas v Secretary of State for the Home Department* [2002] EWCA Civ 74, [2002] 1 WLR 1891 [54] (Simon Brown LJ), cited with approval in *Januzi v Secretary of State for the Home Department* [2006] UKHL 5, [2006] 2 AC 426 [21] (Lord Bingham).

[39] *Minister for Immigration and Multicultural Affairs v Khawar* [2002] HCA 14 [21], [62] (Gleeson CJ). See Fortin, A. (2000) 'The Meaning of "Protection" in the Refugee Definition', *International Journal of Refugee Law*, 12(4): 548–576.

[40] See for example *DM (Majority Clan Entities Can Protect) Somalia* [2005] UKAIT 00150, *AM and AM (Armed Conflict: Risk Categories) Somalia CG* [2008] UKAIT 00091 and *MOJ (Return to Mogadishu) CG* [2014] UKUT 442 (IAC). This approach is not confined

Kosovo was found to be capable of providing protection within the meaning of the Refugee Convention but not, at one time, the government of the Kurdish Autonomous Region of northern Iraq.[41] The European Union's Qualification Directive states that protection can be provided by the state or by 'parties or organisations, including international organisations, controlling the State or a substantial part of the territory of the State'. This is subject to considerable qualification, however, as the protection must be 'effective and of a non-temporary nature' and should be capable of 'operating an effective legal system for the detection, prosecution and punishment of acts constituting persecution'.[42] In at least some jurisdictions, state-like bodies are considered capable of providing the requisite protection.

Degree of protection

The refugee definition makes international surrogate protection available where a state (or, as discussed earlier, a state-like body) is 'unable or unwilling' to provide protection itself. The UNHCR Handbook suggests that where acts of serious harm originate from 'the local populace', they may amount to persecution 'if they are knowingly tolerated by the authorities, or if the authorities refuse, or prove unable, to offer effective protection'.[43] The degree of protection which must be provided by a state has proven to be controversial. Some jurisdictions have adopted a version of a 'due diligence', 'best efforts' or 'system of protection' approach in which it is considered a person does not qualify for refugee status if their home state will diligently attempt to protect them but may nevertheless fail to do so. Other jurisdictions have preferred to remain fixed on the question of whether protection is sufficient to reduce the risk of being persecuted below the threshold of being well-founded, what might be described as an 'effective protection' approach. Individual asylum assessors have at times veered between the two approaches depending on the circumstances of the individual case and country under consideration.

---

to the United Kingdom: see *Elmi v Minister of Citizenship and Immigration* 163 FTR 122 (Federal Court, 3 March 1999) for a Canadian equivalent.

[41] *Dyli* [2000] Imm AR 652 (UK IAT) and *Gardi v Secretary of State for the Home Department* [2002] EWCA Civ 750, [2002] 1 WLR 2755 respectively. The judgment in *Gardi* was later held to be void but a similar conclusion was reached by the Court of Sessions in the same case in *Saber v Secretary of State for the Home Department* [2003] ScotCS 360, [2004] INLR 222.

[42] Directive 2011/95/EC (recast). See also Case C-255/19 *United Kingdom v OA* interpreting the similar provision in Directive 2004/83/EC (original).

[43] UNHCR, *Handbook on Procedures and Criteria for Determining Refugee Status and Guidelines on International Protection under the 1951 Convention and the 1967 Protocol Relating to the Status of Refugees*, HCR/1P/4/ENG/REV.4 (1979, reissued 2019) [65].

The leading 'system of protection' case is *Horvath*.[44] The interpretation and meaning of the various judgments in the case have proven to be somewhat problematic, which is particularly unfortunate given the gravity of the issues arising in refugee status claims and the desirability of clear and consistent decision-making. Rather than a single judgment, as has become the practice of the successor Supreme Court, five separate judgments were handed down by the Law Lords hearing the case, three of which were fully and diversely reasoned.

KEY CASE

Horvath involved a Roma citizen of Slovakia. He, his family and other neighbouring Roma had experienced extreme violence at the hands of skinheads in his local area from which the police had failed to protect him. He and his family had also experienced discriminatory denial of employment opportunities and discrimination in the provision of education and other public services. A majority of the Law Lords, endorsing the judgment of Lord Hoffman in *R v Immigration Appeal Tribunal, ex p Shah* the previous year, held that persecution requires not just serious harm but also failure of state protection. On what was meant by state protection the outcome was considerably less clear. Lord Hope, giving the leading judgment, held that the duty of protection was 'to establish and to operate a system of protection against the persecution of its own nationals'.[45] Such a system would not have to eliminate all risk and thus guarantee protection: '[c]ertain levels of ill-treatment may still occur even if steps to prevent this are taken by the state to which we look for our protection'. Instead, Lord Hope describes this issue as being whether there is 'sufficiency of state protection', which amounts to 'a practical standard, which takes proper account of the duty which the state owes to all its own nationals'. Lord Clyde's concurring judgment – which was not the majority judgment – appeared to go further by holding explicitly that a person might be at risk but still not qualify for refugee status: '[t]he sufficiency of state protection is not measured by the existence of a real risk of an abuse of rights but by the availability of a system for the protection of the citizen and a reasonable willingness by the state to operate it'.[46] Given that 'real risk' is considered a synonym for 'well-founded fear', Lord Clyde appeared explicitly to be suggesting that a person with a well-founded fear might be denied refugee status if the person's home state was operating a system of protection even if that system of protection did not, in fact, protect the person concerned. Lord Hope did not appear to go so far, although what he meant by 'system' or 'sufficiency' of protection or the relevance of 'the duty which the state owes to all its own nationals' is not clear on the face of the judgment.

---

[44] *Horvath v Secretary of State for the Home Department* [2001] AC 489 (UK HL).
[45] *Horvath v Secretary of State for the Home Department* [2001] AC 489 (UK HL) (Lord Hope).
[46] *Horvath v Secretary of State for the Home Department* [2001] AC 489 (UK HL) (Lord Clyde).

Whether the differences between the judgments are or are not 'more a matter of semantics than substance', the *Horvath* case definitively entrenched the concept of a 'system of protection' in the jurisprudence of the United Kingdom.[47] The characteristics of such a system were broadly sketched out in subsequent case law, much of which arose in claims based on Article 3 of the ECHR, from which the system of protection approach had arguably been derived in the first place.[48] Criminal law must make violence punishable, appropriate penalties must be imposed on offenders, classes of victim should not be exempted in law or practice from protection and the authorities must be reasonably willing to investigate, detect and prosecute.[49] The law and its enforcement should have a deterrent effect, although need not deter all crime.[50] However, a person is not automatically excluded from refugee status 'where the law enforcement agencies are doing their best and are not being either generally inefficient or incompetent (as that word is generally understood, implying lack of skill rather than lack of effectiveness)' and there need not be 'a total collapse of the state's protective machinery'.[51] What amounts to sufficient protection has been held to depend on the level of risk faced.[52] By the time the issue of state protection returned to the House of Lords in the context of the ECHR, Lord Brown was able to say without apparent trace of irony that it was 'plainly established' that 'the asylum seeker must establish not merely the risk of severe ill-treatment but also that his home state was unwilling or unable to provide a reasonable level of protection'.[53]

The system of protection approach has been adopted outside the United Kingdom. In Australia, the High Court held in *S152/2003* that a state is required 'to take reasonable measures to protect the lives and safety of its citizens and those measures would include an appropriate criminal law, and the provision of a reasonably effective and impartial police force and justice system'.[54] The European Union's Qualification

---

[47] *Dhima v Immigration Appeal Tribunal* [2002] EWHC 80 (Admin) [16] (Auld LJ); *Banomova v Secretary of State for the Home Department* [2001] EWCA Civ 807 [28] (Clarke LJ).

[48] *R (on the application of Bagdanavicius) v Secretary of State for the Home Department* [2005] UKHL 38, [2005] 2 AC 668.

[49] *Dhima v Immigration Appeal Tribunal* [2002] EWHC 80 (Admin) [16]; *Banomova v Secretary of State for the Home Department* [2001] EWCA Civ 807 [29].

[50] *McPherson v Secretary of State for the Home Department* [2001] EWCA Civ 1955, [2002] INLR 139. For example, see Arden LJ [35]–[38].

[51] *Noune v Secretary of State for the Home Department* [2000] All ER (D) 2163 [28] (Schiemann LJ).

[52] *Dhima v Immigration Appeal Tribunal* [2002] EWHC 80 (Admin) [35] (Auld LJ).

[53] *R (on the application of Bagdanavicius) v Secretary of State for the Home Department* [2005] UKHL 38, [2005] 2 AC 668 [29] (Lord Brown).

[54] *Minister for Immigration and Multicultural Affairs v Respondents S152–2003* [2004] HCA 18 [26] (Gleeson CJ, Hayne and Heydon JJ).

Directive states that protection will be provided where 'reasonable steps' are taken to prevent persecution '*inter alia*, by operating an effective legal system for the detection, prosecution and punishment of acts constituting persecution'.[55] In Canada, it is presumed that a state is capable of protecting its citizens; La Forest J held in *Ward* that 'clear and convincing proof of a state's inability to protect must be advanced' by a refugee to displace this presumption.[56]

Criticisms have been made of the system of protection approach, however. It not only in effect adds words but also a new concept into the Refugee Convention, a concept imported from the very different context of human rights instruments such as the ECHR. Human rights instruments are in their modern form, unlike the Refugee Convention, very much concerned with state responsibility. Reference to the case of *Osman v United Kingdom*, in which the European Court of Human Rights recognized that 'account should be taken of the operational responsibilities and the constraints on the provision of police protection and accordingly the obligation to protect must not be so interpreted as to impose an impossible or disproportionate burden upon the authorities', was made both by Lord Clyde in *Horvath* and by the majority of the Australian High Court in *S152/2003*, for example.[57] This approach tends in practice to refocus the refugee inquiry away from future risk onto past conduct by the refugee claimant in exhausting avenues of protection before departure. It invites an inquiry into state responsibility, despite a near-universal agreement that in principle state responsibility need not be established. The problem is particularly acute in claims for refugee status made by citizens of democracies. Asylum assessors will often assume that protection is sufficient in a mature democracy, forcing claimants to refugee status to prove otherwise.[58] In the Canadian case of *Kadenko*, for example, the Federal Court held that '[t]he burden of proof that rests on the claimant is, in a way, directly proportional to the level of democracy in the state in question: the more democratic the state's institutions, the more the claimant must have done to exhaust all the courses of action open to him or her'.[59] A series of Canadian cases have rejected claims for refugee status on the basis of prior failure to exhaust domestic remedies, an argument that at one time featured prominently in United Kingdom initial decisions

---

[55] Directive 2004/83/EC, Article 7(2). This was amended in 2011 to provide also that protection 'must be effective and of a non-temporary nature': see what follows.

[56] *Canada (Attorney-General) v Ward* (1993) 103 DLR (4th) 1.

[57] *Osman v United Kingdom* [1998] 29 EHRR 245.

[58] A formal presumption to this effect was introduced into Canadian jurisprudence by *Canada (Attorney-General) v Ward* (1993) 103 DLR (4th) 1.

[59] *Kadenko v Canada (Solicitor General)* (1996) 143 DLR (4th) 532.

but which was not endorsed in the higher courts.[60] The New Zealand Refugee Status Appeals Authority declined to follow *Horvath* on the issue of sufficiency of protection, with Rodger Haines QC characterizing the *Horvath* position as being that 'an individual can be returned to his or her country of origin notwithstanding the fact that the person holds a well-founded fear of persecution for a Convention reason'.[61] Hathaway and Foster argue that what they label the 'due diligence' analysis of state protection is also inappropriate because 'it is ultimately a duty of process, not of result', it is largely retrospective and it is unclear, all of which render it singularly ill-suited to the task of determining future risk.[62] Lack of clarity is certainly an issue, as the deluge of sufficiency of protection case law subsequent to *Horvath* testifies.

While United Kingdom jurisprudence has continued in principle to espouse a position suggesting a person with a well-founded fear of being persecuted by non-state actors would not qualify for refugee status if a general system of protection were in place in their country, in practice judges often flinch from the consequences of this logic. As Collins J said in the much-cited case of *Kacaj*, '[i]t may be said that it is no consolation to an applicant to know that if he is killed or tortured, the police will take steps to try to bring his murderers or assailants to justice'.[63] In response to a finding that a person who suffered severe ill-treatment but nevertheless could afterwards have recourse to the courts was not entitled to refugee status – a finding based firmly on the logic of the system of protection analysis – the Court of Appeal in *Kinuthia* held that '[r]ecourse after mistreatment does not provide adequate protection'.[64] That such an exception proved to be necessary suggests either or both that the original principle was flawed or that judges are unconstrained by it in practice. The sufficiency of protection test is flexed, fudged or even abandoned depending on the facts of a case, with reliance placed on Lord Hope's 'practical standard' rather than Lord Clyde's more absolutist position. The notoriously unconstrained, judicially-empowering and therefore appeal-resistant word 'reasonable' was appended to 'protection' in a number of key cases, a formulation gratefully embraced by the House of

---

[60] For the Canadian cases see Hathaway, J. and Foster, M. (2014) *The Law of Refugee Status* (2nd edn), Cambridge: Cambridge University Press, pp 323–330.

[61] *Refugee Appeal No. 71684/99* [2000] INLR 165 (NZ RSAA) [62] (Rodger Haines QC).

[62] Hathaway, J. and Foster, M. (2014) *The Law of Refugee Status* (2nd edn), Cambridge: Cambridge University Press, pp 314–315.

[63] *Secretary of State for the Home Department v Kacaj* [2001] UKIAT 00018, [2002] INLR 354.

[64] *Kinuthia v Secretary of State for the Home Department* [2002] INLR 133 [26] (Tuckey LJ), [20]-[21] (Pill LJ) and [28] (Jonathan Parker LJ).

Lords itself in *Bagdanavicius*.⁶⁵ Similarly, the European Union's Qualification Directive was amended in 2011 to add that protection must be 'effective'.⁶⁶

Internal flight, relocation or protection

The Refugee Convention requires that a person have a well-founded fear of being persecuted for one of the convention reasons and be unable or unwilling to avail themselves of the protection of their country of nationality. Although it is not expressly addressed in the refugee definition, it is considered in many jurisdictions that a person who could safely and reasonably relocate within their country of origin will not qualify as a refugee. The UNHCR Handbook puts it another way: 'a person will not be excluded from refugee status merely because he could have sought refuge in another part of the same country, if under all the circumstances it would not have been reasonable to expect him to do so'.⁶⁷ The use of the past tense seems misplaced given that the refugee status enquiry is forward-looking. While the development of a doctrine of internal relocation or protection may pre-date the near-universal embrace of the principle that the Refugee Convention provides surrogate protection, it is certainly consistent with the notion that a refugee may only turn to the international community if domestic protection is not available.⁶⁸ This concept is variously described as internal flight, internal relocation or internal protection. Terminology matters here because each label tends to signal a different approach. The words 'internal flight' arguably encourage consideration of past conduct over future risk. In jurisdictions adopting the rubric of 'internal relocation', the focus tends to be on whether it is reasonable for the individual to relocate. The term 'internal protection' is favoured by those who advocate robust standards of protection for a refugee based on the Refugee Convention itself. As Lord Carswell commented in *Januzi*, the key United Kingdom case on internal relocation, 'the choice … may be critical, for it may lead to different results in individual cases'.⁶⁹

---

⁶⁵ See also the prior influential cases of *Noune* [2000] All ER (D) 2163 ('there had to be in place a justice system that provided reasonable protection in practical terms') and *Dhima* [2002] EWHC 80 (Admin) ('what is critical is a combination of a willingness and ability to provide protection to the level that can reasonably be expected to meet and overcome the real risk of harm from non-state agents').

⁶⁶ Directive 2011/95/EU, Article 7(2).

⁶⁷ UNHCR, *Handbook on Procedures and Criteria for Determining Refugee Status and Guidelines on International Protection under the 1951 Convention and the 1967 Protocol Relating to the Status of Refugees*, HCR/1P/4/ENG/REV.4 (1979, reissued 2019) [91].

⁶⁸ See for example the influential Federal Court of Australian case of *Randhawa v Minister for Immigration Local Government and Ethnic Affairs* (1994) 124 ALR 265 [8]-[10] (Black CJ).

⁶⁹ *Januzi v Secretary of State for the Home Department* [2006] UKHL 5, [2006] 2 AC 426 [65] (Lord Carswell).

Internal flight or relocation

In early refugee law jurisprudence in Canada and the United Kingdom, judges often referred to 'internal flight' or the 'internal flight alternative'.[70] The word 'flight' is evocative, suggesting as it does that some subjective fear is required (see discussion in Chapter 2). Encouraged by the use of the past tense in the relevant paragraph of the UNHCR Handbook, early cases tended to fixate on the past actions of the applicant for refugee status. The issue tended to be whether the applicant did or could have lived in specific areas of their home country before their departure. While the past might legitimately offer some guidance to the future, this retrospective approach risks the assessor being distracted from 'the real question', which is 'whether a person liable to persecution in one part of the country would be adequately protected by the state if relocated in another part to which he would in practice be returned'.[71] For this reason, the term 'internal relocation' is now generally used in the United Kingdom. The asylum assessor will have to consider what might actually happen on return in future, such as how the applicant would enter the country, to where they would relocate and how they would travel there after what might be several years of absence from the country in circumstances where it may be obvious the person has claimed asylum abroad. These can be critical issues in some cases, as where it is suggested that a person can relocate away from central government controlled areas to reach a hypothetical safe haven yet would have to pass through such areas in order to reach it.[72] The existence of a 'safe' place which a person cannot reach or can only reach by exposing themselves to great danger is no proper basis for refusal of a claim to refugee status. But the question then arises of whether anything less than a well-founded fear of being persecuted for a convention reason will suffice to rule out the possibility of relocation.

---

[70] For example *Rasaratnam v Canada (Minister of Employment and Immigration)* [1992] 1 FC 706, *Thirunavukkarasu v Minister of Employment and Immigration* (1993) 109 DLR (4th) 682, *R (on the application of Robinson) v Secretary of State for the Home Department* [1997] 4 All ER 210 (CA).

[71] See for example *R v Secretary of State for the Home Department, ex p Yogathas* [2002] UKHL 36, [2003] AC 920 [6], [40] and [111].

[72] In the United Kingdom this issue has arisen in Iraqi and Somali claims, for example: *AAH (Iraqi Kurds – internal relocation) CG* [2018] UKUT 212 (IAC) and *AMM and others (conflict; humanitarian crisis; returnees; FGM) Somalia CG* [2011] UKUT 445 (IAC).

KEY CASE

Januzi v Secretary of State for the Home Department involved one appellant from Kosovo and three from Darfur in Sudan.[73] It was accepted that all four had experienced persecution in their home areas. The question for the court was whether they qualified for refugee status or should be returned to their home countries and expected to relocate and, if so, under what circumstances. The parties agreed that the relevant test was whether it would be 'reasonable' to expect a person to relocate. This was the test required under European Union law, which was at that time binding in the United Kingdom.[74] The question remained how this test should be interpreted.

After considering the conflicting domestic and international authorities on the question of the legal basis for the principle, Lord Bingham held that

> if a person is outside the country of his nationality because he has chosen to leave that country and seek asylum in a foreign country, rather than move to a place of relocation within his own country where he would have no well-founded fear of persecution, where the protection of his country would be available to him and where he could reasonably be expected to relocate, it can properly be said that he is not outside the country of his nationality owing to a well-founded fear of being persecuted for a Convention reason.

Internal relocation is on this analysis considered to be rooted in the 'well-founded fear' causative condition of the refugee definition, not in the protection element of the definition. Lord Bingham, therefore, rejected the proposition that the proposed place of relocation must provide basic norms of civil, political and socio-economic rights derived from the other articles of the Refugee Convention. A principal concern of the court appeared to be that a claimant for refugee status should not be entitled to rely on a comparison between the conditions in the country of refuge and the conditions in the place of relocation. The correct approach was held to be to ask 'Can the claimant, in the context of the country concerned, lead a relatively normal life without facing undue hardship?', a question derived from UNHCR guidelines.[75] If so, it would be reasonable for the person to relocate.

---

[73] *Januzi v Secretary of State for the Home Department* [2006] UKHL 5, [2006] 2 AC 426.
[74] Directive 2004/83/EC, Article 8, which was then in force in the United Kingdom, provides that 'Member States may determine that an applicant is not in need of international protection if in a part of the country of origin there is no well-founded fear of being persecuted or no real risk of suffering serious harm and the applicant can reasonably be expected to stay in that part of the country'.
[75] UNHCR, *Guidelines on International Protection No. 4: 'Internal Flight or Relocation Alternative' Within the Context of Article 1A(2) of the 1951 Convention and/or 1967 Protocol Relating to the Status of Refugees*, 23 July 2003, HCR/GIP/03/04.

> Conditions breaching non-derogable human rights like the prohibition on torture, cruel or inhuman treatment or punishment would be likely to meet this test, as would a situation where the person concerned was unable to earn a living or access any accommodation. But in a later case, *AH (Sudan)*, it was clarified that it is not a prerequisite that the conditions be so harsh.[76]

A similar approach to that in *Januzi* is also followed in Australia and the United States.[77] In practice, it appears to be settled law that the approach in the venerable Canadian case of *Thirunavukkarasu* is broadly the right one.[78] The enquiry into internal relocation should be forward-looking. It is axiomatic that the person concerned must have no well-founded fear of being persecuted there, whether from the original risk or some new risk arising in the place of relocation. The degree of state involvement in persecution is highly likely to be relevant to this question, particularly if the state is in 'full control of events and its agents of persecution are active everywhere within its border'.[79] As with the failure of state protection element of 'being persecuted', though, this is generally not a formal presumption as such, other than in the United States. The spectrum analysis deployed in a different but related context in the case of *Svazas* is probably preferable here as well for the same reasons (see earlier discussion).[80] It is also important to consider the reasons why the person faced persecution in the first place and the purpose of the Refugee Convention; it is no answer to a political activist, religious adherent or a gay man fearing persecution in his home area to tell him he should move to another if the same risk will arise there unless he behaves discreetly.[81] The place of safety must be reasonably accessible to that person, any barriers in reaching the place must be reasonably surmountable and the person cannot be required to expose themselves to great physical danger

---

[76] This was clarified when the case returned again to the House of Lords as *Secretary of State for the Home Department v AH (Sudan)* [2007] UKHL 49, [2008] AC 678.

[77] *SZATV v Minister for Immigration and Citizenship* [2007] HCA 40 (Aus HC) [24]-[26] and domestic regulations 8 CRF § 208.13(b)(2)(ii) cited in Hathaway, J. and Foster, M. (2014) *The Law of Refugee Status* (2nd edn), Cambridge: Cambridge University Press, p 336 n 291.

[78] *Thirunavukkarasu v Canada (Minister of Employment and Immigration)* (1993) 109 DLR (4th) 682.

[79] *Januzi v Secretary of State for the Home Department* [2006] UKHL 5, [2006] 2 AC 426 (Lord Hope).

[80] *Svazas v Secretary of State For the Home Department* [2002] EWCA Civ 74, [2002] 1 WLR 1891.

[81] *HJ (Iran) v Secretary of State for the Home Department* [2010] UKSC 31, [2011] 1 AC 596; *SZATV v Minister for Immigration and Citizenship* [2007] HCA 40 (Aus HC); (2007) 233 CLR 18 [38] (Kirby J).

or undue hardship in travelling there by, for example, having to cross battle lines. On this basis, it has been held in the United Kingdom that an Iraqi Kurd could not be expected to relocate internally from a point of arrival of Baghdad International Airport to the Kurdish Autonomous Region in northern Iraq without possession of an identity document which would enable safe passage, nor could a Somali citizen being returned to the airport in Mogadishu be expected to travel through a conflict zone to reach a safe area.[82] Finally, refugee status should not be denied on the basis that the applicant could 'hide out in an isolated region of their country, like a cave in the mountains, or in a desert or a jungle' if those are the only areas of internal safety available. This final consideration is so firmly embedded in jurisprudence that it is rarely if ever now expressed in practice.[83]

Internal protection

An alternative analysis is advocated by Hathaway and Foster, who propose the use of the rubric of 'internal protection'. This is also the terminology deployed in the EU's Qualification Directive.[84] They argue that the concept should be located in the last part of the refugee definition, which requires a refugee to be unable or unwilling to avail themselves of protection.[85] There is no textual or other basis in the Refugee Convention for exempting a refugee from relocation on the basis of a test of reasonableness or undue harshness: it is an invention of case law, albeit now incorporated into European Union law as well. If there is a place where a person would not have a well-founded fear of being persecuted, even if it is in a desert or jungle, then on the face of the Refugee Convention there is no basis for the person to qualify as a refugee. The origins of the additional enquiry into whether relocation would be unreasonable or unduly harsh lie outside the Refugee Convention itself in the UNHCR Handbook in a passage which is backwards-facing to the conduct of the refugee before their departure and is more in the nature of an exhortation to state parties than a legal principle derived from the text of the Convention. Even if the additional, extrinsic criterion of reasonableness is accepted – which it very widely is, fortunately – the framing of relocation

---

[82] *AAH (Iraqi Kurds – internal relocation) CG* [2018] UKUT 212 (IAC) and *AMM and others (conflict; humanitarian crisis; returnees; FGM) Somalia CG* [2011] UKUT 445 (IAC).

[83] For an early example, see *R v Immigration Appeal Tribunal, ex p Jonah* [1985] Imm AR 7 (EW HC).

[84] Qualification Directive 2011/95/ EU, Article 8.

[85] Hathaway, J. and Foster, M. (2014) *The Law of Refugee Status* (2nd edn), Cambridge: Cambridge University Press, pp 332–342 and 351–361. This is also the terminology preferred in Schultz, J. (2019) *The Internal Protection Alternative in Refugee Law: Treaty Basis and Scope of Application under the 1951 Convention Relating to the Status of Refugees and Its 1967 Protocol*, Leiden and Boston, MA: Brill Nijhoff.

as being inherent to well-founded fear, coupled with the ambiguity of the term 'reasonable', encourages asylum assessors to require proof of country-wide persecution.[86] Finally, there is no objective or principled standard by which reasonableness can be measured or decided. This risks inconsistent and unpredictable decision-making within and between jurisdictions and the inherent subjectivity of the word invites consideration of factors that ought to be properly irrelevant. The preoccupation of some Law Lords in both *Januzi* and *AH (Sudan)* with ensuring applicants for asylum 'cannot take advantage of past persecution to achieve a better life in the country to which they have fled' might be thought one such consideration, for example.[87]

It is therefore preferable, Hathaway and Foster argue, to source the issue of relocation in the concept of state protection in the second part of the refugee definition. This not only provides a proper textual anchor in the refugee definition itself without introducing an extrinsic concept but also provides a principled framework for decision-making which goes beyond the elusive and inherently subjective concept of 'reasonableness'. The standard they propose is that of the Refugee Convention itself, whose articles impose duties of non-discrimination in relation to a limited range of rights including freedom of religion, property rights, rights of association, access to the courts, employment and self-employment, housing, education, social assistance and freedom of movement. These rights were those considered by the drafters of the convention to be essential to a person trying to make a new life for themselves in a new location, after all. The approach has been embraced in New Zealand, where Rodger Haines QC held that 'the appropriate minimal standard of effective protection for the purposes of Art 1A(2) of the Refugee Convention is the standard of human rights set by the Refugee Convention itself, ie, the rights owed by State parties to persons who are refugees'.[88] In contrast, what has been labelled 'the Hathaway/New Zealand rule' was explicitly rejected by the House of Lords in the United Kingdom on the basis that the Refugee Convention is addressed to the rights of those outside not within their country of origin.[89] The approach is not one that has been adopted in case law outside New Zealand.

---

[86] For examples see Hathaway, J. and Foster, M. (2014) *The Law of Refugee Status* (2nd edn), Cambridge: Cambridge University Press, p 337 n 304.

[87] *Secretary of State for the Home Department v AH (Sudan)* [2007] UKHL 49, [2008] AC 678 [27] (Baroness Hale). See also *Januzi v Secretary of State for the Home Department* [2006] UKHL 5, [2006] 2 AC 426 [19] (Lord Bingham) and *Secretary of State for the Home Department v AH (Sudan)* [2007] UKHL 49, [2008] AC 678 [40]-[41] (Lord Brown).

[88] *Refugee Appeal No. 71684/99* [2000] INLR 165 (NZ RSAA); see also *Butler v Attorney-General* [1997] NZCA 309.

[89] *Januzi v Secretary of State for the Home Department* [2006] UKHL 5, [2006] 2 AC 426 [15]-[19] (Lord Bingham).

Suggested further reading

Hathaway, J. and Foster, M. (2014) *The Law of Refugee Status* (2nd edn), Cambridge: Cambridge University Press, Chapter 4.

Fortin, A. (2000) 'The Meaning of "Protection" in the Refugee Definition', *International Journal of Refugee Law*, 12(4): 548–576.

Kälin, W. (2001) 'Non-State Agents of Persecution and the Inability of the State to Protect', *Georgetown Immigration Law Journal*, 15(3): 415–431.

UNHCR, *Guidelines on International Protection No. 4: 'Internal Flight or Relocation Alternative' Within the Context of Article 1A(2) of the 1951 Convention and/or 1967 Protocol Relating to the Status of Refugees*, 23 July 2003, HCR/GIP/03/04.

UNHCR, *Handbook on Procedures and Criteria for Determining Refugee Status and Guidelines on International Protection under the 1951 Convention and the 1967 Protocol Relating to the Status of Refugees*, HCR/1P/4/ENG/REV.4 (1979, reissued 2019) [97]-[105].

Wilsher, D. (2003) 'Non-State Actors and the Definition of a Refugee in the United Kingdom: Protection, Accountability or Culpability?', *International Journal of Refugee Law* 15(1): 68–112.

Horvath v Secretary of State for the Home Department [2001] AC 489 (UK HL).

Refugee Appeal No. 71684/99 [2000] INLR 165 (NZ RSAA).

Svazas v Secretary of State for the Home Department [2002] EWCA Civ 74, [2002] 1 WLR 1891.

5

Reasons for Persecution

As we have seen in the preceding chapters, the Refugee Convention does not protect against all harm, only harm that reaches the threshold necessary to amount to being persecuted and which, in some jurisdictions, is accompanied by a failure of state protection. Even then, there must be a causal link between the persecution and the five specific reasons that engages the Refugee Convention. These reasons are often referred to as the 'convention reasons' or 'convention grounds' for convenience. They are race, religion, nationality, membership of a particular social group and political opinion. The convention grounds represent protected characteristics which the person concerned cannot or should not be expected to change. There are two broad themes to discuss in this chapter, which addresses these reasons. Firstly is the way in which the convention grounds operate within the scheme of the Refugee Convention. The issue of causation requires exploration, as does the way in which the convention grounds can transform some forms of serious harm into persecutory harm. Secondly is the meaning and scope of the individual convention grounds themselves. Their very existence indicates that the purpose of the Refugee Convention is limited and they can be and have been interpreted both narrowly and expansively.

Causation

The Refugee Convention requires that a refugee have a well-founded fear of being persecuted *for reasons of* race, religion, nationality, membership of a particular social group or political opinion. The words 'for reasons of' clearly require a causal link between the being persecuted and at least one of the convention grounds. Analysis of this requirement has sometimes veered off into importing alien concepts of 'effective cause' or 'but for' causation from the law of tort or discrimination.[1] It is now widely but not universally

---

[1] *Montoya v Secretary of State for the Home Department* [2002] EWCA Civ 620 [8] and *R v Immigration Appeal Tribunal, ex p Shah* [1999] 2 AC 629 (UK HL) (Lord Steyn).

accepted that a simpler approach is preferable, either with no gloss at all to the words 'for reasons of' or to elaborate only by saying the convention ground must be a (not 'the') 'real reason' or 'effective reason' for the persecuted experienced. If a convention ground is genuinely incidental, coincidental or 'remote to the point of irrelevance' then the necessary nexus will not be established and the person will not be eligible for refugee status.[2] The causal link can be located in express or implied conduct: a refugee can manifest their protected characteristic by words or deeds. For example, the refusal of a person to perform compulsory military service may be interpreted as an expression of political opinion, as discussed later, or refusal to join a gang can be interpreted as political opposition, or even as the expression of a feminist, anti-patriarchal opinion.[3]

Intention of persecutor

Deliberate intention on the part of the persecutor will definitively establish causation. In the most straightforward examples, the persecutor will clearly, obviously and provably be motivated by the refugee's protected characteristic. For example, a repressive government may target a political activist because of the activist's political opinion in order to silence that activist, or the religious zealot may target a person of a different religion because of their religion in order to suppress that religion. The causal connection may literally be declared by the persecutor in some cases. In others, the connection may be self-evident from the facts of the case and the available country information, which may document similar cases. The connection may not always be so clear, though, and whether intention is *necessary* to establish causation is controversial. The motive of the persecutor has been held in the United States to be 'critical' to the issue of causation.[4] The United States is something of an outlier in this respect, however, and in the United Kingdom it has been said that 'the law is concerned with the reasons for the persecution and not with the motives of the persecutor'.[5] One risk is that claims based on structural, systemic, societal or institutional discrimination are undermined. Focus on

---

[2] *Klawitter v Immigration & Naturalization Service* 970 F2d 149 (1992); *Michigan Guidelines on Nexus to a Convention Ground* [13]; *Refugee Appeal No. 72635/01* (NZ RSAA) (6 September 2002) [173].

[3] *Alvarez-Lagos v Barr* 927 F3d 236 (2019); *Hernandez-Chacon v Barr* 948 F3d 94 (2020).

[4] *Immigration and Naturalization Service v Elias-Zacarias* (1992) 502 US 478 (US SC), albeit here interpreting the domestic statutory equivalent of 'on account of' instead of 'for reasons of'.

[5] *R (on the application of Sivakumar) v Secretary of State for the Home Department* [2003] UKHL 14, [2003] 2 All ER 1097 [41] (Lord Rodger).

the intentions of the alleged persecutor can make some refugee claims very hard to prove, lead to perverse outcomes and can particularly disadvantage victims of non-state persecution and child and women refugees. Forced sterilization or forced abortion have been held to have been motivated by an intention to control population rather than for reasons of a convention ground, for example, and domestic violence against women and children has been argued to have resulted from personality defects in the persecutor rather than the protected status of the persecuted.[6] Persecutors seldom stop to explain their motive, even more rarely furnish their victims with proof of that motive, and 'an inquiry into the motives and feelings of the alleged "persecutors" will be extremely difficult or impossible to perform'.[7] Even where intention is considered relevant, it is at least widely accepted that no enmity or malignity is required on the part of the persecutor: laws of general application or conduct intended by the persecutor to benefit the victim might still be persecutory.[8] In jurisdictions where the bifurcated definition of persecution has been adopted (persecution = serious harm + failure of state protection: see Chapters 3 and 4), the motive of the persecutor or the state which fails to provide protection is considered sufficient to establish the necessary causal link.[9] As discussed previously, this ensures that protection is available where the persecutor acts for personal or other reasons but in doing so takes advantage of the lack of protection offered by the state.

Predicament of persecuted person

It has been suggested that a search for rules or principles which add a gloss to the 'for reasons of' wording of the Refugee Convention is 'neither practicable nor desirable'.[10] It is not an explicit requirement of the Refugee Convention that the persecutor must intend to persecute their victim for reasons of a convention ground. To require provable intention on the part of the persecutor as necessary to establishing causation is therefore to add an additional, extraneous criterion. All that should be required is

---

[6] *In re Chang* 20 I & N Dec 38, 39–40, 45 (BIA 1989); *In re R-A-22* I & N Dec 906, 926 (BIA 2001); *Gomez-Romero v Holder* 475 F App'x 621 (2012).
[7] *Chen Shi Hai v Minister for Immigration and Multicultural Affairs* [2000] HCA 19 (Aus HC) [64].
[8] *Chen Shi Hai v Minister for Immigration and Multicultural Affairs* [2000] HCA 19 (Aus HC) [33]-[35] and [72]; *Fornah v Secretary of State for the Home Department* [2006] UKHL 46, [2007] 1 AC 412 [17].
[9] *R v Immigration Appeal Tribunal, ex p Shah* [1999] 2 AC 629 (UK HL) (Lord Hoffman); Directive 2011/95/EC, Article 9(3).
[10] *Chen Shi Hai v Minister for Immigration and Multicultural Affairs* [2000] HCA 19 (Aus HC) [68] (Kirby J). See also *Sepet and Bulbul* [2001] Imm AR 452 (EW CA) [92] (Laws LJ).

that a convention ground explains the risk to the refugee. This simpler causation test is more consistent with the 'being persecuted' language of the Refugee Convention as well as with its overall protective purpose. On this approach, the focus shifts from the intention of the persecutor to the predicament of the refugee. There is no need to prove that the persecutor declared the reason for their persecutory actions or to imply their motive from circumstantial evidence.

Multiple grounds

A convention ground need not be the only or even the primary reason for the risk of the refugee being persecuted.[11] All that is necessary is that a convention ground be 'an effective reason'.[12] There may also be multiple convention grounds engaged in a single case. For example, no purpose is served in attempting to discern the supposed primary or main operative convention ground if a female activist for a political party which exists primarily to represent an ethnic minority faces being persecuted for reasons of her gender, political opinion and race.[13] The statutory requirement in the United States that a convention reason must be 'one central reason', which was deliberately introduced in 2005 to reverse previous case law, adds an extrinsic requirement to the Refugee Convention.[14] The same is also true of the Australian statutory requirement that a convention reason must be 'the essential and significant reason' for the risk of being persecuted.[15]

Imputed or attributed convention grounds

The refugee need not actually have, hold or possess the relevant protected characteristic in order for that refugee to be persecuted for reasons of that convention ground. A person can qualify for refugee status if persecuted

---

[11] *R (on the application of Sivakumar) v Secretary of State for the Home Department* [2003] UKHL 14, [2003] 2 All ER 1097 [41] (Lord Rodger), citing *Suarez v Secretary of State for the Home Department* [2002] EWCA Civ 722, [2002] 1 WLR 2663.

[12] *Fornah v Secretary of State for the Home Department* [2006] UKHL 46, [2007] 1 AC 412 [17] (Lord Bingham); *R (on the application of Sivakumar) v Secretary of State for the Home Department* [2003] UKHL 14, [2003] 2 All ER 1097.

[13] UNHCR, *Handbook on Procedures and Criteria for Determining Refugee Status and Guidelines on International Protection under the 1951 Convention and the 1967 Protocol relating to the Status of Refugees*, HCR/1P/4/ENG/REV.4 (1979, reissued 2019) [66].

[14] Immigration and Nationality Act 1158(b)(1)(B)(i); see *Barajas-Romero v Lynch* (US Court of Appeals, 9th Circuit, 18 January 2017).

[15] Migration Act 1958 s 91R(1)(a), repealed and replaced in 2015 with an equivalent provision at s 5J(4)(a).

for reasons of a political opinion the persecutor incorrectly imputes or attributes to the person.[16] The same applies to the other convention grounds. As the European Union's Qualification Directive states, 'it is immaterial whether the applicant actually possesses the racial, religious, national, social or political characteristic which attracts the persecution, provided that such a characteristic is attributed to the applicant by the actor of persecution'.[17] Attribution of a protected characteristic may be particularly important in gender-related and child refugee claims, where a convention ground may be ascribed irrespective of the refugee's own views on the basis of their circumstances, for example as family members, couriers or camp followers who provide medical care, cook or similar. There is no requirement that such attribution has a rational basis: repressive regimes often behave in ways which appear to defy logic.[18] Choice of dress, speech, make-up, hairstyle, ornaments, music or other manifestations of personal preference which appear apolitical to a foreign observer or asylum assessor may be loaded with significance in the context of a given country and may attract persecutory treatment for reasons of a convention ground.

Concealment of convention grounds

It has never been suggested that a person conceal their race, nationality or sex in order to avoid being persecuted. It has, however, been suggested that a person conceal their religion, political opinion or sexuality.[19] While it might be argued that concealment of race, nationality or sex is simply impractical or impossible, it is hard to see how it can be legitimate to draw a distinction between some convention grounds and others on the basis of practicality rather than principle. There is no legitimate basis for treating the convention grounds differently or to rank them in order of importance. Indeed, the jurisprudence defining the meaning and scope of the 'membership of a particular social group' convention ground draws on the *ejusdem generis* (of the same kind) principle and holds that each is an immutable characteristic,

---

[16] See for example *Chan v Minister for Immigration and Ethnic Affairs* [1989] HCA 62 (Aus HC) [41] (McHugh J); *Attorney General of Canada v Ward* [1993] 2 SCR 689 (Can SC) (La Forest J); *RT (Zimbabwe) v Secretary of State for the Home Department* [2012] UKSC 38, [2013] 1 AC 152 [53].

[17] Directive 2011/95/EU, Article 10(2).

[18] *Suleyman* (16242) (UK IAT, 11 February 1998); *Minister for Immigration & Ethnic Affairs v Guo* [1997] HCA 22 (Aus HC) (Kirby J).

[19] Religion: *Ahmad v Secretary of State for the Home Department* [1991] Imm AR 61 (EW CA); political opinion: *R v Immigration Appeal Tribunal, ex p Jonah* [1985] Imm AR 7 (EW HC); sexuality: *J v Secretary of State for the Home Department* [2006] EWCA Civ 1238, [2007] Imm AR 73.

'a characteristic that either is beyond the power of an individual to change or is so fundamental to individual identity or conscience that it ought not be required to be changed'.[20] As discussed in Chapter 2, it is therefore now widely recognized that a suggestion that a person should conceal their protected characteristics or otherwise be 'discreet' about expression of their protected characteristics 'is unacceptable as being inconsistent with the underlying purpose of the Convention since it involves the applicant denying or hiding precisely the innate characteristic which forms the basis of his claim of persecution'.[21]

Role of the convention grounds

It has been said that the issue of whether a person has a well-founded fear of being persecuted for reasons of a convention ground raises 'a single composite question' and therefore it is 'unhelpful and potentially misleading to try to reach separate conclusions as to whether certain conduct amounts to persecution, and as to what reasons underlie it'.[22] However, any analysis and exploration of the definition of a refugee must necessarily address the words of Article 1A(2) of the Refugee Convention in a sequence. It might be added that some degree of analytical compartmentalization might promote more rigorous decision-making.[23] This should not distract from the reality that the convention grounds interact with the 'being persecuted' concept, having a transformative effect on some forms of serious harm. The interaction is not one way. It has also been suggested that particularly severe persecution of a person should cause an asylum assessor carefully to consider the reasons for that persecution and may suggest that a convention ground is one of the effective reasons for it.[24]

---

[20] *In re Acosta* (1985) 19 I & N 211, since widely cited, for example in *R v Immigration Appeal Tribunal, ex p Shah* [1999] 2 AC 629 (UK HL).

[21] *HJ (Iran) v Secretary of State for the Home Department* [2010] UKSC 31, [2011] 1 AC 596 [76] (Lord Rodger). See also *Appellant S395/2002 v Minister for Immigration* [2003] HCA 71 (Aus HC) [41] (McHugh and Kirby JJ), *Atta Fosu v Canada (Minister of Citizenship and Immigration)* 2008 FC 1135 [17] (Zinn J) and Joined Cases C-71/11 and C-99/11 *Germany v Y and Z*.

[22] *Ravichandran and Sandralingham v Secretary of State for the Home Department* [1996] Imm AR 97 (UK CA) (Simon Brown LJ), frequently cited with approval in subsequent cases including *Sepet v Secretary of State for the Home Department* [2003] UKHL 15, [2003] 3 All ER 304.

[23] *Svazas v Secretary of State For the Home Department* [2002] EWCA Civ 74, [2002] WLR 1891 [30] (Sedley LJ).

[24] *R (on the application of Sivakumar) v Secretary of State for the Home Department* [2003] UKHL 14, [2003] 2 All ER 1097.

Transformative effect

Imprisonment and the total loss of liberty it occasions will always amount to serious harm, but it is only sometimes persecution. As discussed in Chapter 3, a person who is prosecuted, convicted and sentenced to a proportionate period of imprisonment in humane conditions for the crime of murder following due process of law has no entitlement to the protection of the Refugee Convention. The UNHCR Handbook states:

> Persecution must be distinguished from punishment for a common law offence. Persons fleeing from prosecution or punishment for such an offence are not normally refugees. It should be recalled that a refugee is a victim – or potential victim – of injustice, not a fugitive from justice.[25]

A person who is prosecuted, convicted and sentenced to imprisonment because of their race, religion, political opinion or other convention ground may, however, have a claim to refugee status. In this second instance, the convention ground has a transformative effect. As Lord Justice Laws put it in his judgment in the Court of Appeal in the case of *Sepet and Bulbul*, 'the existence of a Convention reason is what *defines* the treatment as persecutory ... The putative act of persecution – imprisonment – is only such if it is inflicted for a Convention reason'.[26] In effect, some imprisonment is legitimate and some is not, although it is important to recall that it is not the role of the Refugee Convention or the asylum assessor to pronounce on the legitimacy of measures as such. It is therefore critically important to have a clear and objective means by which to determine persecutory from non-persecutory imprisonment. In practice, it is not sufficient to say simply that the existence or otherwise of a convention ground will determine this issue. This is because it is not always straightforward to discern whether or not there is a convention ground engaged. Is it persecution if a person is prosecuted, convicted and sentenced for a crime as defined in the national law of their country of origin? What if the crime is that of committing a homosexual act, apostasy or a politically inspired murder or a terrorist attack? Marginal cases may well arise, such as whether a short period of imprisonment for carrying out banned political activities such as attending

---

[25] UNHCR, *Handbook on Procedures and Criteria for Determining Refugee Status and Guidelines on International Protection under the 1951 Convention and the 1967 Protocol relating to the Status of Refugees*, HCR/1P/4/ENG/REV.4 (1979, reissued 2019) [56].

[26] *Sepet v Secretary of State for the Home Department* [2001] EWCA Civ 681, [2001] Imm AR 452 [64]-[65] (Laws LJ).

a demonstration or delivering leaflets amounts to being persecuted. An asylum assessor needs some objective legal basis for determining whether national law is persecutory or not. This issue is often framed in refugee law as being one of whether the conduct in question amounts to prosecution or to persecution, where 'prosecution' acts as a shorthand for the full criminal process including conviction and sentence.

The definition and extent of the convention grounds may also have an important transformative effect. The convention grounds encompass not just the holding of beliefs or opinions or even identifying with a particular religion or political party. They also include the expression of those beliefs or opinions or identity. A restriction on what a person wears on going out in public to meet other people will not normally amount to being persecuted, but it may do so where a convention ground is engaged and, for example, that restriction interferes with a person's religion or political opinion.

Prosecution and persecution

In general, prosecution is not persecution. However, some prosecutions will also amount to persecution. More pertinently, given that prosecution alone may not always be of sufficient severity to reach the threshold for serious harm, some convictions and sentences also amount to persecution. Whether a convention ground is engaged will in principle distinguish one situation from the other, but determining whether a convention ground is engaged may be difficult on the facts of a case.

The measure of whether a law is itself or in its application persecutory is often said to be whether the law is disproportionate or discriminatory or is applied in a disproportionate or discriminatory way. This is the approach adopted in the European Union's Qualification Directive, for example, and advocated in the UNHCR Handbook.[27] This begs the question of how to judge whether a law or its application is or is not disproportionate or discriminatory. An objective measure is needed, otherwise asylum assessors are left having to make subjective judgments about the laws and customs of other countries. International human rights law can provide the necessary measure. Even if a country is not a signatory to any of the principal treaties, so many counties are signatories that the standards of the

---

[27] See Directive 2011/95/EU at Article 9(2)(b), (c) and (d); UNHCR, *Handbook on Procedures and Criteria for Determining Refugee Status and Guidelines on International Protection under the 1951 Convention and the 1967 Protocol Relating to the Status of Refugees*, HCR/1P/4/ENG/REV.4 (1979, reissued 2019) [56]-[60], referring to 'excessive' punishment and discriminatory application of laws.

Universal Declaration of Human Rights, International Covenant on Civil and Political Rights and International Covenant on Economic, Social and Cultural Rights (ICESCR) that they can be taken to be an objective measure of internationally agreed minimum standards. The regional treaties like the European Convention on Human Rights, the elaborating treaties like the Convention on the Elimination of Discrimination against Women and Convention on the Rights of the Child and various court and committee decisions can all provide guidance.

Disproportionality or discrimination, measured against international human rights standards, may reveal the otherwise invisible but transformative hand of a convention ground. For example, a law which in theory is of universal application might be used disproportionately or even exclusively to target certain groups. Otherwise, sentences disproportionate to the crime committed may be imposed on individuals with protected characteristics such as a specific political opinion or a particular race. It is the existence of discrimination on a convention ground that means the person concerned is being persecuted rather than merely prosecuted.

Military service cases

Cases in which a person claims that their punishment under criminal law for refusing to perform military service would amount to being persecuted illustrate vividly the intersection of the persecution and discrimination elements of the Refugee Convention. As the UNHCR Handbook states, '[f]ear of prosecution and punishment for desertion or draft-evasion does not in itself constitute well-founded fear of persecution under the definition'.[28] The question is essentially how to judge whether a law of general application in reality discriminates against a person because of their protected characteristics. Ultimately, the answer to that question lies in whether international human rights law recognizes a right to conscientious objection and, if so, in what circumstances. On the face of it, international human rights conventions forbid forced labour but an explicit exception is made for military service. No explicit right to conscientious objection on religious or other grounds can be located in other protected rights in the major human rights instruments.[29]

---

[28] UNHCR, *Handbook on Procedures and Criteria for Determining Refugee Status and Guidelines on International Protection under the 1951 Convention and the 1967 Protocol Relating to the Status of Refugees*, HCR/1P/4/ENG/REV.4 (1979, reissued 2019) [167].

[29] International Convention on Civil and Political Rights, Article 8(3); European Convention on Human Rights, Article 4(3), American Convention on Human Rights, Article 6(3)(b); the African Charter on Human and Peoples' Rights is entirely silent on military service and conscientious objection.

KEY CASE

Sepet v Secretary of State for the Home Department involved two asylum applicants of Kurdish origin and Turkish nationality.[30] They sought asylum on the basis that they would have to perform compulsory military service on return or, if they refused, would be convicted of a criminal offence and imprisoned. No non-combatant alternative to military service was available and draft evaders were liable to a prison sentence of between six months and three years, which was agreed not to amount to disproportionate or excessive punishment. Their objection to performing military service was based on their political objections to the policies of the Turkish government and their wish to avoid being required to take part in military action, possibly involving atrocities and abuse of human rights, in Kurdish areas.

The House of Lords reviewed the state of international law and jurisprudence on military service and concluded that at that time, in 2003, the applicants could not show there existed 'a core human right to refuse military service on conscientious grounds which entails that punishment of persons who hold such views is necessarily discriminatory treatment'. The existence of such a right was held not to be supported by either a moral imperative or international practice. The applicants were therefore not entitled to refugee status. Their Lordships reached the conclusion with reluctance, recognizing that the international consensus of tomorrow might be otherwise.

In 2009, the Charter of Fundamental Rights of the European Union came into effect and, with it, a right of conscientious objection.[31] In 2011, the European Court of Human Rights held in the landmark case of *Bayatyan v Armenia* that refusal to perform military service was protected by the right to freedom of thought, conscience and religion and that prosecution and imprisonment for refusal to perform military service when no non-combatant alternative was provided was an interference with that right which could not be justified in the circumstances of the case.[32] Whether these subsequent developments would lead to a different outcome in *Sepet* were it heard today is unclear given that the case turned on a partial rather than complete objection to military service.

Aside from cases of principled conscientious objection based on freedom of thought, conscience and religion, a person subject to criminal sanction for refusal to perform military service will normally be a victim of

---

[30] [2003] UKHL 15, [2003] 3 All ER 304.
[31] Charter of Fundamental Rights of the European Union, 2012/C 326/02, Article 10(2).
[32] *Bayatyan v Armenia* [2011] ECHR 1095. See also *Yeo-Bum Yoon and Myung-Jin Choi v Republic of Korea*, CCPR/C/88/D/1321-1322/2004, UN Human Rights Committee, 23 January 2007.

prosecution rather than persecution. There are two further recognized exceptions to the general rule.[33] The first arises where a person refuses to perform compulsory military service and is subjected to a disproportionate or discriminatory sanction or particularly arduous or dangerous service for reasons of a convention ground. This might arise where those from a particular religious or racial group are singled out because of their religion or race. This situation, in which the military service is essentially incidental or contextual, may potentially engage the Refugee Convention if the sanction is sufficiently severe. The second exception arises where there is a real risk the person concerned will have to serve in an armed conflict and be required to commit atrocities or gross human rights abuses or participate in a conflict condemned by the international community.[34] Refusal to serve in these circumstances amounts to an actual or implied political opinion as to the limits of governmental authority and therefore attracts the protection of the Refugee Convention.[35] There is no need for the specific conflict in question to have actually been condemned by the international community, although this adds weight to an applicant's case: it is sufficient that the conflict involves breaches of international law.[36] The degree of involvement necessary before a person will be eligible for refugee status on this basis has proven difficult to define more precisely. The Court of Justice of the European Union takes the view that any military personnel are eligible, including logistical or support personnel, but that there must be a real risk the person will be required to commit or provide indispensable support for the preparation or execution of war crimes.[37] It is arguable that any sanction for refusal to serve which is more than negligible, including a non-custodial sanction, will still amount to being persecuted in these circumstances.[38]

---

[33] See UNHCR, *Handbook on Procedures and Criteria for Determining Refugee Status and Guidelines on International Protection under the 1951 Convention and the 1967 Protocol Relating to the Status of Refugees*, HCR/1P/4/ENG/REV.4 (1979, reissued 2019) [169] and [171]; *Sepet and Bulbul v Secretary of State for the Home Department* [2003] UKHL 15 [2003] WLR 856; Directive 2011/95/EU, Article 9(2)(e); Case C-472/13; *Andre Lawrence Shepherd v Germany*.

[34] *Sepet v Secretary of State for the Home Department* [2003] UKHL 15, [2003] 3 All ER 304 [8] (Lord Bingham).

[35] *Krotov v Secretary of State for the Home Department* [2004] EWCA Civ 69, [2004] WLR 1825 [46]; *Canas-Segovia v Immigration and Naturalization Service* (1990) 902 F2d 717.

[36] *Krotov v Secretary of State for the Home Department* [2004] EWCA Civ 69, [2004] WLR 1825 [20], [30], [37]-[38], [51]-[52].

[37] Case C-472/13 *Andre Lawrence Shepherd v Germany*.

[38] *BE (Iran) v Secretary of State for the Home Department* [2008] EWCA Civ 540 [40]; *Davidov v Secretary of State for the Home Department* [2005] 1 SC 540 [17]; *PK (Ukraine) v Secretary of State for the Home Department* [2019] EWCA Civ 1756.

The convention grounds

The preamble to the Refugee Convention begins by citing the principle that 'human beings shall enjoy fundamental rights and freedoms without discrimination'. The five convention grounds of race, religion, nationality, membership of a particular social group and political opinion represent the grounds for discrimination against which the Refugee Convention offers protection. They are not hierarchical in any sense. All are accorded equal importance and weight. Each represents an immutable characteristic, 'a characteristic that either is beyond the power of an individual to change or is so fundamental to individual identity or conscience that it ought not be required to be changed'.[39]

The major instruments of international human rights law – and the jurisprudence that has explored and developed them – can act as an aide to the interpretation and understanding of the meaning and scope of the convention grounds. Given that the Refugee Convention is now regarded as an integral part of this post-war system of international human rights protection, the omission from the five convention grounds of sex and other potential grounds for discrimination seems curious. The Universal Declaration of Human Rights of 1948, which preceded the Refugee Convention, cites 'race, colour, sex, language, religion, political or other opinion, national or social origin, property, birth or other status' as impermissible grounds for discrimination.[40] The grounds for impermissible discrimination in the ECHR of 1950 are similar.[41] The omission from the Refugee Convention of the other potential grounds for discrimination was not, therefore, because such grounds were inconceivable at that time. The omission can be explained, although not excused, by the original focus of the Refugee Convention on refugees arising from events prior to 1 January 1951. The drafters were concerned with refugees who had fled from or been displaced by the Nazi regime and with those unwilling to return to Soviet-controlled countries. The pre-war and post-war definitions of refugees were tied to these events and this time period. As discussed in the Introduction, the definition incorporated into the 1951 Refugee Convention was an evolution from those earlier definitions. Put simply, refugees prior to the Second World War were considered to have been persecuted because of their race, religion or political opinion. The ground of nationality was

---

[39] *In re Acosta* (1985) 19 I & N 211, since widely cited for example in *R v Immigration Appeal Tribunal, ex p Shah* [1999] 2 AC 629 (UK HL).
[40] Universal Declaration of Human Rights, Article 2.
[41] Convention for the Protection of Human Rights and Fundamental Freedoms, Article 14.

added after the war in the definition adopted by the IRO. The ground of 'membership of a particular social group', which as discussed in what follows has come to be regarded as encompassing sex and some other grounds for discrimination, at least in some cases, was only added very late in the drafting process and with very little discussion.

Race

The whole notion and concept of biological race is now discredited, and it is widely understood that the concept is a social construct.[42] The inclusion of race as a ground for refugee status in the text of the Refugee Convention in some ways makes the instrument appear antiquated. However, if a wide definition of race is used in a non-biological sense and the historical context of the Refugee Convention is borne in mind, then it serves as an important tool for protecting refugees against persecution. Or, from another perspective, so long as perceived 'race' continues to motivate the persecution of others – which, sadly it most certainly does – its inclusion in the Refugee Convention serves a useful and important purpose.

When the Refugee Convention was drafted and adopted, the paradigm refugee was the Jewish victim of Nazi persecution.[43] The word was used in a wide sense of ethnicity, irrespective of the Jewish person's religious observance, and this is consistent with modern international legal usage of the term. The International Covenant on the Elimination of All Forms of Racial Discrimination refers to 'race, colour, descent, or national or ethnic origin'.[44] The European Union's Qualification Directive states that the concept of race 'shall, in particular, include consideration of colour, descent, or membership of a particular ethnic group'.[45]

Religion

The Convention ground of religion is broadly understood as applying to, more or less, any system of belief and to its expression in private or in a community with others. International human rights law groups religion with

---

[42] See for example Saini, S. (2019) *Superior: The Return of Race Science*, London: Penguin.
[43] See Introduction. Race was first proposed and then later adopted as one of the qualifying criterion for refugee status in the pre-war years after the rise of the Nazi Party to power in Germany.
[44] International Covenant on the Elimination of All Forms of Racial Discrimination, Article 1(1).
[45] Directive 2011/95/EU, Article 10(1)(a).

freedom of thought, conscience and belief.[46] While this might conceivably be taken to suggest these are related but separate concepts, it is more sensible and consistent with the purpose of the Refugee Convention to regard religion as encompassing them all. The Human Rights Committee has stated that the right to freedom of thought, conscience and religion 'protects theistic, non-theistic and atheistic beliefs, as well as the right not to profess any religion or belief' and that the right 'is not limited in its application to traditional religions or to religions and beliefs with institutional characteristics or practices analogous to those of traditional religions'.[47] Perhaps because of its breadth, the scope of the concept of religion is seldom contested, but in one United Kingdom case a judge held that '[t]he notion that a "devil cult" practising pagan rituals of the sort here described is in any true sense a religion I find deeply offensive'.[48]

Freedom of religion is defined in international human rights law as including the right to change religion or belief and freedom to practice 'either individually or in community with others and in public or private, to manifest his religion or belief in worship, observance, practice and teaching'.[49] The importance of the form and content of communal rites and practices and a faith's system of governance has been emphasized in refugee law, with Wilcox J observing in one case that '[m]any wars have been fought, and many people martyred, because of disagreements on such matters'.[50] Outside the context of refugee law, the European Court of Human Rights has observed that manifestation of religious belief may take the form of worship, teaching, practice and observance and that '[b]earing witness in words and deeds is bound up with the existence of religious convictions'.[51] The European Union's Qualification Directive draws all of these threads together into a usefully concise yet also very broad written definition as including 'the holding of theistic, non-theistic and atheistic beliefs, the participation in, or abstention from, formal worship in private or in public, either alone or in community with others, other religious acts or expressions of view, or forms of personal or communal conduct based on or mandated by any religious belief'.[52]

---

[46] See for example Universal Declaration of Human Rights at Article 18, International Covenant on Civil and Political Rights at Article 18 and European Convention on Human Rights at Article 9.
[47] UN Human Rights Committee (1993) *General Comment No. 22: The Right to Freedom of Thought, Conscience and Religion (Art. 18)* (UN Doc CCPR/C/21/Rev.1/Add.4).
[48] *Omoruyi v Secretary of State for the Home Department* [2000] EWCA Civ 258.
[49] International Covenant on Civil and Political Rights, Article 18.
[50] *Wang v Minister for Immigration and Multicultural Affairs* [2000] FCA 1599 (Aus FC).
[51] *Eweida v United Kingdom* [2013] ECHR 37 [80].
[52] Directive 2011/95/EU, Article 10(1)(b).

It is a mistake to draw a distinction between core and peripheral aspects of religious freedom. As Lord Dyson has said,

> [t]here is no support in any of the human rights jurisprudence for a distinction between the conscientious non-believer and the indifferent non-believer, any more than there is support for a distinction between the zealous believer and the marginally committed believer. All are equally entitled to human rights protection and to protection against persecution under the Convention.[53]

A prohibition on public communal worship has been accepted as being capable of amounting to being persecuted, and it has been recognized that risk of prosecution or serious harm can constitute persecution in this context.[54] It does not follow that any interference with freedom of religion automatically engages the Refugee Convention, however. Where religious practice is banned, it tends to be enforced through violence so the question seldom arises in practice. The human rights analysis discussed in Chapter 4 provides a principled means by which cases of persecution can be identified: through *breach* of the qualified, non-absolute right of freedom of religion, not mere *interference* with it. This still leaves asylum assessors with the difficult task of assessing when a breach has occurred, but international human rights law and decided cases can provide guidance.[55]

Nationality

Before and during the Second World War, national borders were redrawn in war and peace and many people moved both voluntarily and involuntarily within Europe. In the aftermath, there was a plain risk that those who found themselves in the 'wrong' country might be targeted by the local population for this reason. In this context, it is easy to see why nationality was included as a convention ground. Pre-war denaturalization (removal of citizenship) of groups of citizens by the Soviet and Nazi regimes may well also have loomed large in the thinking of the drafters. Today, however, the convention ground is infrequently relied on, not least because it overlaps considerably with the more readily understood ground of race. Nationality is not redundant as a convention ground, though.

---

[53] *RT (Zimbabwe) v Secretary of State for the Home Department* [2012] UKSC 38, [2013] 1 AC 152 [45] (Lord Dyson). See also Joined Cases C-71/11 and C-99/11 *Y and Z v Germany* [62].

[54] *Kazemzadeh v Attorney General* (11th Circuit, 6 August 2009); Joined Cases C-71/11 and C-99/11 *Y and Z v Germany* [65]-[72].

[55] See for example *Eweida v United Kingdom* [2013] ECHR 37.

In international law, the concept of nationality is a narrow one, a 'politico-legal term denoting membership of a State'.[56] It can also be used in a wider 'historico-biological' sense denoting 'membership of a nation'. The concept of nationality in the context of the Refugee Convention is now broadly understood as including both of these usages. The European Union's Qualification Directive provides a useful reference point, defining nationality as including 'cultural, ethnic, or linguistic identity, common geographical or political origins or ... relationship with the population of another state'.[57] As Fripp observes, military occupation of a country and subsequent targeting of its citizens might well provide an example of persecution for reasons of nationality, as might targeting of dual-nationals (those who hold more than one nationality) or the creation and targeting of distinct classes of nationality within a country, as occurred in apartheid South Africa.[58] Applying the composite approach to the refugee definition, the existence of the convention ground of nationality also informs us as to what constitutes persecuted. Denationalization and statelessness are more readily understood as constituting persecution given that nationality is characteristic specifically protected by the Refugee Convention.[59] On this basis, stateless Kuwaiti Bidoons have been recognized as refugees, for example.[60] Palestinians resident outside Israel and the occupied territories who are not excluded from refugee status by Article 1D of the Refugee Convention, as discussed in Chapter 6, have fared less well. Rather rubbing salt in the wound of statelessness, it has been said that denial of re-entry into a country of former habitual residence to a stateless person 'does not interfere with a stateless person's rights in the way that it does with the rights of a national'.[61] In contrast, expulsion from a person's country of nationality has been described as

---

[56] Weis, P. (1956) *Nationality and Statelessness in International Law*, cited in Fripp, E. (2016) *Nationality and Statelessness in the International Law of Refugee Status*, London: Hart, pp 5 and 145.

[57] Directive 2011/95/EU, Article 10(1)(c). See also UNHCR, *Handbook on Procedures and Criteria for Determining Refugee Status and Guidelines on International Protection under the 1951 Convention and the 1967 Protocol Relating to the Status of Refugees*, HCR/1P/4/ENG/REV.4 (1979, reissued 2019) [27].

[58] Fripp, E. (2016) *Nationality and Statelessness in the International Law of Refugee Status*, London: Hart, pp 146–147.

[59] *Tesfamichael v MIMIM* [1999] FCA 1661 (Aus FC); *Thabet v Canada (MCI)* [1998] 4 FC 21 (Can FC); *EB (Ethiopia) v Secretary of State for the Home Department* [2009] QB 1, [2007] EWCA Civ 809.

[60] *Refugee Appeal No. 74467* (NZ RSAA, 1 September 2004); *BA and others (Bedoon–statelessness–risk of persecution) Kuwait CG* [2004] UKIAT 00256.

[61] *MA (Palestinian Territories) v Secretary of State for the Home Department* [2008] EWCA Civ 304 [26] (Maurice Kay LJ).

'a particularly acute form of persecution' and the same reasoning would apply to denial of a right of return.[62]

Membership of a particular social group

The convention ground of membership of a particular social group was added to the text of the Refugee Convention very late in the drafting process after the related UNHCR statute had already been finalized and adopted. Its meaning is not self-evident. Introducing the new ground, the Swedish delegate to the conference said only that 'experience had shown that certain refugees had been persecuted because they belonged to particular social groups. The draft convention made no provision for such cases, and one designed to cover them should accordingly be included'.[63] Considerable judicial time and energy have since been expended in exploring, defining and restraining the concept. The application of positive and negative rules of legal interpretation combined with extensive transnational judicial dialogue has resulted in broad agreement on some principles but a degree of divergence on others. In particular, two different means by which a particular social group can be identified have emerged: the immutable characteristic and social perception approaches. These may be regarded as alternatives ('or') but have become cumulative conditions ('and') in some jurisdictions.

Firstly, the points of consensus. The particular social group ground should not be interpreted as a 'catch all' category because this would render redundant the other grounds enumerated in the Refugee Convention, thus offending against the interpretative rule of surplusage.[64] It is therefore important not to define a particular social group solely by reference to the persecution suffered because to do so would have precisely this effect. Further, a particular social group need not be small nor need be homogenous or cohesive. There does not need to be a 'voluntary, associational relationship': the other convention grounds might apply to very large numbers of disparate individuals.[65] There is no requirement that all members of the social group experience or are at risk of persecution; some members of any social group may escape persecution, for whatever reason.[66] There is no stipulation that persecution originate from outside the particular social group as defined; the persecution

---

[62] *Haile v Gonzales* 421 F3d 493 (7th Circuit, 2005), reiterated later in the same case in *Haile v Holder* 591 F3d 572 (7th Circuit, 2010).

[63] UN Doc A/CONF.2/SR.3.

[64] Hathaway, J. (1991) *The Law of Refugee Status*, Toronto: Butterworths Canada, p 159; *Attorney General of Canada v Ward* [1993] 2 SCR 689.

[65] *R v Immigration Appeal Tribunal, ex p Shah* [1999] 2 AC 629 (UK HL); *Applicant A v Minister for Immigration and Ethnic Affairs* [1997] HCA 4 (Aus HC).

[66] *R v Immigration Appeal Tribunal, ex p Shah* [1999] 2 AC 629 (UK HL).

may be conducted by other members of the group.[67] While these negative considerations are widely agreed, disagreements remain on the principles that apply to positive identification of a particular social group.

On the immutable characteristic analysis, a particular social group should be understood as being of the same kind ('*ejusdem generis*') as the other Refugee Convention grounds. Each of the other convention grounds represents 'a characteristic that either is beyond the power of an individual to change or is so fundamental to individual identity or conscience that it ought not be required to be changed'.[68] A particular social group must also, therefore, be regarded as having a similarly immutable quality to it that person cannot change or, for reasons of conscience, should not have to change. Pioneering this approach in the influential case of *Acosta*, the United States Board of Immigration Appeals went on to say that

> [t]he shared characteristic might be an innate one such as sex, color, or kinship ties, or in some circumstances it might be a shared past experience such as former military leadership or land ownership. The particular kind of group characteristic that will qualify under this construction remains to be determined on a case-by-case basis.[69]

The *Acosta* analysis was championed by Professor Hathaway and has become widely accepted despite the relatively lowly status of the Board of Immigration Appeals.[70] It is consistent with the broad objective of the Refugee Convention to protect against discriminatory harm. Having enumerated race, religion, nationality and political opinion, '[i]t would have been remarkable if the draftsmen had overlooked other forms of discrimination'.[71] By including this additional ground, the framers of the convention were 'intending to include whatever groups might be regarded as coming within the anti-discriminatory objectives of the Convention'.[72] This focus on discrimination has enabled the identification of particular social groups including social classes, women, LGBTQ+ people, children, the

---

[67] *Fornah v Secretary of State for the Home Department* [2006] UKHL 46, [2007] 1 AC 412 [31] (Lord Bingham) and [110] (Baroness Hale).
[68] *In re Acosta* (1985) 19 I & N 211.
[69] *In re Acosta* (1985) 19 I & N 211.
[70] Hathaway, J. (1991) *The Law of Refugee Status*, Toronto: Butterworths Canada; see for example *Attorney General of Canada v Ward* [1993] 2 SCR 689 (Can SC), *R v Immigration Appeal Tribunal, ex p Shah* [1999] 2 AC 629 (UK HL), *Appeal No. 1312/93 Re GJ*; *Refugee Appeal 71427/99* [2000] NZRSAA 337 and *Jian-Qiang Fang v Refugee Appeal Board et al*, Case No. 40771/05, 15 November 2006 (South African HC).
[71] *R v Immigration Appeal Tribunal, ex p Shah* [1999] 2 AC 629 (UK HL) (Lord Steyn).
[72] *R v Immigration Appeal Tribunal, ex p Shah* [1999] 2 AC 629 (UK HL) (Lord Hoffman).

family, victims of trafficking, disabled people and others.[73] Legal controversies have arisen along the way, though, and the immutable characteristic approach has denied recognition to some other cohorts that might be considered colloquially to be 'social' groups.

The extent to which a social group based on employment, occupation or land ownership – which can be characterized as forms of voluntary association – will be recognized as a particular social group is contested. The outcome in *Acosta* itself was rejection of the proposition that Salvadoran taxi drivers formed a particular social group and it has been said that '[a] common employment does not ordinarily have that impact upon individual identities or conscience necessary to constitute employees a particular social group'.[74] Hathaway and Foster question this analysis, observing that freedom to choose one's occupation is an internationally protected human right and that willingness to recognize particular social groups based on professional or 'worthy' occupations reflects something of a class bias.[75] Claims are more likely to succeed based on former status, association or occupation as this is a characteristic which cannot now be changed. In a society where people working in a job or occupation are targeted for persecution for ideological reasons irrespective of whether they continue working in that job or occupation – as for example with teachers, lawyers, doctors and others in Pol Pot's Cambodia – then this is an immutable characteristic that the person concerned cannot change and the test may therefore be met.[76] Historical examples have been postulated that might also constitute a particular social group in a particular time and place, such as landlords after revolutions in

---

[73] Social class: *R v Immigration Appeal Tribunal, ex p Shah* [1999] 2 AC 629 (UK HL), *Fornah v Secretary of State for the Home Department* [2006] UKHL 46, [2007] 1 AC 412 [98]; women: *R v Immigration Appeal Tribunal, ex p Shah* [1999] 2 AC 629 (UK HL), *Minister for Immigration v Khawar* [2002] HCA 14 (Aus HC), *Fornah v Secretary of State for the Home Department* [2006] UKHL 46, [2007] 1 AC 412; LGBTQ+ people: *Attorney General of Canada v Ward* [1993] 2 SCR 689 (Can SC), *Appellant S395/2002 v Minister for Immigration and Multicultural Affairs* [2003] HCA 71 (Aus HC), *HJ (Iran) v Secretary of State for the Home Department* [2010] UKSC 31, [2011] 1 AC 596, Joined Cases C-199/12, C-200/12 and C-201/12 *Netherlands v X, Y and Z*; children/age: *VFAY v Minister for Immigration* [2003] FMCA 35, *Xiao v Canada (Minister of Citizenship and Immigration)* [2001] FCT 195, *LQ (age: immutable characteristics) Afghanistan* [2008] UK AIT 00005; family: *Chan v Minister for Immigration and Ethnic Affairs* [1989] HCA 62 (Aus HC), *Sarrazola v Minister for Immigration and Multicultural Affairs* [2000] FCA 919 (Aus FC), *Fornah v Secretary of State for the Home Department* [2006] UKHL 46, [2007] 1 AC 412; victims of trafficking: *SM (PSG, Protection Regulations, Regulation 6) Moldova CG* [2008] UKAIT 00002; disability: *DH (Particular Social Group: Mental Health) Afghanistan* [2020] UKUT 223 (IAC).

[74] *Secretary of State for the Home Department v Ouanes* [1998] Imm AR 76 (EW CA) (Pill LJ).

[75] Hathaway, J. and Foster, M. (2014) *The Law of Refugee Status* (2nd edn), Cambridge: Cambridge University Press, p 457.

[76] *Nouredine v Minister for Immigration and Multicultural Affairs* (1999) 91 FCR 138 (Aus FC).

Russia and China or ballet dancers and others associated with Western culture during the Cultural Revolution in China. Contemporary examples include former victims of trafficking, former child soldiers and former police officers.[77]

The alternative means for identifying a particular social group is often labelled the 'social perception' approach, whereby a group is identified by reference to a common characteristic which makes them a recognizable group and sets them apart from society as a whole. The word 'social' can be read as a reference not to the internal qualities of the group but rather to the society in which the group manifests. On this analysis, a requirement that the identifying common characteristic be an immutable one may be seen as an additional, unnecessary gloss on the wording of the Refugee Convention.[78] In the Australian case of *Applicant A*, for example, Dawson J held that a particular social group is 'a collection of persons who share a certain characteristic or element which unites them and enables them to be set apart from society at large'.[79] Goodwin-Gill and McAdam argue this is a more straightforward means of identifying groups in society in the sociological sense or 'in the ordinary, everyday sense which describes the constitution or make-up of the community at large', such as 'the landlord class, the working class, the ruling class, the bourgeoisie, the middle class or even the criminal class'.[80] While the House of Lords case of *Islam* is often held out as an example of the 'immutable characteristic' approach, the judgment also encourages an asylum assessor to consider the context of the relevant society.[81] Lord Hoffman stated that to identify a social group, 'one must first identify the society of which it forms a part'. Or, as Lord Hope put it,

> In general terms a social group may be said to exist when a group of people with a particular characteristic is recognised as a distinct group by society. The concept of a group means that we dealing here with people who are grouped together because they share a characteristic not shared by others, not with individuals. The word 'social' means that we are being asked to identify a group of people which is recognised as a particular group by society. As social customs and social attitudes

---

[77] *SM (PSG, Protection Regulations, Regulation 6) Moldova CG* [2008] UKAIT 00002; *Lukwago v Ashcroft* 329 F3d 157 (3rd Cir 2003); *Cruz-Navarro v INS* 232 F3d 1024 (9th Cir 2000).
[78] *Applicant A v Minister of Immigration and Ethnic Affairs* [1997] HCA 4 (Aus HC) (Brennan CJ).
[79] *Applicant A v Minister for Immigration and Ethnic Affairs* [1997] HCA 4 (Aus HC).
[80] Goodwin-Gill, G. and McAdam, J. (2021) *The Refugee in International Law* (4th edn), Oxford: Oxford University Press, p 118.
[81] *R v Immigration Appeal Tribunal, ex p Shah* [1999] 2 AC 629 (UK HL).

differ from one country to another, the context for this inquiry is the country of the person's nationality.

A particular social group may therefore be identified in one country and society but not in another.

Advocates for refugees have sometimes attempted to frame particular social groups in narrow terms in order to encourage acceptance by asylum assessors. 'Women who experience domestic violence' or 'girls at risk of Female Genital Mutilation' have been advanced as particular social groups, for example.[82] These narrowly framed groups potentially offend against the principle identified earlier, that a particular social group must not be defined solely by reference to the persecution suffered. This is not to say that discrimination or persecution against a group excludes the possibility of identifying a particular social group for the purposes of the Refugee Convention; the Refugee Convention does not feature a Catch 22.[83] Discrimination against a group in society may well serve to highlight the existence of a particular social group. Where, for example, women are discriminated against and persecuted in a country because they are women, gender can be the immutable shared characteristic to define the group. But it can also be argued that the discrimination indicates that women are perceived in that society to be inferior and therefore that they constitute a particular social group. On either analysis, the relevant particular social group is 'women', not a more narrowly drawn group. It may be appropriate and permissible in some contexts to define a particular social group more narrowly based on a criterion separate to the persecution, such as age, ethnic group or class, for example.[84] Similarly, Pobjoy sets out recognized examples of what he terms 'age-plus' cases involving children, such as orphaned children, abandoned children, impoverished children, disabled children, westernized children and others.[85]

As the example of women shows, it will often be the case that a particular social group is identifiable both by an immutable characteristic *and* social perception and it has therefore been argued that the two approaches are not inconsistent.[86] This will not always be the case. An issue may arise where

---

[82] *R v Immigration Appeal Tribunal, ex p Shah* [1999] 2 AC 629 (UK HL) and *Fornah v Secretary of State for the Home Department* [2006] UKHL 46, [2007] 1 AC 412.

[83] *Fornah v Secretary of State for the Home Department* [2006] UKHL 46, [2007] 1 AC 412 [113] (Baroness Hale).

[84] *Fornah v Secretary of State for the Home Department* [2006] UKHL 46, [2007] 1 AC 412.

[85] Pobjoy, J. (2017) *The Child in International Refugee Law*, Cambridge: Cambridge University Press, p 179.

[86] UNHCR (2002) *Guidelines on International Protection No 2: 'Membership of a Particular Social Group' within the Context of Article 1A(2) of the 1951 Convention and/or Its 1967 Protocol Relating to the Status of Refugees* (HCR/GIP/02/02).

a group is perceived as being different by society but does not share an immutable characteristic. The two routes to recognition are therefore best seen as alternatives, not as cumulative requirements. The European Union's Qualification Directive appears on the face of it to require both approaches to be satisfied but this has been held to be 'more stringent than is warranted by international authority'.[87] At the time of writing, the United Kingdom was in the process of legislating to require both approaches to be satisfied before a particular social group might be recognized.[88]

Political opinion

For many, the political refugee is the paradigm refugee: a principled party activist opposing a repressive regime who flees state oppression. In common with the other convention grounds, though, political opinion should be broadly interpreted. It is not restricted only to political activists for recognized political parties, for example. As a starting point, political opinion should be understood to include 'any opinion on any matter in which the machinery of state, government, and policy may be engaged'.[89] Political opinion is not restricted to opinions of this nature, though. It may apply to opinions concerning non-state or private actors.[90] It is also understood as applying broadly to opinions concerning power relationships and power structures within a country and policies or methods.[91] A person need not be a member of a political party; what matters is whether a person risks being persecuted for their political beliefs.[92] This includes a risk arising from a neutral opinion or a refusal to express support for a cause.[93]

A person can express their political opinion explicitly or implicitly through their actions. Similarly, a political opinion may be attributed to a person – whether correctly or incorrectly is irrelevant – on the basis of their actions. Choice of association, dress, speech, make-up, hairstyle, ornaments, music

---

[87] Directive 2004/85/EC and Directive 2004/95/EU at Article 10(1)(d) and *Fornah v Secretary of State for the Home Department* [2006] UKHL 46, [2007] 1 AC 412 [18] (Lord Bingham), [100]-[103] (Baroness Hale) and [118] (Lord Brown of Eaton-Under-Heywood).

[88] Nationality and Borders Bill 2021.

[89] Goodwin-Gill, G. (1983) *The Refugee in International Law*, Oxford: Oxford University Press, p 31, cited in cases including *Attorney General of Canada v Ward* [1993] 2 SCR 689 and *Gomez v Secretary of State for the Home Department* [2000] INLR 549 (UK IAT).

[90] Directive 2011/95/EU, Article 10(1)(e), *Gomez v Secretary of State for the Home Department* [2000] INLR 549 (UK IAT).

[91] Directive 2011/95/EU, Article 10(1)(e), *Gomez v Secretary of State for the Home Department* [2000] INLR 549 (UK IAT).

[92] *Osorio v INS* 18 F3d 1017 (2nd Cir 1994).

[93] *RT (Zimbabwe) v Secretary of State for the Home Department* [2012] UKSC 38, [2013] 1 AC 152.

or other manifestations of personal choice may be politically charged in a given society. Recognition that political opinion may be attributed on account of conduct may be particularly significant in refugee claims made by women and children among others, for example through support roles for political organizations.

There is no requirement that a person has expressed their political opinion or acted upon it in order to succeed in a claim to refugee status.[94] The assessment of risk is forward-looking and therefore it is sufficient to show that a person's political opinion will place them in danger if returned to their home country. It may be the case that the political opinion was held previously and is in danger of being discovered by the authorities in the home country, for example, or that the person wishes in future to express their previously unexpressed political opinion, or that the person has developed a political opinion since leaving the country concerned which they wish to express on their return. Issues of proof may arise in such situations (see Chapter 2) but in principle, there is no bar to a claim succeeding on these grounds.

Suggested further reading

Goodwin-Gill, G. and McAdam, J. (2021) *The Refugee in International Law* (4th edn), Oxford: Oxford University Press, Chapter 3.

Hathaway, J. and Foster, M. (2014) *The Law of Refugee Status* (2nd edn), Cambridge: Cambridge University Press, Chapter 5.

UNHCR, *Guidelines on International Protection No. 2: 'Membership of a Particular Social Group' within the Context of Article 1A(2) of the 1951 Convention and/or Its 1967 Protocol Relating to the Status of Refugees*, HCR/GIP/02/02 (7 May 2002).

UNHCR, *Guidelines on International Protection No. 6: Religion-Based Refugee Claims under Article 1A(2) of the 1951 Convention and/or the 1967 Protocol Relating to the Status of Refugees*, HCR/GIP/04/06 (28 April 2004).

UNHCR, *Guidelines on International Protection No. 9: Claims to Refugee Status based on Sexual Orientation and/or Gender Identity within the context of Article 1A(2) of the 1951 Convention and/or Its 1967 Protocol Relating to the Status of Refugees*, HCR/GIP/12/09 (23 October 2012).

UNHCR, *Guidelines on International Protection No. 10: Claims to Refugee Status related to Military Service within the Context of Article 1A (2) of the 1951 Convention and/or the 1967 Protocol Relating to the Status of Refugees*, HCR/GIP/13/10 (12 November 2014).

---

[94] UNHCR, *Handbook on Procedures and Criteria for Determining Refugee Status and Guidelines on International Protection under the 1951 Convention and the 1967 Protocol Relating to the Status of Refugees*, HCR/1P/4/ENG/REV.4 (1979, reissued 2019) [82].

UNHCR, *Guidelines on International Protection No. 12: Claims for Refugee Status Related to Situations of Armed Conflict and Violence under Article 1A(2) of the 1951 Convention and/or 1967 Protocol Relating to the Status of Refugees and the Regional Refugee Definitions*, HCR/GIP/16/12 (2 December 2012).

UNHCR, *Handbook on Procedures and Criteria for Determining Refugee Status and Guidelines on International Protection under the 1951 Convention and the 1967 Protocol Relating to the Status of Refugees*, HCR/1P/4/ENG/REV.4 (1979, reissued 2019), [66]-[86].

Fornah v Secretary of State for the Home Department [2006] UKHL 46, [2007] 1 AC 412.

HJ (Iran) v Secretary of State for the Home Department [2010] UKSC 31, [2011] 1 AC 596.

Joined Cases C-71/11 and C-99/11 *Y and Z v Germany*.

R v Immigration Appeal Tribunal, ex p Shah [1999] 2 AC 629 (UKHL) (Lord Hoffman).

RT (Zimbabwe) v Secretary of State for the Home Department [2012] UKSC 38, [2013] 1 AC 152.

Sepet v Secretary of State for the Home Department [2003] UKHL 15, [2003] 3 All ER 304.

6

Cessation and Exclusion

As well as being gained, refugee status can be lost, taken away or denied. Refugee status may be lost when it is no longer needed because the refugee can return home. In some situations, this may be voluntary on the part of the refugee but the Refugee Convention also provides for countries of asylum to terminate refugee status on certain grounds even if this is against the refugee's wishes. The provisions in the Refugee Convention addressing loss of refugee status are often referred to as the cessation clauses and are found at Article 1C. Refugee status is also denied in some limited circumstances. Denial of refugee status is aimed at those who would normally be entitled to refugee status but who are considered either not to need it or not to deserve it. These provisions denying refugee status are often referred to as the exclusion clauses and are found at Articles 1D, 1E and 1F of the convention. Article 1D excludes Palestinian refugees on the basis that they are entitled to protection from a different United Nations agency. Article 1E was intended to apply to historic groups of ethnic Germans in post-war Europe but is framed more widely so as potentially to apply to those who have rights equivalent to the citizens of the country in which they reside. Article 1F excludes certain individuals on the grounds of moral opprobrium in order to protect the reputation and integrity of the Refugee Convention.

Cessation of or exclusion from refugee status are conceptually distinct from formal retention of refugee status but loss of the *benefits* of refugee status, including protection from expulsion or *refoulement*. Denial of the benefits of refugee status can occur on grounds of national security or public order and the relevant provisions are found at Articles 32 and 33 of the Refugee Convention. For a refugee – and indeed for a country of asylum – this may feel like a distinction without a difference, but the grounds for cessation of status, exclusion from status and expulsion are all different. Expulsion of a refugee from a country of asylum as distinct from cessation or denial of refugee status is addressed in Chapter 7 on refugee rights.

Cessation clauses

Refugee status is not intended to be permanent. The Refugee Convention recognizes two broad potential outcomes for a refugee: assimilation into a new country or safe return to the country of origin. These two outcomes are reflected in what are often referred to as the 'cessation' clauses at Article 1C of the Convention. Both outcomes lead to loss of refugee status on the basis that it is no longer necessary. This is the theory. In practice, many refugees achieve neither solution. Instead, they spend many years, perhaps their whole life, in a supposedly temporary refugee camp in a country adjacent to their own. This is the outcome where the home country remains unstable or otherwise unwelcoming, the host country is unwilling to facilitate assimilation and naturalization – perhaps not being a signatory to the Refugee Convention – and the refugee is not resettled elsewhere.[1]

Returning to how refugee status is intended to work, the Refugee Convention's cessation clauses set out six distinct circumstances in which refugee status ends. These can be grouped into circumstances where, firstly, the refugee is considered to have voluntarily reavailed themselves of the protection of their country of origin either in practice or in law and, secondly, where the refugee cannot 'continue to refuse to avail himself of the protection' of the country or origin. These circumstances are exhaustive in the sense that no other reasons are permissible under the Refugee Convention for cessation of refugee status, aside from an implied right for state parties to annul refugee status granted on the basis of misrepresentation. They are also intended to be limited in nature, so as to assure refugees of continuity of status absent specific conditions being met:

> Once an asylum application has been formally determined and refugee status officially granted, with all the benefits both under the Convention and under national law which that carries with it, the refugee has the assurance of a secure future in the host country and a legitimate expectation that he will not henceforth be stripped of this save for demonstrably good and sufficient reason.[2]

---

[1] Article 34 of the Refugee Convention reads: 'The Contracting States shall as far as possible facilitate the assimilation and naturalization of refugees. They shall in particular make every effort to expedite naturalization proceedings and to reduce as far as possible the charges and costs of such proceedings.' See further Chapter 7.

[2] *Hoxha v Secretary of State for the Home Department* [2005] UKHL 19, [2005] WLR 1063 [65] (Lord Brown of Eaton-under-Heywood). See also UNHCR, *Handbook on Procedures and Criteria for Determining Refugee Status and Guidelines on International Protection under the 1951 Convention and the 1967 Protocol Relating to the Status of Refugees*, HCR/1P/4/ENG/REV.4 (1979, reissued 2019) [112].

Nevertheless, the language of the cessation clause is, at least in part, mandatory and automatic. Article 1C begins 'This Convention shall cease to apply ...'. This is the mirror image of the constitutive nature of refugee status discussed in the Introduction. Refugee status may therefore be considered to lapse automatically where the conditions in the cessation clauses are met.[3] However, a recognized refugee will (or should) have been granted formal refugee status and a residence permit. For these to be revoked a determination will need to be made as to whether the circumstances of cessation have or have not arisen. Cessation is therefore not usually automatic or immediate in practice.

Voluntary acquisition of protection

There are four circumstances in which a refugee is considered voluntarily to cease being a refugee.[4] Three relate to the country of origin or nationality: where the refugee 'has voluntarily re-availed himself of the protection of the country of his nationality', where the refugee, having lost their nationality, voluntarily requires it and where the refugee 'voluntarily re-established himself in the country which he left or outside which he remained owing to fear of persecution'. The other is where the refugee acquires a new nationality and enjoys the protection of the country in question.[5] This might be the country of refuge or it might be some other, third country. Of these, it is voluntary reavailment of protection and voluntary re-establishment that have proven most problematic for refugees.

The meaning of the word 'protection' in the cessation clauses at both Article 1C(1) and Article 1C(5) is, as with its use in the definition clause, contested. Use of the same word in multiple locations in the same legal instrument strongly suggests that the same meaning should be attributed to that word throughout. This is not how the clauses have been interpreted in practice, however. The original meaning of 'protection' was in the sense of diplomatic protection, for example by applying for a passport or identity document through consular authorities in the country of refuge.[6] Hathaway and Foster describe this usage of the word in the context of cessation as 'highly formalistic and outmoded' on the basis that many of those applying

---

[3] *Minister for Immigration, Multicultural and Indigenous Affairs v QAAH* [2006] HCA 53 (Aus HC) [44]; *ZN (Afghanistan) v Entry Clearance Officer, Karachi* [2008] EWCA Civ 1420, [2009] Imm AR 352 [32] (Laws LJ) (on appeal, the Supreme Court allowed the appeal but expressed no view on this issue: *ZN (Afghanistan) v Entry Clearance Officer, Karachi* [2010] UKSC 21, [2010] WLR 1275).

[4] Refugee Convention, Article 1C(1)–(4) respectively.

[5] Refugee Convention, Article 1C(5).

[6] See Chapter 4.

for such documents do so as a matter of routine or practical convenience without regard to the international law ramifications of doing so.[7] They propose that cessation should therefore only be triggered in this way if a request for diplomatic protection was genuinely voluntary, was genuinely intended as an act of reavailment of protection and the protection sought was actually forthcoming. The UNHCR Handbook is unhelpful to refugees in this regard, stating that where a refugee applies for and obtains or renews a national passport then 'it will, in the absence of proof to the contrary, be presumed that he intends to avail himself of the protection of the country of his nationality'.[8] The presumption may be rebuttable but this approach, which goes beyond the wording of the cessation clauses themselves, unnecessarily shifts the onus to the refugee. Realistically, a refugee will rarely have good reason to fear diplomatic or consular staff outside their country, although the assassination of Saudi Arabian dissident Jamal Khashoggi at a consulate in Turkey in 2018 provides a salutary example to the contrary. It might also be observed that it is not unknown for a repressive regime to desire an exile to return home so that they might be made an example of. In such cases, diplomatic services could conceivably be made available to an exile as a means of securing their return by triggering cessation of their refugee status.

The provision for cessation through voluntary reacquisition of citizenship is less problematic as it is by its nature less likely to occur by accident and more likely to signal an actual intention on the part of a refugee to throw in their lot with that country again. It also seldom arises in practice, given that denaturalization of refugees is no longer commonplace, in contrast to the interwar period. Automatic loss of a prior citizenship may occur where a country's laws prohibit dual citizenship and a refugee acquires a new citizenship, but refugee status is normally lost in such circumstances anyway owing to another of the cessation clauses and so citizenship reacquisition will normally be irrelevant in practice.[9]

There should be no difficulty with the idea that a refugee who genuinely returns to live long-term in their country of origin no longer requires refugee status. This cessation provision applies to both nationals of a country and stateless former residents. In practice, however, voluntary re-establishment has presented similar problems to reavailment of protection: it is ambiguous and can occur by accident rather than design on the part of the refugee. The term 're-establishment' was adopted by the drafters of the Refugee Convention

---

[7] Hathaway, J. and Foster, M. (2014) *The Law of Refugee Status* (2nd edn), Cambridge: Cambridge University Press, p 465.

[8] UNHCR, *Handbook on Procedures and Criteria for Determining Refugee Status and Guidelines on International Protection under the 1951 Convention and the 1967 Protocol Relating to the Status of Refugees*, HCR/1P/4/ENG/REV.4 (1979, reissued 2019) [121].

[9] Refugee Convention, Article 1C(3).

rather than an alternative such as 'return', indicating very strongly that a mere visit or a forcible repatriation or push-back does not engage this clause. UNHCR advocate the view that this clause refers to return to the country of nationality or former habitual residence with a view to permanently residing there.[10] Low-profile and short-term visits – for example to visit a sick or dying relative or bring abroad a family member, possessions or property – should not be considered to amount to re-establishment. A pattern of prolonged and frequent visits, perhaps for holidays or business purposes, might however indicate something more substantial than transitory presence and therefore constitute re-establishment.[11] The test should be substantive re-establishment and reintegration consistent with the international commitment to enable refugees to return home freely in safety and dignity in exercise of a free and informed choice.[12] Sadly, this has not prevented some countries of refuge from considering cessation and revocation of refugee status simply on the basis of a single physical visit, apparently as a means of absolving themselves of responsibility for hosting refugees.[13]

Voluntary acquisition of an entirely new nationality is most likely to arise in respect of the country of refuge. In such circumstances, it is appropriate that refugee status ends on the basis that it is no longer needed. This is not to say that a refugee is necessarily entirely restored to their former condition before flight or that the person concerned will cease to be a refugee in ordinary parlance. But the protection of an international legal instrument will no longer be necessary and is therefore appropriately withdrawn. Problems have arisen where a person who was a refugee but has acquired citizenship of the country of refuge is not in reality fully integrated, assimilated or settled into their country of refuge and seeks reunification with family members who are still abroad.[14] The Refugee Convention does not include an explicit right of family reunification and a former refugee will have to adapt as best they can to life in the new country (see further Chapter 7).

---

[10] UNHCR, *Handbook on Procedures and Criteria for Determining Refugee Status and Guidelines on International Protection under the 1951 Convention and the 1967 Protocol Relating to the Status of Refugees*, HCR/1P/4/ENG/REV.4 (1979, reissued 2019) [134].

[11] UNHCR, *Handbook on Procedures and Criteria for Determining Refugee Status and Guidelines on International Protection under the 1951 Convention and the 1967 Protocol Relating to the Status of Refugees*, HCR/1P/4/ENG/REV.4 (1979, reissued 2019) [125].

[12] See Global Compact on Refugees (UN Doc A/73/12 (Part II)) (2 August 2018) [87].

[13] See for example United Kingdom Home Office, *Asylum Policy Instruction: Revocation of Refugee Status* (version 4.0, 19 January 2016): 'Where a refugee has obtained a passport and travelled to their country of origin or former habitual residence, the circumstances of the case must be reviewed to consider whether refugee status should be revoked.'

[14] See for example *ZN (Afghanistan) v Entry Clearance Officer (Karachi)* [2010] UKSC 21, [2010] WLR 1275.

The risk of absurd and dangerous outcomes, from the reavailment and re-establishment of cessation clauses in particular, can be mitigated by emphasizing that the action on the part of the refugee must be genuinely voluntary.[15] Involuntary reavailment or re-establishment, for example through a short visit or unknowing, ill-considered action or an action at the behest of the country of refuge, should not trigger cessation. A strict approach whereby the mere fact of return or application for a passport has sometimes been applied in some countries but is not justified on the face of the wording of the cessation clauses.[16]

Change of circumstances

The Refugee Convention ceases to apply to a recognized refugee if he 'can no longer, because the circumstances in connection with which he has been recognized as a refugee have ceased to exist, continue to refuse to avail himself of the protection of the country of his nationality'.[17] An equivalent provision applies to a stateless person who has been recognized as a refugee in respect of their return to their country of former habitual residence.[18] Cessation due to change of circumstances can therefore be triggered by a host state irrespective of the wishes or actions of a refugee. In other words, it may lead to involuntary cessation of refugee status. A natural reading of the reference to 'protection of his country of nationality' suggests that the protection in question must be provided by state authorities, a conclusion supported by the text and the purpose of the Refugee Convention.[19] Despite this, the European Union's Qualification Directive has been read as permitting non-state protection to justify cessation, albeit that mere social and financial support would be inadequate.[20] The reference to 'circumstances in connection with which he has been recognized as a refugee' can be read as referring to either or both the general political conditions in that person's home country and some aspect of that person's personal characteristics.[21]

---

[15] UNHCR, *Handbook on Procedures and Criteria for Determining Refugee Status and Guidelines on International Protection under the 1951 Convention and the 1967 Protocol Relating to the Status of Refugees*, HCR/1P/4/ENG/REV.4 (1979, reissued 2019) [120]; Hathaway, J. and Foster, M. (2014) *The Law of Refugee Status* (2nd edn), Cambridge: Cambridge University Press, p 465.

[16] See for example United Kingdom Home Office, *Asylum Policy Instruction: Revocation of Refugee Status* (version 4.0, 19 January 2016).

[17] Refugee Convention, Article 1C(5).

[18] Refugee Convention, Article 1C(6).

[19] See previous discussion and Hathaway, J. and Foster, M. (2014) *The Law of Refugee Status* (2nd edn), Cambridge: Cambridge University Press, pp 289-292.

[20] Case C-255/19 *United Kingdom v OA* [47].

[21] *Secretary of State for the Home Department v MM (Zimbabwe)* [2017] EWCA Civ 797.

A change in either or both may be sufficient. It is generally considered that the change should be significant and durable in nature and not transitory or temporary.[22] While assuring continuity of residence for refugees in the absence of a durable change is to be welcomed on a humanitarian basis, the legal basis for the idea the change must be durable is not clear. In many jurisdictions a refugee who no longer has a well-founded fear is considered to have undergone a change of circumstances that amounts to cessation.[23] The onus lies with the host state to show that conditions for cessation are satisfied and it is usually considered that the relevant standard of proof is the balance of probabilities (more probable than not).[24] Hathaway and Foster argue that the reference to 'protection' in the cessation clauses 'requires consideration of the sorts of rights critical to reintegration and re-establishment in the home country'.[25] It is not an argument yet to have found favour in the courts. The English Court of Appeal has explicitly said that 'humanitarian standards are not the test for a cessation decision'.[26]

The change of circumstances clauses are subject to a proviso stating that they 'shall not apply to a refugee falling under section A(1) of this article who is able to invoke compelling reasons arising out of previous persecution' for refusing to avail himself of the protection of the country of nationality or former habitual residence. Section A(1) refugees are those who had been recognized as refugees under previous legal instruments prior to the adoption

---

[22] UNHCR, *Handbook on Procedures and Criteria for Determining Refugee Status and Guidelines on International Protection under the 1951 Convention and the 1967 Protocol Relating to the Status of Refugees*, HCR/1P/4/ENG/REV.4 (1979, reissued 2019) [135]; Directive 2011/95/EU, Article 11(2); *Hoxha v Secretary of State for the Home Department* [2005] UKHL 19, [2005] WLR 1063 [63]; *EN (Serbia) v Secretary of State for the Home Department* [2009] EWCA Civ 630 [95]-[96]; *Secretary of State for the Home Department v MM (Zimbabwe)* [2017] EWCA Civ 797 [24].

[23] *Hoxha v Secretary of State for the Home Department* [2005] UKHL 19, [2005] WLR 1063 [56]; *Minister for Immigration, Multicultural Indigenous Affairs v QAAH* [2006] HCA 53 (Aus HC) [39]; Joined Cases C-175/08, C-176/08, C-178/08 and C-179/08 *Salahadin Abdulla and Others v Germany* [66]; *Secretary of State for the Home Department v MA (Somalia)* [2018] EWCA Civ 994 [2] and [47]. See criticism of this approach in Hathaway, J. and Foster, M. (2014) *The Law of Refugee Status* (2nd edn), Cambridge: Cambridge University Press, pp 476–490.

[24] Directive 2011/95/EU, Article 14(2); *Hoxha v Secretary of State for the Home Department* [2005] UKHL 19, [2005] WLR 1063 [66]; *Németh v Canada (Minister of Justice)* [2010] 3 SCR 281 [106]-[112]; there is said to be no burden on either party in Australia.

[25] Hathaway, J. and Foster, M. (2014) *The Law of Refugee Status* (2nd edn), Cambridge: Cambridge University Press, p 488. See also UNHCR, *Guidelines on International Protection No. 3: Cessation of Refugee Status under Article 1C(5) and (6) of the 1951 Convention Relating to the Status of Refugees* (the 'Ceased Circumstances' Clauses) (10 February 2003).

[26] *Secretary of State for the Home Department v MA (Somalia)* [2018] EWCA Civ 994 [56] (Arden LJ).

of the Refugee Convention in 1951 and so the proviso has no continuing effect.[27] Some regional and national legal instruments have nevertheless for humanitarian reasons applied the proviso to contemporary refugees despite being under no international law obligation to do so.[28]

In the United Kingdom, cessation decisions have been relatively rare despite a policy that a recognized refugee be granted a residence permit of five years, at the end which status should be reviewed.[29] The exception to this norm has arisen where the government wishes to deport on the basis of criminal conduct a person previously recognized as a refugee. Under the scheme of the Refugee Convention, expulsion of refugees on grounds of national security or public order is governed by a separate provision at Article 32 (see further Chapter 7). Some governments have found it more convenient to proceed on the basis of selective – and therefore potentially discriminatory – cessation of refugee status rather than engage with the stricter test for expulsion of a person who continues to be recognized as a refugee.[30]

Exclusion clauses

The Refugee Convention includes at Article 1 a number of exclusion clauses which disapply the Convention from certain groups or individuals.[31] These exclusion clauses are to be contrasted with the *non-refoulement* and non-expulsion protections later in the Refugee Convention, which do not disapply the whole Refugee Convention, only the right of *non-refoulement* or non-expulsion (see Chapter 7).

The first and most significant of the exclusion clauses in terms of the number of people it affects is Article 1D. Despite the opacity of its language, it is well established that this provision applies to Palestinian refugees assisted by the United Nations Relief and Works Agency for Palestinian Refugees in the Near East, or UNRWA. The second exclusion clause is the least well known, at Article 1E. Again, the language of this provision is far from clear. The *travaux préparatoires* show that the clause was intended by the drafters of

---

[27] *Hoxha v Secretary of State for the Home Department* [2005] UKHL 19, [2005] WLR 1063.
[28] See for example EU Qualification Directive 2011/95/EU, Article 11(3); Canadian Immigration and Refugee Protection Act, SC 2001, c 27, s 108.
[29] Home Office, *Asylum Policy Instruction: Settlement Protection* (version 4.0, 2 February 2016).
[30] See Chief Inspector of Borders and Immigration, *An Inspection of the Review and Removal of Immigration, Refugee and Citizenship 'Status'* (January 2018) and, for example, *Secretary of State for the Home Department v MA (Somalia)* [2018] EWCA Civ 994. The inspection report revealed 309 cessations of refugee status in cases of previous criminality between 1 January 2015 and 31 March 2017 compared to 25 non-criminal cases in the same period.
[31] Refugee Convention, Articles 1D–1F.

the Refugee Convention to apply to ethnic Germans who had been living outside the territory of post-war Germany and relocated there after the war. The last exclusion clause, at Article 1F, is the most frequently litigated. It excludes from the protection of the Refugee Convention certain individuals adjudged to be ineligible on moral grounds to benefit from refugee status.

Article 1D: Palestinian refugees

In 1948, the conflict in Palestine and the foundation of the state of Israel caused the displacement of around 750,000 Palestinian Arabs. The United Nations, having precipitated the crisis with a plan for partition of the territory, appointed an official mediator and then, recognizing that the displaced Palestinians were refugees, created a temporary relief agency, the United Nations Relief for Palestinian Refugees (UNRPR).[32] This was followed by UN Resolution 194, which resolved that 'refugees wishing to return to their homes and live at peace with their neighbours should be permitted to do so at the earliest practicable date' and created the United Nations Conciliation Commission for Palestine (UNCCP) 'to facilitate the repatriation, resettlement and economic and social rehabilitation of the refugees and the payment of compensation'.[33] The temporary relief agency was replaced in 1949 by the United Nations Relief and Works Agency for Palestine Refugees in the Near East (UNRWA).[34] The function of this new body was to carry out 'direct relief and works programmes' in order to 'prevent conditions of starvation and distress … and to further conditions of peace and stability'. UNCCP remained responsible for achieving what is now commonly referred to as a 'durable solution' for the refugees. But it became increasingly clear that repatriation was not going to happen and funding for UNCCP was eventually terminated. Palestinians had previously been citizens of British Mandate Palestine, but the Israeli Citizenship Act 1952 did not extend citizenship of the new Israeli state to Palestinians who remained outside the territory, meaning that 'almost the totality of Palestinian refugees were effectively denationalized en masse'.[35] For various reasons, the countries in which Palestinian refugees settled have refused to enable them to naturalize as citizens, with the exception of those who fled to Jordan in 1948 (but not those who arrived in Jordan subsequently, for example in 1967). Today, the vast majority of Palestinian refugees – those who fled in

---

[32] A/RES/186 (S-2), 14 May 1948; A/RES/212 (III), 19 November 1948.
[33] A/RES/194 (III), 11 December 1948.
[34] A/RES/302 (IV), 8 December 1949.
[35] Albanese, F. P. and Takkenberg, L. (2020) *Palestinian Refugees in International Law* (2nd edn), Oxford: Oxford University Press, p 158.

1948 and subsequently their descendants – remain stateless. They are assisted by UNRWA, which provides schools, hospitals, utilities and social services in Gaza, the West Bank, Jordan, Syria and Lebanon.

At the time the Palestinian refugee crisis began, it was not unusual for the international community to address the situation of specific groups of refugees with specific, tailored measures. In the interwar years, national groups of refugees had been identified on an ad hoc basis.[36] During the drafting of what was to become the Refugee Convention, a fierce debate broke out as to whether the old group-status approach should continue in the new era or whether a 'universal' and individual definition of a refugee should be agreed upon. The final text of the 1951 convention represented a compromise: the definition had universal elements to it and was not restricted to certain national groups. But it was limited temporally to events occurring before 1 January 1951 and (optionally) geographically to events occurring in Europe. It was only with the 1967 protocol that these restrictions were removed and the definition of a refugee became genuinely universal.

While the 1951 regime was being debated and created, a specific national group of refugees had already been identified: Palestinian refugees. Two United Nations agencies had been created to address their short- and long-term needs: UNRWA and UNCCP. Delegates from Arab states argued that the situation of Palestinian refugees was caused by the United Nations itself, with the proposed partition plan and then recognition of the state of Israel. Palestinian refugees were, therefore, a 'direct responsibility on the part of the United Nations and could not be placed in the general category of refugees without betrayal of that responsibility'.[37] Intending to maintain special attention on their plight and maintain the pressure to repatriate rather than disperse them, the delegates of Egypt, Lebanon and Saudi Arabia therefore proposed a clause excluding Palestinians from the new regime.[38] Initially a simple exclusion clause, a second sentence was later added to the version incorporated into the Refugee Convention, transforming it into what has been described as a 'deferred inclusion' or 'contingent inclusion' clause.[39] Article 1D of the convention provides:

---

[36] See Introduction.
[37] Statement of Mr Azkoul of Lebanon, UNGAOR, 5th session, 3rd committee, 328th meeting, paragraph 47 (UN Doc A/C.3/SR.328) (27 November 1950).
[38] Statements of Mr Azmi Bey of Egypt and Mr Baroody of Saudi Arabia, UNGAOR, 5th session, 3rd committee, 328th meeting, paragraphs 39 and 52 (UN doc A/C.3/SR.328) (27 November 1950).
[39] Statement of Mr Rochefort of France, Conference of Plenipotentiaries on the Status of Refugees and Stateless Persons: summary record of the 3rd meeting, held at the Palais des Nations, Geneva, on Tuesday (UN Doc A/CONF.2/SR.3) (3 July 1951) p 10; Goodwin-Gill, G. and McAdam, J. (2021) *The Refugee in International Law* (4th edn), Oxford: Oxford University Press, p 185.

> This Convention shall not apply to persons who are at present receiving from organs or agencies of the United Nations other than the United Nations High Commissioner for Refugees protection or assistance.
>
> When such protection or assistance has ceased for any reason, without the position of such persons being definitively settled in accordance with the relevant resolutions adopted by the General Assembly of the United Nations, these persons shall *ipso facto* be entitled to the benefits of this Convention.

The intention behind Article 1D was to maintain the special status of Palestinian refugees, to avoid duplication of institutional responsibility and legal status and to ensure that, in the event that United Nations protection or assistance ceased, Palestinians would benefit from the general refugee assistance and protection regime put in place for other recognized refugees. The mandate of UNHCR, which was adopted before the final amendments to the Refugee Convention were made, reflects the initial simple exclusion clause: 'the competence of the High Commissioner ... shall not extend to a person ... who continues to receive from other organs or agencies of the United Nations protection or assistance'.[40] The same applies to the Convention Relating to the Status of Stateless Persons 1954.[41]

The scope and interpretation of Article 1D has proven to be controversial, however. Firstly, the meaning and intention behind its wording is not at all self-evident. The text does not even refer specifically to Palestinians. Secondly, comprehension of the interpretation and effect of Article 1D is complicated by the duration of the Palestinian refugee crisis and by events subsequent to 1951. While relatively few of the original 750,000 or so Palestinian refugees of 1948 may remain alive today, the legal status of their descendants is unresolved. The Arab-Israeli war of 1967, the Israeli occupation of Gaza and the West Bank and subsequent conflicts have caused many more Palestinians to flee their homes. There are now nearly six million Palestinian refugees falling within the expanded mandate of UNRWA. Meanwhile, UNCCP exists only on paper in the modern world, its funding having been ended in the early 1950s. All of this, along with a straightforward lack of awareness of the existence and application of Article 1D, led to significant divergence of approach between different countries.

A broad consensus on the interpretation of parts of Article 1D has nevertheless begun to emerge in recent years. It is accepted that Article 1D

---

[40] Statute of the Office of the United Nations High Commissioner for Refugees, UNGA Res 428(V), 14 December 1950, Article 7(c).
[41] Article 1(2)(i).

is concerned only with Palestinian refugees.[42] The protection or assistance to which Article 1D refers is understood to be that provided by UNCCP and UNRWA.[43] The words *ipso facto* ('by that very fact') are interpreted as meaning that a person qualifies for refugee status automatically without having to undergo assessment of whether they have a well-founded fear and so on, subject to the cessation and other exclusion clauses at Articles 1C, 1E and 1F.[44] A basic tension remains between interpretations of Article 1D which regard it as an exclusion clause or a deferred inclusion clause, however. If regarded as an exclusion clause, a protection-oriented approach requires a narrow interpretation of the first sentence of Article 1D so that as few Palestinians are excluded as possible. On this analysis, Palestinians should not be discriminated against compared to other stateless persons and should not be prevented from qualifying as a refugee if they have a well-founded fear of being persecuted in their country of former habitual residence.[45] If Article 1D is regarded as a deferred inclusion clause, though, Palestinians are seen as being a special case: they have already been recognized as refugees by the United Nations and if the special arrangements for their assistance and protection cease, they should automatically benefit from the general regime put in place for other refugees. In short, Article 1D is 'another pathway' to recognition as a refugee.[46] On this analysis, a protection-oriented approach interprets the first sentence of Article 1D as widely as possible. This tension manifests in different approaches to understanding the words 'at present receiving'. One approach is to regard 'at present' as referring only to Palestinians who were alive at the time that the Refugee Convention was adopted, 28 July 1951.[47] The normal Refugee Convention regime would therefore apply to all other Palestinians, who would qualify as refugees if they met the criteria at Article 1A(2) of the convention. The alternative reading regards the words 'at present' as referring to the present day. The

---

[42] See for example *El-Ali v Secretary of State for the Home Department* [2002] EWCA Civ 1103, [2003] WLR 95 [22] (Laws LJ).

[43] Albanese, F. P. and Takkenberg, L. (2020) *Palestinian Refugees in International Law* (2nd edn), Oxford: Oxford University Press, p 80.

[44] *El-Ali v Secretary of State for the Home Department* [2002] EWCA Civ 1103, [2003] WLR 95 [36] and [49] (Laws LJ); Case C-364/11 *El Kott v Hungary* [71]-[74]; UNHCR, *Guidelines on International Protection No. 13: Applicability of Article 1D of the 1951 Convention Relating to the Status of Refugees to Palestinian Refugees*, HCR/GIP/17/13, December 2017 [29].

[45] Hathaway, J. and Foster, M. (2014) *The Law of Refugee Status* (2nd edn), Cambridge: Cambridge University Press, p 515.

[46] *AD (Palestine)* [2015] NZIPT 800693 [242].

[47] *Minister for Immigration and Multicultural Affairs v WABQ* [2002] FCAFC 329; *El-Ali v Secretary of State for the Home Department* [2002] EWCA Civ 1103, [2003] WLR 95; Hathaway, J. and Foster, M. (2014) *The Law of Refugee Status* (2nd edn), Cambridge: Cambridge University Press, pp 513–515.

continuing approach is advocated by Goodwin-Gill and McAdam, endorsed by UNHCR and has been adopted by the Court of Justice of the European Union and the New Zealand Immigration and Protection Tribunal.[48] However, the Court of Justice of the European Union regards the word 'receiving' as applying to 'persons who have actually availed themselves of the assistance provided by UNRWA'.[49] UNHCR adopts the position that the clause applies to all those eligible to receive assistance from UNRWA as well as those actually receiving it. To do otherwise would 'result in denial of protection for many Palestinian refugees, *whose refugee character is already established*, leaving gaps in the protection regime' [emphasis in original].[50]

The debate matters considerably to Palestinian refugees who leave the UNRWA-administered refugee camps, as three cases concerning Palestinian refugees heard by the Court of Justice of the European Union demonstrate.

KEY CASES

Bolbol v Hungary concerned a Palestinian woman who had left the Gaza Strip and later claimed asylum on the basis that clashes between Fatah and Hamas made it too dangerous for her to return. She had not availed herself of protection from UNRWA but was eligible and entitled to such protection. The court decided that 'at present receiving' in Article 1D should be interpreted in the continuing sense to all Palestinians actually receiving assistance and protection from UNRWA in the present day.[51] The effect was that Mrs Bolbol was not automatically entitled to refugee status.

In *El Kott v Hungary*, three Palestinian refugees from different UNRWA-administered refugee camps in Lebanon had fled their homes there because of violence and what arguably amounted to persecution.[52] In one case, the person's house had been burned down and he had been threatened. In the second, the person's home had been destroyed in clashes between the Lebanese army and Islamic Fatah and then he and his family had been insulted, mistreated, arrested arbitrarily, tortured and humiliated by the Lebanese authorities. In the third, the applicant had refused to allow extremists to use

---

[48] Goodwin-Gill, G. and McAdam, J. (2021) *The Refugee in International Law* (4th edn), Oxford: Oxford University Press, p 187; UNHCR, *Guidelines on International Protection No. 13: Applicability of Article 1D of the 1951 Convention Relating to the Status of Refugees to Palestinian Refugees*, HCR/GIP/17/13, December 2017 [13] and n 13; Case C-31/09 *Bolbol v Hungary* [47]; *AD (Palestine)* [2015] NZIPT 800693 [154]–[160].

[49] Case C-31/09 *Bolbol v Hungary*.

[50] UNHCR, *Guidelines on International Protection No. 13: Applicability of Article 1D of the 1951 Convention Relating to the Status of Refugees to Palestinian Refugees*, HCR/GIP/17/13, December 2017 [14].

[51] Case C-31/09 *Bolbol v Hungary*.

[52] Case C-364/11 *El Kott v Hungary*.

his roof during armed clashes, had been threatened with death and suspected as an enemy agent, left the camp and then left Lebanon completely. In all three cases, the applicants remained entitled to UNRWA assistance and protection but argued that it had ceased in their cases and therefore they qualified automatically for refugee status.

The court held in *El Kott* that the assistance and protection of UNRWA could cease in individual cases even if UNRWA continued to exist as an institution. The words 'for any reason' were considered to mandate this conclusion. However, '[m]ere absence from such an area or a voluntary decision to leave it cannot be regarded as cessation of assistance'. Refugee status would therefore require individual evaluation for Palestinians. The court went on to hold that protection can be found to have ceased for a person 'if his personal safety is at serious risk and if it is impossible for that agency to guarantee that his living conditions in that area will be commensurate with the mission entrusted to that agency'. If the applicants could show that they had been forced to leave their UNRWA camps, they were entitled to refugee status in their current country of residence.

The subsequent case of *Aletho v Bulgaria* erected yet another new barrier by finding that where a Palestinian refugee can be readmitted to a UNRWA area of operation other than that from which they fled, the person is not entitled to refugee status if the protection in the second area will be effective.[53]

On the interpretation of Article 1D advocated by UNHCR and broadly accepted by the Court of Justice of the European Union, all Palestinian refugees today are potentially eligible for refugee status in countries that have ratified the Refugee Convention if they can show that the protection of UNRWA has effectively ceased in their case. This includes not just those who qualify as Palestinian refugees displaced from what became the state of Israel by the 1948 Arab-Israeli conflict but also their descendants and Palestinians displaced by the 1967 Arab-Israeli war and subsequent conflicts.[54] However, the cessation and exclusion clauses would apply to a Palestinian in this situation. A Palestinian refugee who has acquired a new nationality and enjoys the protection of the country of their new nationality would therefore not be considered a refugee under the terms of the Refugee Convention, for example.[55]

---

[53] Case C-585/16 *Aletho v Bulgaria* [134], [140].
[54] The United Nations has never adopted a formal definition of 'Palestinian refugee' although one was in development by UNCCP before it ceased operating. The definition normally used today is that employed by UNRWA in its Consolidated Eligibility and Registration Instructions (CERI). See further Albanese, F. P. and Takkenberg, L. (2020) *Palestinian Refugees in International Law* (2nd edn), Oxford: Oxford University Press, pp 90–91.
[55] Refugee Convention, Article 1C(3).

Ambiguity remains as to what amounts to a cessation of assistance and protection by UNRWA. Some early cases suggest that only formal termination of the existence of UNRWA would mean such protection or assistance has ceased.[56] This view is now considered outdated and incorrect, with UNHCR and the Court of Justice of the European Union both considering that cessation of protection is to be assessed on the facts of the case. The New Zealand Immigration and Protection Tribunal has pointed to the potential effects of severe constraints on UNRWA on the entitlement of Palestinians to refugee status outside UNRWA areas of operation:

> Given the long-standing and continuing reality of funding deficits, should UNRWA continue to exist but in fact be unable to provide effective protection or assistance due to a lack of funding, there is no reason in principle why this should also not qualify as a cessation of activities under Article 1D, which expressly contemplates cessation 'for any reason' as activating the inclusion clause. The temporary suspension of Palestine refugees from the Refugee Convention was predicated on the provision of assistance. It is entirely in keeping with the intention of the drafters that the inability of UNRWA to provide assistance due to financial constraints should be regarded as constituting a de facto cessation by an absence of effective protection or assistance.[57]

The withdrawal of funding for UNRWA by the government of the United State in 2018, which at a stroke cut the pre-existing budget by around 25 per cent, caused the situation to deteriorate further. It is increasingly questionable whether UNRWA can provide effective assistance and protection to Palestinian refugees. In a case in 2019, the New Zealand tribunal held that on the facts of the case and in light of 'the inability of UNRWA to guarantee access to even the most basic living allowance and adequate medical services' assistance and protection was considered to have ceased for one Palestinian refugee, with the effect that he was automatically entitled to refugee status in New Zealand.[58] In another case, the New Zealand tribunal found that protection had effectively ceased 'through the sheer inability of the appellants to return to the West Bank and avail themselves on any effective protection or assistance from UNRWA'.[59]

---

[56] *El-Ali v Secretary of State for the Home Department* [2002] EWCA Civ 1103, [2003] WLR 95 [47].
[57] *AD (Palestine)* [2015] NZIPT 800693 [172].
[58] *AE (Lebanon)* [2019] NZIPT 801588 [85]–[86].
[59] *AQ (Jordan)* [2019] NZIPT 801469 [99] and [109].

Article 1E: Equivalent protection

Where a person does not need refugee status because they have 'taken residence' in a country of which they are not a citizen but have been accorded 'the rights and obligations which are attached to the possession of the nationality of that country' then they are excluded from the benefits of the Refugee Convention by Article 1E.[60] The original purpose of this provision was narrow and specific: the exclusion from refugee status of ethnic Germans living in central and eastern Europe who had voluntarily or been forcibly relocated to Germany during or following the Second World War.[61] This purpose is plain from the *travaux préparatoires* to the Refugee Convention and the context of the explicit exclusion of Germans under the constitution of the prior IRO.[62] Nevertheless, the final language adopted is potentially of broader and ongoing application. Some countries have adopted provisions purportedly based upon or derived from Article 1E to prevent what is sometimes termed 'forum' or 'asylum shopping' by refugees seeking preferable residence conditions.[63]

The requirement to have 'taken residence' indicates that continuing residence more substantial than a visit or temporary stay is necessary before the provision is engaged. Similarly, a potential but so far unrealized right of residence in a country is insufficient. There is no further definition of the relevant 'rights and obligations' but the wording makes plain that the person concerned must have a status substantially similar to a citizen.[64] They must therefore at a minimum be protected from deportation or expulsion. On this basis, Canadian law excludes from refugee status those who already hold refugee status in another country.[65] Going far beyond the language and intention of Article 1E, Australian law excludes even a person who has not taken all possible steps to avail themselves of a right to enter or reside permanently or temporarily in another country.[66]

---

[60] Refugee Convention, Article 1E.
[61] UNHCR, *Handbook on Procedures and Criteria for Determining Refugee Status and Guidelines on International Protection under the 1951 Convention and the 1967 Protocol Relating to the Status of Refugees*, HCR/1P/4/ENG/REV.4 (1979, reissued 2019) [144] n 19.
[62] Goodwin-Gill, G. and McAdam, J. (2021) *The Refugee in International Law* (4th edn), Oxford: Oxford University Press, pp 192–193; Hathaway, J. and Foster, M. (2014) *The Law of Refugee Status* (2nd edn), Cambridge: Cambridge University Press, pp 500–502.
[63] *SZMWQ v Minister for Immigration and Citizenship* [2010] FCAFC 97; *Canada (Citizenship and Immigration) v Zeng* [2010] FCA 118.
[64] *Canada (Citizenship and Immigration) v Zeng* [2010] FCA 118 [28].
[65] Immigration and Refugee Protection Act SC 2001, s 98.
[66] Migration Act 1958, ss 36(3)–(5).

Article 1F: Exclusion on moral grounds

While the language of moral condemnation sits uneasily in the age of universal human rights, the drafters of the Refugee Convention deliberately denied its protection to those considered undeserving or unworthy.[67] Where a person is thus excluded, they can be returned to their country of origin to face a well-founded fear of being persecuted.

No exclusion clauses had existed under the refugee regimes in force before the Second World War.[68] The horrors of that conflict, the atrocities committed and the prospect that some of the individuals responsible might rely on the new Refugee Convention persuaded the drafters of the need to excise them from the new protection regime. Similarly, the Universal Declaration of Human Rights states that the right of asylum 'may not be invoked in the case of prosecutions genuinely arising from non-political crimes or from acts contrary to the purposes and principles of the United Nations'.[69] The motivation to exclude certain individuals was not driven simply by their being undeserving of protection. The *travaux préparatoires* show that the drafters were concerned that countries would not agree to be bound by the Refugee Convention if it required them to admit very serious criminals.[70] The object of Article 1F is one of 'system integrity' rather than safety or security: the purpose is to protect the international refugee protection regime as a whole rather than to protect a host state from any specific risk posed by a refugee.[71] It is Article 33(2), read with Article 32 that performs the latter function by allowing for expulsion of a refugee in certain circumstances: see Chapter 7.[72]

Because of the drastic consequences that might in theory flow from exclusion from refugee status, the exclusion criteria should be interpreted

---

[67] UNHCR, *Handbook on Procedures and Criteria for Determining Refugee Status and Guidelines on International Protection under the 1951 Convention and the 1967 Protocol Relating to the Status of Refugees*, HCR/1P/4/ENG/REV.4 (1979, reissued 2019) [140]; Goodwin-Gill, G. (1983) *The Refugee in International Law*, Oxford: Oxford University Press, p 85.

[68] UNHCR, *Handbook on Procedures and Criteria for Determining Refugee Status and Guidelines on International Protection under the 1951 Convention and the 1967 Protocol Relating to the Status of Refugees*, HCR/1P/4/ENG/REV.4 (1979, reissued 2019) [147].

[69] Universal Declaration of Human Rights, Article 14(2).

[70] See Hathaway, J. and Foster, M. (2014) *The Law of Refugee Status* (2nd edn), Cambridge: Cambridge University Press, citing statements from the Belgian, British, French, German and Yugoslav delegates, pp 525–526.

[71] Dauvergne, C. and Lindy, H. (2019) 'Excluding Women', *International Journal of Refugee Law*, 31(1): 1–29. See also Joined Cases C-57/09 and C-101/09 *Germany v B and D* [115]; *Ezokola v Canada (Citizenship and Immigration)* [2013] 2 SCR 678 [36], *Attorney-General (Minister of Immigration) v Tamil X* [2011] 1 NZLR 721 [33].

[72] *T v Secretary of State for the Home Department* [1996] AC 742 (UK HL) at 771 (Lord Mustill); *Pushpanathan v Canada (Minister of Citizenship and Immigration)* [1998] 1 SCR 982 (Can SC) [58].

restrictively rather than expansively.[73] In reality, as discussed in Chapter 1, the evolution of *non-refoulement* protection under international human rights law has ameliorated the risk that a person excluded from refugee status might be returned to their country of origin to face torture or inhuman or degrading treatment or punishment. Nevertheless, the other benefits of the Refugee Convention at Articles 2 to 34 can – and indeed must – be denied an excluded individual. The use of the words 'shall not apply' indicate that such denial is required by the Refugee Convention of a signatory state.[74] Typically, the exclusion clauses will be considered as part of the initial refugee status determination procedure. They are effective at all times, though, and where it emerges later that a recognized refugee may fall for exclusion from that status then this may justify later cancellation of refugee status.[75] One of the exclusion clauses, at Article 1F(b), specifically applies to events 'outside the country of refuge prior to his admission to that country as a refugee'. The plain language and intentions of the drafters expressed in the *travaux préparatoires* have not prevented some countries from providing for the possibility this clause might apply to events within the country of refuge.[76] The other exclusion clauses at Article 1F(a) and (c) do not include this explicit 'outside the country of refuge' provision, leading to their application after the grant of refugee status to justify revocation notwithstanding that Article 33(2) exists to permit the expulsion of refugees where they are judged to be a danger to the security of the country of refuge.[77]

Article 1F provides that where there are 'serious reasons for considering' that certain acts have been committed, the person is excluded from refugee status. This is widely considered to amount to a standard of proof lower than that of the normal civil standard of the balance of probabilities (more probable than not).[78] While advocating adherence to the wording of Article 1F itself, Baroness Hale and Lord Dyson in a joint judgment for the whole United Kingdom Supreme Court held that the words

---

[73] UNHCR, *Handbook on Procedures and Criteria for Determining Refugee Status and Guidelines on International Protection under the 1951 Convention and the 1967 Protocol Relating to the Status of Refugees*, HCR/1P/4/ENG/REV.4 (1979, reissued 2019) [149]; *Al-Sirri v Secretary of State for the Home Department* [2013] 1 AC 745, [2012] UKSC 54 [16] and [75].

[74] *Attorney-General (Minister of Immigration) v Tamil X* [2011] 1 NZLR 721 [13].

[75] UNHCR, *Handbook on Procedures and Criteria for Determining Refugee Status and Guidelines on International Protection under the 1951 Convention and the 1967 Protocol Relating to the Status of Refugees*, HCR/1P/4/ENG/REV.4 (1979, reissued 2019) [141].

[76] See for example Directive 2011/95/EU, Article 12(2)(b); *Minister for Immigration and Multicultural Affairs v Singh* [2002] HCA 7.

[77] *RB (Algeria) v Secretary of State for the Home Department* [2009] UKHL 10, [2010] 2 AC 110 [127]-[129].

[78] *JS (Sri Lanka) v Secretary of State for the Home Department* [2010] UKSC 15, [2011] 1 AC 184 [39].

indicate a higher standard than mere suspicion or reasonable grounds for considering. The 'considered judgment' of the asylum assessor is required and the evidence from which the reasons are derived must be clear and credible or strong.[79] They concluded by saying: 'The reality is that there are unlikely to be sufficiently serious reasons for considering the applicant to be guilty unless the decision-maker can be satisfied on the balance of probabilities that he is.'

Individuals claiming asylum are usually low-ranking participants in a conflict. The required degree of involvement, responsibility or complicity of the person concerned to fall for exclusion from refugee status has therefore arisen on numerous occasions. The Rome Statute of the International Criminal Court specifically provides for the assessment of individual criminal responsibility. This is the appropriate starting point for applying the Refugee Convention exclusion clauses, although the Rome Statute 'cannot be considered as a complete codification of international criminal law'.[80] Broadly speaking, a person will be disqualified from refugee status under the exclusion clauses 'if there are serious reasons for considering him voluntarily to have contributed in a significant way to the organization's ability to pursue its purpose of committing war crimes, aware that his assistance will in fact further that purpose'.[81] The person must have had knowledge that their act or omission would facilitate the act in question.[82] Guilt by association is insufficient.[83] A person who personally carries out war crimes or crimes against humanity, acting alone or jointly with others, will be excluded. A person who incites or otherwise participates in such acts will also be excluded.[84] This includes ordering, soliciting or inducing the commission of such a crime or aiding, abetting or otherwise assisting in its commission, including providing the means for its

---

[79] *Al-Sirri v Secretary of State for the Home Department* [2012] UKSC 54, [2013] 1 AC 745 [75]. See also *Ezokola v Canada (Minister of Citizenship and Immigration)* [2013] 2 SCR 678 [102].

[80] UN General Assembly (1998) *Rome Statute of the International Criminal Court* (UN Doc A/CONF.183/9 as amended) Article 25; *Attorney-General (Minister of Immigration) v Tamil X* [2011] 1 NZLR 721 [27]; *Ezokola v Canada (Minister of Citizenship and Immigration)* [2013] 2 SCR 678 [51].

[81] *JS (Sri Lanka) v Secretary of State for the Home Department* [2010] UKSC 15, [2011] 1 AC 184 [38] (Lord Brown). See also *Attorney-General (Minister of Immigration) v Tamil X* [2011] 1 NZLR 721 [70], Joined Cases C-57/09 and C-101/09 *Germany v B and D* [94], *Al-Sirri v Secretary of State for the Home Department* [2012] UKSC 54, [2013] 1 AC 745 [15] and *Ezokola v Canada (Minister of Citizenship and Immigration)* [2013] 2 SCR 678 [8].

[82] *Al-Sirri v Secretary of State for the Home Department* [2012] UKSC 54, [2013] 1 AC 745 [15] and *Ezokola v Canada (Minister of Citizenship and Immigration)* [2013] 2 SCR 678 [8].

[83] *Ezokola v Canada (Minister of Citizenship and Immigration)* [2013] 2 SCR 678 [3] and [9].

[84] Directive 2011/95/EU, Article 12(3) and *JS (Sri Lanka) v Secretary of State for the Home Department* [2010] UKSC 15, [2011] 1 AC 184 [33].

commission.⁸⁵ Knowingly controlling the funds or providing the 'physical, logistical support that enable modern, terrorist groups to operate' will also justify exclusion, as will 'the recruitment, organization, transportation or equipment of individuals' who travel to another country to carry out terrorist acts.⁸⁶ Mere membership of an organization that carries out acts falling within the exclusion clauses is an insufficient basis for exclusion.⁸⁷ If the organization *only* promotes its objectives by carrying out acts of terrorism, voluntary and active membership of such an organization may well justify exclusion once the facts are carefully considered, but there is no presumption to this effect.⁸⁸ A commander may be criminally responsible for the acts committed by forces under their effective command and control where they knew or should have known such crimes would be or were being committed and they failed to take all necessary and reasonable measures to prevent those crimes.⁸⁹ A defence of following superior orders is available against some war crimes in some circumstances. Where such a defence exists this will be relevant to the issue of exclusion under the Refugee Convention.⁹⁰ Similarly, a defence of duress has been presumed to exist in this context, given that the acts concerned must not only be knowing but also voluntary.

KEY CASE

JS (Sri Lanka) v Secretary of State for the Home Department concerned a Tamil from Sri Lanka who had become a member of the Liberation Tigers of Tamil Eelam (LTTE) at the age of 10, had quickly joined the Intelligence Division and thereafter been appointed to positions of increasing seniority.⁹¹ He led other soldiers directly in military operations against the Sri Lankan army and eventually became second in command of the

---

⁸⁵ See in full UN General Assembly (1998) *Rome Statute of the International Criminal Court* (UN Doc A/CONF.183/9 as amended) Article 25 and *JS (Sri Lanka) v Secretary of State for the Home Department* [2010] UKSC 15, [2011] 1 AC 184 [33].

⁸⁶ *McMullen v INS* 685 F2d 1312 (9th Cir 1981); *JS (Sri Lanka) v Secretary of State for the Home Department* [2010] UKSC 15, [2011] 1 AC 184 [35]; Case C-573/14 *Louani v Belgium* [69].

⁸⁷ Joined Cases C-57/09 and C-101/09 *Germany v B and D* [88].

⁸⁸ *KJ (Sri Lanka) v Secretary of State for the Home Department* [2009] EWCA Civ 292 [37]; *JS (Sri Lanka) v Secretary of State for the Home Department* [2010] UKSC 15, [2011] 1 AC 184 [31].

⁸⁹ UN General Assembly (1998) *Rome Statute of the International Criminal Court* (UN Doc A/CONF.183/9 as amended) Article 28.

⁹⁰ UN General Assembly (1998) *Rome Statute of the International Criminal Court* (UN Doc A/CONF.183/9 as amended) Article 33.

⁹¹ [2010] UKSC 15, [2011] 1 AC 184.

Intelligence Division's combat unit. He was sent in plain clothes and under an assumed identity to the capital city, Colombo, to await further instructions, but after his presence was discovered he fled the country and claimed asylum in the United Kingdom.

His claim to refugee status was rejected on the basis that the LTTE was an organization that has been responsible for 'widespread and systemic war crimes and crimes against humanity' and his 'voluntary membership of an extremist group could be presumed to amount to personal and knowing participation, or at least acquiescence, amounting to complicity in the crimes in question'.

The Supreme Court held Article 1F excludes from refugee status not only those who personally commit war crimes and similar but also – based on the test for responsibility in the Rome Statute – those who order, solicit or induce, aid, abet or otherwise assist or in any other way intentionally contribute to its commission. The nature of the organization concerned was not the key issue. Rather, it is better to consider indicators of personal responsibility such as how the person came to join, how long they remained involved, their position, rank, standing and influence in the organization, knowledge of the organization's war crimes and personal involvement including any contributions made towards the commission of such crimes.

There are three separate although potentially overlapping grounds for exclusion on the basis that the person concerned is not morally deserving of the protection of the Refugee Convention.

The first is that the person concerned has committed a crime against peace, a war crime or a crime against humanity, as defined in the international instruments drawn up to make provision in respect of such crimes.[92] The wording of this provision is both specific, in that it refers to certain recognized classes of crime, but also general in that the recognition is not tied to a specific legal instrument. This was a deliberate decision on the part of the drafters and has enabled understanding of this exclusion clause to evolve alongside international criminal law. The main reference point today for determining whether a crime is one against peace, a war crime or a crime against humanity is the Rome Statute.[93] The decisions of international war crimes tribunals prior to and interpreting and applying the Rome Statue are also considered relevant, such as the International Criminal Tribunal for the Former Yugoslavia and the International Criminal Tribunal for

---

[92] Refugee Convention, Article 1F(a).
[93] *JS (Sri Lanka) v Secretary of State for the Home Department* [2011] 1 AC 184 [8]; *Attorney-General (Minister of Immigration) v Tamil X* [2011] 1 NZLR 721 [47]; *Ezokola v Canada (Minister of Citizenship and Immigration)* [2013] 2 SCR 678 [48].

Rwanda as well as the International Criminal Court itself. A crime against peace is understood as entailing high-level involvement in the planning, preparation, initiation or execution of an aggressive international war which 'by its character, gravity and scale, constitutes a manifest violation of the Charter of the United Nations'.[94] This is unlikely to arise in the ordinary course of refugee status determination. War crimes are essentially either grave breaches of the Geneva Conventions regulating the conduct of armed conflict or attacks during an armed conflict against non-combatants or their property.[95] Such violations may include – but are not limited to – murder or ill-treatment of civilian populations or prisoners of war, the killing of hostages, wanton destruction of cities, towns or villages, or a deliberate policy of devastation that is not justified by any military necessity. The armed conflict concerned may be an international or domestic one. Crimes against humanity consist of certain atrocious crimes or inhumane acts causing great suffering or serious injury to body or mental or physical health, including murder, enslavement, torture and rape, carried out as part of a widespread or systematic attack directed against a civilian population.[96] The Rome Statute makes clear that a crime against humanity can be committed during war or peacetime.[97] The crime of genocide is not specifically listed in the Refugee Convention exclusion clauses but would undoubtedly amount to a crime against humanity. The *travaux préparatoires* support this conclusion, with the British and French delegates expressly saying as much.[98] The first convention adopted by the United Nations was the Convention on the Prevention and Punishment of the Crime of Genocide 1948, which notes that genocide 'is a crime under international law, contrary to the spirit and aims of the United Nations and condemned by the civilized world'. Genocide is listed alongside crimes against humanity, war crimes and the crime of aggression in the jurisdiction of the International Criminal Court.[99] Finally, UNHCR guidance classes genocide as a crime against humanity.[100]

---

[94] See the crime of aggression as defined at Article 8 *bis* of the UN General Assembly (1998) *Rome Statute of the International Criminal Court* (UN Doc A/CONF.183/9 as amended by resolution RC/Res.6 of 11 June 2010).

[95] UN General Assembly (1998) *Rome Statute of the International Criminal Court* (UN Doc A/CONF.183/9 as amended) Article 8.

[96] UN General Assembly (1998) *Rome Statute of the International Criminal Court* (UN Doc A/CONF.183/9 as amended) Article 7.

[97] UN General Assembly (1998) *Rome Statute of the International Criminal Court* (UN Doc A/CONF.183/9 as amended) Article 7(2)(a).

[98] UN Doc A/CONF.2/SR.24, p 5; UN Doc E/AC.7/SR.160, p 15.

[99] UN General Assembly (1998) *Rome Statute of the International Criminal Court* (UN Doc A/CONF.183/9 as amended) Article 5.

[100] UNHCR, *Guidelines on International Protection No. 5: Application of the Exclusion Clauses: Article 1F of the 1951 Convention Relating to the Status of Refugees* (HCR/GIP/03/05) [13].

The second exclusion clause applies to a person who has committed a serious non-political crime outside the country of refuge prior to their admission to that country as a refugee.[101] These are what might be characterized as 'common crimes' and this exclusion clause reflects the principle that fugitives from justice are not refugees. The *travaux préparatoires* and the context in which the Refugee Convention was drafted show that the intention of the drafters was primarily to prevent those who had committed serious extraditable crimes from claiming protection as refugees.[102] The limitation of exclusion to 'serious' crimes which are 'non-political' in nature indicates that not every criminal is undeserving of protection, however. The 'serious' proviso at Article 1F(b) is notably lesser than the 'particularly serious' provision at Article 33(2), but, beyond that, there is little context to guide an asylum assessor as to what crimes might be sufficiently serious as to qualify. Adopting an *ejusdem generis* (of like kind) approach to the exclusion clauses, in particular, the grave nature of the other excluded acts of Article 1F and the consequences to the individual of being excluded from the Refugee Convention and thereby exposed to a well-founded fear of being persecuted, suggests that a high level of seriousness should be required. The UNHCR Handbook states that only 'a capital crime or a very grave punishable act' will qualify, not minor offences punishable by moderate sentences.[103] Goodwin-Gill and McAdam argue that crimes against physical integrity, life and liberty are considered serious for this purpose.[104] Hathaway and Foster suggest that guidance might be derived from what amounts to an extraditable crime, albeit with caution given that the drafters did not intend *all* extraditable crimes to lead to exclusion and that the scope of extradition has expanded considerably in the years since 1951.[105] Lord Justice Laws has suggested that the words 'serious crime' in this context denote 'especially grave offending'.[106] Domestic delineations of seriousness should be treated with caution on the grounds that the Refugee Convention is international in

---

[101] Refugee Convention, Article 1F(b).
[102] See Hathaway, J. and Foster, M. (2014) *The Law of Refugee Status* (2nd edn), Cambridge: Cambridge University Press, pp 541–543; Goodwin-Gill, G. and McAdam, J. (2021) *The Refugee in International Law* (4th edn), Oxford: Oxford University Press, pp 207–211.
[103] UNHCR, *Handbook on Procedures and Criteria for Determining Refugee Status and Guidelines on International Protection under the 1951 Convention and the 1967 Protocol Relating to the Status of Refugees*, HCR/1P/4/ENG/REV.4 (1979, reissued 2019) [155].
[104] Goodwin-Gill, G. and McAdam, J. (2021) *The Refugee in International Law* (4th edn), Oxford: Oxford University Press, p 212.
[105] See Hathaway, J. and Foster, M. (2014) *The Law of Refugee Status* (2nd edn), Cambridge: Cambridge University Press, pp 548–554.
[106] *AH (Algeria) v Secretary of State for the Home Department* [2012] EWCA Civ 395 [35].

nature.[107] That said, the Canadian Supreme Court held that crimes attracting a maximum sentence of ten years or more in Canada will generally be sufficiently serious to warrant exclusion but went on to say that 'the ten-year rule should not be applied in a mechanistic, decontextualized, or unjust manner'.[108] Homicide, rape, child molesting, wounding, arson, drug trafficking and armed robbery were cited as 'good examples of crimes that are sufficiently serious to presumptively warrant exclusion from refugee protection'. The ruling was much needed given that crimes including international child abduction, use of false or forged documents or identity theft, economic offences such as fraud and drugs offences are reported to have led to exclusion from refugee status in Canada.[109]

It has been argued that expiated crimes (a crime for which the person concerned has already been punished) do not engage the 'serious crime' exclusion clause. While the argument is logical, there is no textual basis for it in the text of the exclusion clauses and it is not an argument that has found favour in international jurisprudence.[110] Similarly, the argument that it is necessary 'to strike a balance between the nature of the offence presumed to have been committed by the applicant and the degree of persecution feared' has been widely rejected.[111]

The requirement that the serious crime be 'non-political' in nature is an echo of a long-standing feature of extradition law and serves a similar purpose: to ensure that only legitimate criminal law prosecution or punishment excludes a person from the scope of protection.[112] Drawing on

---

[107] *AH (Algeria) v Secretary of State for the Home Department* [2012] EWCA Civ 395 [31].
[108] *Febles v Canada (Minister of Citizenship and Immigration)* [2014] 3 SCR 431 [62].
[109] Dauvergne, C. and Lindy, H. (2019) 'Excluding Women', *International Journal of Refugee Law*, 31(1): 1–29.
[110] Weis, P. (1987) 'The Concept of the Refugee in International Law', 87 *Journal du Droit International* 928 and Hathaway, J. and Foster, M. (2014) *The Law of Refugee Status* (2nd edn), Cambridge: Cambridge University Press, pp 543–544 against *Attorney-General (Minister of Immigration) v Tamil X* [2011] 1 NZLR 721, *Febles v Canada (Minister of Citizenship and Immigration)* [2014] 3 SCR 431 [60] and *AH (Algeria) v Secretary of State for the Home Department* [2015] EWCA Civ 1003.
[111] UNHCR, *Handbook on Procedures and Criteria for Determining Refugee Status and Guidelines on International Protection under the 1951 Convention and the 1967 Protocol Relating to the Status of Refugees*, HCR/1P/4/ENG/REV.4 (1979, reissued 2019) [156] against, for example, *T v Secretary of State for the Home Department* [1996] AC 742 (UK HL), *INS v Aguirre-Aguirre* 526 US 415 (1999) (US SC), *Attorney-General (Minister of Immigration) v Tamil X* [2011] 1 NZLR 721, Joined Cases C-57/09 and C-101/09 *Germany v B and D* [109] and *AH (Algeria) v Secretary of State for the Home Department* [2015] EWCA Civ 1003 [19]-[27].
[112] In English law, see for example Extradition Act 1870, s 3(1): 'A fugitive criminal shall not be surrendered if the offence in respect of which his surrender is demanded is one of a political character ...'.

extradition law, a political crime has been defined by two features.[113] Firstly, it must be 'committed for a political purpose, that is to say, with the object of overthrowing or subverting or changing the government of a state or inducing it to change its policy'. Secondly, there must be 'a sufficiently close and direct link between the crime and the alleged political purpose', having regard to the means used to achieve the object, such as whether the target was military or governmental or civilian or whether it was likely to involve the indiscriminate killing or injuring of members of the public. It is this second issue that has proven most problematic in practice. The European Union's Qualification Directive provides that 'particularly cruel actions, even if committed with an allegedly political objective, may be classified as serious non-political crimes'.[114] In the United States, it is considered that 'atrocious' acts are inherently non-political in nature.[115] Despite (some might say because of) the difficulties of definition, 'terrorist' acts are widely considered to be non-political crimes, even if carried out for purportedly political purposes, as is discussed later.[116] The link between the crime and the purported political object was held to be too remote in the case of a person closely associated with a bombing carried out at an airport in which civilians were killed.[117] Similarly, crimes carried out in protest at proposed increases to bus fares in Guatemala were considered politically motivated but 'a lack of proportion between means and ends' rendered the crime non-political in nature for the purposes of Article 1F(b).[118] In contrast, the scuttling of a ship carrying armaments to a rebel group has been held to be a political crime despite some danger to sailors of an unconnected nationality.[119]

The third and final exclusion clause applies to those guilty of 'acts contrary to the purposes and principles of the United Nations'. Understanding of this provision is elusive given the breadth of the purposes and principles of the United Nations. One way to discern some meaning to these words is to refer to the United Nations Charter itself. Article 1 of the charter states that the purposes of the United Nations include maintaining international peace and security, developing friendly relations among nations, achieving international cooperation in solving international problems of an economic, social, cultural, or humanitarian character, and in promoting and encouraging respect for human rights, and harmonizing the actions of nations in the

---

[113] *T v Secretary of State for the Home Department* [1996] AC 742 (UK HL) (Lord Lloyd).
[114] Directive 2011/95/EU, Article 12(2)(b).
[115] *INS v Aguirre-Aguirre* 526 US 415 (1999) (US SC).
[116] *T v Secretary of State for the Home Department* [1996] AC 742 (UK HL); Joined Cases C-57/09 and C-101/09 *Germany v B and D*.
[117] *T v Secretary of State for the Home Department* [1996] AC 742 (UK HL).
[118] *INS v Aguirre-Aguirre* 526 US 415 (1999) (US SC).
[119] *Attorney-General (Minister of Immigration) v Tamil X* [2011] 1 NZLR 721 [90]-[97].

attainment of these ends. Article 2 of the charter sets out a number of principles, including the sovereign equality of all nations, performance of obligations in good faith, settling disputes by peaceful means, refraining from threat or use of force against the territorial integrity or political independence of any state, assisting the United Nations in its actions and non-interference with matters within the domestic jurisdiction of states. The Preamble to the Charter is even broader, referring to faith in fundamental rights, the dignity and worth of the human person, equal rights for men and women, justice, social progress and better standard of life, tolerance, international peace and security and the economic and social advancement of all peoples. It is also possible to conceive of the purposes and principles of the United Nations in a yet wider sense by taking into consideration resolutions made by the UN General Assembly or Security Council, for example condemning terrorism or drugs trafficking. The Canadian Supreme Court has adopted a sort of middle way, not limiting Article 1F(c) to the text of the UN Charter but also not accepting that drug trafficking meets the elusive criteria.[120] The EU's Qualification Directive adopts a similarly flexible position, specifically citing the UN Charter Preamble and Articles 1 and 2 but going on to reference United Nations resolutions regarding combatting terrorism, 'amongst others'.[121]

Self-evidently, the purposes and principles of the United Nations defy easy summary. Articles 1 and 2 of the UN Charter broadly relate to the maintenance of international order and cooperation. UNHCR, influenced by the inter-state level at which the purposes and principles of the United Nations are expressed and the intentions of the drafters reflected in the *travaux préparatoires*, argues that for exclusion clause to apply to an individual, they 'must have been in a position of power' and 'instrumental' to their country's infringing these principles.[122] It is, however, widely accepted that those not in a position of governmental power or authority can potentially be guilty of acts contrary to these purposes and principles.[123] Major acts of international terrorism would appear to fly in the face of United Nations purposes and principles, for example, even if carried out by non-state actors. Seemingly lesser actions have in the event attracted exclusion from refugee status, including running a website glorifying terrorism generally without

---

[120] *Pushpanathan v Canada (Minister of Citizenship and Immigration)* [1998] 1 SCR 982.

[121] Directive 2011/95/EU, Preamble [31].

[122] UNHCR, *Handbook on Procedures and Criteria for Determining Refugee Status and Guidelines on International Protection under the 1951 Convention and the 1967 Protocol Relating to the Status of Refugees*, HCR/1P/4/ENG/REV.4 (1979, reissued 2019) [163].

[123] *Pushpanathan v Canada (Minister of Citizenship and Immigration)* [1998] 1 SCR 982; Joined Cases C-57/09 and C-101/09 *Germany v B and D*; *Al-Sirri v Secretary of State for the Home Department* [2012] UKSC 54, [2013] 1 AC 745.

inciting or encouraging any specific piece of violence, or preaching and advocating in favour of terrorist activity.[124] Conviction for downloading prohibited terrorist material and a general 'terrorist mindset' have been held to be insufficient.[125]

The adoption of a wide understanding of the meaning of the purposes and principles of the United Nations combined with acceptance that private individuals can be guilty of acts contrary to those purposes and principles risks the exclusion of a wide range of individuals from the regime of refugee protection. It also risks undermining the restrained nature of the other exclusion clauses and therefore falling foul of the principles of treaty interpretation. The United Kingdom Supreme Court, seeking to reconcile the potentially expansive and disputed definition of 'terrorism' with the restrictive nature of the exclusion clauses, adopted UNHCR guidelines from 2003:

> Article 1F(c) is only triggered in extreme circumstances by activity which attacks the very basis of the international community's coexistence. Such activity must have an international dimension. Crimes capable of affecting international peace, security and peaceful relations between states, as well as serious and sustained violations of human rights would fall under this category.[126]

This approach is appropriately rooted in the international nature of Articles 1 and 2 of the UN Charter but recognizes that private actors might at times be capable of acting in breach of those purposes and principles.

Suggested further reading
Albanese, F. P. and Takkenberg, L. (2020) *Palestinian Refugees in International Law* (2nd edn), Oxford: Oxford University Press, Chapters 2 and 4.
Dauvergne, C. and Lindy, H. (2019) 'Excluding Women', *International Journal of Refugee Law*, 31(1): 1–29.
Goodwin-Gill, G. and McAdam, J. (2021) *The Refugee in International Law* (4th edn), Oxford: Oxford University Press, Chapter 4.

---

[124] *Youssef v Secretary of State for the Home Department* [2018] EWCA Civ 933; *RB (Algeria) v Secretary of State for the Home Department* [2009] UKHL 10, [2010] 2 AC 110 [50]-[51] and [127]-[129].

[125] *Secretary of State for the Home Department v NF* [2021] EWCA Civ 17.

[126] *Al-Sirri v Secretary of State for the Home Department* [2012] UKSC 54, [2013] 1 AC 745 [38], quoting from UNHCR, *Guidelines on International Protection No. 5: Application of the Exclusion Clauses: Article 1F of the 1951 Convention Relating to the Status of Refugees* (HCR/GIP/03/05).

Hathaway, J. and Foster, M. (2014) *The Law of Refugee Status* (2nd edn), Cambridge: Cambridge University Press, Chapters 6 and 7.

UNHCR, *Guidelines on International Protection No. 3: Cessation of Refugee Status under Article 1C(5) and (6) of the 1951 Convention Relating to the Status of Refugees (the 'Ceased Circumstances' Clauses)*, HCR/GIP/03/03 (10 February 2003).

UNHCR, *Guidelines on International Protection No. 5: Application of the Exclusion Clauses: Article 1F of the 1951 Convention Relating to the Status of Refugees*, HCR/GIP/03/05 (4 September 2003).

UNHCR, *Guidelines on International Protection No. 13: Applicability of Article 1D of the 1951 Convention relating to the Status of Refugees to Palestinian Refugees*, HCR/GIP/17/13 (20 December 2017).

UNHCR, *Handbook on Procedures and Criteria for Determining Refugee Status and Guidelines on International Protection under the 1951 Convention and the 1967 Protocol Relating to the Status of Refugees*, HCR/1P/4/ENG/REV.4 (1979, reissued 2019), [111]-[163].

7

Rights of Refugees

The point and purpose of the definition of a refugee so far discussed in the preceding chapters is that a refugee be afforded the rights set out in the Refugee Convention. The most important of these rights is the right of *non-refoulement* set out at Article 33 of the Refugee Convention: the right not to be returned to face persecution. It is far from the only right the Refugee Convention bestows on a refugee, though. This chapter briefly outlines the rights of refugees at Articles 2 to 34 and the way in which the Refugee Convention imparts those rights to refugees at different points in their literal then metaphorical journey as refugees.

The key reference point for analysis and understanding of the rights of refugees is Professor James Hathaway's substantial work on the subject, *The Rights of Refugees under International Law*, at the time of writing in its second edition.[1] Hathaway begins by observing that the rights of refugees were in the past largely uncontroversial in the industrialized world because most such countries admitted refugees as long-term residents, either formally or in practice. In doing so, these countries broadly, if incidentally, imparted rights in compliance with the requirements of the Refugee Convention. It was therefore access to the territory, the definition of a refugee and the refugee status determination process that were controversial. The reverse was true in the developing world, where the vast majority of the world's refugees are hosted. There, large numbers were admitted and tacitly recognized as refugees, but the rights imparted to them by the Refugee Convention were seldom respected. Countries of the Global North are increasingly seeking new ways to limit their liabilities to refugees and the rights at Articles 2 to 34 of the Refugee Convention

---

[1] Hathaway, J. (2021) *The Rights of Refugees under International Law* (2nd edn), Cambridge: Cambridge University Press.

are increasingly contested. Hathaway robustly defends the scheme and content of the Refugee Conventions rights, arguing that they are 'in no sense anachronistic' but rather are 'extraordinarily balanced and resilient'.

Scheme of refugee rights

The Refugee Convention does not directly confer absolute rights on all refugees. Reflecting the transitional nature of the Refugee Convention in bridging the pre- and post-war international legal settlements, rights are framed as obligations on state parties. These obligations become engaged or attached to a refugee at different stages of the literal then metaphorical refugee journey from entering the jurisdiction of a country through to long-term lawful residence. The rights thus acquired are sometimes unequivocal, but more often rights are to be treated equivalently to, or no less favourably than, citizens of the country concerned or other foreign nationals within that country. As Hathaway puts it:

> [T]he refugee rights regime is not simply a list of duties owed by state parties equally to all refugees. An attempt is instead made to grant enhanced rights as the bond strengthens between a particular refugee and the state party in which he or she is present. While all refugees benefit from a number of core rights, additional entitlements accrue as a function of the nature and duration of the attachment to the asylum state.[2]

The rights regime of the Refugee Convention is thus very different to that of other international human rights instruments. It specifically addresses the plight of refugees in particular and closer forms of attachment between a state and a refugee unlock more extensive sets of rights.

Reservations

Opt-outs by state parties from some provisions of the Refugee Convention are permitted by Article 42. No reservation may be made in respect of Articles 1, 3, 4, 16(1), 33 or 36 to 46, however. Respectively, this applies to the refugee definition, the duty of non-discrimination, the rights to freedom of religion, access to the courts, *non-refoulement* and various administrative matters.

---

[2] Hathaway, J. (2021) *The Rights of Refugees under International Law* (2nd edn), Cambridge: Cambridge University Press, p 174.

Degree of attachment

A close look at the language of the rights at Articles 2 to 34 of the Refugee Convention reveals that different rights are imparted to refugees with different forms of residence. To take some examples at random, several articles apply to refugees generally without any residence requirement at all, such as Article 3 on non-discrimination and Article 33 on *non-refoulement*. Other articles apply to refugees within the territory of a country, such as Article 4 on freedom of religion or Article 27 on identity papers. Article 25 on administrative assistance applies to refugees residing in a territory. A further tranche of articles applies to refugees lawfully in the territory of a country, such as Article 18 on self-employment and Article 26 on freedom of movement. Some articles apply where the refugee is lawfully staying in a country, such Article 15 right of association or Article 17 right to wage-earning employment. Others apply to refugees habitually resident in a country, including Article 14 on artistic rights and industrial property.

The various rights are not ordered within the Refugee Convention by the degree of attachment and the use of language largely appears chaotic to a casual reader. Goodwin-Gill and McAdam observe that on this issue 'there is little consistency in the language of the Convention, be it in English or French'.[3] There is a broad structure to be discerned, though. UNHCR identifies four groups of rights based on residence: rights of all asylum seekers and refugees, regardless of status or length of stay; rights of asylum seekers and refugees lawfully in the country (meaning from the moment of application for refugee status); rights of refugees lawfully staying in the country; and rights of refugees habitually resident.[4] Hathaway proposes a slightly different scheme to produce five progressive stages of attachment:

(1) Subject to a state's jurisdiction
(2) Physical presence
(3) Lawful or habitual presence
(4) Lawful stay
(5) Durable residence

Allocating the rights to Hathaway's structure requires a degree of conflating different but similar terminology within the Refugee Convention. A refugee lawfully in a territory is grouped with a refugee habitually resident in a territory, even though in law the two can be and are distinguished. Similarly,

---

[3] Goodwin-Gill, G. and McAdam, J. (2021) *The Refugee in International Law* (4th edn), Oxford: Oxford University Press, p 595.

[4] UNHCR (2017) *A Guide to International Refugee Protection and Building State Asylum Systems: Handbook for Parliamentarians No. 27*, Geneva: UNHCR, p 202.

residence is conflated with physical presence, although neither is a term of legal art in this instance. The reality is that the drafters of the Convention considered that different rights should attach at different times, but the language deployed is variable.[5] But by discerning a structure, a purpose may also be divined: immediate protection and gradual assimilation. In turn, this can help provide guidance as to the interpretation of the terms of the Refugee Convention.

Several rights apply to all refugees regardless of their status or length of stay and with no reference even to physical presence in the territory of a state. This includes the right of non-discrimination between refugees, property rights, access to the courts, rationing, education, taxation, *non-refoulement* and facilitation of naturalization.[6] However, state parties to the Refugee Convention cannot generally interact with refugees entirely outside their jurisdiction, so it makes little sense to conceive of these as rights available to all refugees everywhere in respect of all countries. Further, this set of rights can logically be distinguished from the next set of rights, which attach to refugees physically in the territory of a state. Hathaway therefore proposes that the first set of rights attach to a refugee within the jurisdiction of a state.[7] This would apply to refugees not yet physically present but under the control or authority of a state, as these concepts are understood in international human rights law (see discussion in Chapter 1).

A second set of rights apply to refugees who are physically present in the territory of a state, whether lawfully or unlawfully. This includes the rights to freedom of religion, administrative assistance, identity papers and non-penalization for illegal entry.[8] Where a so-called 'operational border' exists within the actual territory of a state, as with the triple fencing structure Spain has erected within its Melilla enclave adjacent to Morocco, legal pretence under domestic law that a migrant has not entered the territory does not under international human rights law oust the state's responsibility for the rights of that migrant.[9] The same reasoning would apply to the designation of 'international zones' at airports, the Australian designation of 'migration zones' and similar measures around the world.

The third set of rights applies once a refugee has attained lawful presence, including the rights to self-employment, freedom of movement and

---

[5] See Hathaway, J. (2021) *The Rights of Refugees under International Law* (2nd edn), Cambridge: Cambridge University Press, Chapter 3 on the intentions of the drafters and *travaux préparatoires*.

[6] Refugee Convention, respectively Articles 3, 13, 16(1), 20, 22, 29, 33 and 34.

[7] Hathaway, J. (2021) *The Rights of Refugees under International Law* (2nd edn), Cambridge: Cambridge University Press, pp 181–193.

[8] Refugee Convention, respectively Articles 4, 25, 27 and 31.

[9] *ND and NT v Spain* App. No. 8675/15 and 8697/15 (ECHR, 13 February 2020).

non-expulsion. The meaning of 'lawful' is contested, however. UNHCR have adopted the position that a refugee is lawfully in a country from the moment they apply for refugee status 'and may therefore be considered as "authorised" to be present in the territory of the country'.[10] Hathaway argues that this accords with the views of the drafters expressed during the *travaux préparatoires* and makes the point that any other interpretation violates principles of legal interpretation by failing to differentiate between the language of 'lawfully in' and that of 'lawfully staying'.[11] Some courts have adopted this position.[12] Goodwin-Gill and McAdam, however, argue that lawful presence 'implies admission and/or permission to remain in accordance with the applicable immigration law, and generally for a temporary purpose, for example, as a student, visitor, or recipient of medical attention'.[13] The United Kingdom Supreme Court has adopted this latter position, taking the view that what is or is not lawful in this context is to be determined under national law.[14] 'Lawfully in' is equated by the court with being 'entitled to reside', with the result that a refugee was not for the purposes of the Refugee Convention considered lawfully in the United Kingdom until formally recognized as a refugee and issued with a residence permit.[15] Reliance on national law permits or even encourages national divergence of approach to an international instrument, potentially leading to different countries affording different rights to refugees who are in truth similarly situated.

Hathaway includes rights in this third group which accrue to a refugee who is habitually resident in a territory, including the rights of intellectual property and assistance in the courts.[16] The concept of 'habitual residence' originates in private international law and features in, for example, the Hague Convention on the Civil Aspects of International Child Abduction.[17] It is a somewhat flexible concept and, while interpretations vary between jurisdictions and

---

[10] UNHCR (2017) *A Guide to International Refugee Protection and Building State Asylum Systems: Handbook for Parliamentarians No. 27*, Geneva: UNHCR, p 202; UNHCR (2016) *Observations on the Proposed Amendments to the Danish Aliens Legislation* [8].

[11] Hathaway, J. (2021) *The Rights of Refugees under International Law* (2nd edn), Cambridge: Cambridge University Press, pp 197–199 and 205–206.

[12] See Hathaway, J. (2021) *The Rights of Refugees under International Law* (2nd edn), Cambridge: Cambridge University Press, pp 200–201 n 135–142.

[13] Goodwin-Gill, G. and McAdam, J. (2021) *The Refugee in International Law* (4th edn), Oxford: Oxford University Press, p 595.

[14] *ST (Eritrea) v Secretary of State for the Home Department* [2012] UKSC 12, [2012] 2 AC 135 [40].

[15] *ST (Eritrea) v Secretary of State for the Home Department* [2012] UKSC 12, [2012] 2 AC 135 [35] and [39], citing *R v Secretary of State for the Home Department, ex p Bugdaycay* [1987] AC 514 (UK HL).

[16] Refugee Convention, respectively Articles 14 and 16(2).

[17] Hague Convention on the Civil Aspects of International Child Abduction 1980 at Preamble and Articles 3, 4, 5, 8 and elsewhere.

according to the purpose for which the concept is deployed, it is widely understood that lawful status is not necessarily required. In the United Kingdom, habitual residence was for a long time considered synonymous with ordinary residence unless otherwise defined. In the case of *ex p Shah* Lord Scarman held that 'if there be proved a regular, habitual mode of life in a particular place, the continuity of which has persisted despite temporary absences, ordinary residence is established provided only it is adopted voluntarily and for a settled purpose'.[18] This definition has been abandoned, at least in cases involving children, for a more factually sensitive assessment.[19] For a child, the country of habitual residence has been held to be 'the place which reflects some degree of integration by the child in a social and family environment'.[20] Relevant considerations include the duration, regularity, conditions and reasons for the stay, among other things.[21] While this definition cannot translate precisely to the situation of a refugee, it nevertheless indicates that habitual residence is manifestly a different test to that of lawful presence. Hathaway argues that the two tests 'converge to a very significant extent' because they both fall between physical presence and formal authorization to stay.[22]

The fourth group of rights attach when a refugee is lawfully staying in a territory, including rights to freedom of association, wage-earning employment, practice of a profession, public housing and welfare, protection of labour and social security laws and entitlement to travel documents. Logically, 'lawfully staying' must mean something more than physical presence or 'lawfully in' and something less than permanent residence. The term *résidant régulièrement* is deployed in the equally official French language version of the Refugee Convention, which implies a settling down and a certain length of residence; the *travaux préparatoires* reveal that the French term was considered authoritative and there was something of a struggle to translate it accurately into English.[23] A refugee should be considered lawfully staying in a country once the refugee's presence is formally sanctioned and ongoing.[24] Typically, but not necessarily, this will be the case once a refugee has been formally recognized as such.

---

[18] *R (on the application of Shah) v Barnet London Borough Council* [1983] 2 AC 309 (UK HL).
[19] *LC (Children)* [2014] UKSC 1, [2014] 1 AC 1038 [37] (Lord Wilson).
[20] *A v A (Children: Habitual Residence)* [2013] UKSC 60, [2014] 1 AC 1 [54], citing Case C-523/07 *Proceedings brought by A*.
[21] Case C-523/07 *Proceedings brought by A* [44].
[22] Hathaway, J. (2021) *The Rights of Refugees under International Law* (2nd edn), Cambridge: Cambridge University Press, p 212.
[23] Goodwin-Gill, G. and McAdam, J. (2021) *The Refugee in International Law* (4th edn), Oxford: Oxford University Press, p 597.
[24] Hathaway, J. (2021) *The Rights of Refugees under International Law* (2nd edn), Cambridge: Cambridge University Press, p 216; Goodwin-Gill, G. and McAdam, J. (2021) *The Refugee in International Law* (4th edn), Oxford: Oxford University Press, p 597.

Two further rights – exemption from requirements of legislative reciprocity between the country of refuge and country of origin and exemption from labour market restrictions imposed on foreign nationals – attach to a refugee after a period of three years of residence.[25] It is not clear whether this residence must be lawful in the sense of officially sanctioned or might include unlawful residence. The concept of reciprocal treatment of citizens is now somewhat outdated. Essentially, countries have sometimes sought better treatment for their own citizens by agreeing on such treatment to the citizens of other countries on a reciprocal basis. This makes little sense in the context of refugee law and this provision is intended to ensure that refugees are entitled to be treated no less favourably than other aliens.[26]

Standards of equivalence

The Refugee Convention not only sets out different stages at which different rights attach to a refugee but also sets out the degree to which such rights are acquired. Some rights are granted to the equivalent standard as foreign nationals generally, others to the equivalent standard as 'most favoured' foreign nationals, others to the equivalent as the country's own citizens and some to refugees absolutely, irrespective of how foreign nationals or citizens are treated. Further, discrimination between refugees on the grounds of race, religion or country of origin is expressly prohibited.[27]

The minimum standard of treatment for refugees under the Refugee Convention is equivalent to foreign nationals generally.[28] Some of the rights specifically provided for in the Refugee Convention are pegged to the standard of 'as favourable as possible and, in any event, not less favourable than that accorded to aliens generally in the same circumstances'. This includes rights to property, self-employment, to access the liberal professions, housing, to access secondary and tertiary education and to freedom of movement.[29] Where a right is not specified in the Refugee Convention, Article 7 provides that refugees should not generally be treated any worse than foreign nationals generally. Or, as Hathaway puts it, 'refugees cannot be excluded from any rights which the asylum state ordinarily grants to other foreigners'.[30] For example, the Refugee Convention provides no right to vote in any form of election nor does international human rights law provide for a right to vote

---

[25] Refugee Convention, Articles 7(2) and 17(2) respectively.
[26] See Refugee Convention, Article 7(1).
[27] Refugee Convention, Article 3.
[28] Refugee Convention, Article 7.
[29] Refugee Convention, Articles 13, 18, 19, 21, 22(2) and 26.
[30] Hathaway, J. (2021) *The Rights of Refugees under International Law* (2nd edn), Cambridge: Cambridge University Press, p 221.

for foreign nationals. Where a state does confer a right to vote on foreign nationals, though, refugees cannot lawfully be denied this general right.

Two rights are specified to be granted at a level equivalent to 'the most favourable treatment accorded to nationals of a foreign country in the same circumstances': the rights to freedom of association and wage-earning employment.[31] Where a country has put in place preferential arrangements for nationals of another country or countries, refugees are to be accorded the same privileges. This may be by way of a bilateral arrangement with a special partner state or by way of regional arrangements. This level of treatment was considered by the drafters to be too high in respect of most rights but an exception was made for the right to work because of its critical importance to refugees.[32] Several countries have entered reservations against these provisions, however.[33]

A further group of rights are granted at a level equivalent to citizens. These include rights to freedom of religion, intellectual property, access to the courts including legal assistance, rationing, elementary education, public relief, the protection of labour and social security legislation and equality of tax treatment.[34] The standard to which state parties are committed is either 'the same treatment as nationals' or, in the case of freedom of religion, 'at least as favourable as that accorded to their nationals'.

Finally, some rights have to be granted to refugees absolutely. This is in the main because these rights are specific to the situation of a refugee and there is no available comparator group. Such rights include the rights of non-discrimination between refugees, to personal juridical status, to access the courts, to administrative assistance, to travel documents, to identity papers, to transfer of assets, to non-penalization for illegal entry, to *non-refoulement* and to facilitate naturalization.[35]

Substance of rights

The substance of the rights afforded to refugees by the Refugee Convention can be grouped broadly into rights of safety and security and rights of integration. The rights of safety and security are intended to ensure, to some degree at least, that a refugee is able to reach safety and will not be returned to face being persecuted. The rights of integration are intended to ensure,

---

[31] Refugee Convention, Articles 15 and 17.
[32] Hathaway, J. (2021) *The Rights of Refugees under International Law* (2nd edn), Cambridge: Cambridge University Press, p 258.
[33] See treaties.un.org [last accessed 17 January 2022].
[34] Refugee Convention, Articles 4, 14, 16(2), 20, 22(1), 23, 24 and 29.
[35] Refugee Convention, Articles 3, 12, 16(1), 25, 27, 30, 31, 33 and 34.

again to some degree, that a refugee is able to live a relatively normal life and over time assimilate in the country of refuge.

Right to asylum

Article 14 of the Universal Declaration of Human Rights states that everyone 'has the right to seek and enjoy in other countries asylum from persecution'. This is not the same as a right to receive asylum or a right to enter a country for the purpose of seeking asylum. In contrast, as discussed in Chapter 1, the American Declaration, which is not binding, enshrines a right 'to seek *and receive* asylum' (emphasis added) and the American Convention, which is binding, includes a right 'to seek *and be granted* asylum' (emphasis added).[36] At an international level, a right not to be rejected at a frontier was included in the non-binding Declaration on Territorial Asylum in 1967 but an attempt to enshrine this in a binding convention ended in failure in 1977.[37] The New York Declaration for Refugees and Migrants of 2016 states that '[w]e reaffirm respect for the institution of asylum and the right to seek asylum'.[38] In reality, there is no enforceable right in international law to enter a country to claim asylum.[39] The closest the Refugee Convention comes are the rights not to be penalized for illegal entry in certain circumstances and the right not to be subjected to *refoulement* to face persecution at Articles 31 and 33 respectively. These do not amount to a right of entry for the purpose of claiming asylum or a right not to be expelled from a territory because, for example, a signatory state is not prohibited from refusing entry to a refugee as long as that refusal does not cause the refugee to be persecuted. Nor is a signatory state clearly prohibited by the Refugee Convention from removing a refugee to a safe country. This omission from international law has permitted the evolution of the post-Cold War policy of *non-entrée* of refugees to contain them in or near their country of origin by means of visa controls and carrier sanctions.[40]

---

[36] American Declaration of the Rights and Duties of Man 1948, Article 27; American Convention on Human Rights 1969, Article 22(7).

[37] UN General Assembly (1967) *Declaration on Territorial Asylum* (UN Doc A/RES/2312(XXII)) Article 3.

[38] UN General Assembly (2015) *New York Declaration for Refugees and Migrants* (UN Doc A/RES/71/1) [67].

[39] *R v Immigration Officer at Prague Airport, ex p European Roma Rights Centre* [2004] UKHL 55, [2005] 2 AC 1; Case C-638/16 *X and X v Belgium*.

[40] Hathaway, J. (1992) 'The Emerging Politics of Non-entrée', *Refugees*, 91: 40; Chimni, B.S. (1998) 'The Geopolitics of Refugee Studies: View from the South', *Journal of Refugee Studies*, 11(4): 350–374.

Entry without penalization

Although there is no right to asylum in the Refugee Convention, there is a right not to be penalized for illegal entry. This is of considerable importance to refugees. A refugee fleeing persecution will rarely have the time or opportunity, and may not have the resources, to be able to comply with the niceties of immigration laws.

The text of Article 31, the right of entry without penalization, requires close analysis:

> The Contracting States shall not impose penalties, on account of their illegal entry or presence, on refugees who, coming directly from a territory where their life or freedom was threatened in the sense of article 1, enter or are present in their territory without authorisation, provided they present themselves without delay to the authorities and show good cause for their illegal entry or presence.

Firstly, the potentially broad word 'penalties' is used. This undoubtedly applies to criminal sanctions for illegal entry and associated offences such as reliance on false documents for the purposes of entry.[41] It has also been held that providing there was no financial benefit involved, 'a state cannot impose a criminal sanction on refugees solely because they have aided others to enter illegally in their collective flight to safety'.[42] The use of the word 'penalties' rather than an explicit reference to criminalization strongly suggests that other disadvantages falling short of criminal sanction must also be prohibited. Goodwin-Gill and McAdam, drawing on the *travaux préparatoires* and the underlying purpose of the Refugee Convention, argue that the word 'penalties' includes 'any seriously prejudicial measures that have the effect of putting the refugee at a disadvantage in the enjoyment of economic, social and integration rights, when compared to other recognised refugees'.[43] Denying or delaying access to the refugee status determination process has been held to amount to such a penalty, for example.[44] At the time of writing, the United Kingdom's proposal to create two different classes of recognized refugees with different rights based on their means of arrival was

---

[41] *R v Uxbridge Magistrates Court, ex p Adimi* [1999] Imm AR 560 (EW CA); *R v Afsaw* [2008] UKHL 31, [2008] 1 AC 1061.
[42] *R v Appulonappa* [2015] SCC 59 [43].
[43] Goodwin-Gill, G. and McAdam, J. (2021) *The Refugee in International Law* (4th edn), Oxford: Oxford University Press, p 591.
[44] *B010 v Canada (Minister of Citizenship and Immigration)* [2015] SCC 58 [57].

widely argued to be incompatible with Article 31 (and with other articles given the requirement to afford recognized refugees certain other rights).[45]

There are, however, important caveats. The text of Article 31 refers to 'refugees', which could conceivably be understood to refer to refugees who are officially recognized as such. In the absence of explicit wording to that effect, in light of the declaratory nature of refugee status and bearing in mind the sometimes considerable period separating entry from determination of status, 'refugees' is normally understood as referring to those claiming asylum in good faith.[46] In the United Kingdom, a person must present sufficient evidence to support their claim to be a refugee, but thereafter it is for the prosecution to prove beyond reasonable doubt the person is not, in fact, a refugee.[47] A literal and geographical meaning of the words 'coming directly from a territory where their life or freedom was threatened' has been argued to mean that travel through or stay in a third country to the country of refuge will disqualify a refugee from relying on this protection. The shortest distance between a persecutor and a permanent safe haven is seldom a straight line and it is notable that the text refers to 'a territory' rather than the refugee's country of origin.[48] Consideration of the *travaux préparatoires* reveals that 'there was universal acceptance that the mere fact that refugees stopped while in transit ought not deprive them of the benefit of the article'.[49] Legal scholars including Weis, Grahl-Madsen, Goodwin-Gill and Hathaway argue that some element of choice is open to those claiming asylum about where they do so and that the emphasis should be on the 'show good cause' requirement.[50] It is this latter view which has been accepted in case law: it is widely agreed that short stays in third countries do not deprive a refugee of the protection of the non-penalization clause. The extent to which a refugee may stay in countries on their way to a final country of asylum is otherwise unclear, however. The length of stay, the reasons for delaying there, whether the time was spent trying to acquire the

---

[45] See for example UNHCR, *Observations on the Nationality and Borders Bill, Bill 141, 2021–22*, September 2021, Available from: https://www.unhcr.org/6149d3484/unhcr-summary-observations-on-the-nationality-and-borders-bill-bill-141 [last accessed 24 September 2021].

[46] *R v Uxbridge Magistrates Court, ex p Adimi* [1999] Imm AR 560 (EW CA) [16].

[47] *R v Makuwa* [2006] EWCA Crim 175, [2006] 1 WLR 2755 [26]; *R v Mateta* [2013] EWCA Crim 1372, [2014] WLR 1516 [9].

[48] Legomsky, S. (2003) 'Secondary Refugee Movements and the Return of Asylum Seekers to Third Countries: The Meaning of Effective Protection', *International Journal of Refugee Law*, 15(4), pp 567–677.

[49] *R v Afsaw* [2008] UKHL 31, [2008] 1 AC 1061 [56] (Lord Hope).

[50] See for example Goodwin-Gill, G. (1983) *The Refugee in International Law*, Oxford: Oxford University Press, pp 83–84 and Hathaway, J. (2021) *The Rights of Refugees under International Law* (2nd edn), Cambridge: Cambridge University Press, pp 495–507.

means of travelling on and whether the refugee sought or found protection there have all been said to be relevant considerations.[51] The requirement that a refugee 'present themselves without delay to the authorities' clearly requires refugees to come forward promptly if they are to benefit from the non-penalization clause. It is intended to ensure refugees regularize their position 'rather than eking out an existence in an unlawful twilight world on the fringes of society' or, worse, proceed 'by illegal stratagems and using the illegal services of shady agents'.[52] This does not require a person to claim asylum at absolutely the first conceivable opportunity, such as at passport control on arrival, but it does require the refugee to come forward of their own volition if the opportunity has reasonably presented itself.[53] It would be contrary to the language and purpose of the Refugee Convention to impose a mechanistic deadline for making a claim for refugee status.

Non-refoulement

The principle of *non-refoulement* has been described as the cornerstone of international refugee protection.[54] The right of *non-refoulement* is the right of a refugee not to be 'pushed back into the arms of their persecutors'.[55] The word '*refouler*' is used in the Refugee Convention and refugee law generally instead of the English language term 'return' because the French term more clearly denotes that *indirect* return is prohibited as well as direct return.[56] This right not only lies at the heart of the Refugee Convention but has also been extended to international human rights law (see Chapter 1) and has been argued to have become a customary rule of international law.[57] This most

---

[51] *R v Uxbridge Magistrates Court, ex p Adimi* [1999] Imm AR 560 (EW CA) [18] (Simon Brown LJ).

[52] *R v Afsaw* [2008] UKHL 31, [2008] 1 AC 1061 [93] and [113] (Lord Rodger).

[53] *R v Uxbridge Magistrates Court, ex p Adimi* [1999] Imm AR 560 (EW CA) [25].

[54] UNHCR, *Note on the Principle of Non-Refoulement* (November 1997); UNHCR, *Advisory Opinion on the Extraterritorial Application of Non-Refoulement Obligations* (26 January 2007); *Németh v Canada (Minister of Justice)* [2010] 3 SCR 281 [105].

[55] Statement of Mr Chance of Canada, Ad Hoc Committee on Statelessness and Related Problems, 1st session, 21st meeting, paragraph 26 (UN Doc E/AC.32/SR.21) (2 February 1950).

[56] *R v Secretary of State for the Home Department, ex p Bugdaycay* [1987] AC 514 (UK HL) at 532D-E.

[57] See for example, Lauterpacht, E. and Bethlehem, D. (2003) 'The Scope and Content of the Principle of Non-refoulement', in Feller E., Türk, V. and Nicholson, F. (eds), *Refugee Protection in International Law*, Cambridge: Cambridge University Press; *R v Immigration Officer at Prague Airport, ex p European Roma Rights Centre* [2004] UKHL 55, [2005] 2 AC 1 [26]; Goodwin-Gill, G. and McAdam, J. (2021) *The Refugee in International Law* (4th edn), Oxford: Oxford University Press, pp 300–306; *contra* see Hathaway, J. (2021) *The*

fundamental of refugee rights was explicitly reaffirmed in the New York Declaration of 2015.[58]

The text of Article 33 of the Refugee Convention provides:

1. No Contracting State shall expel or return ('refouler') a refugee in any manner whatsoever to the frontiers of territories where his life or freedom would be threatened on account of his race, religion, nationality, membership of a particular social group or political opinion.
2. The benefit of the present provision may not, however, be claimed by a refugee whom there are reasonable grounds for regarding as a danger to the security of the country in which he is, or who, having been convicted by a final judgement of a particularly serious crime, constitutes a danger to the community of that country.

The right of *non-refoulement* applies to both expulsion once a refugee has already entered the territory and also to non-admission. This expansive understanding of the term is reinforced by the inclusion of the words 'in any manner whatsoever'. For example, indirect return by 'chain' *refoulement* might occur by returning a refugee to a third country, which then returns the refugee to another country to face persecution. This could occur directly or perhaps by means of misapplication of refugee law or failures in its refugee status determination process.[59] It might also occur by way of measures which make a refugee's life so intolerable they are effectively forced to return to face persecution, sometimes referred to as 'disguised' or 'constructive' *refoulement*.[60] The duty applies not just to removal or extradition from the territory but also to situations of non-admission and rejection once the border is reached: a refugee cannot be denied entry if the effect is that the refugee will be exposed to a threat to life or freedom.[61] There is notably no requirement in Article 33 that the refugee be physically or lawfully present before the obligation

---

Rights of Refugees under International Law (2nd edn), Cambridge: Cambridge University Press, pp 435–459.

[58] UN General Assembly (2015) *New York Declaration for Refugees and Migrants* (UN Doc A/RES/71/1) [67].

[59] *Ex p Adan and Aitsegur* [2001] 2 AC 477 (UK HL); *R v Secretary of State for the Home Department, ex p Yogathas* [2002] UKHL 36, [2003] 1 AC 920; *MSS v Belgium and Greece* (2011) 53 EHRR 2 [321].

[60] *R (on the application of Joint Council for the Welfare of Immigrants) v Secretary of State for Social Security* [1997] WLR 275 (EW CA); United Nations Committee against Torture, *General Comment No. 4 (2017) on the Implementation of Article 3 of the Convention in the Context of Article 22*, CAT/C/GC/4, 4 September 2018 [14].

[61] *NAGV and NAGW of 2002 v Minister for Immigration, Multicultural and Indigenous Affairs* [2005] HCA 6 (Aus HC); *Németh v Canada (Minister of Justice)* [2010] 3 SCR 281; *ND and NT v Spain* App. Nos. 8675/15 and 8697/15 (ECHR, 13 February 2020) [178].

is engaged. As discussed earlier, however, the right of *non-refoulement* does not amount to a right to enter a country and does not impose an obligation on states to admit refugees.[62] A refugee can be denied entry or turned back, for example to a safe third country, if there is no threat to life or freedom in doing so.[63] Nor is the right of *non-refoulement* a right of non-expulsion for a refugee: see immediately what follows. Nevertheless, it still provides powerful protection for the refugee who is able to reach the jurisdiction of a country of refuge: 'if a refugee has succeeded in eluding the frontier guards, he is safe; if he has not, it is his hard luck'.[64]

The reference in Article 33(1) to a threat to a refugee's 'life or freedom' has been interpreted in the United States as specifying a different and more stringent test to that of 'being persecuted' in Article 1A(2), with the effect that only a subset of refugees is protected from *refoulement*.[65] This approach is not one adopted elsewhere.[66]

Protection against *refoulement* is denied to certain refugees, as Article 33(2) makes clear. There are two potential grounds for such denial, both of which are predicated on the refugee representing a threat to the asylum state. Firstly, a state may expel or return a refugee if there are reasonable grounds for regarding the refugee as a danger to the security of the asylum country. This provision does not require the person to have been convicted of a crime but the founding of this exception on a threat to national security clearly sets a demanding test for the type of conduct required to engage it. Secondly, a refugee is denied protection against *refoulement* where they have been convicted by final judgment of a particularly serious crime and constitute a danger to the community of the country of asylum. In contrast to the refugee status exclusion provisions at Article 1F, there must be a final conviction, the crime must be a 'particularly' serious one, it can have taken place prior to or since entry to the country of asylum and the person concerned must represent an ongoing danger to the community.

The terms of exclusion from protection against *refoulement* in Article 33 appear to overlap with both the terms of Article 1F discussed in Chapter 6

---

[62] *Minister for Immigration v Khawar* [2002] HCA 14; *R v Immigration Officer at Prague Airport, ex p European Roma Rights Centre* [2004] UKHL 55, [2005] 2 AC 1.
[63] *NAGV and NAGW of 2002 v Minister for Immigration, Multicultural and Indigenous Affairs* [2005] HCA 6 (Aus HC).
[64] Robinson, N. (1953) *Convention Relating to the Status of Refugees*, Institute of Jewish Affairs, cited in *R v Immigration Officer at Prague Airport, ex p European Roma Rights Centre* [2004] UKHL 55, [2005] 2 AC 1.
[65] *Immigration and Naturalization Service v Cardoza-Fonseca* 480 US 421 (1987) (US SC).
[66] See for example *R (on the application of Sivakumuran) v Secretary of State for the Home Department* [1988] AC 958 (UK HL); *R v Secretary of State for the Home Department, ex p Adan* [1999] 1 AC 293 (UK HL); *Németh v Canada (Minister of Justice)* [2010] 3 SCR 281 (Can SC) [101].

and the terms of Article 32 to be discussed in more depth later. The three standards are not the same, with Article 32 engaged on 'grounds of national security or public order', Article 1F(b) applying to a 'serious non-political crime' and Article 33(2) to a person whom there are reasonable grounds for regarding as a danger to the security of the country or who has committed a 'particularly serious crime' and is a 'danger to the community of the country'. Importantly, the three provisions perform different functions.[67] Article 1F operates to deny refugee status entirely to a fugitive from justice in order to protect the integrity of the refugee regime itself. The effect is that the person has no protection against expulsion or return to any country including one where the person will face persecution.[68] Article 33 protects all refugees from exposure to being persecuted, which will usually but not necessarily mean expulsion or return to the country of origin. Where the protection of Article 33 is denied a refugee, this is for the purpose of protecting the asylum country. The person remains a refugee but may be returned to face persecution anyway. Confusion arises because in practice this is a similar effect to Article 1F. As a result, the temptation to deploy the lower 'serious non-political crime' test in Article 1F in preference to the higher test of Article 33(2) has proven 'nearly irresistible to states'.[69] Article 32 confers additional rights on a refugee compared to Article 33 but only for certain refugees – those who are lawfully present – by also protecting against expulsion to any other country, not just one where the refugee faces persecution. Article 32 is essentially a right to stay so long as the person concerned continues to qualify as a refugee and does not threaten national security or public order.[70]

Non-expulsion

Protection against expulsion 'save on grounds of national security or public order' is conferred by Article 32 on refugees who are 'lawfully in' the territory of a country. Safeguards for refugees are imposed, meaning that 'due process of law' must be followed, a refugee is entitled to submit

---

[67] See for example *Pushpanathan v Canada (Minister of Citizenship and Immigration)* [1998] 1 SCR 982 on Article 1F and Article 33(2) at [58] and Joined Cases C-57/09 and C-101/09 *Germany v B and D* [103]. But see also *Febles v Canada (Minister of Citizenship and Immigration)* [2014] 3 SCR 431 [35].
[68] Hathaway, J. and Foster, M. (2014) *The Law of Refugee Status* (2nd edn), Cambridge: Cambridge University Press, p 541; Hathaway, J. (2021) *The Rights of Refugees under International Law* (2nd edn), Cambridge: Cambridge University Press, pp 400–406.
[69] Hathaway, J. (2021) *The Rights of Refugees under International Law* (2nd edn), Cambridge: Cambridge University Press, p 405.
[70] *ST (Eritrea) v Secretary of State for the Home Department* [2012] UKSC 12, [2012] 2 AC 135 [1].

evidence (absent 'compelling reasons of national security') and an appeal process is mandated along with the right to representation. In the event that an expulsion order is made, the refugee is to be allowed time to seek legal admission to another country. The effect of Article 32 is that 'once a refugee has been admitted or his presence has been legalized and so long as entitlement to refugee status continues, he is entitled to stay indefinitely in the receiving state'.[71] In contrast to Article 33, which applies to all refugees within a state's jurisdiction, Article 32 only applies to a subset of refugees. The question of when a refugee becomes lawfully present for the purposes of the Refugee Convention was discussed earlier. UNHCR and Hathaway argue that it is registering an asylum application that renders a refugee lawfully present. Goodwin-Gill and McAdam suggest that a grant of temporary status may be required and the United Kingdom Supreme Court has adopted this latter approach.

The distinction between *non-refoulement* and non-expulsion obligations becomes particularly relevant where a state proposes to remove refugees to a safe third country, whether for the purpose of their claim to refugee status being processed or otherwise. This is sometimes referred to as extraterritorial or off-shore processing. Such removal is not barred by the Article 33 *non-refoulement* obligation, assuming the country concerned is genuinely safe and there is genuinely no risk of *refoulement*, including so-called 'chain' or 'constructive' *refoulement* via other countries. Whether such assumptions can really be made in practice is highly questionable given the probable context of such arrangements. The refugees in question would likely be detained or otherwise isolated in a country with few resources in order to prevent their resuming their journey and they would likely be denied their other rights under the Refugee Convention. A real risk of occurrence of future human rights abuses in the 'safe' country would bar removal there under separate provisions of international human rights law. In contrast to the position under Article 33, removal to a safe third country is prohibited by the Article 32 non-expulsion obligation, subject to the caveat of national security or public order. On the UNHCR and Hathaway analysis, Article 32 is engaged as soon as the refugee makes an application for recognition as a refugee and is therefore protected from removal to a safe third country for so-called 'off-shore processing'. On the analysis of Goodwin-Gill and McAdam and the United Kingdom Supreme Court, though, Article 32 only protects a refugee once officially recognized as a refugee.

---

[71] *ST (Eritrea) v Secretary of State for the Home Department* [2012] UKSC 12, [2012] 2 AC 135 [1].

Rights to integration

As well as the rights of safety and security already addressed – the rights to non-penalization, *non-refoulement* and non-expulsion – the Refugee Convention imparts a range of rights intended to enable refugees to integrate and build new lives for themselves in their country of refuge. This includes the right at Article 3 not to discriminate between refugees, meaning that some refugees may not be treated worse than others, the right at Article 4 to freedom of religion and religious education of their children, the rights at Articles 5, 7, 8, 25 and 29 not to be disadvantaged in various ways including by the imposition of additional fiscal charges or taxation, the right at Article 12 to recognition of personal juridical status, the right at Article 16 of access to courts and legal assistance, the rights at Articles 17, 18 and 19 to work and self-employment, the rights at 15, 20, 21, 23 and 24 to join a trade union, welfare, housing, social security and labour law protection, the right at Article 22 to education, the rights at Articles 25 and 27 to administrative assistance and identity papers, the rights at Articles 13, 14 and 30 to property and its transfer, the rights at Articles 26 and 28 to domestic and international mobility and, finally, the right at Article 34 to 'facilitate the assimilation and naturalisation of refugees' including by making every effort to 'expedite naturalisation proceedings and to reduce as far as possible the charges and costs of such proceedings'.

These rights are set out in Table 1 with reference to the level of attachment required before the relevant right is engaged and the degree to which the right is conferred on a refugee equivalent to which comparator group.

Family unity

It is commonplace for refugees to become separated from their families, whether because they were forced to leave them behind in the country of origin or because they became separated during their journey. Once a country of refuge is reached, the desire to be reunited with family members, whether they are spouses, children, parents, siblings or others, can become an overpowering imperative, driven by worry, distress and feelings of guilt. While such separation continues, it can be very hard for refugees to recover from their trauma and settle into new lives. Surprisingly, then, there is no formal right of family unity set out in the articles of the Refugee Convention. Nevertheless, the need to respect the family life of refugees was strongly recommended by the Conference of Plenipotentiaries which adopted the Refugee Convention:

> Considering that the unity of the family, the natural and fundamental group of society, is an essential right of the refugee and that such unity is constantly threatened, and

Table 1

LEVEL OF ATTACHMENT	LEVEL OF EQUIVALENCE			
	Absolute	Equivalent to citizens	Equivalent to most favoured foreigners	Equivalent to foreigners generally
Within state jurisdiction	Art 3: non-discrimination Art 12: personal status Art 16(1): access to court Art 30: transfer of assets Art 33: *non-refoulement* Art 34: Facilitate naturalization	Art 16(2): legal assistance Art 20: Access to rations Art 22(1): Elementary education Art 29: Charges and taxation		Art 7: general right not to be treated worse than foreign nationals Art 13: acquisition of property Art 22(2): Secondary and tertiary education
Physical presence	Art 25: administrative assistance Art 27: identity papers Art 31: non-penalisation for illegal entry	Art 4: freedom of religion		
Lawful presence	Art 32: non-expulsion			Art 18: self-employment Art 26: freedom of movement
Lawful stay	Art 28: Travel documents	Art 14: Artistic rights and industrial property Art 23: Public relief Art 24: Labour legislation and social security	Art 15: Right of association Art 17: Wage-earning employment	Art 19: Liberal professions Art 21: Housing
Durable residence				Art 7(2): exemption from legislative reciprocity Art 17(2): exemption from labour market restrictions

Noting with satisfaction that, according to the official commentary of the ad hoc Committee on Statelessness and Related Problems the rights granted to a refugee are extended to members of his family,

Recommends Governments to take the necessary measures for the protection of the refugee's family, especially with a view to:

(1) Ensuring that the unity of the refugee's family is maintained particularly in cases where the head of the family has fulfilled the necessary conditions for admission to a particular country;
(2) The protection of refugees who are minors, in particular unaccompanied children and girls, with particular reference to guardianship and adoption.[72]

The recommendation – and arguably the absence of express provision for family unity in the text of the Refugee Convention – was based on the assumption by the drafters 'that the family members of a refugee would benefit from the protection of the Refugee Convention, even if not able themselves to show a "well-founded fear of being persecuted"'.[73] UNHCR has repeatedly reiterated 'the fundamental importance of the principle of family reunion' and urged state parties to respect the family lives of refugees.[74] The issue of refugee family life barely features in the United Nations Global Compact on Refugees, however.[75] To some degree, states have generally respected the need for refugees to be joined by close, pre-existing family members. In the absence of a clearly defined right, it is, sadly, unsurprising that the family lives of refugees have nevertheless been severely curtailed in some ways. In the United Kingdom, for example, recognized refugees are able to make free of charge applications to be joined by pre-existing spouses, partners and dependent related children under the age of 18 and the refugee is exempt from the normal minimum income rules.[76] However, there is no right to be reunited with other family members, whether pre-existing or

---

[72] Final Act of the United Nations Conference of Plenipotentiaries on the Status of Refugees and Stateless Persons (UN Doc A/CONF.2/108/Rev.1).
[73] Hathaway, J. (2021) *The Rights of Refugees under International Law* (2nd edn), Cambridge: Cambridge University Press, p 674.
[74] UNHCR Executive Committee Conclusion No. 9, No. 24, No. 47, No. 84, No. 85, No 88, No. 107, UNHCR Guidelines on Reunification of Refugee Families (1983) and Elsewhere.
[75] See Global Compact on Refugees (UN Doc A/73/12 (Part II)) (2 August 2018) [76], [95] and Annex 1 [5(a)].
[76] See Immigration Rules HC 395 [352A], [352D] and [319X].

new. And there is no defined immigration route for a separated child to be joined by parents or siblings.

The Refugee Convention is not the only source of law imparting rights to refugees. International human rights law is a source of rights for all, including refugees. The right to family life is protected by the ICCPR at Articles 17, 23 and 24, the ICESCR at Article 10, the ECHR at Articles 8 and 12 and other international human rights instruments. The CRC acts as a further source of rights for child refugees. These rights apply to refugees in respect of their family members abroad and also within the country of asylum. The right to a family life is generally a qualified right, however, which can make it difficult to enforce. Even the near absolute right of a child not to be separated from their parents has proven ineffective in practice for some refugee children.[77]

Rescue at sea

In the absence of safe and legal routes to sanctuary countries in which they can rebuild their lives, refugees often resort to travel by unsafe means. The issue of rescue of refugees at sea has risen in global prominence. An estimated 40,000 refugees and other migrants died between 2014 and 2020 in the process of moving between countries around the world.[78] Over half of those deaths occurred by drowning in the Mediterranean. The Refugee Convention does not impose any duty on state parties to rescue refugees at sea and it is a long-standing feature of international law that states can control access to their territory. However, there is also a very long-standing custom of rendering assistance at sea. The duty to do so has attained the status of customary international law and is further embedded into the law of the sea by four binding conventions which address the issue.[79] The four conventions perform different functions, but all impose a general duty to rescue those in distress at sea. Three of the four require state parties to establish search and rescue operations. International human rights law is also highly relevant, with the right to life requiring positive measures to safeguard and protect life, including at sea. The law of the sea and human rights law do not stand entirely apart: the two bodies of law

---

[77] UN Convention on the Rights of the Child 1989, Article 9(1). See Pobjoy, J. (2017) *The Child in International Refugee Law*, Cambridge: Cambridge University Press, pp 70 and 72–78.
[78] See missingmigrants.iom.int [last accessed 28 September 2021].
[79] Barnes, R. (2004) 'Refugee Law at Sea', *International and Comparative Law Quarterly*, 53(1): 47–77, 49.

influence each another.[80] Indeed, it has been argued that the existential dilemma of whether to save a stranger's life at sea or let them die can provide a conceptual foundation for human rights law as 'a thin but firm modicum of legal responsibility individuals may experience toward all other individuals upon encounter'.[81]

The United Nations Convention of the Law of the Sea (UNCLOS) purports to settle 'all issues relating to the law of the sea' and establish a 'legal order for the seas and oceans'.[82] Originally agreed in 1982 and coming into force in 1994, it is now very widely ratified in its modern, amended form. Notable non-parties include Iran, Israel, Libya, North Korea, Turkey, the United States and Venezuela. While state parties must agree to allow 'innocent passage' by ships through their territorial waters and contiguous zone, exceptions are made for 'the prevention of infringement of the customs, fiscal, immigration or sanitary laws and regulations of the coastal State'.[83] The convention goes on to impose a general duty on state parties to require their vessels 'to render assistance to any person found at sea in danger of being lost' and 'to proceed with all possible speed to the rescue of persons in distress, if informed of their need of assistance, in so far as such action may reasonably be expected'.[84] No immigration or other exceptions apply. UNCLOS also imposes a duty on state parties to 'promote the establishment, operation and maintenance of an adequate and effective search and rescue service regarding safety on and over the sea and, where circumstances so require, by way of mutual regional arrangements cooperate with neighbouring States for this purpose'.[85]

UNCLOS has been described as a 'quasi-constitution for the oceans', but three further conventions set out the details of search and rescue obligations.[86] The first of these is the International Convention on Maritime Search and Rescue (SAR), which was agreed in 1979 and came into force in 1985.[87]

---

[80] For example, UN Human Rights Committee, *General Comment No. 36: The Right to Life* (UN doc CCPR/C/GC/36) (30 October 2018) [63] refers to UNCLOS when discussing the right to life and sea rescue.

[81] Munn, I. (2016) *Humanity at Sea: Maritime Migration and the Foundations of International Law*, Cambridge: Cambridge University Press.

[82] United Nations Convention of the Law of the Sea 1982, United Nations Treaty Series, Vol. 1833, p 3, Preamble.

[83] United Nations Convention of the Law of the Sea 1982, Articles 19, 21 and 33.

[84] United Nations Convention of the Law of the Sea 1982, Article 98(1). There is some debate whether the duty applies in territorial waters, but that lies beyond the scope of this book.

[85] United Nations Convention of the Law of the Sea 1982, Article 98(2).

[86] Barnes, R. (2004) 'Refugee Law at Sea', *International and Comparative Law Quarterly*, 53(1): 47–77, 48.

[87] International Convention on Maritime Search and Rescue 1979, United Nations Treaty Series, Vol. 1403, p 118. Amendments took effect in 2000 and 2006 other than for Malta, which objected.

It is widely ratified, although not as widely as UNCLOS. SAR requires state parties to establish the basic elements of search and rescue operations, to coordinate and cooperate with neighbouring states regarding the same and 'on receiving information that any person is, or appears to be, in distress at sea' to 'take urgent steps to ensure that the necessary assistance is provided'.[88] Following an amendment taking effect in 2006, the obligation to provide assistance to a person at distress at sea expressly applies 'regardless of the nationality or status of such a person or the circumstances in which that person is found'. Once a person has been rescued, the person must be delivered to a 'place of safety'. The second agreement is the International Convention for the Safety of Life at Sea of 1974 (SOLAS), which is primarily concerned with the seaworthiness of ships. This convention is also widely ratified. SOLAS imposes a duty on the master of a ship at sea 'to proceed with all speed to the assistance of the persons in distress' and an obligation on state parties to 'to ensure that any necessary arrangements are made for coast watching and for the rescue of persons in distress at sea round its coasts'.[89] Mirroring the adjustments to SAR, SOLAS has been amended explicitly to state that the duty to provide assistance 'applies regardless of the nationality or status of such persons or the circumstances in which they are found' and provides that a rescued person should be treated with humanity while on board ship and delivered to a place of safety. Finally, the International Convention on Salvage of 1989 ('Salvage Convention') requires that every ship master, 'so far as he can do so without serious danger to his vessel and persons thereon, to render assistance to any person in danger of being lost at sea' and imposes a duty on state parties to adopt the measures necessary to enforce that duty.[90]

The duty of rescue applies to a person in distress, potentially leaving some room for evaluating whether a person is truly in distress. The term is not further defined, but it must be understood bearing in mind the purpose and object of the conventions, which is clearly to save lives at sea. Where it is reasonably foreseeable that a person will end up in danger, that person would normally be regarded as in distress in this context.[91] The 2006 amendments

---

[88] International Convention on Maritime Search and Rescue, Chapters 2 and 3.

[89] International Convention for the Safety of Life at Sea 1974, United Nations Treaty Series, Vol. 1184, p 3, Chapter V, regulations 33 and 7 as amended by International Maritime Organization resolutions MSC.99(73) and MSC.153(78). Despite the language framing, the obligation is likely on the state party to require the ship master so to act.

[90] International Convention on Salvage 1989, Article 10. See also the similar duty at Article 11 of the Brussels Convention for the Unification of Certain Rules with Respect to Assistance and Salvage at Sea of 1910 ('Brussels Convention').

[91] See discussion in Ratcovich, M. (2019) *International Law and the Rescue of Migrants at Sea*, Stockholm: Stockholm University, p 82.

to SAR and SOLAS also make clear that the duty of rescue applies regardless of the circumstances in which a person is found. The duty, therefore, applies just as much to a person who contributes to or even causes their own distress as to a person who takes all reasonable precautions.

The international law of the sea itself offers no direct means of enforcing the duty of rescue without incorporation into national law.[92] International human rights law and the right to life are relevant to the issues around duty of rescue and may to some extent fill that gap. As discussed in Chapter 1, for the purposes of human rights law, a state's jurisdiction extends to situations of interdiction or rescue at sea. The right to life includes positive obligations to safeguard and protect life.[93] This duty extends to the provision of air-mountain and air-sea rescue facilities, although the obligation is to provide an appropriate regulatory framework and adequate mechanisms in general rather than to save every life in danger.[94]

KEY CASE

Early in 2021, the United Nations Human Rights Committee found that Italy had breached its positive obligations to protect the right to life of 13 people who had drowned in 2013 within the designated SAR area for Malta.[95] It is thought that more than 200 people drowned after a boat carrying migrants from Libya towards Lampedusa, an Italian island, capsized. Passengers on the boat had contacted the Italian coastguard, but there was a significant delay of several hours in assistance being rendered, despite the close proximity of an Italian navy vessel.

In twin decisions, the committee considered by a majority that both Italy and Malta had concurrently held jurisdiction over the boat despite being outside the national territory of either country. The incident took place in Malta's SAR area. Malta had assumed formal responsibility for the rescue and had then 'exercised effective control over the rescue operation, potentially resulting in a direct and reasonably foreseeable causal relationship between the State parties' acts and omissions and the outcome of

---

[92] In the United Kingdom, the relevant provisions of SOLAS are incorporated into law by the Merchant Shipping (Safety of Navigation) Regulations 2020, SI 2020/673.

[93] UN Human Rights Committee, *General Comment No. 36: The Right to Life*, (UN Doc CCPR/C/GC/36) (30 October 2018) [18] and see specifically [63]; *LCB v United Kingdom* App. No. 23413/94, [1998] ECHR 49 [36].

[94] *Furdik v Slovakia* App. No. 42994/05, 2 December 2008; UN Human Rights Committee, *General Comment No. 36: The Right to Life* (UN Doc CCPR/C/GC/36) (30 October 2018) [63]; UN Human Rights Committee, Views adopted by the Committee under Article 5 (4) of the Optional Protocol, Concerning Communication No. 3042/2017.

[95] *AS and others v Italy* CCPR/C/130/DR/3042/2017; *AS and others v Malta* CCPR/C/128/D/3043/2017.

the operation'. The case against Malta was nevertheless held inadmissible for failure to pursue a domestic remedy there.

Italy was found responsible on the basis that 'a special relationship of dependency' had arisen because of the initial contact with the Italian coastguard, the close proximity of the Italian naval vessel and the legal obligations of Italy to render assistance under the SOLAS and SAR conventions. Italy was considered to have breached its positive obligation to protect life by failing with due diligence. There had been a failure to respond promptly to the distress call, a failure to dispatch the relevant naval vessel even once a formal request had been made by the Maltese SAR authorities and a failure to explain telephone records indicating that the navel vessel had in fact been instructed to sail away from the vessel in distress.

The committee members were significantly divided on critical issues of jurisdiction and responsibility. International human rights law is likely to evolve further.

There had been no reported cases from the European Court of Human Rights on these issues at the time of writing, but a case was pending before the court relating the deaths of 63 migrants at sea in a boat left adrift in the Mediterranean in 2011.[96]

Suggested further reading

Chimni, B.S. (1998) 'The Geopolitics of Refugee Studies: View from the South', *Journal of Refugee Studies*, 11(4): 350–374.

Goodwin-Gill, G. and McAdam, J. (2021) *The Refugee in International Law* (4th edn), Oxford: Oxford University Press, Chapters 5, 6 and 11.

Hathaway, J. (1992) 'The Emerging Politics of Non-entrée', *Refugees*, 91: 40.

Hathaway, J. (2021) *The Rights of Refugees under International Law* (2nd edn), Cambridge: Cambridge University Press, Introduction and Chapter 3.

Munn, I. (2016) *Humanity at Sea: Maritime Migration and the Foundations of International Law*, Cambridge: Cambridge University Press.

R v Uxbridge Magistrates Court, ex p Adimi [1999] Imm AR 560 (UK CA).

R v Immigration Officer at Prague Airport, ex p European Roma Rights Centre [2004] UKHL 55, [2005] 2 AC 1.

---

[96] *SS and others v Italy* App. No. 21660/18.

8

Refugee Status Determination

This chapter focuses on the United Kingdom as an example of the state management of refugees as they enter a country and have their claims to refugee status determined.[1] The administration of borders and refugee status determination processes vary from country to country as the Refugee Convention does not mandate any particular method for determining who is or is not a refugee. There are undoubtedly common themes as well as important differences which emerge from a comparative study, but these issues are beyond the scope of this book.[2]

Bureaucratic processes are subject to constant change at the government department responsible for borders, immigration and asylum in the United Kingdom, the Home Office. Many such changes are essentially superficial. At the time of writing, the basic structure of the refugee status determination process and the basic experience of the refugee had remained broadly constant since reforms introduced in the late 1990s and early 2000s. This 'asylum system' taken as a whole consists of several parts. The first is the externalized border, which as far as possible has been exported to external territories through visa regimes, carrier sanctions, juxtaposed border controls and security measures.[3] These expedients prevent refugees from reaching the territory of the United Kingdom but are presented as being morally counterbalanced by a resettlement

---

[1] This chapter is based largely on the author's own experience as a lawyer practising in the United Kingdom. See further Yeo, C. (2020) *Welcome to Britain: Fixing Our Broken Immigration System*, Croydon: Biteback.

[2] Studies of refugee status determination processes in various countries can be found at Hamlin, R. (2012) 'International Law and Administrative Insulation: A Comparison of Refugee Status Determination Regimes in the United States, Canada, and Australia', *Law & Social Inquiry*, 37: 933–968 and in *Forced Migration Review*, Issue 65, November 2020.

[3] Welander, M. (2021) 'The Politics of Exhaustion and the Externalization of British Border Control: An Articulation of a Strategy Designed to Deter, Control and Exclude', *International Migration*, 59(3): 29–46.

programme operated in cooperation with UNHCR which was first launched (at a very small scale) in 2003. The second is an accommodation and support system specific to refugees, into which refugees are forced because they are prohibited from work or self-employment until eventually formally recognized as a refugee.[4] The system consists of actual or de facto immigration detention for some in isolated accommodation centres and, for the rest, destitution-level accommodation and support in economically deprived areas around the country delivered through large-scale private contractors. This centrally-managed but arms-length support is intended to deter refugees from seeking to enter the United Kingdom in the first place and assuage the substantial segment of public opinion hostile to those seeking asylum. The third is a highly bureaucratic two-stage decision-making process in which government officials interview a refugee and make an individualized assessment on the claim, with the burden resting on the refugee to make out their claim for status. If the application is rejected, a new decision is made in an adversarial appeal setting by an independent tribunal judge and the refugee is generally entitled to government-funded legal assistance. The process satisfies formal minimum legal requirements of fairness but is complex and impossible for refugees to navigate alone. The fourth feature of the asylum system is the official apathy shown to successful and unsuccessful refugee applicants alike. Enforced removals of those whose refugee claims failed peaked in 2005 and have declined considerably since, leaving those whose applications are refused physically present but legally proscribed.[5] Integration of recognized refugees has been half-hearted at best. A recognized refugee is afforded all of the rights of the Refugee Convention including the right to work but otherwise mainly left to fend for themselves. There have long been problems with transitioning refugees from the centralized asylum support system to mainstream welfare support and, aside from for a brief period, refugees have been granted short-term residence permits and had to apply later for settlement. Rights of family reunion for refugees have remained broadly stable.

Significant variables over the years from the perspective of the refugee have included the recognition rate of refugees at the administrative stage of assessment, which had increased from 4 per cent in the late 1990s to around 50 per cent at the time of writing (before appeal outcomes are taken into

---

[4] Immigration and Asylum Act 1999, Part VI; Rifa, N.T. and Donà, G. (2021) 'Forced Unemployment or Undocumented Work: The Burden of the Prohibition to Work for Asylum Seekers in the UK', *Journal of Refugee Studies*, 34(2): 2052–2073.

[5] Migration Observatory (2020) *Briefing: Deportation and Voluntary Departure from the UK*, Oxford: The Migration Observatory.

account), level of delays in the decision-making process and the numbers of individuals detained under immigration powers.[6]

Immigration and asylum law applies throughout the United Kingdom and is not within the legislative competence of the devolved administrations of Scotland, Wales or Northern Ireland. Nevertheless, there are in effect three distinct legal systems respectively in (1) England and Wales, (2) Scotland and (3) Northern Ireland. This matters when it comes to legal appeals beyond the tribunal system, public funding of legal representation and on issues which are not strictly immigration laws, such as provision for welfare benefits or housing. The structure of the court systems in these areas are similar to one another but separate. For example, an appeal from the Upper Tribunal for a resident of England or Wales must be made to the Court of Appeal of England and Wales, for a resident of Scotland to the Court of Session and for a resident of Northern Ireland to the Court of Appeal in Northern Ireland. The court structure then converges again at its apex: final appeals from all areas must be made to the Supreme Court of the United Kingdom.

Entry and off-shoring

Since the 1990s, the United Kingdom has, in common with other countries of the Global North, pursued a policy of *non-entrée* to prevent refugees from reaching its territory. This has been coupled with a policy of collective containment of refugees in their country or region of origin.[7] Citizens from poor, unstable or refugee-producing countries have to apply for a visa before they travel to the United Kingdom and airlines and ferry companies are subject to a 'carrier sanction' of a £2,000 penalty fine if they carry a person to the United Kingdom who requires a visa but does not have one.[8] With the exception of a scheme tailored to nationals of Afghanistan who had worked with the British government or armed forces, there is no asylum visa or humanitarian visa available for which a refugee can apply. This makes it impossible for a refugee to travel directly and lawfully to the United Kingdom by air to claim asylum. Some refugees are able to obtain a visa for another purpose, such as visit or study, and then claim asylum on or after entry, but

---

[6] 4 per cent figure given by Michael Howard, Hansard, House of Commons debate, 20 November 1995, Vol. 267, Col. 335. More recent statistics can be accessed in the Home Office Quarterly Immigration Statistics published at https://www.gov.uk/government/collections/immigration-statistics-quarterly-release [last accessed 15 February 2022].

[7] Hathaway, J. (1992) 'The Emerging Politics of Non-entrée', *Refugees*, 91: 40; B.S. Chimni (1998) 'The Geopolitics of Refugee Studies: View from the South', *Journal of Refugee Studies*, 11(4): 350–374.

[8] Immigration (Carriers' Liability) Act 1987, later replaced by Immigration and Asylum Act 1999, Part II.

this almost inevitably requires deceiving the United Kingdom authorities in the course of the application process. A small number of refugees enter the country for another purpose without deception and then, because of a change of circumstance either in their country or personally, claim asylum as a *sur place* refugee. However, between 2015 and 2020, until the scheme was disrupted by the global pandemic, around 5,000 refugees resident in official refugee camps were selected every year with UNHCR for resettlement to the United Kingdom. There was no way to apply for eligibility under this resettlement scheme. A similar scheme was expected to be introduced for an unspecified number Afghan citizens but was yet to be launched at the time of writing.

Meanwhile, externalized and securitized borders have been introduced closer to home to address entry by land and sea. Juxtaposed immigration controls jointly operated by British and French immigration officials have been introduced on the principal routes of entry by land and sea. High levels of security on French territory, funded by the United Kingdom, make it extremely difficult for refugees to board trains or lorries carrying freight into the country. Where informal refugee camps have emerged on the French coast, an agreement has been reached with the French authorities that they be closed or demolished. The introduction of this system in stages between 1987 and 2002 eventually brought about a drastic reduction in the number of refugees reaching the United Kingdom. Numbers of asylum claims rose at the time of the Syrian refugee influx around 2015, fell thereafter and had been gradually rising before the global pandemic began in 2020.[9] From 2018 onwards, rapidly increasing numbers of asylum seekers took to small boats to cross the Channel as a means of avoiding the externalised border, sometimes with predictably disastrous consequences.

Successive governments have expressed interest in the policy of refugee 'off-shoring' pioneered in Australia, whereby refugees are intercepted before arrival or removed after arrival and taken to a third country where their claims are considered. The reduction in numbers of asylum claims from 2002 onwards coupled with practical and legal difficulties and lack of enthusiasm from within the European Union, into the Common European Asylum System of which the United Kingdom committed itself, led to the abandonment of these plans in the early 2000s.[10] The closest analogue to 'off-shoring' of asylum decision-making was through the Dublin arrangement for allocating which country within the European Union would be responsible

---

[9] Migration Observatory (2021) *Briefing: Asylum and Refugee Resettlement in the UK*, Oxford: The Migration Observatory.

[10] UK Home Office, A New Vision for Refugees, referred to in 'Safe havens plan to slash asylum numbers', *The Guardian*, 5 February 2003.

for determining an asylum claim. In short, each country committed to detecting, fingerprinting and registering asylum seekers on its territory, entering the details into a centralized database called Eurodac. If a refugee was detected in a country other than that through which they first entered the European Union they would be sent back to that country. In later years, other allocation criteria were introduced, including the reuniting of children with family members already present within the European Union. The system was subject to a certain level of bureaucratic inefficiency and the strain on the main entry countries of Greece and Italy caused the system to collapse.[11] In reality, despite its relatively isolated geographical position on the periphery of Europe, the United Kingdom was by 2020 receiving more refugees through these amended allocation rules than it was removing to European Union countries.[12] The off-shore concept was revived in 2020, but at the time of writing the practical and legal difficulties and refusal of the European Union or other countries to enter into bilateral arrangements to receive refugees from the United Kingdom meant that no discernible progress towards implementation of the policy had been made.

The legality of so-called 'off-shoring' is disputed. As discussed in Chapter 7, intercepting refugees at sea and transporting them to a genuinely safe third country does not breach the *non-refoulement* obligation imposed by Article 33 of the Refugee Convention because this does not force the refugees back into the arms of their persecutors. Removal of refugees lawfully in the territory of a country does breach the non-expulsion obligation imposed by Article 32, but the construction of lawful presence is disputed. Under the interpretation and understanding of the United Kingdom Supreme Court in the case of *ST (Eritrea)*, such removal is permissible under the Refugee Convention because a refugee only becomes lawfully present once granted a formal residence permit.[13] Under domestic law, as it stood in 2021, such removal would be unlawful.[14] Domestic law can be changed, however. The ECHR might, in practice, present more of a legal barrier, at least so long as the United Kingdom remains a party. If conditions in any detention centre built in a third country to contain refugees were to amount to inhuman or degrading treatment then the transfer of a person into those conditions would be unlawful.

---

[11] See for example Fratzke, S. (2015) *Not Adding Up: The Fading Promise of Europe's Dublin System*, Washington, DC: Migration Policy Institute.

[12] Dathan, M. 'UK Fails in Most Attempts to Remove Asylum Seekers', *The Times*, 8 March 2021.

[13] *ST (Eritrea) v Secretary of State for the Home Department* [2012] UKSC 12, [2012] 2 AC 135. See Chapter 7.

[14] Nationality, Immigration and Asylum Act 2002, s 77. See further *G v G* [2021] UKSC 9 [77]-[106].

The effectiveness of the overall regional refugee containment policy is questionable. Collectively, the *non-entrée* measures no doubt make it more difficult for refugees to travel safely by air to prosperous sanctuary countries. Instead long-distance travel routes by land and sea have opened up to Europe and eventually the United Kingdom through Russia into central and northern Europe and across the Mediterranean from Turkey to Greece, from Libya and Tunisia to Malta and Italy and from Morocco to Spain. Funding is provided by the United Kingdom government and others for refugee camps in transit countries and to 'help address the root causes of mass migration', but it is unclear whether this really operates to prevent people from moving.[15] As discussed in Chapter 7, many have died as a consequence of resorting to dangerous means of travel.

Asylum claim and support

The details of the asylum process in the United Kingdom often change, but the broad shape or structure has remained broadly consistent for around 20 years at the time of writing. Notional responsibility for immigration and asylum has been allocated to various agencies before being returned to direct departmental control; the places at which asylum claims may be registered have been subject to occasional change, 'fast track' processes have come and gone and the priorities and resources allocated to 'clearly unfounded' or 'Dublin' cases have sometimes shifted. The fundamental stability of the system suggests an internal and external equilibrium to the existing arrangements, although this is not to say that this broad *status quo* is unchangeable.

The government department responsible for managing the United Kingdom's asylum system is the Home Office. The responsible legal personality is the head of that department, the Secretary of State for the Home Department, often referred to as the Home Secretary. Border operations such as receiving asylum claims at ports of entry are generally carried out by Immigration Officers and officials of the UK Border Force, who have the legal authority to perform various border functions in their own right, such as grants or refusals of permission to enter.[16] Where an asylum claim is received by an Immigration Officer, that claim is referred to officials acting for the Home Secretary.[17] Processing of asylum claims and asylum decision-making is carried out by these officials acting for the

---

[15] Department for International Development, *UK Aid Tackling Global Migration Crisis* (18 December 2017), Available from: https://www.gov.uk/government/news/uk-aid-tackling-global-migration-crisis [last accessed 13 May 2021].

[16] See Immigration Act 1971 as amended.

[17] Immigration Rules HC 395 [328].

Home Secretary under the legal authority of the Home Secretary. Various other functions, such as the provision of accommodation and support, detention, escort and removal may be and generally are carried out by private contractors.

Claim for asylum

Once a refugee reaches the territory of the United Kingdom, they can make a claim for asylum. Legislation specifies that the Home Secretary may specify where asylum claims may be made.[18] This will either be on arrival at a port or airport, a location to which the person has been directed in order to claim asylum or any other location where an authorized official is present, or after arrival from within the United Kingdom at the designated 'asylum intake unit' in Croydon (or Belfast for those in Northern Ireland), for which a prior appointment must normally be booked by telephone. Asylum claims are not accepted at sea, for example if a vessel is intercepted or boarded, but such vessels are landed in the United Kingdom. An asylum claim may be made without using the words 'refugee' or 'asylum' as long as a desire for international protection is indicated.

When the asylum claim is officially recorded and registered, officials conduct an initial interview to establish the personal and basic biographical details of the person concerned such as their name, age, country of origin and family members both within and outside the United Kingdom.[19] This interview is referred to as a 'screening interview'. Photographs and fingerprints (referred to as 'biometric' details) are also taken and recorded electronically. Asylum applicants are asked to state briefly their reasons for claiming asylum although few details are recorded at this stage.

Streaming

Once an asylum claim is made and registered, officials allocate the case to one of several different 'streams' or processes within the Home Office. These are for children, clearly unfounded cases, detained casework and general. Historically there had been two further processes: detained fast track and 'third country' (or 'Dublin') cases. Both these processes appeared to be defunct at the time of writing, although potentially subject to revival in future. The

---

[18] Nationality, Immigration and Asylum Act 2002, s 113(1) and Immigration Rules HC 395 [327]-[327D]. At the time of writing further provision was due to be made in the Nationality and Borders Bill.

[19] For details of the process, see Right to Remain, *The Right to Remain Toolkit: A Guide to the UK Immigration and Asylum System*, Available from: https://righttoremain.org.uk/toolkit/ [last accessed 28 May 2021].

United Kingdom withdrew from the Common European Asylum System with effect from 31 December 2020, meaning loss of access to the Dublin arrangement or the Eurodac fingerprint database. No agreement had been reached with the European Union as a whole, any individual European Union countries or any other countries to carry out removals of asylum seekers, meaning that third country removals were virtually impossible. The detained fast track process was closed following a court judgment in 2015 that the system then in existence, which included both accelerated decisions and accelerated appeals, was inherently unfair to claimants.[20] At the time of writing, a new fast track process was due to be revived and embedded into primary legislation by the Nationality and Borders Bill.

Assessment of age in order to identify children is imprecise and has been controversial. Pending a full age assessment conducted by two trained social workers, Home Office officials are instructed to proceed on the basis that a person claiming to be a child is indeed a child unless their physical appearance and demeanour very strongly suggest that they are 25 years of age or over.[21] The Home Office is obliged by domestic legislation to have regard to 'the need to safeguard and promote the welfare of children' when performing immigration functions.[22] This obliges officials to have regard to the best interests of a child at all times.[23] If a child who is unaccompanied because they have been separated from their parent or carer is not already known to the relevant local authority's social services department then they will be referred. That child is then supported by the local authority through the asylum process. Various safeguards are put in place during the asylum process, including the use of specially trained officials, an additional opportunity to submit detailed evidence prior to the main interview with the Home Office and that the child be accompanied by a responsible adult at all times.[24] As a consequence, the time for processing child asylum cases is longer than that for adult cases. In England and Wales, there are no limits on the legal aid time a lawyer may spend with a child client, unlike with adult asylum seekers. If an unaccompanied child's application for asylum is refused then the child will still be granted a residence permit up to the

---

[20] *The Lord Chancellor v Detention Action* [2015] EWCA Civ 840. An earlier Strasbourg judgment on a fast-track process applying to initial asylum decisions only had upheld its legality: *Saadi v United Kingdom* [2008] ECHR 79.

[21] Home Office, *Assessing Age* (version 4.0), 31 December 2020. See also *R (on the application of BF (Eritrea)) v Secretary of State for the Home Department* [2021] UKSC 38.

[22] Borders, Citizenship and Immigration Act 2009, s 55.

[23] See Home Office, *Every Child Matters*, statutory guidance made pursuant to Borders, Citizenship and Immigration Act 2009, 55(3) and *ZH (Tanzania) v Secretary of State for the Home Department* [2011] UKSC 4, [2011] 2 AC 166.

[24] Home Office, *Children's Asylum Claims* (version 4.0), 31 December 2020.

date of their becoming seventeen and a half years old. The child can appeal immediately on refugee grounds (which would usually be in their best interests if they have an arguable claim to refugee status) or re-apply on refugee and/or human rights grounds once they have turned seventeen and a half and their residence permit expires.

Asylum seekers whose claims for international protection are considered 'clearly unfounded' are subject to refusal with a right of appeal that can only be exercised from abroad, after removal.[25] Such individuals are more likely to be detained than in other cases. The statutory power includes a general discretion to designate any person's case as clearly unfounded. More commonly in practice, a rebuttable statutory presumption that a person's case is clearly unfounded arises if a person is entitled to reside in one of a specified list of countries and the person meets the other criteria on the list, which may include gender, language, race, religion and other characteristics. Cases certified as clearly unfounded, whether under the general discretion or by reason of not rebutting the statutory presumption, are assessed for asylum by officials acting for the Home Secretary, but if the claim is refused, which will almost inevitably be the case, then the person may only lodge an appeal against this decision after their removal. A decision to certify a case as clearly unfounded can be subject to an application for judicial review. Such applications are heard by the Upper Tribunal and an error of law must be demonstrated (see the following) for the application to succeed. If the application does succeed, the clearly unfounded certificate is cancelled and the asylum applicant may appeal from within the United Kingdom as normal.

In all cases, if any person seeking asylum discloses that they are or may be a victim of trafficking then at any stage of the asylum process they are supposed to be referred by officials to a separate assessment and assistance process called the NRM. See further Chapter 1. This runs in parallel to the asylum process, although the relevant facts inevitably overlap with one another.

Detention

The Home Secretary and her officials are empowered to detain any person subject to immigration control, and indeed to establish whether or not a person is subject to immigration control.[26] The power is used at various stages of the asylum process: to detain on arrival to decide whether or not to admit a person, to detain those encountered within the country in order to consider their cases, to maintain detention at the end of a criminal sentence in order to deport or otherwise to detain pending removal, for

---

[25] Nationality, Immigration and Asylum Act 2002, s 94.
[26] Immigration Act 1971, Schedules 2 and 3.

example when a person is asked to report to the Home Office or subject to a home visit. There is no statutory time limit to the period a person subject to immigration control can be detained, potentially leading to lengthy periods of immigration detention in some cases. Implied restrictions have evolved through case law and the power can only lawfully be exercised for a reasonable period and while there is a realistic prospect of removal.[27]

Aside from immigration control enforcement, immigration detention has periodically been used for administrative purposes in order to decide asylum claims more rapidly and, sometimes, enforce a subsequent removal more conveniently. There have been three broad variations on this use of immigration detention in order to 'fast-track' asylum claims. The first was to detain asylum seekers at the time they were detected, either on arrival or within the country, and to detain them for a relatively short time while an initial decision was taken on their case. This was often referred to as the 'Oakington' process, after the name of the detention centre used for this purpose, and a legal challenge to the use of detention for this purpose was ultimately rejected by the European Court of Human Rights.[28] The second, sometimes referred to as the 'Harmondsworth' process after the name of the principal detention centre used for the purpose, was to detain asylum seekers for the duration of the asylum process, including both the initial decision and the appeal. Very short periods were allowed for preparation of the initial claim and the appeal and appeals were heard in special tribunal hearing rooms within the detention centre. The process was so foreshortened that it was held to be procedurally unfair in 2015.[29] Finally, a general process of detained asylum casework has also been deployed with an accelerated initial decision and then a prioritized appeal hearing, although one that is subject to the normal time limits for non-detained appeals, for example, for lodging appeals, responding to tribunal directions and similar.

Support and accommodation

When an asylum applicant enters the asylum process, they are entitled to apply for support or support and accommodation. Since legislation introduced in 1999, support and accommodation have been provided (or at least funded) by the Home Office.[30] This system is separate from that operated by local government for citizens and long-term residents. Levels of asylum support are far lower than the mainstream equivalent and the

---

[27] *R v Governor of Durham Prison, ex p Hardial Singh* [1984] 1 WLR 704 (EW HC).
[28] *Saadi v United Kingdom* [2008] ECHR 79.
[29] *The Lord Chancellor v Detention Action* [2015] EWCA Civ 840.
[30] Immigration and Asylum Act 1999, Part VI.

accommodation provided is of a far lower standard. At the time of writing, an asylum seeker was normally entitled to £39.63 per week cash support, compared to £74.96 per week standard allowance universal credit for a single person over 25. Accommodation is allocated outside London and any geographical preferences of the asylum applicant are usually irrelevant. Provision of the accommodation itself is contracted out by the Home Office to private companies.

Refugee status determination process

There are broadly two stages to the refugee status determination process. Firstly, a decision is made by an official within the government department responsible, the Home Office. The proportion of decisions to grant refugee status has varied over time, but, at the time of writing, had followed a broad upward trend, rising from just 4 per cent in the 1990s to as high as around 50 per cent by 2020.[31] The recognition rate varies considerably by country. If the decision is a refusal then the asylum applicant may appeal to an independent tribunal, the formal title of which is the First-tier Tribunal Immigration and Asylum Chamber. Again, success rates have varied over time but followed a broad upward trend and stood at around 50 per cent at the time of writing.[32]

Asylum seekers are entitled to legal representation throughout the asylum process and government-funded legal representation if they are eligible.[33] Only a person with a very low or non-existent income and savings is eligible for publicly funded representation. Because most asylum seekers have no income or savings, most are therefore eligible. In England and Wales, only lawyers who have been awarded a contract by the Ministry of Justice may provide legal aid; they may only undertake a specified number of cases, and only a certain amount of work on each case is normally paid for. It can therefore be difficult to find a lawyer in some parts of the country, and the lawyer will not be paid to undertake a considerable amount of work on the case other than in exceptional circumstances or in separated child cases. If the case reaches the appeal stage, a publicly funded lawyer may only provide

---

[31] 4 per cent figure given by Michael Howard, Hansard, House of Commons debate, 20 November 1995, Vol. 267, Col. 335. More recent statistics can be accessed in the Home Office Quarterly Immigration Statistics published at https://www.gov.uk/government/collections/immigration-statistics-quarterly-release [last accessed 15 February 2022].

[32] For latest and historic figures, see https://www.gov.uk/government/collections/tribunals-statistics [last accessed 15 February 2022].

[33] See Wilding, J. (2021) *The Legal Aid Market: Challenges for Publicly Funded Immigration and Asylum Legal Representation*, Bristol: Policy Press.

assistance if the chances of success are considered by the lawyer to be over 50 per cent.

Administrative stage

Following the initial screening interview to establish an asylum applicant's basic biographical details and allocate them to an administrative process within the Home Office, the next main stage is an in-depth interview concerning the details of the asylum applicant's account of what happened to them in the past and why they fear to return now and in the future. The interview is conducted by an official from the Home Office and an interpreter is provided where one is requested. The Home Office interviewer reads out a number of standard statements concerning, for example, the confidentiality of the asylum process and then asks questions of the asylum applicant and makes a written record of the questions and answers. Interviews vary in length and a duration of three or four hours is not unusual. Short breaks usually are provided at the discretion of the official and on request by the asylum applicant. The audio from the interview is recorded and made available to the asylum applicant afterwards on request.[34]

Following the interview, the asylum applicant is provided with the written record of the interview, can request the audio recording and has an opportunity to submit clarifications or further evidence prior to a decision being made. An official other than the one who conducted the interview will usually make the asylum decision. A decision to grant asylum is not accompanied by reasons, although concise reasons are recorded on the Home Office file. A decision to refuse asylum is accompanied by a lengthy explanation letter often referred to as a 'reasons for refusal letter'. This assesses the truthfulness of the asylum applicant's account of past events and also assesses future risk of harm if the asylum applicant were to be removed to their country of origin. In doing so, the letter will often reference information about and evidence from the country of origin, the asylum applicant's own various accounts of past events and future fears and any documentary or other evidence that the asylum applicant has submitted. The country information referred to in decisions will usually be drawn exclusively from reports compiled by a team within the Home Office which are based on a range of sources including governmental, non-governmental and media organizations. The decision letter will normally evaluate the eligibility of the applicant under other potential immigration and protection routes,

---

[34] *R (on the application of Dirshe) v Secretary of State for the Home Department* [2005] EWCA Civ 421, [2005] 1 WLR 2685.

including humanitarian and human rights protection and Home Office discretionary policies.

Throughout the entire asylum process, officials are supposed to be guided by a range of 'policy guidance' documents. Each of these is addressed to different aspects or stages or themes of the asylum process. For example, one such document sets out guidance for officials on conducting interviews, another provides guidance on assessing the truthfulness (often referred to as 'credibility') of the asylum applicant and there are also guidance documents on gender issues in asylum claims, asylum claims by children and other so-called 'cross cutting' issues.

Appeal stage

If an asylum applicant's initial application is rejected at the administrative stage, they have the right to lodge an appeal against that decision. The appeal is managed, heard and decided by an independent immigration tribunal, the First-tier Tribunal Immigration and Asylum Chamber.[35] The tribunal's processes are regulated by a set of procedure rules made by the Tribunal Procedure Committee, the membership of which is itself regulated by law.[36] The deadline for lodging an appeal is 14 days from being sent the decision, although late appeals can be accepted by the tribunal if there are good reasons. If the asylum applicant is subject to the 'clearly unfounded' out-of-country appeal process, the deadline is 28 days from the date of departure from the country. Fees normally have to be paid to lodge an appeal but not where the asylum applicant is being assisted by a legal aid lawyer.

The hearing date and location is decided by the tribunal and notice is sent to the asylum applicant and the Home Office. The Home Office is directed to send to the asylum applicant and the tribunal a copy of all the relevant documents including interview notes, decision letter, any material submitted by the asylum applicant to the Home Office and any country information relied on by the Home Office. The asylum applicant then has an opportunity to respond by submitting any further evidence or statements and country information to the Home Office and tribunal.

Hearings are adversarial in nature, with a judge impartially presiding over a process in which both sides call any relevant evidence they wish, subject opposing witnesses to cross-examination and make submissions on the law, facts and outcome.[37] In practice, the Home Office very rarely calls

---

[35] Tribunals, Courts and Enforcement Act 2007.
[36] Tribunals, Courts and Enforcement Act 2007, s 22 and Schedule 5; Tribunal Procedure (First-tier Tribunal) (Immigration and Asylum Chamber) Rules 2014.
[37] Campbell, J. (2017) *Bureaucracy, Law and Dystopia in the United Kingdom's Asylum System*, Abingdon: Routledge.

any witnesses of its own, meaning that the hearing consists primarily of the asylum applicant and any supporting witnesses giving evidence and being cross-examined and then both sides making submissions. Decisions are rarely reached by a judge on the day of a hearing. Instead, both parties normally receive the decision in writing at the same time some two or three weeks after the hearing.

A further appeal can be pursued by the unsuccessful party, whether that is the asylum applicant or the Home Office.[38] This second stage of appeal is not automatic and an application for permission to appeal must first be made in which the appealing party attempts to identify an arguable error of law in the decision under appeal. A disagreement with the outcome is insufficient; an error of law is generally a flaw in the way in which the decision was reached, such as overlooking important evidence or failing to take account of relevant considerations.[39] An application for permission must first be made to the First-tier Tribunal, in which case it will be considered by a judge other than the one who heard the original appeal. If that is rejected, an application can then be made to the Upper Tribunal. If that is also rejected, an application for judicial review can be made in England and Wales to the Administrative Court, albeit it will be subject to an abbreviated form of procedure.[40] In Scotland, the application is to the Outer House of the Court of Session and in Northern Ireland to the High Court of Justice in Northern Ireland. If permission to appeal is granted, a hearing will be held in the Upper Tribunal. The test for permission to appeal is whether there is an arguable error of law, so if permission is granted, the tribunal's first task will be to establish whether or not there was an error of law. If not, the original appeal decision will stand and be confirmed. If an error of law is found, the tribunal can either remit the appeal to be reheard in the First-tier or can proceed to decide the appeal for itself.

If the Upper Tribunal dismisses the appeal, the unsuccessful party can apply for permission to appeal to the Court of Appeal in England and Wales. In Scotland, this appeal is to the Outer House of the Court of Session and in Northern Ireland to the Court of Appeal in Northern Ireland. As well as identifying an arguable error of law, the appealing party must also demonstrate that the appeal raises an important point of principle or practice or there is

---

[38] Tribunals, Courts and Enforcement Act 2007, s 11. For administrative processes, see Tribunal Procedure (Upper Tribunal) Rules 2008.

[39] See *R (Iran) & others v Secretary of State for the Home Department* [2005] EWCA Civ 982, [2005] Imm AR 535 [9] for a summary of commonly pleaded errors of law.

[40] See *R (Cart) v Upper Tribunal; R (MR (Pakistan)) v Upper Tribunal* [2012] 1 AC 663 and *Eba v Advocate General for Scotland* [2012] 1 AC 710. At the time of writing, the government proposed to curtail even this abbreviated judicial review procedure by means of the Nationality and Borders Bill 2021.

some other compelling reason why permission should be granted.[41] A similar process is followed of applying for permission first to the Upper Tribunal then, if unsuccessful, to the relevant appeal court. As before, if permission to appeal is granted then the first issue is whether there was or was not an error of law and then, if so, whether the case should be remitted to the Upper Tribunal or decided by the appeal court itself. For the unsuccessful party, a right of appeal from a final decision of the Court of Appeal of England and Wales, Court of Session or Court of Appeal in Northern Ireland exists to the Supreme Court. Permission is rarely granted beyond the Upper Tribunal and even more seldom to the Supreme Court.

Refusal

There are two potential outcomes from rejection of an asylum claim: removal from the country or unlawful residence. Removal at the conclusion of an unsuccessful asylum claim is historically unusual, other than for those asylum seekers subject to a detained casework process. The number of enforced removals from the United Kingdom peaked at around 20,000 per year in 2006 and at the time of writing had been in long-term decline since then, falling to just over 7,000 in 2019. These figures include not just asylum seekers but all removed migrants.[42] Recorded voluntary departures of migrants had also been trending downward. In contrast, the number of asylum seekers (including dependents) entering the country peaked at over 100,000 in 2002, has never since then been lower than 20,000 per year, and in 2019 stood at over 35,000 applications.[43] Unlawful residence following the unsuccessful conclusion of an asylum application is not, therefore, unusual.

Where an asylum applicant reaches the end of the asylum process and has no further option to appeal or the deadline for appealing has passed, the Home Office labels them as 'appeal rights exhausted'. If the asylum applicant was in receipt of asylum support and/or accommodation then this will be terminated after 21 days. The unsuccessful asylum applicant will normally be directed to attend a Home Office reporting centre at least once per month but will normally receive no support to do so. They may be detained at any time. Given the asylum applicant will usually be homeless and therefore difficult to find, this is most likely to be at the time they report to the Home

---

[41] Tribunals, Courts and Enforcement Act 2007, s 13(6).
[42] Migration Observatory (2016) *Briefing: Deportations, Removals and Voluntary Departures from the UK*, p 6; for more recent figures see https://www.gov.uk/government/collecti ons/immigration-statistics-quarterly-release [last accessed 15 February 2022].
[43] Migration Observatory (2021) *Briefing: Asylum and Refugee Resettlement in the UK*, Oxford: Migration Observatory.

Office. In practice, the low number of enforced removals means that the threat of removal hangs over an unsuccessful asylum applicant, but actual detention and removal is unusual.

Unauthorized residence

Most unsuccessful asylum seekers become unlawfully resident at the conclusion of their claims, at least for a short time. Often, though, this unlawful residence is for a very protracted period. The physical presence of unsuccessful asylum seekers is unofficially tolerated by the government, given that they are rarely removed in practice, but they have no right lawfully to work, to rent accommodation, to open a bank account or pursue other normal activities required for a minimum acceptable life. The set of policies introduced in the United Kingdom with the intention of making life intolerable for unauthorized migrants, including unsuccessful asylum seekers, is often referred to as the 'hostile environment' or more recently in official government communications as the 'compliant environment'.[44] This state of limbo is not considered to breach the person's human rights because it is considered to be a voluntary state of affairs the person can bring to an end at any time by departing from the country should they choose. Essentially, government policy is to encourage unsuccessful asylum seekers to leave of their own volition, a policy sometimes referred to in the United States as 'self-deportation'. On these terms, the policy is a dismal failure given that voluntary returns of asylum seekers have followed a downward trend since 2006 and, before the global pandemic beginning in 2020, had reached an historic low.

Some welfare support and accommodation is made available to unsuccessful asylum seekers who can demonstrate that they are taking all reasonable steps to leave the United Kingdom but that there are barriers or delays beyond the person's control preventing their departure.[45] This will include agreeing to the voluntary return scheme discussed later.

Removal or return

If efforts are made to remove an unsuccessful asylum applicant, the Home Office will need to ensure the receiving country consents to the arrival of the person concerned, otherwise, the asylum applicant will simply be returned to the United Kingdom. If the asylum applicant or the Home

---

[44] Griffiths, M. and Yeo, C. (2021) 'The UK's Hostile Environment: Deputising Immigration Control', *Critical Social Policy*, 41(4).
[45] Immigration and Asylum Act 1999, s 4.

Office is in possession of a valid and unexpired passport or travel document, this is straightforward. In reality, this is rarely the case. Asylum seekers may not have had such a travel document at all or may have destroyed it *en route* to the United Kingdom, perhaps on the instruction of an agent. If they did hold such a document, it may be expired. The Home Office will usually, therefore, need to obtain a temporary travel document of some sort to ensure the unsuccessful asylum applicant is admitted to the country concerned. Obtaining such a document will usually involve convincing the authorities of the country in question that the asylum applicant is one of their citizens. This may involve submitting biographical details such as date and place of birth and names of parents so that local records can be checked. Sometimes embassy officials from that country may wish to interview the asylum applicant before agreeing to accept them. Some countries are very slow to conduct such verifications.

Some removals take place by means of a seat being booked by the Home Office on a conventional passenger flight. Escorts will usually accompany the person being removed. A significant proportion of removals of migrants, including asylum seekers, take place by charter flight.[46] These are special flights booked by the Home Office to a particular country, sometimes with a stopover in another country. A number of migrants are removed in this way at the same time. Migrants of a given nationality are often detained in advance and such flights overbooked in order to attempt to maximize the number of actual removals, given that some migrants lodge legal challenges to their removal, as discussed in a moment.

It is a criminal offence to fail to comply with requests to cooperate with one's own removal.[47] Prosecutions are unusual, no doubt because they will rarely do much to encourage the cooperation of an unsuccessful asylum applicant who is already detained and very reluctant to go to the country concerned.

A voluntary returns scheme has been operated for many years under various guises, sometimes contracted out to organizations and sometimes run in-house by the Home Office.[48] Under these schemes, an unsuccessful asylum applicant who agrees to return voluntarily to their country of origin is eligible for a 'reintegration package' usually involving a cash payment.

---

[46] Corporate Watch (2018) *Deportation Charter Flights: Updated Report 2018*, 2 July, Available from: https://corporatewatch.org/deportation-charter-flights-updated-report-2018/ [last accessed 1 December 2021] reported that 1,664 migrants were removed on charter flights in 2017.

[47] Asylum and Immigration (Treatment of Claimants, etc.) Act 2004, s 35.

[48] Thomas, J. (2019) *Between a Rock and a Hard Place: AVR 2.0: The Case for Rebooting Assisted Voluntary Return in the UK's Immigration Control Regime*, London: Social Market Foundation.

Fresh asylum claims

An unsuccessful asylum applicant may at any time make a new claim for asylum. These are often referred to as 'fresh claims'. The Home Office, seeking to avoid an obligation to consider infinitely repeated but weak claims for asylum, has erected a number of barriers to such claims while also recognizing that some such claims may ultimately succeed.[49] For example, the situation in the asylum applicant's country of origin may have changed such that the asylum applicant is now in danger despite a previous unsuccessful claim; new evidence may have come to light that the asylum applicant may have engaged in activities in the United Kingdom which would expose them to risk if returned; or the asylum applicant may have been poorly represented in their earlier asylum application. The Home Office will always consider whether new submissions from a previously unsuccessful asylum applicant demonstrate that they are a refugee. Occasionally, asylum is granted in such cases. Normally, refusal of such a claim will not generate a right of appeal to the tribunal, meaning that the only means of legal challenge is an application for judicial review. Where asylum is refused but the Home Office considers that the new evidence or submissions create a reasonable prospect of success before a tribunal judge, the Home Office will enable the asylum applicant to pursue an appeal to the tribunal.

An unsuccessful asylum applicant may also apply for lawful status on the basis of their human rights. Such applications are beyond the scope of this book. Briefly, such applications are more likely to succeed where the claimant has children or other family members in the United Kingdom who cannot be expected to leave.[50] It is also possible to apply for lawful status on the basis of 20 years of continuous unlawful residence.[51]

Integration

Where an asylum applicant is recognized as a refugee they will be granted a residence permit, be granted permission to work and become eligible for mainstream welfare support. Some integration assistance is also available, including the possibility of being joined in the United Kingdom by some family members. Interest-free refugee integration loans were available at the time of writing, for example, for assistance with a rent deposit, purchase of household items or education or training for work. Support is also available from a range of charities.

---

[49] Immigration Rules HC 395 [353].
[50] For example, Immigration Rules HC 395 [276ADE(1)(iv)].
[51] Immigration Rules HC 395 [276ADE(1)(iii)].

Residence status

Since 2005, recognition as a refugee has been accompanied by a grant of a five-year residence permit.[52] The residence permit enables the refugee to work and live in the United Kingdom and brings with it the other rights conferred on refugees by the Refugee Convention (see Chapter 7). Asylum support from the Home Office will continue for a short period at the end of which the refugee is eligible for mainstream welfare benefits and housing support by the relevant local authority where the refugee resides. A recognized refugee is eligible to apply for a travel document enabling travel to other states which have ratified the Refugee Convention.[53] A recognized refugee is also able to apply to be joined by certain pre-existing family members, including a spouse or partner and children.[54] These family reunion applications can be made on more generous terms than for British citizens or other migrants, in that applications are free of charge and the normal minimum income requirement for the sponsor is waived.

At the end of the five-year period, the refugee is eligible to apply for permanent residence.[55] An application for permanent residence can be granted, refused or, alternatively, a shorter residence permit may be granted instead.

Return reviews

It is official Home Office policy to carry out a 'safe return review' if a refugee applies for permanent residence at the conclusion of their initial five years of residence.[56] This review is intended to determine whether the refugee continues to have protection needs. If any of the cessation clauses of the Refugee Convention are found to apply (see Chapter 6), whether due to the refugee's own actions or due to a significant and non-temporary change of circumstances in the refugee's country of origin, the application for permanent residence can be refused. In practice, these reviews seldom seem to lead to the refusal of an application for permanent residence. However, any criminality by the refugee will lead to a more thorough review and, potentially, revocation of refugee status, detention and deportation. As discussed in the previous chapter, the benefits of refugee status are often withdrawn by inappropriate but administratively simple means of cessation rather than more properly on the basis of expulsion on grounds of national security or public order.

---

[52] Immigration Rules HC 395 [339Q(i)].
[53] Immigration Rules HC 395 [344A(i)]; Refugee Convention, Article 28.
[54] Immigration Rules HC 395 [352A], [352D] and [319X].
[55] Immigration Rules HC 395 [339R].
[56] Home Office, *Asylum Policy Instruction Settlement Protection* (version 4.0), 2 February 2016.

Settlement

If permanent residence is granted to the refugee then refugee status continues. No further review of residence or refugee status will normally be carried out. However, if the refugee comes to the attention of the Home Office through criminality or engagement in activity considered not 'conducive to the public good' then both residence and refugee status may be reviewed as discussed previously and in Chapter 6.

Once a refugee has been permanently resident for one year and has already previously been lawfully resident for four years before that, the refugee becomes eligible to apply for naturalization as a British citizen.[57] The requirements applied to refugees are essentially the same as for other migrants wishing to naturalize, in that no more generous terms or procedures are normally available to refugees (although stateless children born in the United Kingdom are eligible to be registered as British citizens after five years of residence rather than the normal ten years). The requirement that an applicant for naturalization be considered to be of 'good character' has caused problems for some refugees because a refugee's means of entry to the United Kingdom, if involving a breach of immigration laws, may be held against them.

Suggested further reading
Botero, A. and Vedsted-Hansen, J. (2021) 'Asylum Procedure', in Costello, C., Foster, M. and McAdam, J. (eds) *The Oxford Handbook of International Refugee Law*, Oxford: Oxford University Press, pp 586–606.
Campbell, J. (2017) *Bureaucracy, Law and Dystopia in the United Kingdom's Asylum System*, Abingdon: Routledge.
Forced Migration Review, Issue 65, November 2020.
Hamlin, R. (2012) 'International Law and Administrative Insulation: A Comparison of Refugee Status Determination Regimes in the United States, Canada, and Australia', *Law and Social Inquiry*, 37: 933–968.
Griffiths, M. and Yeo, C. (2021) 'The UK's Hostile Environment: Deputising Immigration Control', *Critical Social Policy*, 41(4) pp 521–544.
Right to Remain, *The Right to Remain Toolkit: A Guide to the UK Immigration and Asylum System*, Available from: https://righttoremain.org.uk/toolkit/ [last accessed 28 May 2021].
Yeo, C. (2020) *Welcome to Britain: Fixing Our Broken Immigration System*, Croydon: Biteback, Chapter 6.
R v Governor of Durham Prison, ex p Hardial Singh [1984] 1 WLR 704.

---

[57] British Nationality Act 1981, s 6 and Schedule 1.

Conclusion

The current international regime of the protection of refugees has, quite rightly, been subject to sustained criticism. Many millions of refugees find themselves warehoused for years in refugee camps, where multiple generations are unable to work and are denied many of the minimum rights of a normal human life. While talk of tackling the 'root causes' of refugee crises is commonplace at an international level, the number of refugees worldwide has dramatically increased in the last decade, more than doubling between 2010 and 2020 from 10 million to over 20 million.[1] The distribution of those refugees is incredibly uneven, with some countries bearing a hugely disproportionate responsibility. Just ten countries host 65 per cent of the world's refugees, 86 per cent of refugees are hosted in the Global South and 73 per cent of refugees are hosted in a country adjacent to their own. Emma Haddad's argument that refugees are 'an inevitable if unintended consequence of the international states system' seems borne out, although this cannot itself explain why the numbers of refugees have risen so swiftly in recent years.[2] Crises in Syria and Venezuela have given rise to around seven million refugees and four million other forcibly displaced people but, similarly, cannot wholly explain the overall increase. Meanwhile, thousands of refugees, shut out by *non-entrée* policies, die attempting to reach more prosperous countries of asylum. An estimated 40,000 refugees and other migrants died between 2014 and 2020 in the process of moving between countries around the world, with over half of those deaths occurring by drowning in the Mediterranean.[3]

Refugees have become a hugely controversial issue in contemporary politics in the Global North. A very substantial portion of public opinion in prosperous countries of asylum considers that the refugee protection regime is too generous and that fewer, not more, refugees should be admitted.

---

[1] UNHCR figures: www.unhcr.org/refugee-statistics [last accessed 17 January 2022].
[2] Haddad, E. (2008) *The Refugee in International Society*, Cambridge: Cambridge University Press, pp 1, 3.
[3] See missingmigrants.iom.int [last accessed 17 January 2022].

Some countries, including the United States, have breached even the fairly minimalist requirements of the Refugee Convention not to subject refugees to *refoulement* back into the arms of their persecutors. Other countries, including Australia, have evaded their international legal obligations to refugees by removing or diverting them to third countries. There is no 'International Court of Refugees' or other effective enforcement mechanism to secure state compliance or even to fix a standard interpretation of key terms or concepts. At the same time, many people who might widely be considered to be refugees are not eligible for refugee status under the terms of the Refugee Convention, including those who have not yet managed to leave their own country, victims of civil wars, those experiencing famine or other natural disasters and those who are sometimes considered 'climate refugees'. Some are offered protection by the UNHCR under its extended mandate, but this will usually be in the form of accommodation – some would say containment – in a refugee camp. Some refugee camps are literally closed, with the refugees imprisoned within them.[4]

Attempts to reform: the Global Compacts

It is therefore hard to argue that the international refugee protection regime is working, particularly from the perspective of refugees themselves. Replacing or even amending that regime seems impossible, however, at least without diminishing even the limited protection the regime currently affords to some refugees. An attempt to enshrine a right of asylum in international law, beginning with the Declaration on Territorial Asylum of 1967, ended with failure to agree a full and binding convention ten years later. Even very modest attempts within the European Union in 2015 to negotiate resettlement quotas had failed just two years later when the scheme was prematurely ended, leading to judgment against the Czech Republic, Hungary and Poland in the Court of Justice of the European Union.[5] In 2016, the UN General Assembly adopted the New York Declaration for Refugees and Migrants, a lengthy but non-binding statement of general principles and worthy exhortations.[6] The declaration included a Comprehensive Refugee Response Framework, which again set out no binding legal commitments to refugees or by countries of asylum. It did, though, initiate the process that led to drawing up of a Global Compact on Refugees and a Global

---

[4] Refugee camps in Bangladesh for Rohingya fleeing Myanmar, for example.
[5] Joined Cases C-715/17, C-718/17 and C-719/17.
[6] UN General Assembly (2015) *New York Declaration for Refugees and Migrants* (UN Doc A/RES/71/1).

Compact for Safe, Orderly and Regular Migration in 2018 discussed in the Introduction.[7]

The Global Compact on Refugees does not necessitate any outcomes as such. It does not seek to amend the international protection regime and does not address the definition of a refugee, for example, or controversial issues of a right to asylum, externalization or *refoulement*. The process of drafting and negotiation was led by UNHCR and these omissions were deliberate.[8] It is better understood as a political instrument rather than a legal one, and criticizing its legal shortcomings arguably misses the point. Parallels can be drawn with the Cartagena Declaration, which has arguably succeeded in strengthening the refugee protection regime in Latin America. Admittedly, this was in the context of a degree of regional solidarity which is absent on the global plane. Whether the Global Compact succeeds, and to what degree, in meeting any of these objectives is likely to be contested. At the very least, it provides an ongoing basis for international discussion of how better to meet the needs of refugees and an agenda for that discussion.

Three years on from the adoption of the two compacts, Garlick and Inder optimistically argue that they together represent 'the most significant steps forward by the international community in the field of human mobility in several decades', although they add the important proviso 'if implemented in good faith'.[9] Similarly, Triggs and Wall point to pledges made at the first Global Refugee Forum of 2019 having 'the potential to transform the lives of tens of millions of refugees and their hosts by building self-reliance, promoting socio-economic inclusion, and paving the way to solutions' but conclude that it is too early to declare the endeavour a success.[10] This was before the global pandemic of 2020–21 led to the suspension of refugee resettlement efforts in many countries. UNHCR have reported that a mere 34,400 refugees were resettled in 2020 at a time when 1.4 million refugees were estimated to be in need of resettlement.[11] And this statement of resettlement requirements may well massively understate the true need,

---

[7] Global Compact on Refugees (UN Doc A/73/12 (Part II)) (2 August 2018); Global Compact for Safe, Orderly and Regular Migration (UN Doc A/RES/73/195) (19 December 2018).

[8] Betts, A. (2018) 'The Global Compact on Refugees: Towards a Theory of Change?', *International Journal of Refugee Law*, 30(4): 623–626.

[9] Garlick, M. and Inder, C. (2021) 'Protection of Refugees and Migrants in the Era of the Global Compacts', *Interventions: International Journal of Postcolonial Studies*, 23(2): 207–226.

[10] Triggs, G. and Wall, P. (2020) '"The Makings of a Success": The Global Compact on Refugees and the Inaugural Global Refugee Forum', *International Journal of Refugee Law*, 32(2): 283–339.

[11] UNHCR, *Global Trends: Forced Displacement in 2020* (18 June 2021).

given that UNHCR also state 15.7 million refugees are in a 'protracted refugee situation' of at least five continuous years' exile.

Climate displacement

So-called 'climate refugees' or 'climate change refugees' are only mentioned tangentially in the Global Compact on Refugees, which acknowledges that 'climate, environmental degradation and natural disasters increasingly interact with the drivers of refugee movements'.[12] The issue is more prominently addressed in the Global Compact for Migration, which explicitly recognizes that both sudden-onset and slow-onset natural disasters and environmental degradation are important reasons driving international displacement.[13] Nothing more concrete than amorphous pledges to 'develop coherent approaches' and 'cooperate to identify, develop and strengthen solutions' features in the document, though.[14] Displacement due to environmental factors is certainly becoming more salient: at the time of writing, more people were being forced from their homes by sudden-onset disasters than by conflict and violence.[15] Estimates on the number of people displaced by environmental impacts by 2050 have varied between 25 million and 1 billion, a range which primarily highlights the problems in making such predictions.[16] Even the term 'climate refugee' is controversial, as hinted at by the somewhat grudging nod to the concept in the Global Compact on Refugees. In the absence of an equivalent to the Refugee Convention to provide a universal reference point, various attempts to define the term have been made. Biermann and Boas offer the following definition: 'people who have to leave their habitats, immediately or in the near future, because of sudden or gradual alterations in their natural environment related to at least one of three impacts of climate change: sea-level rise, extreme weather events, and drought and water scarcity'.[17] While this definition may work well for popular understanding or policy purposes, a lawyer might observe that broad concepts such as 'near future' and 'extreme weather' might be problematic. The Environmental Justice Foundation offers a definition

---

[12] Global Compact on Refugees (UN Doc A/73/12 (Part II)) (2 August 2018) [8].

[13] Global Compact for Safe, Orderly and Regular Migration (A/RES/73/195), Objective 2, [19(h)]-[19(l)].

[14] See paragraphs 18(l) and 21(h).

[15] Internal Displacement Monitoring Centre (2020) *Global Report on Internal Displacement 2020*, April, Available from: https://www.internal-displacement.org/global-report/grid2020/ [last accessed 1 December 2021].

[16] International Organization for Migration (2014) *Outlook on Migration, Environment and Climate Change*, Geneva: IOM, p 38.

[17] Biermann, F. and Boas, I. (2008) 'Protecting Climate Refugees: The Case for a Global Protocol', *Environment: Science and Policy for Sustainable Development*, 50: 8.

which is perhaps more tightly drawn yet also conceptually wider in that it does not cite particular effects of climate change: 'persons or groups of persons who, for reasons of sudden or progressive climate-related change in the environment that adversely affects their lives or living conditions, are obliged to leave their habitual homes either temporarily or permanently and who move either within their country or abroad'.[18] The IOM uses the same definition for an 'environmental migrant'.[19] Whatever label or definition is ultimately used, the definitions were not drawn with a view to their being embedded into a formal legal protection regime or as formal triggers for climate refugee protection status. Nevertheless, the definitions would, on the face of it, appear to apply to someone *forced* from their home ('have to leave' or 'obliged to leave') by rising seawater or repeated droughts. The case of Ioane Teitiota, a citizen of Kiribati, a collection of low-lying atolls in the central Pacific Ocean, illustrates the difficulties of the proposed definitions as well as the inability of the existing international regime to provide assistance to those affected by slow-onset climate degradation.

KEY CASE

Mr Teitiota claimed asylum in New Zealand in 2013 on the basis that rising seawater levels, associated environmental degradation and the pressure of over-population had combined to cause him and his family serious harm which amounted to being persecuted and a breach of his human rights.[20] He had previously been lawfully resident and working in New Zealand as an economic migrant but his visa had expired. His claim to refugee status was rejected on the basis that the concept of being persecuted requires some human agency and there was none in his case; he had not established that 'the environmental conditions that he faced or is likely to face on return are so parlous that his life will be placed in jeopardy, or that he and his family will not be able to resume their prior subsistence life with dignity' and, in any event, there was no discrimination on a convention ground causing the harm he had experienced.

The case also failed on human rights grounds, and a related claim based on the right to life and right to freedom from cruel, inhuman or degrading treatment as

---

[18] Environmental Justice Foundation (2007) *Beyond Borders: Our Changing Climate – Its Role in Conflict and Displacement*, London: EJF, p 6.
[19] International Organization for Migration (2011) *Glossary on Migration* (2nd edn), Geneva: IOM, p 33.
[20] The fully reasoned tribunal decision is *AF (Kiribati)* [2013] NZIPT 800413. The case was then considered by the High Court as *Teitiota v Chief Executive of the Ministry of Business, Innovation and Employment* by the Court of Appeal as [2014] NZCA 173 and the Supreme Court as [2015] NZSC 107 on 20 July 2015.

protected by the ICCPR was rejected by the UN Human Rights Committee in a reasoned decision in 2020.[21] The New Zealand tribunal and courts and the committee left open the possibility that a claim for international protection which flowed from the effects of climate change might conceivably succeed, for example because of resulting overcrowding and land disputes causing serious violence or due to the land becoming literally uninhabitable. They found that on the facts of the case neither had yet come to pass. In short, Mr Teitiota had left Kiribati for understandable reasons, but the situation had not been so bad that he had been *forced* to leave. It is therefore not immediately obvious that the various definitions of 'climate refugee' would have assisted.

Jane McAdam forcefully argues that the label of 'climate refugee' is 'both legally and conceptually flawed', an 'inappropriate normative framework for responding to the needs of those forced to move on account of environmental or climate change impacts' and, more recently, 'a well-worn but inaccurate trope'.[22] She also observes that at least some of those labelled by others as climate refugees reject the categorization as offensive to their dignity. Nevertheless, McAdam recognizes that the term may be 'a useful advocacy tool to generate attention and mobilize civil society around the dangers of global warming'.[23]

This is not to say that the effects of climate change are in any way irrelevant to a claim for refugee status. A conventional refugee law analysis based on differential impact may be useful if, for example, a person suffering from drought or flooding has been denied crucial assistance by their government for reasons which engage the Refugee Convention.[24] A person in this situation could argue they have suffered serious harm involving failure of state protection for reasons of a protected characteristic. It is an unusual situation, though, and offers no solace to those who are not discriminated against by their government but nonetheless are still victims of flood, drought or similar. Some refugee claims have succeeded where conflict and violence have ensued from a disaster, as following a drought in Somalia in 2011–12, for

---

[21] *Teitiota v New Zealand* (UN Doc CCPR/C/127/D/2728/2016) (7 January 2020).
[22] McAdam, J. (2012) *Climate Change, Forced Migration, and International Law*, Oxford: Oxford University Press, p 39; McAdam, J. (2020) 'Protecting People Displaced by the Impacts of Climate Change: The UN Human Rights Committee and the Principle of Non-refoulement', *American Journal of International Law*, 114(4): 708–725.
[23] McAdam, J. (2012) *Climate Change, Forced Migration, and International Law*, Oxford: Oxford University Press, p 40, based on research conducted in Kiribati and Tuvalu.
[24] The concept of 'differential impact' is drawn from *R v Secretary of State for the Home Department, ex p Adan* [1999] 1 AC 293 (UK HL).

example.[25] The Environmental Justice Foundation accepts that 'refugee law is not a suitable avenue through which to pursue responses to climate-induced displacement' but use the term climate refugee for campaigning purposes.[26] While recognizing that the Refugee Convention does not currently protect climate refugees, Kent and Behrman advocate in favour of the use of the term on the basis that the word refugee is adaptable and signals that 'others bear a responsibility for the causes of their flight'.[27]

It has been suggested that the disappearance of a state in a 'sinking island' situation could be addressed through international law on statelessness. While this appears logical, Goodwin-Gill and McAdam argue that the statelessness regime 'holds little promise as a normative framework to assist the disaster displaced'.[28] The population of such a state would have to flee long before its physical territory sank finally and irretrievably beneath the waves. It is not clear that the physical disappearance of a state would have the effect of extinguishing the legal entity capable of conferring nationality on individuals. In any event, existing international law and practice on statelessness is simply inadequate as it stands. The Stateless Persons Convention is not widely ratified, even those countries that have ratified it have not implemented a statelessness determination procedure and the convention does not include a right of admission or *non-refoulement*. Very substantial reforms of international law and practice would be necessary and none are currently proposed.

States have not stood entirely idle but they have been reluctant to frame climate migration as a matter of international law. Following the Cancún Climate Change Conference of 2010, a climate migration project led by UNHCR petered out in 2011 for the very reason that it was led by UNHCR, an international agency focused on international solutions.[29] To revive discussion, Norway and Switzerland jointly sponsored a new state-led forum they called the Nansen Initiative on Disaster-Induced Cross-Border Displacement, commonly referred to simply as the Nansen Initiative. Following a series of consultations, the non-binding Agenda for

---

[25] Wood, T. (2014) *Protection and Disasters in the Horn of Africa: Norms and Practice for Addressing Cross-border Displacement in Disaster Contexts*, Technical Paper, Geneva: Nansen Initiative, pp 32–33.

[26] Environmental Justice Foundation (2007) *Beyond Borders: Our Changing Climate – Its Role in Conflict and Displacement*, London: EJF, p 41.

[27] Kent, A. and Behrman, S. (2018) *Facilitating the Resettlement and Rights of Climate Refugees: An Argument for Developing Existing Principles and Practices*, Abingdon: Routledge, Chapter 2.

[28] Goodwin-Gill, G. and McAdam, J. (2021) *The Refugee in International Law* (4th edn), Oxford: Oxford University Press, p 658.

[29] McAdam, J. (2016) 'From the Nansen Initiative to the Platform on Disaster Displacement: Shaping International Approaches to Climate Change, Disasters and Displacement', *University of New South Wales Law Journal*, 39(4): 1518–1546.

the Protection of Cross-Border Displaced Persons in the Context of Disasters and Climate Change was produced in 2015. This more bottom-up approach has proven more effective in securing agreement, with the protection agenda being endorsed by 109 states and proving influential in parallel regional fora such as the Central and Northern American Regional Conference on Migration (RCM) and the South American Conference on Migration (SCM). Examination of state practice reveals that many countries have been admitting those displaced by disasters on a responsive, ad hoc basis for many years.[30] Rather than seeking to impose binding international law obligations or rights, these state-led international and regional discussions have focused on sharing and harmonizing national solutions to disasters which are rooted in discretionary admission and pre-existing immigration law. A successor to the Nansen Initiative, the Platform on Disaster Displacement, was launched in 2016 and has continued in the same vein. In parallel, parties to the United Nations Framework Convention on Climate Change established in 2015 a Task Force on Displacement under the Warsaw International Mechanism on Loss and Damage.[31] Its primary focus is to avert and minimize impacts, but it has also recognized the need to 'facilitate, initiate and/or manage migration as a positive strategy and planned relocated as a last resort option'.[32] The task force's mandate was renewed for a further five years in 2018 and its work continues. As with the Nansen Initiative, its successor and the American conferences, the purpose is not to produce a new international legal instrument but to incubate and disseminate new norms. There is little appetite for a new international legal instrument and many question whether there is a real need for one.

Last words

None of this is to say that the international refugee protection regime has not had important successes. The definition of a refugee has proven durable. It has evolved alongside international human rights law and apparent omissions at the time of drafting, such as specifying sex as a convention ground, have, in effect, been made good by a principled but adaptable interpretation of the particular social group ground. The principle of *non-refoulement* may be breached on occasion but it is now so widely accepted that it has been

---

[30] Cantor, D. (2021) 'Environment, Mobility, and International Law: A New Approach in the Americas', *Chicago Journal of International Law*, 21(2): 263–322.

[31] Report of the Conference of the Parties on its twenty-first session, held in Paris from 30 November to 13 December 2015 (UN Doc FCCC/CP/2015/10/Add.1).

[32] Task Force on Displacement, *Report of the Task Force on Displacement*, 17 September 2018, available at: https://unfccc.int/sites/default/files/resource/2018_TFD_report_17_Sep.pdf [last accessed 30 September 2021], p 14.

argued to have become a feature of customary international law. Countries including Bangladesh, Colombia, Ethiopia, Turkey and Uganda have kept their borders open and saved countless lives even as other wealthier countries have sought to close their own. The rights conferred on refugees by the Refugee Convention are generally respected in the prosperous countries of the Global North, enabling at least those lucky few refugees who safely reach those countries through resettlement or irregular journeys to integrate and rebuild their lives. For those able to access and navigate the refugee status determination process in a country which complies with its international commitments under the Refugee Convention, the system is life-saving and life-changing.

Suggested further reading

Garlick, M. and Inder, C. (2021) 'Protection of Refugees and Migrants in the Era of the Global Compacts', *Interventions: International Journal of Postcolonial Studies*, 23(2): 207–226.

Goodwin-Gill, G. and McAdam, J. (2021) *The Refugee in International Law* (4th edn), Oxford: Oxford University Press, Chapter 12.

McAdam, J. (2020) 'Protecting People Displaced by the Impacts of Climate Change: The UN Human Rights Committee and the Principle of Non-refoulement', *American Journal of International Law*, 114(4): 708–725.

Special Edition: 'The 2018 Global Compacts on Refugees and Migration', *International Journal of Refugee Law*' 30(4), December 2018.

Teitiota v New Zealand (UN Doc CCPR/C/127/D/2728/2016) (7 January 2020).

Index

References to footnotes show both the page number and the note number (e.g. 62n125).

A

academic works 33, 37–38
accountability of states 64–65, 115
Acosta analysis 38, 166–167, 173, 179, 180
African human and peoples' rights system 43–45, 62, 66
African Refugee Convention 1969 40–43, 44–46, 48, 56, 58, 115, 148
Aga Khan, Sadruddin 9
age assessments 245
agents of the state 147–149
Aletho v Bulgaria (ECJ) 199
alternative protection *see* complementary protection regimes
American Convention on Human Rights 1969 50, 62, 66, 222
American Declaration of the Rights and Duties of Man 1948 50, 222
Andrade, Fischel de 50
apostasy *see* religious freedom
Arab Convention on Regulating Status of Refugees in the Arab Countries 1994 45
Arendt, Hannah 5, 18–19
arrest *see* criminal sanctions
AS and others v Italy and Malta (UNHRC) 236–237
Assange, Julian 52–53
asylum claims
 burden of proof 26, 83–84, 224
 credibility assessments *see* credibility assessments
 diplomatic asylum claims 52–53
 future risk assessments *see* future risk assessments
 motives of applicant, relevance of 15–16, 106–107
 off-shore processing 29, 35, 217, 229, 241–242, 259
 omissions from Refugee Convention on 15, 29
 right to make 31, 44, 50, 59–60, 202, 222
 standard of proof *see* standard of proof
 UK case study *see* United Kingdom, asylum claims processing
attribution of protected characteristic 165–166
Australia
 exclusions from refugee status 201
 off-shore processing of asylum claims 217, 241, 259
 particular social group 181
 persecution claims 102–103, 107, 110, 112, 115, 117, 126–127, 145
 refugee definition 12, 60, 82, 87, 165
 state protection failure jurisprudence 152, 153, 158
autonomy right 95, 134–138

B

bad faith claims 105, 106–107
Bank, Roland 59
Behrman, S. 264
'being persecuted'
 actors of persecution 114–115
 bifurcated approach 111–114, 145, 164
 dignity and autonomy loss 134–138
 and discrimination 122–123
 EU Qualification Directive on 115, 121, 123, 124–125
 generally 27, 108–109, 125–127
 grounds of persecution *see* 'convention grounds'
 human rights standards, role of 63, 111–113, 116–121, 135–138, 153
 liberty loss 131–134
 physical harm 127–131, 133
 and state protection failure 145, 150
 subjective dimension 109–111
 'sustained or systemic' harms 121–122
Betts, Alexander 9, 19–20, 25, 34
Biermann, F. 261

Bingham, Thomas 92
Boas, I. 261
Bolbol v Hungary (ECJ) 198
burden of proof
  asylum claims 26, 83–84, 224
  ongoing protection needs 74
  see also standard of proof

C

Canada
  exclusion from refugee status 209, 211
  persecution claims 129
  refugee definition 60, 87, 201
  state protection failure jurisprudence 18, 111–112, 115, 143, 153–154, 156, 158
Cantor, David 47, 48, 122, 127
Caracas Conventions on Territorial and Diplomatic Asylum 1954 46
Cartagena Declaration on Refugees 1984 45, 46–50, 56, 58, 115, 148, 260
cessation of refugee status *see* loss of refugee status
change of circumstances 191–193
Charter of Fundamental Rights of the European Union 55, 58, 171
Chetail, V. 31
children
  age assessments 245
  education, denial of right 126–127, 138
  family unity/reunion right 28, 190, 230, 232–233, 239, 256
  'habitual residence' of 219
  refugee definition applied to 87, 164, 182
  unaccompanied minors 54, 232, 245–246
Chimni, B.S. 23, 34
China 135–136
climate displacement 46, 47–48, 259, 261–265
collective deportations 71
Collier, Paul 19–20, 34
Common European Asylum System (EU) 53–59, 241–242
complementary protection regimes 26
  of African Refugee Convention 40–42, 46
  of Cartagena Declaration 46–49
  of EU Qualification Directive 56–58
conscientious objection right 7, 39, 62n125, 64, 125, 163, 170–172
constitutional rights to asylum 59–60
consular or diplomatic protection loss 20, 114, 141, 143–144, 145–146, 149
'convention grounds'
  concealment of 102–105, 158, 166–167
  criminal sanctions, effect on *see* criminal sanctions
  discrimination-based account 122–123, 169–170
  generally 27–28, 121, 162–163, 167
  imputation or attribution of 165–166

intentions of persecutors 163–165
multiple grounds 165
nationality *see* nationality-based persecution
omissions from 173–174
particular social group *see* particular social group
political opinion *see* political opinion-based persecution
race 112–113, 129, 174
religion *see* religious freedom
Convention on Action against Trafficking in Human Beings 2005 (Council of Europe) 76–77
Convention on the Reduction of Statelessness 1961 80
Convention relating to the International Status of Refugees 1933 6
Convention relating to the Status of Refugees of 1951 *see* Refugee Convention 1951
Convention relating to the Status of Stateless Persons 1954 78–79, 264
Costello, C. 31, 69
country reports 83, 93, 249
credibility assessments
  bad faith claims 105, 106–107
  'benefit of the doubt' approach 83
  corroborative evidence 93–95, 106
  and future risk assessments 89, 104
  generally 26, 82, 88–91
  plausibility *versus* probability 91–93
  quality of narrative 95–98
  see also future risk assessments
criminal sanctions
  death penalty 57, 67, 128
  denial of refugee status 202–212
  expulsion as sanction 186, 193, 202, 226–229, 256–257
  extradition cases 52–53, 67
  illegal entry right 223–225
  military service cases 39, 62n125, 64, 125, 163, 170–172
  whether persecution 123, 132–133, 168–170
Crisp, Jeff 45
cruel, inhuman or degrading treatment *see* inhuman or degrading treatment

D

Dauvergne, Catherine 34
death penalty 57, 67, 128
Declaration for Refugees and Migrants 2016 25, 222, 226, 259
Declaration on Territorial Asylum 1967 24, 259
deportation
  as criminal sanction 186, 193, 202, 226–229, 256–257
  following failed UK asylum claim 252–254
detention, criminal *see* criminal sanctions

INDEX

detention of UK asylum seekers 239, 246–247
dignity right 95, 134–138
diplomatic asylum claims 52–53
diplomatic or consular protection loss 20, 114, 141, 143–144, 145–146, 149, 189
disaster and climate displacement 46, 47–48, 123, 259, 261–265
'discreet' future behaviour 102–105, 158, 166–167
discrimination 122–123, 169–170
  see also 'convention grounds'
domestic law refugee definitions 2, 59–61
domestic servitude 133–134
domestic violence 131, 164, 182
dual nationality holders 141–143
Dublin system (EU) 53–55, 241–242

E

Ecuador 52–53, 59–60
education, denial of right 126–127, 138
Einarsen, Terje 24
employment see work and social assistance
Environmental Justice Foundation 261–262, 264
equivalent protection 201
ethnicity-based persecution 112–113, 129, 174
EU law
  Charter of Fundamental Rights of the European Union 55, 58, 171
  Common European Asylum System 53–59, 241–242
  Qualification Directive see Qualification Directive (EU)
European Convention on Human Rights 1950 62, 71, 124–125, 170, 233
  Article 3 57–58, 66, 67
  see also inhuman or degrading treatment
European Volunteer Worker scheme (UK) 24
evolution of refugee definition 4–8, 21–22, 173–174
exclusions from refugee definition
  dual and multiple nationality holders 141–143
  equivalent protection 201
  under EU Qualification Directive 56, 57–58, 210, 211
  generally 12–13, 28, 65–66, 186, 193–194
  internal relocation/flight alternative 27, 104, 114, 155–160
  on moral grounds 202–212
  Palestinian refugees 194–200
  pre-Refugee Convention exclusions 7–8
  voluntary returns possible 106
  see also loss of refugee status
expert evidence 94–95
expulsion as criminal sanction 186, 193, 202, 226–229, 256–257
extradition cases 52–53, 67

F

fair trial right 51–52, 72
family-based rights
  family unity/reunion 28, 190, 230, 232–233, 239, 256
  private and family life right 66, 71, 74, 80, 95, 233
fear of being persecuted see 'being persecuted'; 'well-founded fear'
female genital mutilation 131, 182
forced labour 75, 133–134, 170
forced marriage 131
'forced migrants' 3
forced sterilization or abortion 131, 164
Fortin, A. 20
forum shopping concerns 39, 53, 201
Foster, Michelle 38, 63–64, 118, 137
  see also Hathaway and Foster, *The Law of Refugee Status* (2nd edn)
freedom of thought, conscience and religion see religious freedom
Fripp, E. 177
future risk assessments
  and credibility assessments 89, 104
  future activities 102–105, 158, 166–167
  generally 88, 98–99
  past events, relevance of 89, 99–100
  risk factors 100–102
  standard of proof 86, 102
  sur place refugees 15, 42, 100, 105–106, 241
  see also credibility assessments

G

Garlick, M. 260
gender-based persecution 63–64, 113, 116, 131, 164, 182
Ghezelbash, Daniel 35
Gibney, Matthew 19, 121
Global Compact for Migration 25–26, 259–260, 261
Global Compact on Refugees 10, 25–26, 38, 259–260, 261
Goodwin-Gill, Guy
  on illegal entry right 224
  influence of 37–38, 39
  on refugee definition 17–18, 63, 108
  on refugee law regime 6, 36, 134
Goodwin-Gill and McAdam, *The Refugee in International Law* (4th edn)
  on denial of refugee status on moral grounds 208
  on 'lawful presence' in a state 229
  on Palestinian refugees 198
  on particular social group 181
  on rights of refugees 216, 218, 223
  on state protection failure 65
  on statelessness 264
Grahl-Madsen, Atle 38, 108, 224
Greece, reception conditions 55, 69

grounds of persecution *see* 'convention grounds'
group-based persecution *see* particular social group

H

'habitual residence' 218–219
Haddad, Emma 19, 258
Hamlin, R. 3
Hathaway, James
  on 'being persecuted' 63, 109–110, 111, 116, 121, 134, 145
  on Global Compact on Refugees 25
  on human rights law 117–118
  influence of 37–38, 39, 99, 122
  on 'lawful presence' in a state 229
  on particular social group 38, 179
  on rights of refugees 214–215, 216, 218, 219, 220, 224
  surrogate protection thesis 18, 111
Hathaway and Foster, *The Law of Refugee Status* (2nd edn)
  on denial of refugee status on moral grounds 208
  on human rights law 119, 120, 132
  on loss of refugee status 188–189, 192
  on particular social group 180
  on refugee definition generally 14
  on state accountability 65
  on state protection failure 114, 154, 159–160
  on 'well-founded fear' 88
history of refugee definition 4–8, 21–22, 173–174
HJ (Iran) case (UK Sup. Ct) 103–104
Horvath v Secretary of State for the Home Department (UK HL)
  influence of 38, 152
  on state accountability 64–65
  on state protection failure generally 18, 20, 111, 112, 145, 147
  on sufficiency of state protection 151–152, 153, 154
  on treaty interpretation 39
human dignity right 95, 134–138
human rights law
  African system 43–45, 62, 66
  Charter of Fundamental Rights of the European Union 55, 58, 171
  ECHR *see* European Convention on Human Rights 1950
  Inter-American system 50–53, 62, 66, 73, 222
  international law framework 31, 61–62, 65, 170
  see also treaty and agreement names
  and judicial interpretations of refugee definition 63–66, 111–113, 116–121, 135–138, 153
  and law of the sea 233–234

Refugee Convention's citation of 31–32, 61, 62
territorial application 72–73, 217
see also rights of refugees
human trafficking victims 75–78, 133–134, 246
humanitarian protection *see* complementary protection regimes

I

illegal entry right 223–225
immigration detention in UK 239, 246–247
imprisonment *see* criminal sanctions
imputation of protected characteristic 165–166
inchoate nationality 142
Inder, C. 260
India 60
inhuman or degrading treatment
  hierarchical status of right 117, 118, 119
  human rights instruments prohibiting 66
  medical treatment cases 68–69
  physical harm as persecution 127–131, 133
  at reception and detention centres 55–58, 67, 69, 242
  religious freedom, interaction with 72, 120
  see also non-refoulement
integration/ongoing protection rights 14, 73–74, 219–221, 230, 231
intentions of persecutors 163–165
Inter-American human rights system 50–53, 62, 66, 73, 222
internal relocation/flight alternative 27, 104, 114, 155–160
internally displaced persons 3
international community of refugee law practitioners 32–35
International Covenant on Civil and Political Rights 1966 41, 61–62, 65, 66, 119, 128, 170, 233
International Covenant on Economic, Social and Cultural Rights 1966 61–62, 137, 170, 233
international criminal liability 204–207
international human rights law *see* human rights law
International Organization for Migration 3, 10, 262
International Refugee Organization 7–8
interpretations of refugee definition *see* judicial interpretations of refugee definition
Iraq 150, 159

J

Januzi v Secretary of State for the Home Department (UK HL) 155, 157–158, 160
Jews, Nazi persecution 100, 112–113, 129, 174

INDEX

Jorro, Peter 38
JS (Sri Lanka) v Secretary of State for the Home Department (UK Sup. Ct) 204, 205–206
judicial dialogue 38–39
judicial interpretations of refugee definition
  credibility assessments *see* credibility assessments
  elements of definition *see* 'being persecuted'; 'convention grounds'; state protection failure; 'well-founded fear'
  future risk assessments *see* future risk assessments
  generally 26
  human rights standards influencing 63–66, 111–113, 116–121, 135–138, 153
  scholarship influencing 33
  UNHCR guidance influencing 35–37
  Vienna Convention rules 16–17, 33, 47, 62, 109, 144
jurisdiction of human rights law 72–73

K
Kadesh Treaty 4
Kälin, Walter 89–90
Kent, A. 264
Khashoggi, Jamal 189
Kiribati 262–263
Kosovo 149–150
El Kott v Hungary (ECJ) 198–199

L
Lambert, Hélène 33n8
Latin America
  Cartagena Declaration on Refugees 1984 45, 46–50, 56, 58, 115, 148, 260
  Inter-American human rights system 50–53, 62, 66, 73, 222
  Refugee Convention ratifications 48
  Venezuelan refugee crisis (2014-current) 49–50, 258
law of the sea 233–236
'lawful presence' in a state 218, 229
League of Nations 5–6
LGBTQ+ persons *see* sexuality-based persecution
Loescher, Gil 9
loss of liberty as persecution 131–134
loss of refugee status
  under African Refugee Convention 43
  change of circumstances 191–193
  disapplication of cessation clauses 99
  under EU Qualification Directive 56, 191
  generally 28, 140, 186–188
  return reviews in UK 256
  voluntary acquisition of protection 188–191
  see also exclusions from refugee definition

M
Macklin, Audrey 33
McAdam, Jane 38, 263
  see also Goodwin-Gill and McAdam, *The Refugee in International Law* (4th edn)
medical expert evidence 94–95
medical treatment cases 68–69
Mexico 60
Michigan Guidelines 37
migrant/refugee binary 2–4, 16
military service, conscientious objection 39, 62n125, 64, 125, 163, 170–172
minimum standards of treatment 55–58, 220
Montevideo Treaty on International Penal Law 1889 46
motives of persecutors 163–165
motives of refugees 15–16, 106–107
multiple 'convention grounds' 165
multiple nationality holders 141–143

N
Nansen, Fridtjof 5
Nansen Initiative 264–265
nationality-based persecution
  concept 176–178
  statelessness 78–80, 114n25, 138, 140–141, 177, 191, 264
natural disaster and climate displacement 46, 47–48, 123, 259, 261–265
New York Declaration for Refugees and Migrants 2016 25, 222, 226, 259
New Zealand
  climate displacement case 262–263
  Palestinian refugee claims 198, 200
  persecution claims 112, 115, 118, 119
  refugee definition 60–61
  state protection failure jurisprudence 154, 160
non-refoulement
  African Refugee Convention on 43, 45
  customary international law status 22, 69–70, 225, 265–266
  definition 13, 120, 225
  evolution of 5, 63, 203
  and expulsion of refugees 226–229
  human rights jurisprudence on 51–52, 66–72, 74
  interpretation and application of right 226–229
  Latin American regional instruments on 47, 50, 66
  and off-shore processing of asylum claims 242
  procedural safeguards 70–71
  territorial application 72–73, 217
  United States, *refoulement* by 259
  see also inhuman or degrading treatment
NS v United Kingdom and ME v Ireland (CJEU) 55

O

off-shore processing of asylum claims 29, 35, 217, 229, 241–242, 259
ongoing protection/integration rights 14, 73–74, 219–221, 230, 231
Owen, D. 19

P

Pacheco Tineo Family v Bolivia (IACHR) 51–52
Palermo Protocol 2000 75–76
Palestinian refugees 194–200
particular social group
  concept 178–183, 265
  gender-based persecution 63–64, 113, 116, 131, 164, 182
  group-based persecution generally 100
  immutable characteristics *(Acosta)* analysis 38, 166–167, 173, 179, 180
  LGBTQ+ persons *see* sexuality-based persecution
  stateless persons 80
  trafficked persons 77
penalties *see* criminal sanctions
persecution *see* 'being persecuted'
physical harm as persecution 127–131, 133
Platform on Disaster Displacement 265
plausibility assessments *see* credibility assessments
Pobjoy, Jason 87, 109–110, 119, 182
political crimes 209–210
political dimension of asylum 19, 24, 148
political opinion-based persecution
  concept 183–184
  conscientious objection right 7, 39, 62n125, 64, 125, 163, 170–172
  corroborative evidence 97, 106
  future political activities 89, 102, 104–105, 158, 166–167
  in Latin America 46
  manifestations of 133, 135, 168–169
Price, Matthew 19, 24
private and family life right 66, 71, 74, 80, 95, 233
prosecutions *see* criminal sanctions
protection element of refugee definition *see* state protection failure
Protocol Relating to the Status of Refugees 1967 2, 11, 40
public perceptions of refugees 1, 258
punishment *see* criminal sanctions

Q

Qualification Directive (EU)
  on bad faith claims 106–107
  exclusions from refugee definition under 56, 57–58, 210, 211
  generally 33, 99
  loss of refugee status under 56, 191
  on nationality 177
  on particular social group 183
  refugee definition 56, 115, 121, 123, 124–125, 166
  on religious freedom 175
  on state protection failure 147, 150, 152–153, 155, 157, 159
  subsidiary protection regime 56–58

R

race-based persecution 112–113, 129, 174
Ramasubramanyam, J. 22
rape 91, 96, 122, 131
re-entry right denial 177–178
'real risk' of persecution 67, 85, 151
  see also 'well-founded fear'
refoulement prohibition *see* non-*refoulement*
Refugee Convention 1951
  cessation clauses *see* loss of refugee status
  criticisms of 18, 19–20, 20–24
  drafting of 11, 21–23, 108, 144, 173–174
  EU law, relationship with 56, 58–59
  exclusion clauses *see* exclusions from refugee definition
  human rights law cited in 31–32, 61, 62
  omissions from 14–15, 28–29, 264
  Protocol 1967 2, 11, 40
  purpose 16–20, 27
  ratifications 2, 22, 48
  reform of 24
  refugee definition *see* refugee definition (Refugee Convention Art.1A(2))
  on rights of refugees *see* rights of refugees
  see also complementary protection regimes
refugee definition
  of African Refugee Convention 40–42, 44–45, 48, 58, 115
  of Cartagena Declaration 46–49, 58, 115
  domestic law definitions 2, 59–61
  of EU Qualification Directive 56, 115, 121, 123, 124–125, 166
  evolution of 4–8, 21–22, 173–174
  exclusions from *see* exclusions from refugee definition
  forum shopping concerns 39, 53, 201
  loss of status *see* loss of refugee status
  of philosophers and ethicists 19–20
  public perceptions of refugees 1, 258
  of Refugee Convention *see* refugee definition (Refugee Convention Art.1A(2))
refugee/migrant binary 2–4, 16
refugee definition (Refugee Convention Art.1A(2))
  elements of *see* 'being persecuted'; 'convention grounds'; state protection failure; 'well-founded fear'
  exclusions from *see* exclusions from refugee definition

INDEX

generally 1–2, 11–13
judicial interpretations *see* judicial interpretations of refugee definition
motives of applicant, relevance of 15–16, 106–107
status recognition under 14
temporal and geographical limitations removed 2, 11, 40
UNHCR guidance on 35–37
refugee law and practice
academic works 37–38
and human rights law *see* human rights law
judicial dialogue 38–39
practitioners 32–35
UNHCR guidance as source 35–37
see also complementary protection regimes; Refugee Convention 1951
refugees *sur place* 15, 42, 100, 105–106, 241
religious freedom
beliefs, corroborative evidence 97
concept 174–176
conscientious objection right 7, 39, 62n125, 64, 125, 163, 170–172
future religious activities 102, 104–105, 158, 166–167
inhuman or degrading treatment, interaction with 72, 120
religious persecution, manifestations 133, 135–136, 169, 176
standard of equivalence 221
removal orders
as criminal sanction 186, 193, 202, 226–229, 256–257
following failed UK asylum claim 252–254
rescues at sea 72–73, 233–237
rights of refugees
complementary regimes protecting *see* complementary protection regimes
to conscientious objection 7, 39, 62n125, 64, 125, 163, 170–172
and degrees of attachment 216–220, 231
to fair trial 51–52, 72
to family unity/reunion 28, 190, 230, 232–233, 239, 256
generally 13–14, 28–29, 214–215, 221–222
to human dignity 95, 134–138
to illegal entry 223–225
to inhuman or degrading treatment protection *see* inhuman or degrading treatment
to integration/ongoing protection 14, 73–74, 219–221, 230, 231
to life 57, 67, 127–128
to *non-refoulement see non-refoulement*
to private and family life 66, 71, 74, 80, 95, 233
to religious freedom *see* religious freedom
to rescues at sea 72–73, 233–237

to seek (and obtain) asylum 31, 44, 50, 59–60, 202, 222
standards of equivalence 220–221, 231
state reservations 215
see also human rights law
Robinson, Nehemiah 38

S

Schengen Agreement system (EU) 53–54
scholarship 33, 37–38
sea rescues 72–73, 233–237
Sepet v Secretary of State for the Home Department (UK HL) 62, 64, 122, 144, 168, 171
'serious crime' 208–210
'serious harm' 57, 101–102, 111–112, 115–125, 128
see also 'being persecuted'
sexuality-based persecution
criminalization of homosexuality 168
future sexual activities 102–105, 158, 166–167
and human dignity 95, 137–138
Shacknove, A.E. 19
Sharpe, Marina 45
slavery and servitude 75, 133–134
social assistance *see* work and social assistance
Soering v United Kingdom (ECtHR) 67
Somalia 69, 128–129, 149, 159, 263–264
South Africa 177
South America *see* Latin America
standard of proof
for denial of refugee status on moral grounds 203–204
statelessness determinations 79–80
'well-founded fear' determinations 67, 84–86, 102
see also burden of proof
state accountability 64–65, 115
state protection failure
agents of the state 147–149
diplomatic or consular protection loss 20, 114, 141, 143–144, 145–146, 149, 189
dual and multiple nationality holders 141–143
equivalent protection 201
generally 27, 140–141
internal protection loss 144–145, 159–160
internal relocation/flight alternative 27, 104, 114, 155–160
source of protection 149–150
sufficiency of protection 150–155
surrogate protection thesis 18, 20, 27, 111, 114–115, 141
'unwilling or unable' 146–147
statelessness 78–80, 114n25, 138, 140–141, 177, 191, 264
subsidiary/supplementary protection *see* complementary protection regimes

sur place refugees 15, 42, 100, 105–106, 241
surrogate protection thesis 18, 20, 27, 111, 114–115, 141
'survival migration' 3
'sustained or systemic' harms 121–122
Symes, Mark 38
Syrian refugee crisis 2, 54–55, 241, 258
'systemic or sustained' harms 121–122

T
Teitiota case (NZ Sup. Ct) 262–263
territorial application of human rights law 72–73, 217
terrorism 210, 211–212
threats of harm 131
torture prohibition *see* inhuman or degrading treatment; *non-refoulement*
trafficked persons 75–78, 133–134, 246
transnational judicial dialogue 38–39
treaty interpretation rules 16–17, 33, 47, 62, 109, 144
Triggs, G. 260
Trimiño Mora, D. 47, 48
truthfulness assessments *see* credibility assessments
Turkey 2

U
UN Charter 1945 31, 61, 207, 210–212
UN Convention relating to the Status of Refugees of 1951 *see* Refugee Convention 1951
UN Global Compact for Migration 25–26, 259–260, 261
UN Global Compact on Refugees 10, 25–26, 38, 259–260, 261
unaccompanied minors 54, 232, 245–246
UNHCR (United Nations High Commissioner for Refugees)
  criticisms of 10, 35
  foundation 8
  guidance 35–37
  information resources 33, 36
  mandate and functions 8–10, 17, 45–46, 196, 259
  refugee resettlement data 260–261
United Kingdom
  asylum claims in *see* United Kingdom, asylum claims processing
  denial of refugee status on moral grounds 203–204, 205–206, 212
  early refugee legislation 4
  European Volunteer Worker scheme 24
  'habitual residence' in 219
  Horvath case *see* Horvath v Secretary of State for the Home Department (UK HL)
  human trafficking regime 77–78, 246
  internal relocation/flight jurisprudence 155, 156–158

'lawful presence' in 218, 229
loss of refugee status 193
particular social group 183
refugee definition 61, 115, 124
residence status of refugees 256, 257
sexuality-based persecution claims 103–104
statelessness regime 79–80
United Kingdom, asylum claims processing
  administrative stage 249–250
  appeal stage 250–252
  burden of proof 224
  detention 239, 246–247
  entry restrictions 223–224, 240–243
  fresh claims 255
  generally 29, 238–240
  human trafficking victims 77–78, 246
  initial procedures 243–246
  legal representation 248–249
  refusal, outcomes of 252–255
  return reviews 256
  standard of proof, prospective reform 86
  support and accommodation 239, 247–248, 252, 254, 255–256
United Nations *see* entries beginning UN
United States
  causation, approach to 163, 165
  denial of refugee status on moral grounds 210
  extraditions to 67
  Inter-American human rights system 50–53, 62, 66, 73, 222
  non-ratification of Refugee Convention 2, 24
  particular social group (*Acosta* analysis) 38, 166–167, 173, 179, 180
  refoulement by 259
  refugee definition 61, 87, 110, 112, 115
Universal Declaration of Human Rights 1948
  on discrimination 173
  hierarchy of rights lacking 118
  on inhuman or degrading treatment 66
  on right to human dignity 134
  on right to seek asylum 31, 202, 222
  status of 61, 62, 170
UNRRA (UN Relief and Rehabilitation Agency) 7
'unwilling or unable' 146–147

V
Venezuelan refugee crisis (2014-current) 49–50, 258
Vienna Convention on the Law of Treaties 1969 16–17, 33, 47, 62, 109, 144
voluntary acquisition of protection 188–191
voluntary returns 106, 253, 254

W
Wall, P. 260
Weis, Paul 38, 134, 224

'well-founded fear'
  burden of proof 83–84
  credibility assessments *see* credibility assessments
  future risk assessments *see* future risk assessments
  generally 26–27, 82
  grounds for *see* 'convention grounds'
  of human trafficking victims 78
  and internal relocation/flight alternative 157
  standard of proof 67, 84–86, 102
  and state protection failure 141, 145
  subjective dimension 86–88
  synonyms 67, 85, 151
withdrawal of refugee status *see* loss of refugee status
women, persecution of 63–64, 113, 116, 131, 164, 182
work and social assistance
  denial as persecution 137
  occupational membership of particular social group 180–181
  as ongoing protection needs 14, 73–74, 219–220, 221, 231
  UK asylum seekers 239, 247–248, 252, 254, 255–256